PREHISTORIC AVEBURY

AUBREY BURL

KT-499-102

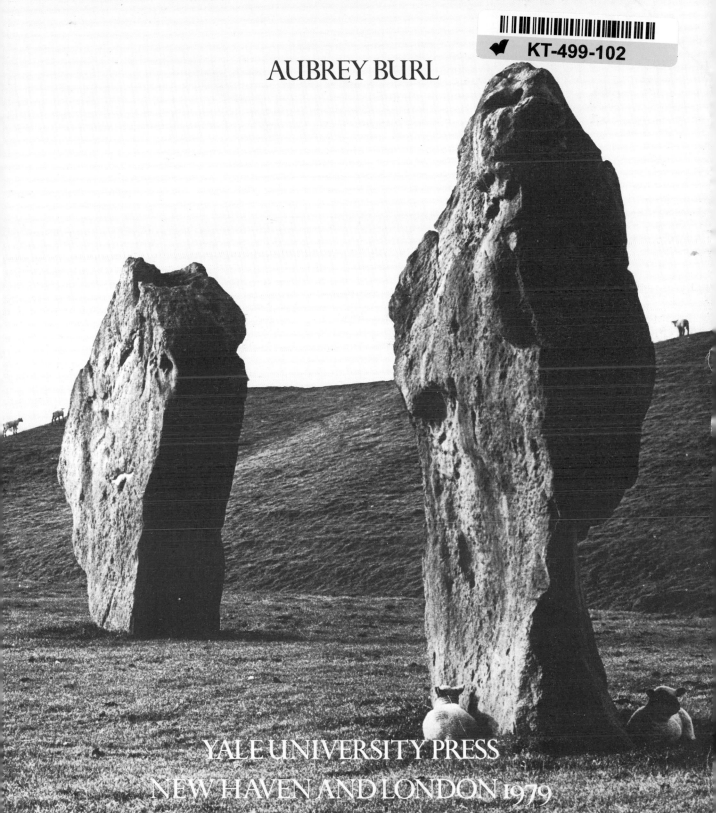

YALE UNIVERSITY PRESS

NEW HAVEN AND LONDON 1979

53544

Dedicated to the Memory of

WILLIAM STUKELEY

1687–1765

of Holbeach, Lincolnshire,
who gave us

*an ample and accurate description of that stupendous temple . . . at Abury in
North Wiltshire, the most august work at this day upon the globe of the earth.*

1. (*half-title page*) The 'Cove' at Avebury.
2. (*title page*) Stones of the south-west quadrant at Avebury.

THE LIBRARY

THE SURREY INSTITUTE OF ART & DESIGN

Farnham Campus, Falkner Road, Farnham, Surrey GU9 7DS

Copyright © 1979 by Yale University.

Second printing, 1986

All rights reserved. This book may not be reproduced, in whole or in part, in any form (beyond that
copying permitted by Sections 107 and 108 of the U.S. Copyright Law and except by reviewers for
the public press), without written permission from the publishers.

Printed in Yugoslavia by Mladinska knjiga, Ljubljana.

Designed by John Nicoll

Published in Great Britain, Europe, Africa, and Asia (except Japan) by Yale University Press, Ltd.,
London. Distributed in Australia and New Zealand by Book & Film Services, Artarmon, N.S.W.,
Australia; and in Japan by Harper & Row, Publishers, Tokyo Office.

Library of Congress Cataloging in Publication Data

Burl, Aubrey.
Prehistoric Avebury.

Bibliography: p.
Includes index.
1. Megalithic monuments—England—Avebury. 2. Avebury, Eng.—Antiquities. 3. England—
Antiquities. I. Title.
GN790.B87   936.2'3'12   78-31589
ISBN 0-300-02368-5 (cloth)
ISBN 0-300-03622-1 (pbk)

571 BURL

Preface

What I have done, I look upon as very imperfect, and but as opening the scene of this very noble subject.

William Stukeley. Abury, iii.

THIS book is about two mysteries. The first is why Avebury whose stone circles were for centuries the proudest monuments of their time should have been so neglected by writers. Stonehenge, not far to the south, has been endlessly described, analysed, painted. As long ago as 1901 a list of books and articles about it was over a hundred and fifty pages long. In contrast, very few works have been solely devoted to Avebury and the best of them was written more than two centuries ago by William Stukeley. It is surprising that Avebury's huge stones and massive bank should have received so little attention.

The second mystery is what Avebury was used for. The difficulty is not that there has been a lack of speculation about the purpose of prehistoric stone circles but that most of it has been by people with only a superficial knowledge of pre-Roman societies. Like chameleons of Time, Avebury and other stone circles change with every year of history. They have become centres of escapist cults. One could ignore the treasure-hunter with surreptitious metal-detector lurking in the nearest hollow. He is following a long-established though reprehensible tradition. But there are also the mystics, some of them peacefully sitting in eye-closed contemplation at the centre of the ring. Others sensitively touch the stones hoping to receive a finger-tipped tingle generated by the spirits of the circle. Dowsers with upturned wrists and sagging rods search for subterranean streams or psychic emanations or both, tripping over a network of strings tied from stone to opposite stone by a surveyor working out the geometrical design of the ring.

Theodolites wink towards every skyline notch where the sun once set or moon rose or where Arcturus for a brief year or two shimmered dimly down into the mists of a prehistoric evening. Ley-liners draw impossibly accurate alignments from Avebury through Silbury Hill to a random barrow or church or mile-wide hill that God happened to place in the correct position. There are even those who believe that the rings were landing-bases for flying saucers.

None of this is destructive and, certainly, to the archaeologist it is encouraging to realise that so many people sense the fascination of these ancient rings. But any single-minded preoccupation with astronomy or measuring-rods or extra-sensory perception must limit an investigation of the past. Prehistory should encompass all of man's activities, not just one or two aspects of our ancestors' lives, and too often in recent books the people who built the stone circles have been ignored.

This book is not about astronomy, geometry, psychometry or any one little and improbable piece of the past. It is about people. It is a book about the people who built the most spectacular prehistoric monument in the British Isles and it is meant for the general reader who has little or no archaeology but who is interested in

Avebury, one of the marvels of our heritage, and who wishes to know more about its importance in prehistoric Britain. Much of the information comes from the writings of earlier antiquarians and archaeologists and from repeated visits to the many ancient sites on the Marlborough Downs. Burial mounds, traces of old fields, circles lay around in ruined emptiness, most collapsing, mouldering, and now utterly spoiled. Fieldwork has been the background to research.

The book is not just a rewriting of what has already been said. It does contain new interpretations fashioned from a study of excavation reports and museum material, from my own researches into the more general problems of stone circles, and from the belief that to understand a place like Avebury it is essential to know both the countryside and, above all, the way of life of the people who raised the great stones.

Dates are a problem. Since it was discovered that radio-carbon or Carbon-14 'dates' obtained from prehistoric organic material are too young and need recalculating the archaeologist has had to refer to calibration tables to convert the Carbon-14 assay to a more accurate form. In this book all dates are expressed in 'real' years, that is, for the time when the event actually occurred. Such dates are always followed by BC. Where these dates are based on radio-carbon determinations they have been revised and the determination quoted in the Notes. Such Carbon-14 'dates' are followed by bc.

It would be improper not to state my sincere thanks to my friends and colleagues who have contributed so much to this book. The opinions are mine but what scholarship there is comes largely from their kindness and guidance. It would be even more improper to select one person above others and it is best simply to say how grateful I am for all their help: Professor Richard Atkinson for reading and correcting the section about Silbury Hill; the staff of the Bodleian Library, Oxford, and the prehistorians of the British Museum, London; Dr David Coombs for material about Callis Wold; Devizes Museum and its fine library; Mrs Patricia Drummond of the National Monuments Record; the Department of the Environment; Mr Deric Evans for providing scarce literature on the Gambian stone circles; Dr Kirk Huffman who telephoned me about Malekula the day before he left for the New Hebrides; Dr Ed Krupp who constantly sent me details of palaeo-American astronomy; Lt Col and Mrs McCarthy for showing me their lovely house on the site of John Aubrey's old home; the Ordnance Survey, Southampton; Professor Stuart Piggott for reading Chapter III and defending the excavation techniques of St. George Gray; Peter Reynolds of the Butser Experimental Farm for conversations about prehistoric farming; Salisbury Museum; Mrs Cred Snow of the National Trust bookshop at Avebury; Mr Peter Tate, most courteous of custodians; Professor Alexander Thom and his son, Archie, for their plan of the Sanctuary; and Dr Geoffrey Wainwright for a largescale plan of Mount Pleasant.

Perhaps I may be excused for offering special thanks to my friends, the late Faith de Mallet Vatcher and her husband, Lance, of Avebury Museum for their generosity and advice, unstintingly given, during a most difficult time for them.

To my wife, Margaret, who tolerated so many dreadful caravans, weather and despondency, and to Miss Ann Farmer who coped with an unbelievable typescript and reshaped it into a piece of literature, to both of them I must offer my personal thanks as I must to John Nicoll, my editor, who tended this book with enthusiasm and care.

To my archaeology students who did so much work at Avebury I must write a special note. Without complaint they surveyed, drew, plane-tabled, checked bearings time and again. They suffered the biting winds of West Kennet, the November chill of Stonehenge and the icing cold of the Marlborough Downs. They also knew rain, mist and, very occasionally, sunshine. I like to think it was prehistory that made them so keen although I suspect it was the evening call of Wadworth's excellent beer. Whatever the incentive, with them fieldwork was a particular pleasure.

Finally, to the reader. This book is not intended to be an archaeological report or a catalogue of finds. It is meant to be read. Continually in my mind have been the wise words of William Stukeley: 'The writers on antiquities generally find more difficulty, in so handling the matter, as to render it agreeable to the reader, than in most other subjects. Tediousness in any thing is a fault, more so in this than other sciences.' *Abury*, 1.

I hope I have handled the matter agreeably.

Photographic Acknowledgements

Permission to reproduce plates has kindly been given by the following who retain the copyright:

Colour photographs. II, IV, V, VII, VIII and XII are by Fay Godwin. I, III, VI, X and XI are by J. S. Nicoll. IX and XIII are by the author.

Black and white photographs. Aerofilms Ltd, 98; The Bodleian Library, Oxford, 20, 23, 25, 38, 53, 54, 60, 62, 63, 84, 85; Dr D. Coombs, 51; the Department of the Environment, 3, 12; The Thomas Gilcrease Institute of American History and Art, Tulsa, Oklahoma, 86; P. V. Glob, 89, 96, 97; Fay Godwin, 1, 2, 7, 8, 9, 10, 19, 21, 28, 86, 88, 93, 99, 106; the estate of H. St. G. Gray, 31; the estate of A. Keiller, 18; National Museum, Denmark, 95; J. S. Nicoll, 11, 14, 66; Mick Sharp, 13, 17, 27, 35, 39, 40, 42, 43, 46, 49, 50, 57, 71, 75, 80, 83, 87, 101; the Society of Antiquaries, 32, 36, 52; the estate of Alan Sorrell, 47, 100; West Air Photography, Weston-super-Mare, 5. The other black and white photographs were taken by the author.

Gratitude is also expressed to the Department of the Environment for permission to photograph plates 35, 46, 56 and 75 in Avebury Museum; and to Devizes Museum who allowed Mick Sharp to take plates 49, 50, 64 and 80 and the author to take plate 91.

Contents

3. An aerial view of Avebury from the north, showing the stones and village within the earthwork. At the top left, above the road, can be seen the stones of the Kennet Avenue.

Introduction

And this stupendous fabric, which for some thousands of years, had brav'd the continual assaults of weather, and by the nature of it, when left to itself, like the pyramids of Egypt, would have lasted as long as the globe, [has] fallen a sacrifice to the wretched ignorance and avarice of a little village unluckily plac'd within it.

William Stukeley. *Abury*, 16.

IN 2600 BC the stone temples of Avebury were the wonder of the British Isles. One day's journey to the south, skirting the marshes and then up the slopes of Salisbury Plain, and a traveller would have come to Stonehenge, its low irregular bank enclosing a ring of freshly cut pits. There were no stones. It would be five hundred years before any great sarsen was raised inside the earthen ring. Just one pillar, unshaped and rough, stood beyond the entrance at a point where the sun rose at midsummer but this was an unspectacular place made by workers in wood, diggers of earth, and even the dozen or more long grass-grown mounds in the neighbourhood, covering ancient burials, were not impressive.

North-westwards, fourteen days along the trackways overlooking rivers and forests, then a crossing of the sea, and he would have arrived at the Irish valley of the River Boyne where a multitude of circular tombs, one of them walled white with quartz, clustered together, some of them hillocks higher than trees. Many had carved kerbstones around their bases, decorated in patterns that few people understood. Inside each tomb a passage led to a dark chamber, its roof rising high above the head, and in the gloomy side-cells the dead had been laid, burned, their bones placed on stone basins in the blackness. It was said that at midwinter dawn the sun penetrated the sepulchre, bringing life to the bones.

A further two weeks more, this time northwards past islands green in the Atlantic waters, and a voyager would have come to the Orkneys and to another tomb, Maes Howe, aligned on the midwinter sunset and close to a pair of rings of standing stones put up in the narrow land between two lochs. The circles of Stenness and Brodgar formed one of the great religious centres of the British Isles like the Boyne cemetery with its passage-graves of Dowth, Knowth and New Grange and the smaller mounds on the plain around them. Here in the Orkneys also, at times marked by the movements of the sun, people came for ceremonies that would safeguard their lives.

There were other cult places in Britain, some newly-built rings of stones, others old and decaying on hillsides, their earthen banks weathered, their ditches sour and sticky with leaves, the people who had erected them gone away or their customs changed. But nowhere was like Avebury. Nowhere was there so big a mound made by man higher than many of the hills around it, nowhere else was there a stone tomb and barrow so long, nowhere was there a hilltop enclosure so large, and nowhere was there a ditch so deep inside a bank so vast around a stone circle so enormous. There was nowhere like Avebury. Four and a half thousand years later this is still true.

Avebury stands in a skyline of low, rolling hills at the centre of the Marlborough Downs in North Wiltshire, the ploughed fields speckled with chalk. The soil is rich but on the higher ground innumerable boulders of local sandstone still defy the farmer. These are known as 'sarsens', probably a corruption of 'saracen' or 'heathen stones', because of their association with un-Christian monuments. Whether one approaches Avebury from the north-east through Bishopstone, or from the north through Swindon and Wroughton, or from Alton to the south there are always sarsens to be seen, some split in modern times for gateposts or for farmhouse foundations, others laid by mediaeval masons for their churches, still others set up in circles by prehistoric peasants, and even more lying solid and untouched in the dry valleys where drenched chalk sludged them down from the hills millions of years before man. Sarsens everywhere. Only to the west are they rare, thinning out before one reaches the bacon-factory town of Calne through which Cobbett rode with a disgusted glance at 'an ill-looking, broken-winded place, called the Town Hall, I suppose. I poured out a double dose of execration upon it. "Out of the frying pan into the fire." For in about ten miles more, I came to another rotten hole called Wootton Bassett. This also is a mean vile place.'

Four thousand years before the unhappy Cobbett other people dragged sarsens to Avebury for reasons that this book attempts to explain. With crude picks of antler they prised out ton after ton of chalk, shouldering it in basketloads up onto the rising ring of the bank encircling the stones, back-straining, muscle-breaking labour that continued for years, perhaps through generations so that those who had begun it did not live to see it done, a giant monument amongst other gigantic structures erected in this oddly obsessive colossus of prehistory.

The region is, perhaps always was, strange, a world almost of its own. To the east is Marlborough, a market town lying in a wide hollow beneath the downs, one of the coldest places in the country, half-confined in the widenesses of Savernake Forest. To the west, near Devizes, is the village of Bishops Cannings, lost in a long valley, whose inhabitants gave the nickname of Moonrakers to all Wiltshiremen when one winter night in the early nineteenth century an excise man riding through the village street came upon some locals raking at the bottom of a dewpond on which the moon was brightly reflected. 'Oh, zur', said one of them excitedly, 'Zomebody has been and lost a cheese, and we'm a-rakin of un out thic thur pond.' Smiling at their simplicity the excise man rode on. Smiling at his simplicity the Cannings men raked out the concealed whisky casks that had been smuggled in from the south coast.

Wiltshire is a paradox. Its quiet hills promise peace but army tanks crush large areas of Salisbury Plain. White Horses decorate the hillsides, designed and cut by farmers and parsons one hundred and fifty or more years ago, and yet between Tilshead and Lavington 'Mr. Dean of Imber was attacked and robbed by Four Highwaymen in the evening of October 21, 1839.' In the pursuit that followed this inauspicious Trafalgar Day attack one robber fell dead. The others were transported.

Today the little villages are hardly awakened by the threads of road that twist through them. On the hillsides at sunset shadows magically reveal ancient settlements whose timber houses and stockades have long since disappeared. Yet in

4. Sarsens at Lockeridge Dene in scrubland reminiscent of a prehistoric landscape.

this quietness there is the astonishment of Stonehenge and the equally amazing but less well-known presence of Avebury.

The book is much concerned with the beliefs of the people who built Avebury. Like all problems concerned with matters sunk in the deepness of our remote past it is like trying to touch shadows to see in the dark the people who have gone and who left no word or sound behind them. It is because of this very absence of any firm background for so many of our most interesting sites that the composers of strange theories about them have prospered, creating their own Utopian or UFOnian fantasies, more phony than factual, that distort some of our ancestors' most splendid works. Archaeologists, quite rightly, have condemned this spurious scholarship with its half-truths and misrepresentations and some of the eccentric books about Avebury will be referred to. They are mentioned at this point only because several of them have put forward ideas about Avebury which are entirely untenable but which nevertheless do have a quaint appeal because of a mongreloid mixture of outdated notions, omissions, forthright errors and over-emphatic claims of gods from other worlds.

5. (*over page*) Avebury from the north-north-west, showing the houses inside the earthwork. Top right is Silbury Hill, to its left the gentle slope of Waden Hill, and left again beside the road is the Kennet Avenue.

There never was a 'Golden Age' at Avebury. Spacemen did not visit it. Streams of extra-sensory perception did not infuse the minds of the Neolithic peasants who lived there. To the contrary, life was demanding, insecure, sometimes dangerous. But men were adaptable, changing their way of life as conditions required, seeking solutions to their problems, allaying their fears of the unknown, the darkness, the winter cold, disease, death, by finding new ways of living, new ceremonies and new patterns of ritual to forestall the terrors which always lingered in their unprotected minds. Their imaginations, suspended between savagery and science, had images stalking in them of a primordial existence through which a terrible ancestor moved, Chesterton's being who 'has no name, and all true tales of him are blotted out; yet he walks behind us in every forest path and wakes within us when the wind wakes at night. He is the origins—he is the man in the forest.' To overcome him and other dreads these early people developed elaborate rituals designed to appease the malevolent powers of nature, and often enacted these rites in specially built religious monuments.

At Avebury there are vast ruins of monuments built so that people nearly five thousand years ago could meet on black winter nights and on summer days to take part in rituals that would provide them with some safeguards against the inexplicable perils of their ordinary lives. Today, from this wreckage, with care we may be able to rediscover what those perils were and perhaps even reconstruct what actions were performed to overcome them. From the decaying debris its builders left behind, broken pottery, flints, antlers, chipped stone axes, from a study of the weatherworn banks and mounds, the burial-places around Avebury, and from an understanding of the landscape itself the archaeologist can compose a fuller, truer outline of Avebury's past. The outline may be coloured in from a knowledge of the customs of other, modern primitive societies. But one has to start by putting Avebury in its contexts of geography and archaeology.

We need to know about the other sites in the area, the long barrows with their human burials, the later round barrows with their skeletons and pots and daggers, to know how people lived from day to day if we are to understand what their religious places were. To understand Avebury we must understand the countryside in which the people lived, almost cut off from other groups, farming the chalk soil, using the sarsen stones for building, watering their cattle by the little streams that fed the land. It is necessary to realise that over the centuries of prehistory the climate changed, slightly but decisively. Moulded in their lives by the landscape and by the subtleties of sun, snow and rain the people themselves changed as contacts with other, outside groups created new customs whereby gifts of stone tools, cattle and, maybe, women were exchanged in order to form social links between the communities. Over the years new people brought in new practices. It is from this interaction of people, land, weather and time that the concept of Avebury grew, so that it is only by knowing them that Avebury can be known.

Archaeology offers a passage back into the past although archaeologists know very well that the bits of a smashed pot can tell us very little about the thoughts of the potter. But as all we have left are the very few, broken fragments of things that the Avebury people used we must manage with them. It is, after all, a rigorous but not uninteresting method, this gathering up of all the evidence, omitting nothing, looking for patterns amongst an antique jigsaw from which nine-tenths of the pieces are missing. To it can sometimes be added the results of other enquiries into the mystery of Avebury, however bizarre some of them may have been.

In 1948 Giuseppe Cocchiara wrote, 'Before being discovered, the savage was first invented',[1] something particularly true of early antiquarians who devised the idea of the 'noble savage'. The same has been true of many investigators who have attempted to explain Avebury, and who have inserted their own sometimes grotesque interpretations of prehistoric life in order to buttress their 'explanations' of what Avebury was. Some have been serious, well-researched essays, others simply silly.

William Stukeley, Avebury's first proper chronicler,[2] thought the monument to have been built by the Druids, a mistake of the magnitude of some two thousand years, but this came about because of Stukeley's own realisation that Avebury must belong to a period actually before the Romans arrived in Britain, a thought almost unthinkable in the classically based education of the early eighteenth century. Stukeley was indebted to the perception of that brilliant fieldworker, John Aubrey, for the insight that megalithic structures like Stonehenge and Avebury were prehistoric. But having come to this conclusion Stukeley could go no further. Almost nothing was known of pre-Roman Britain. Yet Avebury was so obviously an important place that it must have been used by powerful priests. Caesar in his *Gallic Wars* had recorded that the chief lawgivers and spiritual leaders in Iron Age Britain when the Romans arrived in 55 BC were the Druids who were 'responsible for all sacrifices, public and private, and they decide all questions of ritual'.[3] As there were no other known candidates it must have been these, Stukeley reasoned, who were the architects of Avebury. He was wrong. The Druids in fact belonged to a society far later than the tribesmen who helped put up the bank and ditch and stones of Avebury. But Stukeley's was an honest and unavoidable error.

His field-observations have provided us with a store of information about the monuments that would otherwise have vanished forever. Modern researchers are also indebted to other pioneers: Sir Richard Colt Hoare and his companion, William Cunnington; William Long; the Revd A. C. Smith; to the excavations of St George Gray and Alexander Keiller; and to the current writings and investigations of Dr Isobel Smith and Mrs Faith Vatcher. These will all be acknowledged with gratitude in their rightful places. But what are we to make of the author who has asserted that Avebury was built as 'England's first city' by a Mediterranean expedition intent on constructing an astronomical observatory at Stonehenge to be used for the prediction of solar eclipses in Egypt?[4] Very little, I fear. There was also the Revd R. Warner's belief, expounded in *The Pagan Altar* (1840), that Stonehenge and Avebury were Phoenician in origin, a mistake comparable to Stukeley's inasmuch as in Victorian times the Phoenicians were regarded as adroit sea-merchants who introduced many aspects of civilisation into Britain. Warner's supposition, therefore, had some merit, more than can be given to W. S. Blacket who in 1883 published his astonishing *Researches into the Lost Histories of America* from which one learns it was Appalachian Indians and their priests who 'must have been the builders of Stonehenge', a pre-Columbian enterprise that surely brought prickles to some prehistoric scalps.

At about the same time as Blacket, James Fergusson[5] was obdurately asserting that Avebury was a memorial to King Arthur's last battle, being the burial-place of his slain warriors, an opinion from which Fergusson was not deflected even after an excavation failed to discover even one skeleton in or near the stone circles within Avebury's enclosing bank.[6]

But if some of these suggestions were ridiculous this is not true of other, quite recent ideas. Since 1955 there has been an increasing acceptance by some archaeologists that the people who erected the stone circles and rows of standing stones actually used a measure when laying out the ground-plans of these sites, not a casual series of paces but a finely defined yardstick, the Megalithic Yard of 0.829 metre, whose length was acknowledged all over Britain. More than this, an extension of the theory claims that the designers of these stone monuments had a knowledge of geometry which they employed to create intentional non-circular forms for some of the rings—ovals and egg-shapes amongst them. Above all, these people, late in the New Stone or Neolithic Age and in the Early Bronze Age, an overall period from about 3000 to 1700 BC, are supposed to have had an advanced understanding of astronomy from which they were able to predict solar and lunar eclipses and to detect minor movements of the moon. Most of these hypotheses come from the stimulating work of Professor Alexander Thom,[7] and they must be considered in this book, something all the more necessary because Thom has also claimed that the asymmetrical shape of Avebury's great stone circle was not accidental but the result of 'the remarkable accuracy with which the whole ring was set out'.[8]

If Thom is right—and there are continuing doubts in the minds of many archaeologists—then a reassessment of the societies that built stone circles and the related earthen rings known as henges is necessary. An unsuspected, authoritarian upper class of priests and astronomers might have existed. Dr Euan MacKie has written, following the excavations of three large earthwork enclosures in Wessex near to Stonehenge and Avebury, that

> the results from these three large henge sites could in my view, have provided the crucially important, direct evidence for the existence of that specialist class of astronomer–priests and wise men in populous lowland Britain which is required by Thom's theories ... The great henges could have been ... the exact counterparts of the Maya ceremonial centres of Central America—the residences, temples and training schools of the learned orders which undertook ... the decades or even centuries of work at the standing stone observatories.[9]

Although, because of the lack of widescale excavation at Avebury, MacKie does not claim it directly Avebury might also have been such a priestly centre. It is very similar to the sites on which MacKie does base his arguments: Marden, Mount Pleasant and Durrington Walls. Instead of being a place for the enacting of barbarous and fearsome rites by superstitious natives it could have been an early

8

form of academy in which novices acquired astronomical lore from their priestly tutors.

If Thom and MacKie are right then the traditional view of peasant communities attempting to protect themselves from the unpredictable dangers of their world by performing acts of savagery and sacrifices amongst the bonfires of autumn must be abandoned as a misleading, old-fashioned picture. If the traditional view is correct then the Megalithic Yard, refined celestial observations and astronomer–priests are no more than illusions created from the mistaken use of statistics.

Quite different from MacKie's learned society of priests and sky-watchers is Michael Dames' vision of a people within a living landscape in which the very shapes of hills, outlines of valleys, wanderings of streams blended into a composition of a godlike torso, artificially enhanced by the erection of burial mounds and ritual centres at significant positions on the countryside's anatomy: 'the Avebury monuments were created as a coherent ensemble to stage a religious drama which took one year to perform, with each edifice offering in turn a special setting for the celebration of a particular event in the farming year'.[10]

These, then, are some of the ways in which Avebury has been visualised. Strangely, despite its grandeur and its invariable mention in books about prehistoric Britain, there have been very few works devoted exclusively to it. Since Stukeley's major study in 1743 only three objective books have appeared. In the mid-nineteenth century William Long[11] collected all the data he could, including unpublished material from John Aubrey's field-notes in the Bodleian Library at Oxford.[12] A hundred years later Dr Isobel Smith prepared a meticulous account of the excavations of the late Alexander Keiller at Windmill Hill and Avebury,[13] an exemplary record of the work done by this rich amateur archaeologist and member of the family Dundee marmalade firm. It is relevant to add that the description of Avebury is contained within less than one-third of the book because of the small proportion of his time that Keiller spent excavating there. Finally, in 1976, Faith de Mallet Vatcher, Curator of Avebury Museum, published an admirable booklet, *The Avebury Monuments*, which provided up-to-date information about the visitable sites in the district. Necessarily her account was limited to a very few pages so that much detail had to be left out. Most of this minutiae, fascinating but hardly known, is contained within learned journals, antiquarian books and manuscripts reaching back three hundred years. A different kind of 'unconscious' information comes from the excavated material, in the pots and implements stored in the delightful museums of Devizes and Salisbury, the British Museum in London, and at Avebury itself.

For many years it was an article of faith that stone circles were built by the Beaker Folk, the first users of metal in this country, whose skeletons have been so often discovered at the foot of standing stones. These people who first entered these islands around 2500 BC have lost some of their mystique. Once regarded as warriors, metalsmiths and conquerors, one recent suggestion has been that their fine pots were not objects of prestige to match their own awe-inspiring weaponry but were vessels to hold Britain's first intoxicating drink, reducing Beaker people from war-leaders to prehistoric hooch-pedlars akin to bootleggers and the sellers of red-eye to simple but eager Indians.

9

THE LIBRARY

 THE SURREY INSTITUTE OF ART & DESIGN

Farnham Campus, Falkner Road, Farnham, Surrey GU9 7DS

6. 'An Ancient Briton', drawn by John White for Hariot's *Briefe and True Report of the New Found Land of Virginia*, 1590. This is the kind of picture many scholars of the sixteenth and seventeenth centuries had of prehistoric people.

It is now known that stone circles were being built in this country long before the first Beaker sandal disturbed our beaches, and it is archaeological revision such as this that makes a reassessment of Avebury necessary. The only intelligent means to investigate the past is to assemble all the evidence, much of it obtained through the painstaking recovery of decayed rubbish by archaeologists: potsherds, corroded bronze, flints, skeletons of the long dead. To this can be added the less reliable evidence of place-names and folklore. Then the landscape within which the people of Avebury lived has to be brought into the story, and one should also take note of modern primitive societies, their fears, social customs, their ceremonies and festivals.

It has already been mentioned that of late it has become fashionable to hint of a golden age of science, advanced mathematics and astronomy. This is 'soft' primitivism, reshaping our forebears into the image of the noble savage, Einstein in a sheepskin. But it is as legitimate and possibly more trustworthy to turn to 'hard' primitivism, the comparison of prehistoric people with today's primitive communities, the sort of analogy that seventeenth- and eighteenth-century historians made between the recently encountered Indians of America and the suspected condition of prehistoric Britain.

> For Mr. Speed, in his chronicle, pictureth an old Briton, naked. Lions, Beares, Serpents painted on him to terrifie enemies, with a lance in his hand, and on the butt end whereof is such a bell screwed fast, which served in steade of a Trumpett to alarme, and a clubb to dash out the enemies braines, and this bell was, I suppose, the permanent part of that old Briton's weapon there buried with its owner.

Even if exaggerated such a comparison in 1722 by the unknown author of *A Fool's bolt soon shott at Stonage* does animate the picture of Avebury and its stones, and gives a lively impression of a remote people. Such anthropological parallels, if not overstated, provide yet another way back into the murk of prehistory.

Above all, one should look at the monuments themselves, shattered, wrecked, bleached of humanity by a million rains:

> a dismal cirque
> Of Druid stones, upon a forlorn moor,
> When the chill rain begins at shut of eve,
> In dull November, and their chancel vault,
> The Heaven itself, is blinded throughout night.
>
> John Keats. *Hyperion*, II. i. 31.

Keats was writing of the stone circle near Keswick in the Lake District, the Castlerigg ring, and his words remind us that Avebury is not alone. There are comparable earthworks and stone circles in Wiltshire, Dorset, Somerset, even as far north as Yorkshire and Northumberland. From them may come further clues to help solve Avebury's mystery. Nor is Avebury isolated in its own countryside. Within a radius of three miles, an hour's walk over the low, climbing hills, there are long burial mounds, round barrows, field boundaries, sites of prehistoric market-fairs. Traces of settlement survive. Within seven miles there were once three enormous man-made hills piled up alongside water by the people to whom Avebury was the religious centre. All this is contained in an area of thirty square miles, far smaller than modern London. As we look at the map and at the pattern that the circles and burial-places make then the questions to be asked are clarified.

1. How old is Avebury? Is it possible for us to be sure that we know the time when it was built?

2. How was it built? What techniques were used to heave stones over fifty tons in mass-weight upright? How was a ditch ten metres deep dug into rock-hard chalk?

3. Which people built Avebury? What do we know, not only of their way of life, the places where they lived, the tools they used, but of the people themselves, what they looked like, how long they lived?

4. And, in conclusion, the most important question of all, what was Avebury used for? What did people do inside the rings of stones, at what time of the year, and did they have priests, witch-doctors? What alien beliefs fashioned their rituals?

To answer any of these questions we have to put together all the information we can find about Avebury and look at everything, not just one or two aspects such as the geometry or astronomy but the total evidence of the remains of the people. Thompson, the doyen of Mayan archaeology has remarked, 'Maya astronomy is too important to be left to the astronomers.' The same archaeologist's advice to those who proposed to make a study of Mayan astronomy would apply equally well to the student of Avebury. Of Thompson's attitude towards any investigation of prehistory Aveni has written:

> We would do well to follow the path he mapped out for us in pursuing our future studies . . . His advice is simple: we must immerse ourselves in the knowledge of the culture and history of these people. Together with an understanding of astronomy, we must also pay close attention to the findings of archaeology, and finally, we must try not to look at their astronomy through European eyes. Only then can we begin to 'get inside the skin' of the priest–astronomer.[14]

This, then, is the story of Avebury as it may be told today. And it is with today that the story must begin.

CHAPTER ONE

Avebury Today

To take in all the beautys of Abury we must widen our imagination and think with the antients.

William Stukeley. *Great Prospect* (Keiller MSS)

AVEBURY was built near the inland edge of the high country, almost in an island of chalk. The clay lowlands of Oxford and the Thames Valley stretched to the north and east, and to the south there was the flatness of the Vale of Pewsey with Salisbury Plain beyond. Far to the west the hills of Somerset separated Avebury from the waters of the Severn Estuary. Only to the north-east could one follow the limestone ridges through the Midlands to where the chalk reappeared on the Lincolnshire and Yorkshire Wolds. For much of their history the downlands of Avebury must have been encircled by forests and swamps that discouraged travelling.

Today there are many ways to reach Avebury. By car one can arrive from the north, climbing the steep escarpment from Swindon then driving along the twisted road to the first sight of the earthwork framed in its tall trees. From the west cars thrust along the Devizes–Marlborough highway up to the Beckhampton traffic island where the Avebury road turns away from Silbury Hill, no longer a highway but a lane that rises to a panorama of the downs with Avebury resting at the bottom of the near slope. From the south another lane at the foot of Overton Hill also ascends, slowly, quietly, finds the stones of the Kennet Avenue alongside it, edges in and then out of them, and sinks to join the western lane at Avebury's entrance.

Only from the east is there no motor road, strange because until the mid-eighteenth century this was the main thoroughfare, marching the Saxons westwards on their conquest of Wessex, carrying the London stage-coaches on their travels to Bath. And it is from the east, if one has time and choice, that Avebury is best approached, walking down the ancient path from the Ridgeway, between the fields and up to the fourth of Avebury's entrances where a gigantic sarsen lies by the ditch. Ideally, if one were to approach as many of the first travellers approached, slowly, on foot, in the open air of the high downs, an enthusiast would start six miles away at the exposed north-western corner of the Marlborough Downs at Barbury Castle. He could leave his car at this Iron Age hillfort and follow the prehistoric Ridgeway, which was already at least three thousand years old when the first Roman road in Britain was being laid out. Here it scrambles up the sides of Barbury to a point from which one can depart easily for Avebury. The view is astonishing. From this shoulder of Hackpen Hill the chalk falls seventy metres to a three-mile-wide shelf of scattered villages amongst the inverted saucers of the hills. At its far edge the land slips down as steeply and deeply again into the wooded, thickly farmed greensands, gaults and clays around Clyffe Pypard, Hilmarton and Bremhill.

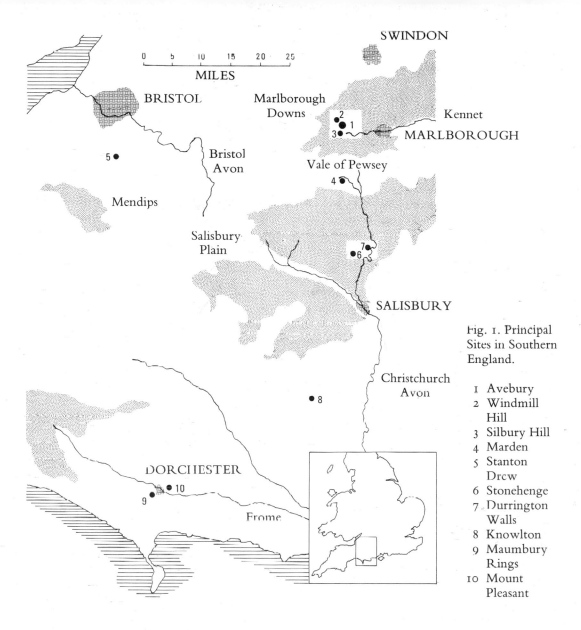

Fig. 1. Principal Sites in Southern England.

1 Avebury
2 Windmill Hill
3 Silbury Hill
4 Marden
5 Stanton Drew
6 Stonehenge
7 Durrington Walls
8 Knowlton
9 Maumbury Rings
10 Mount Pleasant

So spectacular and quiet are these heights that years ago the poet and naturalist Richard Jefferies often went for contemplation to the hillforts of Barbury and of Liddington which has been proposed as the site of Arthur's greatest battle, Mount Badon.[1] On Barbury a sarsen carries an inscription to Jefferies:

> It is Eternity now.
> I am in the midst of it.
> It is about me in the sunshine.

From Barbury the Ridgeway treads along a high slope sharp against the horizon, 'seeming to touch it, and every footstep opens up a slightly different view of the never-changing, always subtly changing countryside of the high Downs'.[2] It crosses the Broad Hinton–Rockley road near a White Horse cut a couple of centuries ago

7. The Ridgeway near the chambered tomb of Waylands Smithy in Berkshire.

on the chalk hillside, passes between humid hedgerows and then opens out into the space of the sarsen-spread downs with their harebells, rock-roses and trefoils, knuckle-gnarled trees, wide miles to the left hand of folded downland while to the west the low-lying country stretches green from the foot of the hills.

Along the skyline the circular mounds of barrows, sometimes in groups, show where Bronze Age people buried their important dead. Fields are fenced with barbed wire. Sarsens tumble round trees where farmers have dragged them. It is a silent place. Nor is there much movement except for the fragile hovering of a lark. The Ridgeway, moving downwards, meets the Herepath, the Saxon army-road down which Avebury lies off to the right at the end of the farm-track, its bank just visible in the haze of the plain, darkened by the trees that grow around it.

Walking down this old path with its ruts and patches of clay the antiquity of the landscape reaches everywhere, in the church towers and deeper still in the barrows now silhouetted against the sky from the lower slopes, on Windmill Hill straight

14

8. From the Ridgeway, looking down to the western shelf of chalk on which Avebury stands.

ahead where men were farming five and a half thousand years ago, and as the track changes to a metalled, hedged road at the vast bank of Avebury itself, solid and heavy on the heart of the land.

Despite contrary claims Avebury is not a particularly attractive village. It cannot match the thatched, honey-coloured loveliness of Sandy Lane a few miles to the west. It straddles a crossroads with the Red Lion pub at one corner. During the summer the few houses to the east are almost cut off from the west by the simultaneous traffic from north and south of cars, lorries, vans, buses, motorcycles and coaches lurching and accelerating round the two bends in a madman's rally that never stops. Even the visitors to Avebury turn off as though for a reluctant pit-stop before re-entering the noise of the race.

Walking in from the east one is soon aware of this bustle, an irritation which the first houses do not assuage. Once past the bank and the massive, prostrate stone there is little sign that this is one of the most intriguing prehistoric temples in the British

9. The South Circle at Avebury with the village beyond.

Isles. Instead, one sees a dirty brick cottage with a rusting lean-to shed, another with weather-stained stucco, a gap, a barn, a fallen sarsen, a final stone-built cottage by the site of the old Catherine Wheel Inn where Stukeley stayed on his yearly visits. Opposite the barn there is an attractive half-timbered cottage, then a flurry of private 'No Parking' signs, and the United Reform Church, established in 1670 just after the visit of Charles II and John Aubrey. 'Heretofore nothing but religious houses . . . now nothing but Quakers and Fanatiqs', Aubrey wistfully wrote thinking of such Puritan chapels and of the golden traditional days before the Civil War. Beyond the chapel and built two hundred years after it is a little general shop, the only one, cobble-fronted, with paintings of Avebury in the 1930s.

Rather oddly there are no houses on the north or south roads, just fields, but beyond the main road the village extends westwards and things are better. Because the National Trust has discouraged commercialism there is almost no trace of the customary gaudiness that infiltrates most famous places, just a couple of pleasant souvenir shops with books, pots of mustard and local pottery. Nearby are lavatories, a small carpark and a discreet telephone box convenient for making notes in the rain. Hardly a hundred yards from the busy road Avebury is a hamlet again. It is very much a country place and from this lane the only indication that one is standing in an ancient temple is the sight of one of the courteous, uniformed custodians strolling unobtrusively amongst the crowds of visitors. Otherwise this could be just another Wiltshire village.

There is a bewilderment of architecture. A cottage with a buckling, dark-tiled roof looks across to a stately brick house with mansard roof and dormer windows. Near a reconstructed stone a corrugated shack stares at a row of terraced cottages of uncertain style with ornate tiles and lumpish archways that contrast with the imposing stone gateway surmounted by stone balls that leads to the manor and the pigeon-house. Beyond a superfluous swing-gate there is the church's lych-gate, erected in memory of Hannah Price, and there is the church itself with its tower and gilt clock, and a glimpse of Avebury Manor. The street continues its ribbon development. It attracts the eye because of the changing heights made by the trees, the roofs, the blend of tiles and thatch, crossed with wires like a rain-beaten spider's web. Over the road from a *mélange* of nineteenth-century cottages is a mixture of more thatch, whitewashed façades, an antique collapsing porch, climbing roses, television aerials and an ultimate attractive eighteenth-century house before the lane ends at a clapboard greenish fence and a wall where lavender grows.

The alleyway on the right has a pebbledashed shop whose thatched roof looks like two sagging haystacks and the impression is of a village that has grown with no thought of its fame. Yet its past has not escaped it. Fragments of sarsen are everywhere, like lucky charms, at the corners of the houses, along the alleys, in walls, greys, browns, tans, smoky-whites, deep reds, a pile of broken pieces lying like a breakwater behind the gate of Manor Farm. But it was not sarsen that brought people to this place over a thousand years ago but the existence of the earthwork that offered protection from the Saxon marauders who came again and again to this region. Then the Saxons themselves settled here and in mediaeval times more people still until a whole village was here 'like some beautiful parasite grown up at the expense, and in the midst of the ancient temple'.

And yet the truly casual visitor wandering up and down this one lane could almost miss this temple entirely. Looking idly at the buildings one could wonder what all the people were doing here except that at just one point where the rusting shed lurks in its bushes there is a grassy space, fenced but with a gate, and here one can see a smooth arc of great standing stones curving around the side of a valley-like ditch with an embankment on its far rim, bending out of sight a good two hundred metres from the viewer. It is these remains and not the village that people mean when they speak of Avebury, described by one of Avebury's earliest chroniclers, Sir Richard Colt Hoare, as 'the supposed parent of Stonehenge, the wonder of Britain, and the most ancient, as well as the most interesting relict which our island can produce'.[3] Anyone who has seen the awesome stones and the sheer size of the bank would think this no exaggeration.

Over a quarter of a million people every year come to Avebury to saunter around the crest of the bank and look down on the ruined stone circles below them. Nearly one in three visits the museum with its vividly displayed exhibits from Keiller's excavations. Some of the tourists have been brought here by evocative television

10. The southern Entrance Stones with the bank beyond.

programmes. Others come to walk between the stones, dowsing rods akimbo, to absorb the psychic emanations. Most come from a vague interest in the past that remains ill-defined because there is not much available to make the focus clearer. For such visitors Avebury offers an emotional response, not an informed answer to their questions.

The first impression of Avebury from the village lane is of hugeness, of the massiveness of the bank and ditch and then, as one wanders past stone after stone, of heaviness, the weight of these thick sarsens. Finally, on the far side of the main road one is aware of vastness, of the enormous space in which the village and trees and fields are microcosmic.

From the western entrance the site seems impressive but uncomplicated. Children run along the top of the worn bank, chase and totter down its sides, down the slopes into the deep ditch and look back up, amazed at the height of the bank above them where their parents stand dwarfed against the sky. Daunted, the children haul themselves up the inner face of the ditch to the curve of standing stones. The stones are so big that even adults seem like six-year-olds alongside them. At this point it is clear that they are part of a circle so big that the eye cannot encompass it.

11. The bank and ditch at the south-east arc of Avebury.

At the south-east there is another entrance and the road must be crossed, more hazardous this time because of the nearness of the corner and absence of a footpath. Two fantastic stones rise here, each one big enough to be the side of a cottage. The bank and ditch continue to curve away to the left but now without their accompanying stones, just one prostrate block, an ash tree growing halfway down the ditch, a line of sycamores with bark like peeling red tobacco, and one more half-buried stone at the eastern entrance where the Herepath comes in from the downs.

Outside this entrance, mutilated by a disused pond, the ground rises quite steeply towards the downs so that anyone approaching Avebury would look down to the entrance, the bank, the great sarsen. Northwards the bank is rippled like Doric fluting as though some incredible pillar overgrown with moss had fallen sideways. No stones stand here. This is a field where the grass is long and the ditch and bank are at their wildest.

It is an aspect that changes as one recrosses the road at the north entrance. This is where the Swindon Stone stands, a mountainous lozenge of sarsen whose inner face is a swirl of pastel colours, pinky-brown at the base, fawns above, that merge into the grey elephantine wrinkles of its west shoulder. This smooth side contrasts

12. Circle stones in the north-west arc of Avebury. The Swindon Stone is on the left.

harshly with the savagely torn outer face, pocked and ravaged by a million years of weather, dark-grey and dead. This gross, unshaped block, balanced delicately on one corner, demonstrates yet another of Avebury's mysteries. It measures about four by three metres along its sides and is over a metre thick of solid sandstone. It weighs nearly fifty tons and must have demanded the muscles of scores if not hundreds of people to heave upright. The very dragging of it over a mile or more from the upper downs must have been a major piece of engineering. Most onlookers today, staring in wonderment at its bulk, must ask themselves what compulsive need, what obsessions, forced people into such effort.

Beyond this stone more sarsens turn in an arc past a row of dying elms back to the western entrance. Here the bank has been levelled to make room for a barn, and on the other side of the ditch a house has been built where stones once stood so that the visitor must descend some wooden steps and walk back to the main street.

All this can be seen from a walk around the bank's top and it is obvious from the bared earth of the trail that many people have followed this path. Even more have gone straight to the centre of the ring where the fields are marked by the worn-down lines of old hedgerows and walls, and where other stones stand on the shattered circumferences of two other, smaller circles. Their remains are hard to decipher. In the north-east quarter of Avebury two more unbelievably large stones

13. The smooth, inner face of the Swindon Stone at Avebury's northern entrance.

stand at right-angles to one another, all that is left of what Stukeley called the 'Cove' which once had a third stone opposite the first making a construction like an unroofed sentry box with an open face towards the Marlborough Downs. Virtually nothing is preserved of the concentric rings of stones that originally surrounded this peculiar feature of the North inner circle. The South Circle has been more fortunate.

In the southern field where cattle graze there is an almost perfect arc of stones, the survivors of this south inner ring. One wide pillar has a notched top like a rifle-sight. Near it a straightish line of lower stones extends towards the cottage gardens that have digested the northern segment of the circle. Close to its centre a concrete obelisk, shaped like a diminutive Mayan pyramid, marks the position of a missing stone. But there is nothing to explain the relationship of one stone to another, of the circles to each other, of the inner rings to the ditch and bank, nothing to make clear why a double row of stones can be seen leading to Avebury from the south. Even in the relatively well-preserved South Circle the puzzle of what Avebury was remains with the visitor. He has seen the stones. There is little else. An isolated fallen pillar. Some concrete markers to show where other stoneholes have been located, the stones themselves long vanished. Trees on the bank. Cars. A sense of emptiness, of history itself in ruins.

21

14. The two remaining stones of the Cove of the North Circle.

I. (*right*) The Kennet Avenue, looking towards Avebury.
II. (*over page*) The south-west arc of the Outer Circle, looking north-west.

Outside the earthwork a more recent past and the battered fragments of older monuments intermingle. Near the manor-house and church some thatched cottages nudge together against the nettle-thick path that goes westwards to the footbridge over the Winterbourne, past Truslowe Manor, a lovely sixteenth-century house with mullioned windows and hip roof, and up to Avebury Trusloe village. This is on higher ground than Avebury with the stream in between on wet winter land. There is a huddle of pleasing brown brick houses and then, across the open fields and crops, there are two more great sarsens, almost camouflaged by the oak wood behind them. Beyond is the bush-covered hillock of the Longstones long barrow in which Neolithic skeletons still lie. Other long barrows nearby, South Street, Beckhampton, have been ploughed and destroyed but in the other direction the edge of Silbury Hill slides out half a mile behind the trees that shadow the thatched stonework of the Waggon and Horses pub with its flowerboxes and cobbled forecourt. Near the Hill, at the summit of a long ridge, the finest megalithic tomb in England and Wales, West Kennet, stands against the skyline, plucked of its human bones but with its stone chambers restored and standing as they did when Neolithic farmers were planting crops and tending their cattle at the springs near Silbury.

All this, the earthen long barrows, the megalithic tombs, Silbury Hill, Avebury itself, belongs to a period five thousand years ago when there was no writing, no way nor any intention of recording the thoughts of the people who raised these monuments. Now even the sites themselves are so damaged that it seems an impossibility ever to find out what they were meant for. Indeed, it appears unlikely that even their original appearance can be rediscovered, let alone the beliefs of their builders. Yet the attempt must be made. Avebury is important. Those who made it are part of our heritage and their thoughts have in part shaped our own just as well-established plants affect the growth of seedlings. The Christian Church did not weed out paganism. It came to terms with it and the two grew together, intertwined, so that even today some of our most ancient past is still with us.

This provides even more reason to explore the roots of these prehistoric places as far as scholarship will permit. Even here the alternatives are many. One archaeological view is that Avebury was put up as a general meeting-place for ceremonies connected with the fertility of the land 'and it has been hazarded that it may have been used by the tribesmen when they gathered at Avebury for seasonal festivals; standing or sitting on the sloping bank, much like the audience in a Roman amphitheatre or a bull-ring they could have watched the rituals celebrated within'.[4] The part astronomy is thought to have had in this sort of interpretation was only a very general one. 'Of the nature of this cult we can only guess by analogy that an open sanctuary is appropriate to a sky-god, and that some may have been planned in relation to a celestial phenomenon such as sunrise at the summer solstice.'[5]

Other researchers, however, look upon Avebury as something much more scientific.

The high degree of organisation and administration responsible for the impressive Breton alignments and the presence in Brittany and Scotland of identical units [of

III. (left) The bank and ditch with the Entrance Stones, and the south-west arc beyond.

measurement] suggests a common culture. Which area was the Center of this culture? The extensive remains in Brittany are suggestive, but Thom and Thom indicate that so far none of the Breton sites examined affords a geometry comparable to that of Avebury.[6]

The suggestion here is of a priestly caste inhabiting Avebury, very different from Jacquetta Hawkes' tribesmen squatting on the bank. These hypothetical experimenters and teachers are supposed to have disseminated from their megalithic temple the rules of measurement, geometry and astronomy that enabled less learned people to erect their own circles and observatories in distant regions as far away as Brittany and the Orkneys. It is a tempting theory. It is easy to reconcile this idea of a priesthood with the size of the earthwork and the grandeur of the megaliths because such works could surely only have been built at the orders of a powerful and intelligent authority.

It is doubtful, though, whether this really is the explanation for Avebury. However easy it may be to associate an erudite priesthood with the architecture of the stone circles it is far less easy to identify them with the actual people whose remains have been discovered in the burial mounds around Avebury. As far as we can tell these barrows were used for the burial only of privileged people whose wisdom, wealth, courage or family connections entitled them to distinctive treatment. It can be taken for granted that had a priestly elite existed its members would assuredly have been included in this special class and that their remains would be found in some of the earlier long barrows and later round tumuli of the Avebury district. If this is so it is very difficult to detect them.

15. A romanticised nineteenth-century sketch of the Roundway Down burial with a beaker at its feet. In reality the bones would have been much more disarranged.

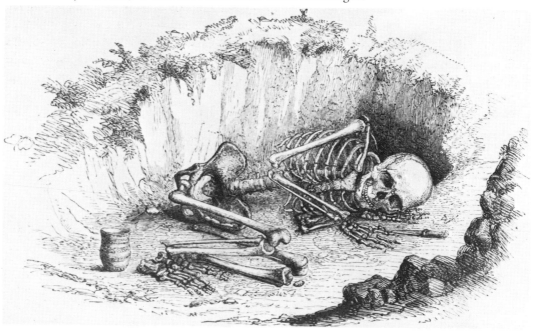

28

On Roundway Down, not many miles from the circles, one of these round barrows was excavated in the mid-nineteenth century. It was a small artificial hillock of chalk and earth that had been heaped over a pit lined with stones in which the skeleton of a very old man lay with his most valued possessions: a bronze dagger and pin; a flint arrowhead; an elegantly decorated beaker pot; a perforated rectangle of stone to protect his wrist from the lacerating bow-string. Lying there on his hillside overlooking the Vale of Pewsey his powerful bones caused the excavator to write: 'The skull possesses all the characteristics of that of a man of great physical power, who through a long career in a rude and barbarous state of society had maintained a successful struggle with, and supremacy over the wild animals from which he obtained food and clothing.'[7]

However romantic this picture it does fit better with other archaeological evidence than the idea of a scholarly priesthood. So does the diagnosis of another elderly male whose bones were found in the West Kennet megalithic tomb itself only two miles from Avebury. The man's left arm had been fractured and had healed. He had a supernumerary toe. He may have suffered from spina bifida and a later spinal breakdown caused by physical stress. There was what looked like an arrow-wound in his left arm. He may even have been deliberately murdered. A flint arrowhead lay near his throat.[8] It is hard to think of this injured cripple as a scientific observer of the skies. Yet, as will be seen in later chapters, his is not an extraordinary and selected case. Most people of his time had similar deficiencies. At Avebury itself, in the ditch to the east of the South Entrance the skeleton of a woman was unearthed, a woman about thirty years of age, the bones of her head heavy, her teeth worn down, one already lost in her lifetime, almost a dwarf less than a metre and a half tall, buried in the rubble that had tumbled into the ditch in its early years.[9]

Undoubtedly these were people who knew Avebury in its lifetime. The man from West Kennet may have helped build it. The man from Roundway Down, the woman at Avebury not only knew it but probably went to it for their ceremonies. We need to know about these people as well as about the architecture of the monument. The first question, however, is to determine what Avebury looked like before it was so badly damaged. To do that we must understand how this damage occurred.

> The Druid's groves are gone—so much the better:
> Stone-henge is not—but what the devil is it?
>
> Lord Byron. *Don Juan*, XI. 25

CHAPTER TWO

The Destruction of Avebury

When I frequented this place, as I did for some years together, to take an exact account of it, staying a fortnight at a time, I found out the entire work by degrees. The second time I was here, an avenue was a new amusement. The third year another. So that at length I discovered the mystery of it.

William Stukeley. *Abury*, 18.

UNLIKE Stonehenge in the undisturbed wildness of Salisbury Plain Avebury's past was restless. From Saxon battles to juggernaut lorries thumping against stones the village has known lawsuits, robbery, violent death and murder. Because of its isolation Stonehenge has almost no written history, only occasional disruptions by Romans, Christians or eighteenth-century curio-seekers but Avebury has chronicles reaching back to Saxon settlers, records that show what has happened to this prehistoric temple since the Iron Age. Mysteries remain. We still do not know who built the church or who ordered the first burying of the stones. But we do have a good idea of what today's ruin looked like when the Romans came.

Avebury was erected around 2600 BC and was used as a temple for nearly a thousand years. During those years customs inevitably changed and with a deterioration in the climate this enormous open-air sanctuary gradually lost its importance. By the Iron Age, that period of tribal warfare when most hill-forts were constructed, few people came to Avebury. What lingering ceremonies there were, thinly attended, were probably only distortions of the original rites. Avebury had been forgotten.

Two thousand years ago it was very much as it had been when it was built. Maybe a stone or two had fallen amongst the thick grass. Trees, bushes, undergrowth made it a wilderness. Yet it is likely that a Roman visitor saw the circles in their entirety uncluttered by huts or barns. Since at least 1000 BC they had been deserted. No Iron Age pottery or equipment has been excavated here and any native in Roman times being asked what Avebury was might have replied as African negroes did when questioned about the ancient Gambian stone circles, simply and with a shrug of ignorance, 'that the olden people did it', adding vaguely that the circles were the haunt of a powerful Earth Spirit.[1] Avebury survived in the safety of neglect.

The Romans altered nothing. In the early centuries AD tourists came from the nearby towns of Cunetio (Marlborough), Durocornovium (Wanborough) and the villa and farms near Devizes, travelling along the new road that had been aligned on the landmark of Silbury Hill. They were fascinated by prehistoric places just as their contemporaries were by the pyramids. One visitor lost a bronze brooch almost immediately after the invasion of AD 43.[2] Over the centuries sherds of Romano-British pottery washed down into the ditch. Sometimes these semi-Romanised

Britons continued native traditions, placating the local gods by dropping offerings into the wells around Silbury or in the spring alongside the prehistoric Marlborough Mound. 'Roman coins have been found in shaping the mount', wrote Stukeley. Then in the troubled fourth and fifth centuries people concealed hoards of coins in conspicuous prehistoric monuments: in the forecourt of West Kennet megalithic tomb; and in the top of a round barrow on Overton Down a mile from Avebury. A century ago one of these hoards was noted at Beckhampton.

> When instructing a labourer in Avebury as to searching for ancient relics for me, I happened to have a few 3rd century British Roman coins in my pocket, which I showed him, and asked if he had ever found any like them, he replied, 'When I were digging them big stones at Beckhampton I dug up lots on 'em, but I thought na one took no notice on 'em so I let 'em bide.'[3]

Many of the hoards were never recovered by their owners. Towns decayed. Bands of mercenaries raped the countryside. Late in the fifth century a rebellion of Saxons devastated western Britain and it may have been around 490 that Arthur's triumphant battle of Mount Badon was fought, repelling the Saxons for a further fifty years. It must have been near Avebury. Whether the fight took place at Liddington hill-fort nine miles north-east or on a hilltop near Bath twenty miles to the west Avebury lay directly on the line of the Saxon advance and the earthwork may have been used as a temporary defence by the Britons just like some hill-forts on the Welsh border at this time.[4]

Despite Badon Britain was doomed. An outbreak of plague preceded another onslaught, this time from the south. A Saxon victory near Carisbrooke Castle on the Isle of Wight in 530 was followed by successes at Old Sarum in 552 and at Barbury Castle in 556. A few years later a decisive British defeat at Dyrham twenty-five miles west of Avebury left much of western Britain under Saxon control. What is of interest in these forgotten clashes between Saxon spears and British horsemen is that in these southern campaigns the British often fought from ancient defensive sites, perhaps from the Roman fort at Carisbrooke, maybe from the hill forts at Mount Badon, Old Sarum and Barbury that stood by trackways that the Saxons followed.

Avebury was on a trackway, the Herepath or army-way along which the few-score men that made up a Saxon host trudged warily through the hostile country, and there is a hint that Avebury was used as a defence by the British. We do not know the prehistoric name for Avebury. But in an Assize Roll of 1289 it was called Waledich,[5] a name that was repeated as Waldich in 1307 and 1309. It was still being called Wall-dyke as late as the nineteenth century. The most likely derivation for this is the Saxon *weala-dic*, the moat of the Britons, a vivid title if Avebury had been used, however temporarily, to hold up the invaders. If this is so then Fergusson's suggestion that this was the site of Arthur's great battle was not wholly nonsensical. The bank and deep ditch would have offered protection from surprise attack at a time when a Saxon 'army' was the size of a Red Indian war party, and a British 'cavalry unit' hardly bigger than a sheriff's posse.[6]

One wonders what they thought, these shabby veterans, as they straggled past the godlike stones that seemed to be the work of otherworld beings, lonely now, mouldering. Saxon poets had elegiac eyes.

> Wondrous is this wall-stone;
> broken by fate, the castles have decayed;
> the work of giants is crumbling.
>
> *The Ruin*

Nothing was eternal.

> . . . day by day
> All this Earth ages   and droops unto death.
>
> *The Wanderer*

More battles were fought. Only a few miles south of Avebury the Ridgeway squeezes between the hills and the land drops steeply, an ideal place for an ambush. Adam's Grave, a long prehistoric mound, overlooks the track. The Saxons called it Wodnesbeorh (Wodin's Barrow), thinking it the grave of their god. The Anglo-Saxon Chronicle for 592 says, 'In this year there was a great slaughter at Wodnesbeorh and Ceawlin was expelled.'

Maybe at this time the colossal Wansdyke was dug, twelve miles of trench and bank from Morgan's Hill in the west where it lay on top of the Roman road across to Savernake Forest, an equal distance to the east from Avebury, where it meandered unsurely through the trees and petered out just below Marlborough. An impressive section of it can still be seen from the main road four miles west of Avebury. Bonney has written:

> Furthermore, the concentration of Woden names in the vicinity of Wodnesbeorg
> . . . has been attributed to the existence of a pagan sanctuary sacred to the god, and
> perhaps intimately connected with the building of the dyke. A further possibility
> is that such a sanctuary did exist, that the district became a centre of Woden's cult,
> and that the dyke simply acquired its name by association.[7]

We do not know whether Avebury itself was the focus of pagan religion but the evidence of Saxon place-names seems significant. A place-name was, of course, nothing more than a description of the place in current language, Celtic, Saxon, early English—'the wooded hill', 'the swift river', 'the cottage by the marsh'. As the language changed and as dialect led to mispronunciation so the meaning became obscure and it now requires place-name experts to demonstrate that Piggledean near Avebury was once *pyttel-denu*, the valley of the hawks, and that Chittoe may have been *coed-yw*, the yew wood. Such explanations are invaluable to any student of the distant past. Once the language is recognised then the name can be interpreted and the period of its formation deduced.

Within ten miles of Avebury there are several names associated with paganism: Wansdyke (Wodin's ditch); Wodin's Barrow for Adam's Grave; Waden Hill by Avebury; perhaps Wanborough (Wodin's hill). Near Tockenham, seven miles north-west, was Weoland, the place of the heathen temple. In the early seventh century when Christianity was reaching Wiltshire resistance to the new faith may have concentrated around ancient holy places, particularly in those areas where the Britons themselves were not entirely subjugated. The villages of Marden and Cherhill and the river Kennet have Celtic names. Welsh, the Celtic tongue, was being spoken in parts of Wiltshire as late as the Norman Conquest.[8]

32

The name of the Kennet itself may be prehistoric,[9] and names of fields near the river and streams that feed it are as old. A tributary from Yatesbury that joins the Kennet at Avebury is called the Sambourn. There is a Sambourne Field near Horslip and another in West Overton, both within a mile of Avebury. Sambourn is the Sam or Sem stream and has its counterparts elsewhere, not only in Wiltshire where the Sem river flows past Sem Hill and Semley, but also in Somerset where the Semington brook runs by Seend and in Wales where the Synfynwy rises. In France there is a Sumène river in the Massif-Central, and there are two other Sumène rivers in France and there is also the Somme. These names all come from the Celtic *sumina* which may have meant 'water' or 'drink' and are extremely old. Within such a background the Wiltshire peasantry, superstitious and conservative, continued in the ways of their forefathers ignoring the cajoling of Christian preachers with their foreign notions.

Pagan Briton, pagan Saxon went on worshipping at the hallowed places at the traditional times of the year. From the activities of churchmen at Avebury in mediaeval times it seems that the stone circles were being used as pagan centres for many centuries after the coming of Christianity.

People had settled at Avebury as long ago as the sixth century AD. A *grubenhaus*, a sunken-floored timber hut, has been excavated just outside the west bank. There cannot have been many early farmers, for it was not for several hundred years, perhaps after 900, that a little church was built between the earthwork and the Winterbourne where the villagers could water their beasts. It is noticeable, however, that it was put up just outside the west entrance as if recognising that Christianity was as yet too feeble to destroy the alien and evil strength of the stone circles inside.[10] It may have been a field-church for the shepherds on the downs, a chapel rather than a church, with no graveyard. Although, strangely, there was no manor here the church appears to have been ordered by a Saxon king, for in Domesday Book it is described as in *terra regis*, the king's land, though by then land and church had been given to Regenbald, possibly the chancellor of Edward the Confessor. The village was small. Only two hides were under cultivation, about half a square mile, just enough to keep two families. Little remains of the early church. In 1880 a pair of round Saxon windows were discovered, still to be seen high in the nave wall. A carved tub font dated somewhere between 880–980 also survives in the church.

Despite the growth of the village it is not until 939 that there is any mention of the circles of stones when, in a charter of Athelstan defining the boundaries of Overton, the parish adjacent to Avebury, the scribe wrote, 'then back again to Kennet. Now this is the boundary of the pastures and the downland at Mapplederlea westward. Thence northward up along the stone row, thence to the burial-places; then south along the road.'[11] This shadowy passage may refer to the part of the Kennet avenue of stones that once climbed from near the river's source at Silbury (Mapplederlea, the marshy place), up Overton Hill to the cemetery of round barrows (the burial-places) where the Ridgeway runs down the southern slope (along the road). It is possible. But the local names in this charter are now so meaningless that interpretation remains unsure.

Still another battle was fought near Avebury when the Danes invaded England in

1006. 'They went to Wallingford and burned it to the ground, and proceeded along the Berkshire Downs . . . Then levies were mustered there at East Kennet, and there they joined battle; but the Danes soon put that force to flight, and bore their plunder to the sea.' The Anglo-Saxon Chronicle omits that Elthelred the Unready paid a fortune in Danegeld to pay them off.

Burne has reconstructed the Danish line of march, bringing the horde along the Ridgeway with Avebury's hamlet away to their right until they came to Overton Hill. 'Thus we may picture the battle, at least in its early stages, as fought astride the Ridgeway a few hundred yards north of the Kennet',[12] on Overton Hill, near the 'Sanctuary', a fancifully named stone circle a mile south of the village.

In 1010 the Danes came again, advancing into Wessex, 'and so on towards the marsh land at All and Bishops Cannings, destroying everything with fire'. These villages are within four miles of Avebury which may also have been burned. So unsettled was the time that timber palisades were put up on Silbury Hill, turning it into a defensive site. A coin of Ethelred the Unready was found in the upper, recut terrace.

With the Norman Conquest there is a minor mystery. There is no indication in Domesday Book that there was yet a village at Avebury, only a passing reference that the church was held by 'Rainbold the priest' and was worth forty shillings. Otherwise it was apparently only part of the larger desmesne of Kennet and less important than the nearby Beckhampton which itself was a mere hamlet. Yet it was growing. Remains of timbered structures, stockades, grain-pits and pottery of the tenth and eleventh centuries have been found outside the west entrance and it may be that village and earthwork remained separate, even had different names. The early Saxon term for the bank and ditch, *weala-dic*, was still used in the fourteenth century and later, a long overlap with the new name of Avebury. The first record of this is the Avreberie of Domesday Book in 1086 followed by Avesbiria (1114), Aveberia (1180), Avesberia (1253) and Avenesbur' (1268). What meaning Avebury has is rather unclear but one translation is 'Afa's burh', the stronghold of Affa, presumably one of the first settlers by the earthwork.[13] The use of *burh* reaffirms the belief that the enclosure had been used defensively. It is ironical that the name of Avebury, younger by at least three hundred years than *weala-dic* and Wallditch, and which for centuries referred only to the huddle of crofts outside the bank, should today have replaced the real name so utterly.

Cultivation extended as the population increased. Villeins and bordars ploughed the long fields of Beckhampton, Kennet and Overton for their overlords. Freemen worked their own plots of land, dragging away the natural sarsens that cluttered the slopes.

In 1114 some of the Avebury lands were given to the Benedictine monastery of St. Georges de Boscherville near Rouen and a priory was built where Avebury Manor now stands. Bones of monks were found there in Elizabethan times when a cellar was added. In the 'skull of one was a nayle driven'. This priory was right against the church. When, in 1133, the church and some other lands were granted to Cirencester Abbey the proximity of French priory and English church inevitably led to the confrontations between ecclesiastical rivals for which the Middle Ages are

16. The font in Avebury church. The head of a serpent or a dragon lies under the bishop's crozier. The face of the bishop has been damaged.

notorious. Although the Benedictine foundation was smaller, never more than a prior and two or three monks, it had the advantage of being at Avebury whereas the Abbot of Cirencester was twenty miles away, dependent on reports from his priest at Avebury.

In 1180, despite the protests of Cirencester, the priory was allowed to have its own oratory, and in 1183, in a dispute that lasted a hundred and fifty years, it agreed to pay Cirencester all the tithes from its lands. Sheep grazed on the meadows inside the earthwork. Crops grew between the stones. Carts lumbered across the causeway of the western ditch and down the muddy lane.

Aisles had been added to the church and it is in the early twelfth century that the font was intriguingly carved, the west side bearing a bishop in a Norman cassock wounding a serpent with his staff. Much has been read into this.[14] Some writers have claimed that this symbolised the triumph of Christianity over the pagan dragon and that at Avebury it was a statement of the Church's domination over the devil's stones outside.

Whatever the font's significance Avebury had other problems. In 1249 the prior was in Marlborough gaol with his brother Robert and nephew Ralph—accused of murder. Then in 1282 Avebury had a murder of its own. 'In the tenth year when Philip Strug was coroner, Thomas Crespyn and Ralph Brond waylaid John the Spinner at Waledich and they killed John and at once fled and by suit of the countryside took sanctuary in the church of Alyngton', stumbling down the Kennet Avenue these penniless serfs and across All Cannings Down to the distant safety of Allington. At the inquest it was revealed that a John de Meire 'carried off the aforesaid body from Waledich where it was found, and that the same John absconded for the aforesaid death and is under suspicion'. We know little more. Both Cirencester Abbey and the priory had rich flocks of sheep on the downs and the annual shearing and wool-sales were more important than the passing interest of a murder or two.

During all the Roman, Saxon and Norman periods no harm had been done to the prehistoric remains at Avebury but by the late thirteenth century Christianity was becoming less tolerant of these reminders of paganism, so obviously the works of the devil. At Avebury the colossal stone at the south entrance is still called the Devil's Chair. The three stones that once formed the Beckhampton Cove were the Devil's Quoits, and the stones inside the North Circle were known as the Devil's Brand-Irons. Silbury Hill was reputed to have been made by the devil dropping a spadeful of earth, and the massive sarsens of a chambered tomb near Clatford were thought to be the Devil's Den.

That people still superstitiously went to such places infuriated and alarmed the Church. As early as 452 the Lateran Council forbade the worship of stones, a ban repeated by Theodore, Archbishop of Canterbury, in his *Penitentials*: 'no one shall go to trees, or wells, or stones, or enclosures [stone circles?], or anywhere else except to God's church, and there to make vows'. Three hundred years later Canute repeated this: 'It is heathen practice if one worships idols, namely if one worships heathen gods and the sun or the moon, fire or flood, wells or stones or any kind of forest trees, or if one practises witchcraft.'

Yet by the fourteenth century, so far from declining, the belief in witchcraft and black magic was increasing, not only among the peasantry but among educated people who were attempting for personal benefit to conjure up demons.[15] In 1324 Lady Alice Kyteler of Kilkenny was accused of witchcraft and only escaped execution by fleeing to England. A companion, Petronilla of Meath, was flogged six times and burned to death. Even the clergy could be suspected. In 1301 Walter Langton, Bishop of Lichfield, was accused of murder, adultery, sorcery and Devil-worship.

There were also the local customs of the villagers. In many parts of Western Europe there was a belief that prehistoric stones had fertilising powers. At Saint-Renan in Finisterre young brides would go at night to a monolith, 'The Stone Mare', and rub themselves against it.[16] Holed stones, of which there was one at Avebury, were thought to have the same properties. Pregnant women of Kilghane in County Cork passed clothing through such a hole to ensure an easy childbirth.

These are only one or two recent examples of customs, now almost dead, that centuries ago were widespread and fervently believed in. Why people should have associated the stones of Avebury and other stone circles with a cult of fertility is one of the central themes of this book. Other records of similar beliefs are given elsewhere. Here it is sufficient to point out with what indignant horror a priest would regard these abominations and would think it urgent to tear down the places where such obscenities went on.

It is in the early fourteenth century that the first indisputable mention of Avebury's stones occurs. On 23 April 1307 the priory granted Cirencester a pathway between the church and the croft of 'Johannis de la Stone', up to the ditch and 'usque magnas petras veteres inter dictam placiem et croftam predicti' (all the way to the great old stones between the said plot and the aforesaid croft) 'juxta la Waldich' (against the earthwork).[17] But it was also the last time anyone would see the circles entire. The devil's handiwork was to be destroyed. Who ordered it done remains a mystery.

Freemen, villeins, in their short tunics and wide-brimmed hats gathered together to destroy the stone circles. Stone after stone was toppled. Using narrow iron spades and crowbars the men loosened the ground and pushed the stone over. Often they dug a pit, carefully shaped so that the sarsen could be levered in and covered so tidily with chalk rubble that it was almost undetectable from the undisturbed soil around it. In the process bits of broken pottery were buried. These must have come from the rotting middens that reeked outside every cottage where the refuse of day to day living was dumped until such time as the manure was spread over the ploughed interior of the earthwork. None of the pottery is later than the early fourteenth century and so tells us when the circles were overthrown. When one of the stones of the Kennet Avenue was buried an old, worn silver penny of Henry III was lost perhaps sixty or seventy years after it was minted between 1222 and 1237. We can assume that the destruction of the circles was at its height a few years after 1300.

Unrealised damage had been done before then. Remains of mediaeval activity survive within the earthwork: ditches, dry-stone walls, even the suggestion of buildings.[18] The interior must have been ploughed for years, on and off, to account for the many twelfth- and thirteenth-century sherds in the soil. Archaeologically this was destructive. Even natural processes can complicate excavation by washing away topsoil. The tiny, apparently harmless earthworm can, by a thousand tunnellings, churn up layers beneath the turf. Man is worse. Digging trenches for walls and drains he cuts through buried hearths. Ploughing is ferocious. Furrowing deeply the farmer rips away the insubstantial stains where posts of houses once stood. Harrowing breaks, drags and spreads sherds and tools far apart. Yet nothing shows. To most visitors Avebury is composed of stone and bank and ditch. To the archaeologist these are the bones. The flesh and blood of the place lie in the earth where the homes of former people, the implements they used, the ornaments they fashioned remain undisturbed, waiting for discovery and revelation. The peasants of Avebury had unknowingly spoiled much of this. Now, intentionally, and fearfully, they attacked the stones.

It is unlikely that the circles were spoiled just to make more room for ploughing. Many of the pottery sherds, even large fragments, are unweathered and unscratched, showing none of the damage they would have received if repeatedly dragged up by the plough. In any case, if space were needed it would have been more sensible to drag the stones away, tumbling them into the ditch just as farmers today haul the sarsens on the downs into their hedgerows. Nor need the stones have been so neatly concealed. Certainly they would not have been left lying on the ground.

Christianity is a more persuasive cause. It is easy to visualise the villagers, perhaps at the time of the yearly fair, apprehensively overthrowing the monstrous stones, encouraged by the priest (Thomas Mayn, 1298–1319?; John de Hoby, 1319–24?), other onlookers, the peasants' wives, shepherds from the hills, watching, doubting, even scared of this interference. It is noticeable that not one stone was smashed. They were handled almost with reverence, covered without hurt to the sarsen, doing God's work without upsetting the Devil.

Yearly it continued. All the inner ring of the North Circle went. The outer stones

17. The inner face of the Barber's Stone.

of the North and South Circles near the Marlborough road also were removed. The thick centre stone, the Obelisk, was pushed over. It lay there solidly for four hundred years and was sketched by Stukeley in 1723, trapped in a cage of trees. Of the one hundred or so stones of the great Outer Circle lining the ditch all the northern arc, the north-west, east-north-east arcs and a long segment in the south-east quadrant were buried. So were many of the stones of the two avenues. One that had been thrown down in the fourteenth century lay on the ground at the foot of Overton Hill until it was smashed up just after 1700. Another was discovered in 1968 during the laying of a telephone cable by the Beckhampton roundabout, still lying in its chalk-cut pit. Another, further to the west, rested in a circular hole, the prehistoric burial of a child alongside it. Others of the Outer and North Circles still lie in their pits.

Presumably the work would have gone on until all the stones were down although it is noticeable that it was the smaller ones that had been chosen first. Whether giants like those at the North and South Entrances could have been manhandled in this way is questionable. It was, perhaps, such an attempt that led to the enterprise being abandoned.

Walking westwards from the south entrance one passes a standing stone, then the low concrete marker of a missing pillar, then the best-preserved of all the arcs, seven more cumbrous stones, each over three metres high. The sixth one killed a man.

When this thirteen-ton block, now delicately balanced on its tapering base, was uncovered in 1938 a man's skeleton was found trapped between the stone and the edge of its pit. He was

> an individual who had been accidentally killed while engaged in completing the pit for the burial of the stone, which had apparently slipped or fallen owing to a support giving way, fracturing the victim's pelvis, and also breaking his neck. The right foot was wedged beneath the fallen stone and it had consequently been impossible at the time of death to remove the corpse.[19]

His rotted leather pouch held three silver coins dated about 1320–5, confirming the time when the stones were being buried. His iron scissors and a lance or probe lying beside him suggest he was an itinerant barber–surgeon travelling from one market-fair to another with his knives and leeches, happening to be at Avebury when stone-felling was in progress. Joining in he was crushed and his body was buried in the rubble thrown back over the stone. Nor was this the end of his misfortune. His skeleton was given to the College of Surgeons in London and was destroyed in an air raid during the Second World War.

His death may have stopped further destruction. One of the smallest sarsens, right against the barber's stone, was left standing. The tragedy clearly shocked the village for it was remembered four centuries later when in 1712 a manservant staying at the

18. The barber–surgeon.

manor-house wrote in his diary: 'One Sunday a cobler was mending of shoos under one of these great stones the minute he rose the stone fell down and broke in pieces on the very ground whare he sat.'[20] Even in the nineteenth century William Long was told it was Reuben Horsall, a parish clerk who died in 1728, who had just left the shelter of a stone when it was shattered by lightning.

One sees them, those peasants, small dark men, sharp-nosed, alert as crows, muttering that everyone knew it was ill fortune to disturb the stones. Retribution could be expected. There would be tempests. Over five hundred years later when thunderstorms followed the opening of a round barrow at Beedon not too far away the villagers thought it 'caused by the sacriligious undertaking to disturb the dead. One of the labourers employed left the work in consequence and much alarm prevailed.' Places like this had guardian ghosts. A spirit haunted the barrow at Inkpen nearby. When the mound was dug into the labourers were driven off by thunder and lightning. Closer still to Avebury was Silbury Hill, where an excavation of 1849 was followed by 'one of the most grand and tremendous thunderstorms I ever recollect to have witnessed. [It] made the hills re-echo to the crashing peals, and Silbury itself, as the men asserted who were working in its centre, to tremble to its base.' And the moving of stones was even more dangerous, likely to bring diseases to cattle, to wither the crops, even to kill. Circles, being sanctuaries, were worst of all. When Colonel Lacy tried to blast the stones of the splendid Cumbrian ring, Long Meg & Her Daughters, there 'was thunder, rain and hail so terrible that the workmen fled for their lives'.[21]

With such dreads it is less surprising that the stone-felling ceased than that it had ever begun. And after the appalling visitation of the Black Death in the winter of 1349 when nearly half the population was infected and died agonisingly of the plague there were too few people left. Even Avebury's priest, Robert Durelyng de Faireford, may have succumbed. The remaining stones were left. Village life returned to the drudgery of herding cattle, digging cess-pits inside the circles, quarrying marl for cottage walls. The priory and its lands were repossessed by the king, and Stephen Fosse, the last prior, was expelled. Avebury was written as Abury. A tower was added to the church. A little memorial brass, once in Berwick Bassett church, records that: 'William Bayly lies here, so it pleases the Lord. He left 100 shillings to the Church for ever. He died 9 November, 1427.' One of his descendants was to shatter Avebury.

After the closing of the monasteries by Henry VIII Avebury's main excitement in the sixteenth century was the lawsuit between the Dunches who had bought Avebury Manor from Sir William Sharington, a disgraced Master of the Bristol Mint, and the Truslowes who had taken over the manor-house from Cirencester Abbey. The dispute was won by the Dunches, perhaps because Deborah Dunch took the precaution of marrying Sir James Mervyn, the High Sheriff of Wiltshire. In 1639, just before the Civil War, Avebury Manor was sold to Sir John Stawell.

Quietly, behind the quarrels, Avebury had at last been recognised as an antiquity. John Leland, Henry VIII's chaplain and librarian, who made a famous tour of England searching out documents from the monasteries, rode through Wiltshire around 1541 and came to the Avebury district. 'Kenet risithe north north-

19. Avebury's biggest stones, the pair at the South Entrance. In the background is a sarsen of the South Circle.

west at Selbiri hille bottome, wherby hath ben camps and sepultures of men of warre, as at Aibiri a myle of.' Although this referred only to the earthwork Avebury had become an ancient monument.

It is odd that no one thought the stones important. William Camden, that perceptive Elizabethan antiquarian who published the first general guide to our antiquities, the *Britannia*, did not even mention Avebury in his Latin edition of 1586, and the English version of 1610 only said:

> Within one mile of Silbury is Abury, an uplandish village, built in an old camp, as it seemeth, but of no large compass. It is environed with a fair trench, and hath four gates, in two of which stand huge stones as jambs, but so rude that they seem rather natural than artificial; of which there are some others in the said village.

There was something of a reference to Avebury in Sir John Harington's notes to *Orlando Furioso* of 1634. Then the Civil War interrupted scholarship. Another battle was fought near Avebury on Roundway Down five miles away when Sir Ralph Hopton's royalist cavalry annihilated Waller's roundheads in 1643. Then in 1695 another edition of the *Britannia* appeared and at long last Avebury's stone circles were recorded.

> About half a mile from Silbury, is Aubury, a monument more considerable in it self, than known to the world . . . It is environ'd with an extraordinary Vallum or

41

Rampart . . . The graff [ditch] has been surrounded all along the edge of it, with large stones pitch'd on end, most of which are now taken away; but some marks remaining give one the liberty to guess they stood quite round.[22]

The marginal note to this entry explains who the author was, this archaeological observer of stoneholes, the discoverer of the circles: '*Aubury*. Aubr. Monument. Britan. MS.' The description had been taken from a manuscript, the 'Monumenta Britannica' of John Aubrey.

Today this wealthy young gentleman who died in poverty is remembered as the writer of a compilation of witty biographies, his *Brief Lives*. 'William Sanderson dyed at Whitehall . . . went out like a spent candle.' But Aubrey was not merely a gossip.[23] He was unceasingly curious. He remembered that when the lead-coffined corpse of the theologian John Colet was examined after the Great Fire of London it 'felt to the probe of a stick which they thrust into a chinke, like boylde brawne'. This curiosity Aubrey extended magnificently to the study of antiquities and he was, without question, the first great English fieldworker and archaeologist. Corresponding up to his death with other antiquarians he personally visited sites, many of which have since been destroyed. 'My head was alwaies working; never idle, and ever travelling (which from 1649 till 1670 was never off horseback).' The result was a collection of invaluable though disordered notes that scholars plunder to this day.[24] He was the first to have the imagination and courage to perceive that the stone circles of the British Isles were pre-Roman and he examined them not from the antiquary's study, for he knew there were no documents, but in the field. 'Twas in that deluge of Historie, the accounte of these British Monuments utterly perished: the Discovery whereof I doe here endeavour (for want of written Record) to work out and restore . . . by comparing them that I have seen, one with another . . . to make the Stones give Evidence for themselves.'

It was in a bitter winter that he first saw Avebury on Sunday, 7 January 1649, three weeks before Charles I was executed. Out hunting with Royalist friends he galloped into the village and was 'wonderfully surprized at the sight of those vast stones of which I had never heard before'. Being a Wiltshireman from Lower Easton Pierse fifteen miles to the west he was able to visit Avebury over several autumns noting the positions of stones and the shapes of the enormous rings.

Charles II heard that Aubrey, a Fellow of the newly formed Royal Society of which the king was the patron, believed that Avebury 'did as much excell Stoneheng, as a Cathedral does a Parish church'. Charles had already seen Stonehenge when a fugitive after the Battle of Worcester twelve years before and was intrigued to learn how Avebury could be more impressive. He commanded Aubrey to come to Court and in July 1663 Aubrey came, bringing with him a plan 'donne by memorie alone' which so interested Charles that a fortnight later, while travelling to Bath, he went out of his way to inspect Avebury with Aubrey as his guide. The North Circle at that time stood behind an inn and the king rode through the yard to see it, so exciting the villagers that they told Stukeley about it sixty years later. Amazed at the bulk of the Cove stones inside the ring the king briefly turned archaeologist. 'His Majestie', Aubrey recalled, 'commanded me to digge at the

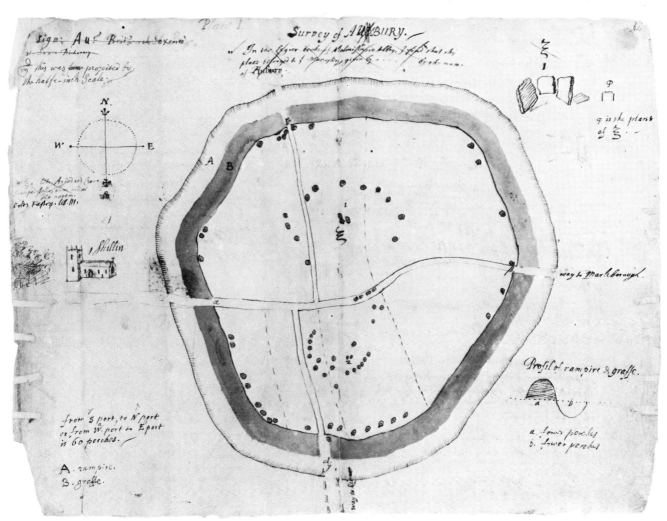

20. John Aubrey's plan of Avebury. There were many more stones of the Outer Circle in 1663 than in Stukeley's time sixty years later. The plan of the irregular ditch and earthwork is very good. Notice the sketch and plan of the undamaged Cove inside the North Circle.

bottom of the stones . . . to try if I could find any humane bones: but I did not doe it.' Charles also walked to the top of Silbury Hill.

That September Aubrey made a plane-table survey of Avebury, 'this old ill-shapen Monument'. Despite the obstacles of houses, hedges and trees his plan is good, far better for the shape of the bank and ditch than Stukeley's schematic representation eighty years later.[25] Following this, 'in obedience to his Majestie's command', Aubrey started to write his 'Monumenta Britannica', a description of ancient remains such as stone circles, barrows and earthworks. Although much of his own fieldwork was done by 1670 he continued to correspond with local people: John Brinsdon, vicar of Winterbourne Monkton who lies buried under a sarsen beside the east end of his church; Dr Toope, the grinder-up of old bones; and Walter Sloper who told him of the fall of the great sarsen outside Avebury's South Entrance. All the information went into his notes. But litigation ruined him, other curiosities

43

diverted him, the king died, and although the dedication to Charles was altered and the book advertised in 1692 at a price of eighteen shillings it was never finished.

We must be thankful to Aubrey first and most simply for his plans and descriptions made before the stone-breakers obliterated so much of Avebury. He not only went to West Kennet and other megalithic tombs, some now destroyed like the Shelving Stones, but his Avebury plans show stones in the circles that had gone by Stukeley's time. Hindered though he was by the clutter inside the earthwork he planned the bank and ditch and the Outer Circle including a run of stones at the south which Stukeley never saw. His plan showed two inner rings north and south of each other. Although the diameters of these circles differ too much as did his dimensions for the interior of Avebury which was too small by a seventh he did include an irreplaceable sketch of the three stones called the Cove inside the North Circle. Not long afterwards one of the stones fell and was split up. In addition Aubrey drew a schematic plan of the Kennet Avenue which rain had prevented him from measuring but which, while riding between the stones in his lace and ruffles, he thought must have been for processions to a concentric stone circle on Overton Hill by a cemetery of round barrows. Slight though his records are, imprecise, they show an awareness of the importance of ordinary things unusual in antiquarians before him.

John Brinsdon told him how villagers were already smashing circle stones.

> I have *verbum sacerdotis*, for it, that these mighty stones, (as hard as marble), may be broken in what part of them you please, without any great trouble : *sc*, make a fire on that line of stone, where you would have it crack; and after the stone is well heated, draw over a line with cold water, & immediately give a knock with a Smyth's sledge, and it will break like the Collets at the Glass-House.

Richard Symonds in his Cavalier *Diary* had already noted that people on Fyfield Down were breaking the 'grey pibble stone of great bignes' for building material in 1644.[26]

Aubrey left us with some puzzles. He must have approached Avebury from the west but made no mention of the Beckhampton Avenue, and when he referred to what was presumably the Beckhampton Cove on the avenue—'three huge upright stones . . . called the Devill's Coytes'—he placed them to the south not the west of Avebury. There was also an enigmatic note about a chambered tomb, like Trefignath on Anglesey, on the east–west road that 'is converted into a pig-stye or cow house—as is to be seen in the road'. No such tomb exists today.

Aubrey's method of investigating the past, his comparisons, his collection of seemingly trivial data were important. He guessed that because Avebury's ditch was on the inner side of the bank the earthwork had not been built for defence. And because Avebury and other stone circles 'are of the same fashion, and antique rudeness' but not always in the same areas as Roman or Saxon sites they had to be even older, 'clear evidence that these monuments were Pagan-Temples, which was not made out before'.

Aubrey's was a time not long after the Pilgrim Fathers when explorers in North America were encountering Indians whose barbaric habits they compared with the

21. The Kennet Avenue leading uphill towards Avebury. The field in the foreground has not been excavated and probably contains other stones.

unknown customs of prehistoric people.[27] Aubrey made similar comparisons. 'Let us imagine', he wrote, 'what kind of countrie this was in the time of the ancient Britons', and went on to draw parallels between Indian tribal warfare and Caesar's descriptions of British warriors of the Iron Age who were 'almost as salvage as the Beasts, whose Skins were their only rayment. They were 2 or 3 degrees I suppose less salvage than the Americans.'

It was an unromanticised view of the past, a hard primitivism that contrasts favourably with some of today's credulous thinking about the life-styles of prehistoric societies.

Archaeologists are well aware of the value of Aubrey's work. He died in poverty in 1697 and is buried somewhere in the church of St Mary Magdalen in the heart of

Oxford. 'John Aubery A stranger was Buryed Jun 7th.' Once he had wistfully written:

> on the southe downe of the farme of Broad Chalk [which had been his], on the top of the plaine, is a little barrow (not very high) called by the name of Gawen's Barrow . . . I was never so sacralegious as to disturbe, or rob his urne, let his Ashes rest in peace: but I have often times wish't that my Corps might be interr'd by it.[28]

Today we are not sure exactly where Aubrey's body lies. Let his work be his memorial.

Stage-coaches were passing through Avebury on their way to Bath and Bristol every Monday and Thursday, fare twenty shillings, 'Flying Machines' that raced the 110 miles from London in three days. Pepys came in 1668 paying a local a shilling to show him round. And destruction went on ever more intensively. John, second Lord Stawell, who had inherited Avebury Manor, levelled a great length of the bank north of the West Entrance to make room for a barn before selling the manor-house to Sir Richard Holford in 1696 for £7500. In a flicker from the past there was an immediate argument between Holford and John White, the parish priest, over tithes.

The destruction of stones was proceeding with almost maniacal zest. It has been suggested that Puritanism, that driver-out of idolatrous faiths, lay behind this iconoclasm and that the driving forces were John Baker, a nonconformist preacher who formed a chapel at Avebury in 1670 and his successor, John Bale, who by 1715 had a congregation of 130 members out of the two hundred or so villagers. It may be symbolical that their Meeting House is built mainly of sarsen fragments from the ravished South Circle.

The demolition was well recorded, systematic and tragic. By the early eighteenth century there were at least thirteen homes inside the earthwork as well as ten pastures. Sarsen was needed for houses, barns, walls and drains, and freed of their fears, the stone-breakers led by Tom Robinson, John Fowler, Green and Griffin got to work just as John Aubrey had described, felling the stones alongside prepared pits of blazing straw. Lines of cold water on the heated sarsen created weaknesses that fractured under the poundings of sledgehammers. Hannibal had used a similar technique when crossing the Alps two thousand years before.[29]

In 1694 Walter Stretch smashed up a stone, one from the outer ring of the North Circle, standing in the main street. From it he got twenty cartloads of pieces for the dining-room of the Catherine Wheel Inn. Already many stones had been taken from the South Circle, for in 1663 Aubrey had noted about twenty-three stones standing there whereas Stukeley in 1724 found only four. In 1700 Robinson broke up most of the stones at the south-east of the Outer Circle and more sarsens were taken from the South Circle. In 1701 some of the Beckhampton Avenue stones were taken for a bridge over the Winterbourne, and two more were removed from a tree-lined paddock the following year. By 1706 all the pillars of the North Circle had fallen and one at the crossroads was used as a fish-stall on market days. By 1710 Fowler and Green had destroyed many of the stones of the South Circle. Between 1711 and 1719 Green, working clockwise around the north ring, broke up stone after stone for his

TAB.XXXIV P.66

22. The Devil's Den. A long mound once covered the area where the ladies are standing.

farm at Beckhampton. The north-east arc of the Outer Circle was taken away in 1718 and other stones on the west side had been 'broke off to the stumps'. Many of the houses in Avebury and Beckhampton today have lumps from these doomed sarsens in their walls. By 1719 when William Stukeley first saw Avebury it was a wreck.

Had it not been for Stukeley, it would be impossible today to write with any accuracy about Avebury. Aubrey discovered it but Stukeley wrote its chronicles. While a young doctor in Boston, Lincolnshire, he became interested in antiquities and made several tours in England and Wales to look at stately homes, Oxford colleges, Roman and prehistoric ruins. Moving to London in 1717 he soon met other antiquarians and was elected a Fellow of the Royal Society the following year.

He heard of Avebury almost by chance. The father of his friend Roger Gale had copied parts of Aubrey's 'Monumenta Britannica' and from these extracts Stukeley made his own transcription in December 1718. Years afterwards in his journal he wrote: 'In 1718 Mr. Roger and Sam. Gale and I took a journey, through my eager desire, to view Avebury, an antiquity altogether unknown.' This is a surprising remark which takes all credit from Aubrey even though Stukeley only visited Avebury because of its description in the 'Monumenta Britannica'. It is, however, a comment entirely in accord with the ungenerous attitude Stukeley had towards Aubrey. He even gave the wrong date for his journey, perhaps deliberately so. His first visit was in 1719, *after* he had entered Aubrey's account in his own 'Commonplace Book'.[30]

Between 1719 and 1724 he went to Avebury six times, sometimes staying for two or three weeks at the Catherine Wheel Inn not far from the present Red Lion, plane-

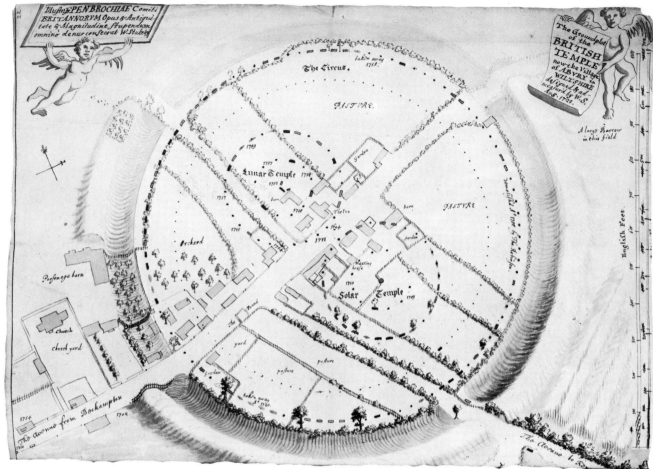

23. William Stukeley's manuscript plan of Avebury. As early as 1721 he was calling the North and South Circles the Lunar and Solar Temples.

24. Stukeley's panorama of the Avebury district. Despite several errors it does give a good impression of the layout of the original megalithic complex.

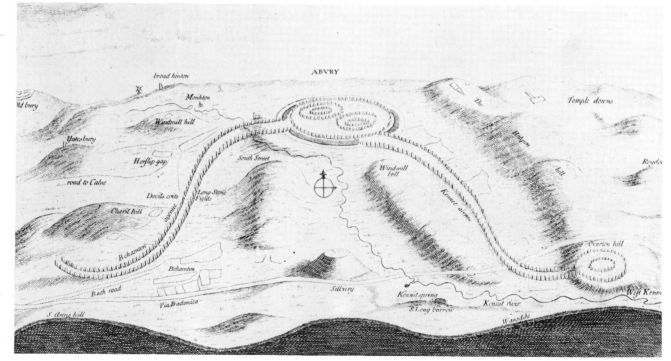

tabling, taking magnetic bearings, making meticulous plans of the circles, measuring the ditch in 1721, plotting the Kennet Avenue but not apparently coming upon the inconspicuous wreckage of the Beckhampton Avenue until 1722. In 1723 he drew the fancifully named Sanctuary stone circle on Overton Hill just twelve months before it was dragged away by Green, and in 1724 he completed his detailed plan of Avebury entitled, 'The Groundplot of the Brittish Temple now the town of Aubury Wilts. Anno 1724.'

In these years Stukeley also explored the surrounding countryside drawing the long burial mounds with their falling stones, excavating a round barrow on Windmill Hill, cantering along the Wansdyke towards Morgan's Hill where a highwayman's gallows swung. Often his pictures include him in his three-cornered hat looking at the Cove, sketching the Beckhampton Avenue from the top of a Neolithic barrow or explaining the wonders of megalithic architecture to satin-gowned young ladies.[31]

Repeatedly he condemned the destruction he saw, describing the burning and battering of stones as barbaric, damning the covetous farmers who smashed them: Green and Griffin; the Fowlers, John of the White Hart alehouse in Kennet, Richard at the Hare and Hounds at Beckhampton who spoiled so much of the Beckhampton Avenue; Mr Ayloff who, Stukeley exulted, broke up a sarsen for a mill-stone 'and employed twenty yoke of oxen to carry it off. Yet so great was its weight, that it repeatedly broke all his tackle to pieces, and he was forc't to leave it.' There was Mr Smith, a lawyer of West Kennet, who planned to take the stones of the chambered tomb for a bridge.[32] Above all, there was the hated 'Herostratus of Avebury', Tom Robinson, a housing speculator, who 'got his wife (an old woman above 50) with child', and who 'is particularly eminent for this kind of execution' and he 'very much glories in it'.

Robinson grumbled that the work was not only exhausting but sometimes uneconomical, costing up to £4 a stone because so many labourers were needed to manoeuvre the sarsens to their burning-pits using heavy and expensive levers which all too often splintered or caught fire. Nevertheless, he continued to smash stones, using the smoke-smeared fragments for the walls of his new cottages. Poetic justice followed. 'The expense of demolishing them was greater than the value of the houses, and after they were built the houses were by some accident burnt and T. R. utterly ruined.'[33]

Although Stukeley recorded all this his work did have some serious demerits. He became obsessed with Druidism and was convinced that the North and South inner circles were temples of the Sun and Moon, a harmless belief in itself but after he took holy orders in 1729 he deliberately used Avebury to prove his own theories about primitive religion, claiming Avebury was a landscaped model of the Trinity, the circle representing the ineffable deity, and the avenues of Beckhampton and Kennet his son 'or first divine emanation' in the form of a serpent.

He falsified measurements and plans to fit these notions.[34] 'Nothing can exceed the effrontery with which Stukeley inserted curved avenues between these circles [at Stanton Drew], so as to make the whole into a serpent form. Nothing of the kind exists.'[35] Rickman more charitably observed that Stukeley's 'imagination too often surpassed even his zeal in antiquarian research'. The circular Sanctuary was redrawn as oval so that it would resemble a serpent's head. His final diorama of Avebury with its distorted perspective, 'A Scenographic view of the Druid Temple', *Abury*, Tab. VIII, looks more like an alert octopus than the megalithic complex it really was. His book on Avebury is half a clear and objective record of his fieldwork, and half a nonsensical jumble from his later years. His biographer has commented on this distinct difference between the quality of his notes before 1725 and his eccentric thinking after then.[36]

He was also notably unfair towards Aubrey who discovered Avebury. 'The mighty carcase of *Stonehenge* draws great numbers of people . . . But Abury a much greater work . . . was altogether overlooked', he wrote on page 15 of his *Abury* (1743), going on to mention Camden, Holland and even a Dr Childrey but ignoring Aubrey until he could accuse him, on page 32, of not realising that the Kennet Avenue ran continuously from Avebury to the Sanctuary. This was manifestly untrue as Aubrey's own plan showed.

What Stukeley can unreservedly be praised for is the series of notes, plans, water-colours and the archaeological contents of his Avebury book. Like Aubrey he noted details but he noted more of them and he noted them more precisely. On his plans he recorded the dates stones had been destroyed. He noticed that the sarsens had a weathered and a smoother face, that it was usually the better side that faced the interior of the circles, and that the largest stones stood at the entrances. He calculated that the Outer Circle had been designed of one hundred stones, and that the inner rings were composed of thirty stones each. He wrote down lesser things. Just outside the South Circle, he said, there was a smallish sarsen with a hole in it, the Ring Stone, of which only the stump now exists. He drew the Obelisk, that fallen central stone of the South Circle, pointing out that when it had been upright it would have been the tallest pillar of the ring. He stated that the North Circle had an inner ring of twelve stones with the Cove at its centre. Although the northern stone of this Cove had fallen and been destroyed he found out from the villagers that 'it was fully seven yards long, of the same shape as its opposite, tall and narrow'. He was in time to see the Kennet Avenue, the spacing of the stones and how they rose in height towards the south entrance of the earthwork. He witnessed the demolition of the Sanctuary: 'The loss of this work I did not lament alone: but all the neighbours (except the person that gain'd the little dirty profit) were heartily griev'd for it. It had a beauty that touch'd them.' But Green took the stones and Griffin ploughed the land. '13 May, 1724. This day I saw several of the few stones left on overton hill carryed downwards towards W. Kennet & two thirds of the temple plowd up this winter and the sods thrown into the cavitys so that next year it will be impossible ever more to take any measure of it.'

Above all, he found the Beckhampton Avenue which for many years afterwards was thought to be a fantasy until recent excavations proved Stukeley, as in so many of his statements, entirely accurate. These sinuous and parallel rows of sarsens, sixteen to seventeen metres apart and some one and a quarter miles long, were not only almost all pushed over but either hidden by hedges, lying obscurely out in the wide fields towards Horslip, or broken and built into cottage walls. It was no wonder that John Aubrey had not noticed them although he had been told by Edward Philips that on the way to Compton Bassett 'are to be seen Houses, part whereof are stones pitched on end'. Stukeley did better. He recognised the avenue and planned it[37] down to its tumbled termination at Fox Covert below Cherhill, 'a most solemn and awful place' from which the Sanctuary could be seen. Two hundred years later Maud Cunnington used Stukeley's notes to rediscover the vanished Sanctuary. She thought Stukeley might have been sitting on the box-seat of a coach when he made his elevated drawing but the truth was humbler: 'I took it, from the top of an haycock.'

On the line of the Beckhampton Avenue he planned the surviving stones of the Cove a mile west of Avebury, Aubrey's three Devil's Quoits. By 1723 one stone had already been burned and broken by Richard Fowler. It is interesting to read Stukeley's original, scrupulous note:

> one of Long Stones ^{was} fell down and a ~~corpse~~ bones
> was found ~~under~~ it when the Landlord of the
> Hare and hounds took it away (burning it) it contained
> 15 load
> Rd Fowler[38]

A second stone was fallen. Today only the eastern stone is preserved of this south-east facing setting. Adjacent to it one stone is left of the two hundred stones or so of the Beckhampton Avenue. Standing together and lonely in the fields these stones more than any others reveal starkly how much we are indebted to Stukeley for our present knowledge of Avebury's design. They have been called the Longstones and also Adam and Eve, not altogether inappropriately, for their significance is not the origin but the downfall of this serpent-like avenue.

Like Aubrey Stukeley made records of other monuments like Old Chapel, a megalithic long mound with a crescentic forecourt high up on Rough Hill and long since dismantled when the ground was 'improved'. Like Aubrey he had insights, wondering what unit of measurement his 'Druids' used when laying-out Avebury. From faulty calculations made at Stonehenge he proposed a Cubit of 20.8 inches (53 centimetres) used by the architects in staffs six cubits long (10 ft 4.8 inches or 3.17 metres), anticipating, quite remarkably, similar modern alternatives.[39]

He even guessed at a date of 1859 BC for the building of Avebury which, although mistakenly based on the year Abraham's wife Sarah died, was a lot closer to the truth than the Roman and Saxon suggestions of some of his later, supercilious critics.[40] And by a peculiar chance he overestimated the diameter of Avebury's interior by about one-seventh just as Aubrey had underestimated it by the same proportion.[41]

Our debt to Stukeley is summarised in his own words: 'Since I frequented the place, I fear it has suffer'd; but at that time, there was scarce a single stone in the original ground plot wanting but I could trace it to the person then living who demolish'd it, and to what use and where.' His book, *Abury, a Temple of the British Druids*, was published in 1743. Before then, in 1723, the Revd Thomas Twining had written a foolish work, *Avebury in Wiltshire, the Remains of a Roman Work*, which Stukeley justifiably ignored.

A View of the valley at the end of Beckhamton avenue from the Cove 26 May 1724
A where was the end of Bekamton avenue.

25. Stukeley is drawn standing by Adam, the one survivor of the Beckhampton Cove. Longstones long barrow is behind him. The fallen stones lead towards the far end of the avenue near Cherhill.

26. The Longstones, sometimes known as the Devil's Quoits or Adam and Eve. To the right of Adam is Eve, the only stone remaining of the Beckhampton Avenue. Windmill Hill with some later round barrows is on the skyline.

27. The inner face of Adam, the eastern side stone of the Beckhampton Cove. Behind it, Eve used to be in the north row of the Beckhampton Avenue.

Destruction continued although more slowly. By 1724 the bank at the south entrance had been cut back to allow stage-coaches to pass through more quickly and in 1762 the truncated end was quarried for material to raise the road, the present ugly hollow being the scar of that mutilation.

In 1725 Mr Caleb Baily almost gained a literary notoriety after he had some stones removed for his manor at Berwick Bassett. Hearing of this the Society of Antiquaries asked Allan Ramsay, a Scottish poet, to lampoon Baily, 'tho the Beast be Realy below satyr and deserves to be shot'. The draft of the resulting poem was almost as bad as the stone-breaking:

> For what the wise have fond regard
> thousands of wasting years had spard
> the monuments wise men regard
> while proven Truths their cares reward
> I like a clown
> to clout the dike arround my Yard
> een Blew them doun.

Either from shame or regret or to spare the Society from further excruciations Baily promised to do no more damage.[42]

28. The quarry in Avebury's bank by the South Entrance.

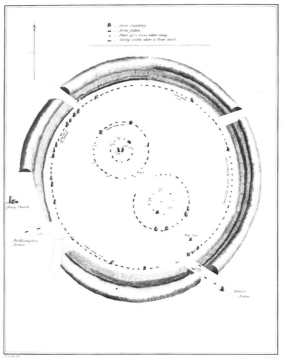

29. (*right*) Crocker's plan of Avebury made for Sir Richard Colt Hoare in 1812.

30. (*far right*) Despite the absence of causeways across the ditch and the incorrect concentric ring inside the South Circle, Crocker's reconstruction does have a good likeness to the original site.

Then the Kennet Avenue suffered. Stones were taken in 1792 'from the neck of the serpent', and other obstructive stones were buried. Another was broken to make a footpath. About 1823 three stones were taken away by order of the Turnpike Trustees because 'horses used to shy at them in the dusk of the evening, and bolt down the bank on the other side of the road'.[43] The Road Commissioners had others at the foot of Overton Hill shattered. Seeing this a passing gentleman told the foreman 'that a man who would undertake such work, ought not to die in bed'. 'The saying of the gentleman was fulfilled, for the man hung himself.'[44]

In 1812 Sir Richard Colt Hoare had his surveyor, Philip Crocker, make a fresh plan of Avebury and a comparison with Stukeley's showed that twelve circle-stones had gone since 1724.[45] The plan and additional information about Avebury appeared in the second volume of Hoare's *The Ancient History of Wiltshire* (1821) which, with its companion, was one of the first works to treat the results of early excavations, mainly directed by Hoare's colleague, William Cunnington,[46] in a serious and helpful manner.

The last stone to be taken from Avebury may have been the single sarsen surviving of the North Circle's inner ring, removed about 1828 because it stood near the entrance to a farmyard. By the mid-nineteenth century there was a growing appreciation of archaeological sites, in part because dreadful excavations were being executed—the most appropriate verb—on burial mounds from which diggers sometimes disinterred a skeleton whose 'mouth was open, and it grinn'd horribly a ghastly smile'. With little shudders of delight people became aware that Britain had an ancient past. More and more the countryside was explored for Roman and prehistoric remains, not always to dig into them but often just to record their

54

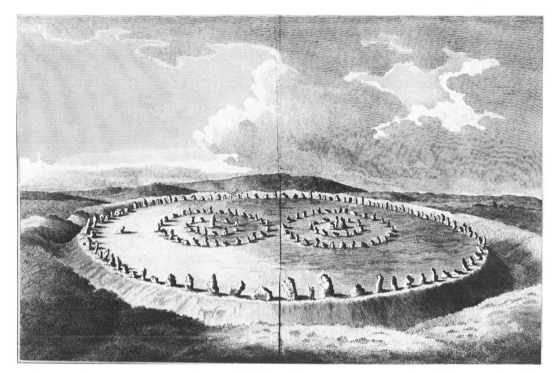

existence. Between 1858 and 1878 William Long wrote several articles based on his researches into the early records of Avebury and the Revd Bryan King, vicar of Avebury, published other papers on the same theme.[47] In 1884, the Revd A. C. Smith, rector of Yatesbury, who for years had ridden over the downs mapping land that was being newly cultivated, 'many of the barrows fast disappearing under the plough', published his *Guide to the British and Roman Antiquities of the North Wiltshire Downs*. When a fire promptly destroyed most of the first edition a second was issued in 1885 with large six-inch maps plotting the location of monuments, many since becoming the victims of today's agriculture. Smith also wrote articles about Silbury and Avebury where he undertook a small excavation.[48]

By Victorian times so few stones were left at Avebury that the chief danger had become the building of more cottages within the earthwork as the population of the village increased. In 1841 just under five hundred people lived there but by 1871 there were half as many again and in 1872 part of the circle was sold as building land. To forestall the catastrophic results Sir John Lubbock, later Lord Avebury, bought part of the village, asking other purchasers to exchange their plots for others in unimportant areas. With some 'small concessions' this was done and the rescue of Avebury had begun.

Well into the twentieth century the earthwork and the stone circles remained in private ownership, always liable to further vandalism. It was not until 1934 when he started excavating there that Alexander Keiller found the answer. After long discussions in the Red Lion with Stuart Piggott, then his young assistant, later Professor of Archaeology at Edinburgh University and one of Britain's greatest prehistorians, Keiller awakened Piggott late one night to announce that he had 'decided' to buy the whole of Avebury and as much of the Kennet Avenue as he could. It was done. Keiller, a rich man who had already purchased Windmill Hill, also obtained Avebury Manor in which he lived until his death in 1955.

In 1937 a public Appeal for £11,000 was started in order to acquire the land from Keiller for the nation. 'If it is agreed that to preserve Avebury is to safeguard a great national heritage for all time, it surely follows that the cost should be a national responsibility.'[49] The Treasury offered nothing. 'The government has not itself come forward with a substantial donation', and the sum was obtained from hundreds of private contributions. In 1942 the National Trust became responsible for Avebury and much of its surroundings. Its attractive shop near the West Entrance reflects its sovereignty.

Now visitors in their thousands come every year to walk along the bank, to photograph the stones, go to the museum. Long ago, in the circles, in the avenues, in the Sanctuary, in this megalithic complex there had been well over six hundred stones. Today there are seventy-six, and little concrete pyramids stand like Passchendaele memorials for some of the others. Thanks to Aubrey and Stukeley we know what the stones of Avebury looked like in prehistoric times. It is our fortune that the latter arrived there during its destruction and was able to speak to the destroyers. After him, less damage was done, perhaps because there was less to do. We should not be complacent and believe it was modern enlightenment that has inhibited injury.

> The importance of Stone 46 [at the North Entrance] cannot be exaggerated and yet passing traffic is allowed to knock into it. This has happened at least twice and we have it on good authority that in one case a lorry knocked it well out of the vertical. It is a disturbing thought that in 1975 we were still allowing the destruction of the Avebury Ring to continue.[50]

The ruins are the relics of an incredible structure. Originally within the bank and Outer Circle were two lesser stone circles, one with a centre stone, the other a double ring with a Cove in the middle. One avenue of stones went southwards then curved uphill to the Sanctuary. The second avenue, virtually erased, led westwards past another Cove down into a 'most melancholy valley' where the round barrows lay not on the surrounding hilltops but crowded together on the lower slopes. A drawing in Hoare's *Ancient Wiltshire* gives some impression, despite the absence of causeways across the ditch, of what the stone circles and earthwork may have looked like to their builders. Today, even in ruin, the monument retains much of its first grandeur.

Quite recently, a scholarly catalogue of Wiltshire prehistoric sites and the results of excavations in them has enabled anyone interested to reconstruct the environment in which Neolithic and Bronze Age people lived in the Avebury district.[51] We can see their monumental handiwork. What we cannot see are the small objects, tools, flints, bones, left behind by those people, lying now beneath the bank or deeply in the ditch or scattered by the plough in the earth around the circles. Some of these objects have been found. To understand what Avebury was meant to be we must know what has been uncovered by excavation.

CHAPTER THREE

Excavations at Avebury

When the lord Stowell . . . levell'd the vallum on that side of the town next the church . . .
they found large quantities of buck's horns, bones, oyster-shells and wood coals.

William Stukeley. *Abury*, 27.

IF John Aubrey had done as Charles II ordered and searched for buried skeletons by the Cove in 1663 he would have made the first scholarly excavation at Avebury. As it was, another two hundred years passed before anyone dug there in a way that could be called archaeological. Aubrey had deduced that the circles were prehistoric but for two centuries more there was no proof that he was right and as late as 1849 researchers like Herbert reasoned that Avebury and Stonehenge could not be pre-Roman because neither Caesar nor Tacitus nor any other Roman writer mentioned them whereas mediaeval historians, Henry of Huntingdon and Geoffrey of Monmouth, did, clear evidence that the circles had been put up at some time between the Romans leaving Britain and the Norman Conquest.[1] Similar reasoning enabled Fergusson to suggest that Avebury was the cemetery of Arthur's warriors. Until excavation could disprove these theories the age of Avebury would remain uncertain.

Yet even in the seventeenth century people had been finding prehistoric remains. Dr Toope digging up human bones near the Sanctuary in 1678 only wanted to turn them 'into a noble medicine that relieved many of my distressed neighbours'[2] much as nineteenth-century Chinese apothecaries ground up teeth from Dragon-Bone Hill for their elixirs, not realising that these were human relics a million years old. And when, around 1685, Lord Stawell had part of Avebury's western bank removed to make space for a barn he was not at all interested in the shells, ashes and antlers his workmen exposed on the blackened turf under the bank where prehistoric people had walked. Stukeley talked with an old man, one of the labourers, who told him 'there was the quantity of a cartload of the horns, that they were very rotten, that there were very many burnt bones among them',[3] and it is possible that Stawell's men had uncovered a place where New Stone Age workers had squatted during the building of Avebury. A similar temporary camp with the rubbish of occupation later covered by the bank was excavated in 1939 far away at the Irish stone circle of the Lios in County Limerick, also on the western side of the ring 'where fires burned and where refuse and filth gathered, occasionally strewn over with earth as the months of labour continued'.[4]

Stawell did not care. Stukeley never saw any of it and could only report that 'these are all the antiquities I could learn to have been found in and about the town of Abury', adding that a bronze axe had been discovered near the church.

For many years little happened. Trees were planted on top of Silbury Hill in 1723 and an iron bridle-bit unearthed, perhaps lost in Ethelred's time when Silbury was fortified against the Danes. In 1776 the Duke of Northumberland had a shaft sunk down the hill by Cornish miners who found only a piece of oak. The Revd Joseph Hunter, distressed to hear that around 1828 two more stones had been taken from Avebury's North Circle, was informed by the farmworker 'that the earth had been examined to the depth of a yard or more, at the foot of the cove stones, to see if there were any evidences of sacrifices having been performed there, but nothing peculiar was observed'.[5]

It was from the mid-nineteenth century onwards that systematic investigation began into the past of Avebury and its region, started by excavators whose techniques did not match their good intentions. In 1849 John Merewether, Dean of Hereford, within four hectic weeks plunged into thirty-three round barrows and West Kennet chambered tomb and had two tunnels thrust into the side of Silbury Hill. Between 1855 and 1860 John Thurnam, Medical Superintendent of the new Wiltshire County Asylum at Devizes, probed into four megalithic tombs near Avebury—Lanhill, Lugbury, West Kennet, and Adam's Grave—discovering human skeletons whose skulls had been split open, 'human victims immolated on the occasion of the burial of a chief', then in 1865, the year Abraham Lincoln was shot, the Revd A. C. Smith, William Cunnington III and the Revd Bryan King, vicar of Avebury, excavated at Avebury itself.[6]

Their aims were good and attainable. They wanted to find where missing stones had stood, to examine the structure of the bank, and to test Fergusson's theory that Avebury was 'a vast burial ground'. During the first week of October these top-hatted Victorian gentlemen made fourteen separate pits and trenches, some in the North Circle where they discovered that the two huge Cove stones were supported on a bed of sarsen stones varying from the size of pebbles to smallish boulders, 'evidently placed there, and rammed in' to keep the pillars upright. In the area of the Cove, after a haystack had been shifted by an obliging farmer, they dug 'four large holes' and below the chalk rubble left by the casual exploration of forty years before they came upon many animal bones, some prehistoric pottery but no human bones whatsoever. They also saw the burnt fragments of the missing northwest stone that had fallen inwards and been broken up.

At the centre of the South Circle they sunk another large, square pit and extended a trench eighteen metres westwards looking for signs of an inner ring. There were none. Finally, they had their workmen dig into the bank in three places, the last being a wide deep ramp at the west-north-west where Lord Stawell had churned up bones and ashes. Work went on here for two days, cutting down through the bank until they came to a layer of 'stiff clay soil of a deep red colour', the undisturbed old land-surface. Again, they found nothing.

By the time they finished they had proved Avebury was not a cemetery. Not one human bone had turned up amongst the plentiful remains of animals just below the turf. Not that this deterred Fergusson. 'In 1865, they tapped the vallum in various places', he jeered, 'and found nothing . . . A man must know very exactly what he is looking for, and where to look for it.'[7] Subsequent excavations, however, have confirmed Smith's beliefs.

The pickaxes and heavy shovels with which their labourers heaved out the soil, the absence of accurate measurements, plans, drawn sections that would have showed how different occupation-layers related to one another, these crudities should not be over-criticised by today's archaeologists. The methods used by Smith were poor. His report lacked detail. But however roughly he had ripped at the shroud of prehistory he had been clear what he was looking for and in part he had succeeded.

Although his finds were few they were important. As well as a piece of antler he discovered many sherds of pottery, especially in and near the North Circle, very different from the mediaeval pottery nearer the surface. 'The fragments of pottery we brought to light from our deeper cuttings were invariably of the British type.' By 'British' he meant prehistoric, probably like that found by Thurnam in the West Kennet tomb six years earlier and illustrated by Smith in his book,[8] pieces that could not be properly dated but which proved that Avebury had been visited by people long before the Romans. Most of the sherds were probably from coarse, flint-gritted pots, handmade and with rounded bases. Nearly all were plain. One or two might have been decorated by the potter digging her fingernails around the drying walls or impressing the clay with a band of twisted cord. And when they were broken the fragments were left lying in the open where rain wore down the sharp fractures until the earth covered them over.[9]

The problem was that little was known about pottery of the Neolithic Age because the dead of the long barrows were rarely buried with pots or other objects to take with them into the spirit world. Even such an experienced digger as Canon Greenwell could comment about the pottery only 'that its absence may be said to characterise the long [barrows]'. John Mortimer, another Yorkshire antiquarian, digging into the long mound at Hanging Grimston three years after Smith's Avebury project, found two Neolithic bowls and had to describe them as of 'uncommon type'.[10] Smith in his *British and Roman Antiquities of North Wiltshire* as late as 1884 had to write of the 'very few earthen vases of any sort' from the eleven long barrows in Wiltshire that had been investigated. Nothing significant could be learned until there were sufficient pots to say what they had been used for and whether they belonged to the Early, Middle or Late Neolithic period of British prehistory.

In 1881 Smith returned to Avebury with five workmen 'who carefully probed the ground with iron bars wherever Stukely had marked fallen stones'. During that summer they located sixteen sarsens in the Outer Circle, some very deeply buried, two more in the North Circle, and detected twenty-five stoneholes as depressions in the ground, showing that Stukeley had sometimes, wrongly, assumed that villains like Robinson were responsible for all the missing stones whereas many sarsens had been piously buried centuries before that time.

While the work progressed the Revd William Lukis was making a largescale plan of Avebury although 'the area is occupied by so many hedges and trees, houses and walled enclosures, that the eye is bewildered'. He was unable later to plan the Kennet Avenue because 'the weather changed, and continued stormy and wet for some time', exactly as rain had prevented John Aubrey from plotting the same stones. Trying again in September 1882, 'the weather was not more favourable' and Lukis had to leave his survey unfinished. Maybe stones and storms do go together.

During his measuring of the stone circles Lukis was told that the previous year, while digging a pit for the annual maypole, Mr Pratt, one of the villagers, chanced upon an unbroken urn 'full of bones' near where the Obelisk had stood in the middle of the South Circle. He put it down by his garden wall and it was smashed some months later, probably by children who took away every piece leaving nothing for Lukis or Smith to examine.[11] Lukis also mentioned 'innumerable fragments of coarse clay vessels of early British or Celtic character' but all of his surviving sherds are mediaeval and none is prehistoric.[12]

If prehistoric pottery was difficult to sort into periods, dating was almost impossible. All that Smith could write about the builders of Avebury was that they were people of a 'low state of civilisation . . . men of small stature, of dark complexion and curly dark hair, and with heads of a peculiar long or oval shape', who 'must have carried on a perpetual struggle with the wild animals by which they were surrounded'. For a prehistorian of the late nineteenth century the only known dates were those from early Mediterranean cultures—Egypt, Greece, Rome, Phoenician—and there were few links between these and events in prehistoric Britain. Estimated dates for the earliest British Bronze Age round barrows ranged from Evans' 3000 BC to Greenwell's 500 BC. Guest thought Stonehenge might have been built as late as 200 BC. Smith simply wrote, 'in all probability the founders of our megalithic monuments in North Wiltshire flourished many centuries before the Christian era'.

It was by now widely accepted that Avebury was prehistoric but there was still disagreement about its function. Lukis doubted Smith's belief that it had been a temple. Colley March thought they were both mistaken, suggesting instead that the bank had been an enormous mortuary enclosure piled up to protect corpses from the gnawing of wild beasts. 'The body, loosely fastened in a case of wicker-work, may have been deposited . . . at the base of monoliths, like those that stand about the enclosed area of Abury.'[13] Written in 1888 these words have some truth in them.

In July 1894, eight years after ten exploratory shafts had been sunk into the ditch of Silbury Hill,[14] Sir Henry Meux of Dauntsey House, eleven miles north-west, had a cutting made through Avebury's south-east bank. The work was done in some secrecy, like an earlier excavation about 1880 on the chambered tomb of West Woods, four miles away, and when Dauntsey House was sold in 1915 all the records, including elaborate plans and sections, disappeared so that the excavation has lost much of its value, all the more to be regretted because of the interesting discoveries made by the workmen.[15]

Just below the bank's crest, some 1.2 metres deep, the diggers found twenty large deer antlers in a 'box' made of lumps of chalk, the tines worn down from being used as levers to quarry out chalk for the bank thousands of years before. These spoiled tools must have been deposited high in the bank when it was almost completed.

Mr Leslie, the supervisor, also recorded a few pieces of pottery, now lost, some shaped animal bones and, at the prehistoric ground level 5.5 metres down, several flint tools including a scraper for cleaning leather and an arrowhead. Perhaps most important of all he noticed a bank within the bank, a smaller rampart whose original grassy surface showed in the side of his cutting as a curved black band about nine centimetres thick a long way back from the lip of the ditch. A dense patch of burnt earth and ashes on its inner slope may show where people rested during the building of Avebury, huddled round an autumn fire, the bank giving some shelter from the chill breezes blowing off the downs.

Leslie also dug into the ditch but not deeply enough to unearth anything except some Romano-British pottery and it was left to the biggest excavation of all at Avebury, just before the First World War, to reveal the fanaticism of those who had laboured year after year hacking out this ditch.

In 1899 the British Association for the Advancement of Science formed a committee to enquire into 'The Age of Stone Circles', and later engaged an archaeologist, Harold St. George Gray, the curator of Taunton Museum, to undertake some exploratory excavations. For eleven years he had worked as an assistant for General Pitt-Rivers, the man who more than any other had revolutionised excavation techniques by his insistence on systematic recording, planning every layer, preserving every find. When the General died in 1900 Gray, with his thorough training, seemed the perfect man to supervise the stone circle project.

In 1901 and 1902 he dug at Arbor Low in the Peak District of Derbyshire, a site with many similarities to Avebury. It was a circle–henge, a roughly circular earthwork with an inner ditch surrounding the remains of a stone circle and Cove. Gray spent three and a half weeks here investigating the rock-cut ditch and the two entrances. In 1905 he went to Bodmin Moor, about fifty miles from Lands End, and passed a fortnight in mixed summer weather excavating the Stripple Stones, another circle–henge spoiled by a hedge and cart-track that sliced between its northern stones.

At each circle Gray made a largescale, contoured plan but the excavations themselves were disappointing. No pottery at all was discovered. At Arbor Low only some thirty flints of various kinds were brought to light and one or two pieces of bone and antler. The Stripple Stones were even less rewarding, yielding only three flint flakes, one burnt flint, an ox bone and some fragments of wood.

Despite this Gray was asked to excavate at Avebury in 1908, the same year that he started digging at the remarkable henge of Maumbury Rings near Dorchester, seventy miles to the south, another circular earthwork with some deep, mysterious shafts sunk into the bottom of its ditch, tapering pits that held objects very revealing about the beliefs of the society that built Avebury.

Altogether Gray spent four short seasons excavating at Avebury: 1908, 1909, 1911, 1914, before the interruption of the First World War, and he returned in 1922 to finish the excavation of the south entrance. In 1912 he planned the whole monument. When one considers the cost and duration of an excavation today, a modern archaeologist spending several thousands of pounds and engaging scores of students and other volunteers for weeks at a time to explore quite small areas of henges or hillforts, then, even allowing for the devaluation of money, Gray's budget was very small. His total grant was £175, made up to £650 by private donations; £130 yearly out of which he had to pay his workforce of up to seventeen men for two or three weeks at a time. His own salary was necessarily small. For Maumbury Rings he was allowed twenty per cent of the excavation fund with a minimum of eight guineas for the first excavation.[16] From the balance he had to pay ten labourers their wages, and obtain spades, pickaxes, wheelbarrows, planking, and surveying equipment.

At Avebury he concentrated his work on the southern side on land owned by Lord Avebury. The north bank and ditch were thick with trees. Even in 1829 Hunter had remarked that the north-west area was so densely planted 'that there is not the means of walking along it'. Gray, fortunately, was able to avoid this unattractive quadrant, and instead started to the west of the southern entrance, sinking three trenches into the ditch, later digging one farther to the west and concluding with a huge excavation at the ditch's terminal on the other side of the entrance causeway.

His cloth-capped labourers, collarless but wearing their habitual waistcoats, without any mechanical assistance picked and shovelled an average of six hundred tons of chalk from each of these trenches, heaving the rubble up ladders as their cuttings sank down through the silt into the darkening shadows of the chalk. Gray watched, recorded and ultimately published his excavation reports.[17] The ditch-sections he drew to show the layers he cut through are the most informative we have of Avebury. They also expose his limitations. He allowed too short a time for examination of the ditch's non-prehistoric layers near the surface and went so rapidly through them that a lot of evidence was thrown away. Nor was he always available while work was in progress and this sometimes led to catastrophe. 'The writer's absence at breakfast was also unfortunate, for on his return some of the bones had been removed, and the skull had been trampled upon before any part of it was actually recognised by the workmen.'[18] It was doubly regrettable because this was the only skeleton found by Gray at Avebury.

He did, however, have a lot of experience in digging in chalk and was able to recognise the effect that weathering had had on the once-sharp lips of the ditch. A modern visitor looking down does not see the ditch-bottom but only the grass-grown surface of material that has accumulated over the years, filling the ditch to within four metres of the present ground-level. Gray proved the original ditch was much deeper. Immediately below the turf his workmen came to a layer of topsoil with bits of eighteenth-century glass bottles and mediaeval pottery in it, and below that a thicker band of loamy earth and small lumps of chalk, the result of rain and wind wearing away the upper edges of the ditch, sending earth, grass and chalk slithering down over many slow centuries. This was the level open in Roman times as pottery sherds revealed, and it was in this mixed silting that the bronze 'avcissa' brooch from Gaul was dropped near where the Barber's Stone still stood.

As they went deeper Gray's labourers dug out crude steps in the chalk for they were now well over five metres below the rim. Under the Roman levels they came to a seam of much finer chalk and soil, not very thick, formed by the imperceptible but perpetual working of nature, grass dying, chalk drifting down, worms tunnelling, weeds blowing in, cattle grazing, leaves rotting, all settling, decomposing, building up millimetre by millimetre over the years. Here the men found signs of prehistoric activity, a medley of flint scrapers, knives, awls, coarse pottery sherds with corded impressions, animal bones, even human arm- and leg-bones, nothing in any discernible order but unmistakable evidence that ancient people had been here. 'The whole group of pottery may be assigned to the overlap period in North Wiltshire between the end of the Neolithic and the dawn of the Bronze Age.'[19]

Because of the increasing number of conscientious excavations much more prehistoric pottery had been recovered and it was becoming possible to arrange the styles in a sequence from early round-based Neolithic bowls, through Bronze Age funerary urns to late Iron Age wheel-turned pots, and, years later, after consulting with Stuart Piggott,[20] Gray could rightly claim that Avebury had been built at a 'very late Neolithic date, Peterborough ware [the cord-impressed pottery] being found on the old surface, and some flint implements'. As the broad, squat flint scrapers and the flat-edged arrowheads were also late Neolithic, Avebury could at last be placed within a definite period although the date of that time remained obscure. Gray's excavations had provided a chronology, in part fulfilling his brief to determine the age of stone circles even though that problem was still being discussed sixty years later.[21] What Gray had not solved was what Avebury had been used for because the flints and bones and pottery in the ditch could be explained in several, quite different ways. They might have been rubbish, thrown into the convenient dump of the ditch. They might have been lying on the ground, slipping into the ditch accidentally as the sides eroded. Or people might solemnly have deposited pot, flint and bone, burying them in some religious ceremony. Without more clues interpretation was little more than guesswork and Gray was content to state that much prehistoric material survived in this layer of mixed silting.

Parts of the layer had been cemented by water so hard that at first the workers thought they had come to the bottom of the ditch much as Sir Henry Meux's labourers had done twenty years before, but when their pickaxes broke through this seam of crystallised chalk they encountered a dense layer of chunks and blocks of chalk, some of them thirty pounds or more in weight. Apart from a few animal bones and potsherds there was little to discover, but three whole metres more had to be dug out before undisturbed chalk was reached and, despite repeated falls of chalk, the floor uncovered nearly ten metres below ground level, so deep that had a telegraph pole been stood upright on the bottom it would not have shown above the top. To someone standing on the floor, the rim of the ditch would have been higher than the chimney-pots of a modern house.

It was obvious that the prehistoric diggers had taken great care in their work. Although the ditch varied a lot in depth yet in cutting after cutting near the entrance Gray's workmen came to a floor so smooth that sections might have been levelled using a water-trough as an improvised spirit-level. The walls also were well cut and Gray wrote of 'no toolmarks on the walls', a 'vertical and smooth face', and 'the

finest example of cut chalk', and he wondered how it had been possible to break away and work the solid, dense chalk with tools of antler. 'The hardest chalk must have been loosened, at least to some extent, by the blows of flint hammers and mauls.'[22] Only in Cutting VIII near the Barber's Stone and farthest from the entrance was the floor irregular, perhaps because of the 'poor quality of the rock in this position, which consisted of a soft, smooth, rotten, pale greenish-grey chalk'.

This desire to create an impressive, well-finished entrance was emphasised in the workmanship uncovered in Cutting IX on the eastern side of the causeway. Here the ditch was even deeper, a full eleven metres below the surface, and the almost sheer lower faces had been 'squared off with the sides of the fosse [ditch], and not rounded off. The face of the solid chalk was excellently cut'. Gray also noticed an apparent pathway along the inner edge of the ditch-bottom trodden by workers carrying rubble to the ditch-end where baskets were hauled up by ropes that left 'two very shallow open channels, or "shutes" scored in each corner'.

On and near the floor of this cutting were some thirty antlers, many of them with tines worn down, or bruised from hammering, or scorched by fire. Similar antlers were found in Cuttings I, II and VIII. These may have been tools thankfully thrown into the ditch when the exhausting work was done but it will be recalled that during

31. (left) This photograph, taken during Gray's excavations, vividly shows the real depth of the ditch.

32. This composite ditch-section shows the depth of the coarse chalk rubble and the mass of antler picks at its bottom. The human bones occur only in the much thinner layer overlying the rubble. The relative positions of all Gray's finds are illustrated here.

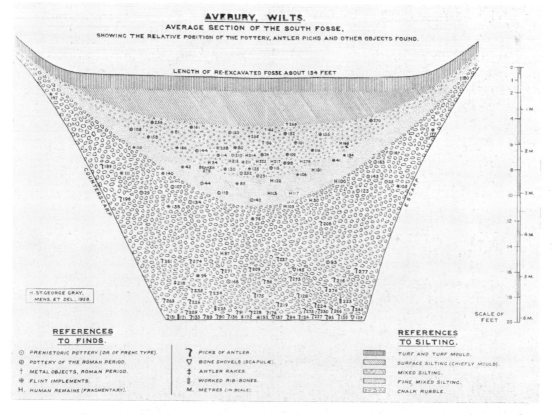

AVEBURY, WILTS.
AVERAGE SECTION OF THE SOUTH FOSSE,
SHOWING THE RELATIVE POSITION OF THE POTTERY, ANTLER PICKS AND OTHER OBJECTS FOUND.

LENGTH OF RE-EXCAVATED FOSSE ABOUT 134 FEET

H. ST.GEORGE GRAY,
MENS. ET DEL, 1928.

SCALE OF FEET

REFERENCES
TO FINDS.

⊙ PREHISTORIC POTTERY (OR OF PREHS. TYPE).
⊕ POTTERY OF THE ROMAN PERIOD.
† METAL OBJECTS, ROMAN PERIOD.
⊕ FLINT IMPLEMENTS.
H. HUMAN REMAINS (FRAGMENTARY).

⌇ PICKS OF ANTLER.
▽ BONE SHOVELS (SCAPULÆ).
‡ ANTLER RAKES.
⌇ WORKED RIB-BONES.
M. METRES (IN SCALE).

REFERENCES
TO SILTING.

⬚ TURF AND TURF MOULD.
⬚ SURFACE SILTING (CHIEFLY MOULD).
⬚ MIXED SILTING.
⬚ FINE MIXED SILTING.
⬚ CHALK RUBBLE.

the excavation by Meux a 'box' of antlers was discovered in the bank, too damaged to be buried 'treasure', but too obviously concealed to be discarded rubbish. Such antlers provide one of the clues to the purpose of Avebury.

Cutting IX had several other interesting features, not least of which was some distinctive stratification. Gray intended to photograph this but 'owing to wind, hail, and rain, this loose and very moist silting would not stand, and a few tons of the material, crashed to the bottom of the fosse, smashing our longest ladder in the fall'. Gray's drawn section shows the 'occasional seams of fine mixed silting' and 'patches of mould' in the thick bottom layer and the great depth of rubble which must certainly have got into the ditch quickly to account for the mass of prehistoric finds in the layer above it. Near the entrance they had been especially numerous, flakes of flint, a knife, scrapers, prehistoric sherds, pieces of antler, ox bones, several human jaw-bones, an arm, fragments of skull, a tooth in a patch of burnt material, and, in the middle of the ditch, not two metres below the grass, a skeleton.

This had been found in almost the worst possible conditions. There was a drizzling rain. The earth had been trampled into sticky, smeared disorder by the boots of too many labourers. The workmen were untrained. The ditch was being chunked out with pickaxes. Gray was not there. Some of the bones had been picked up 'and thrown back'. Even so it was seen that the skeleton lay crouched on its side, head to the south, inside an oval setting of small sarsens. One of the stones seemed to be 'half a ring-stone', a stone with a hole through it. Other, quite large sarsen slabs weighing two or three hundredweights and placed over the skeleton,[23] had been hauled away some days before without anyone realising their significance. The burial was of a woman about thirty years old, almost a dwarf, the bones of her skull excessively thick, her teeth worn down, a front tooth missing, quite unlike a person from a golden age.

With her was a lump of chalk about the size of a table-tennis ball, several flints, a bone from the front leg of a sheep, and some sherds from plain pots, most of them with flecks of quartz in the clay. Just below the skeleton were the remains of a fire with a lot of burnt animal bones and scorched flints. Gray recorded this but made no deductions about its presence in the ditch.

In April 1914 he supervised a cutting through the south-east bank, finding it was composed of blocks of firmly compacted chalk from the ditch, different from the loose rubble noticed in the excavation of 1894 only 120 metres to the north. There was no sign of an inner rampart. Nor were there many finds in the bank itself, just some charcoals from hazel and hawthorn trees but, under the bank, on the prehistoric land-surface there were flints and more late Neolithic Peterborough pottery.

By 1922 Gray's work at Avebury was finished. As well as his ditch and bank cuttings he had examined the causeway across the south entrance and had also uncovered three buried sarsens in the North Circle. He had accomplished his main aim of recovering evidence for the date of the monument, he had revealed both the immensity of the ditch, an average of nearly ten metres deep, and the size of the bank, once about six metres high and twenty-eight to thirty metres wide at its base, and in 1912 he had made what is still the most satisfactory plan of the earthwork. The monument, covering about eleven hectares (28½ acres) inside the bank, had been built on a low dome of chalk and was centred on the highest point in front of which a house now stands at the north-east corner of the crossroads.

It is of some interest to compare the varying measurements of Avebury's surveyors.

	Aubrey (1663)	Stukeley (1724)	Crocker (1812)	Lukis (1881)	Gray (1912) Ft.	Metres	Smith I.F. (1965)	Thom (1976)	Meg. Yds.
Bank	—	1528	1414	1233	1400	426.7	1400	—	—
Ditch	990	1387	—	—	1152	351	1140	—	—
Outer Circle	—	1300	1205	1047	1108	338	1096	1088	400
North Circle	—	—	—	—			—	—	—
—outer ring	355	416	272	270	320	97.5	320	340	125
—inner ring	—	173	166	—	170	51.8	140	—	—
South Circle									
—outer ring	205	416	325	320	336	102.4	340	340	125
—inner ring	—	173	—	—	154	46.9	—	—	—

Table 1. Average Diameters at Avebury (in Imperial Feet).

Gray's largescale plan with its detailed layout of the bank and ditch needs only the addition of stones located and re-erected since 1912 to be the most accurate available. He pointed out the inaccuracy of the Outer 'Circle'. It had an approximate diameter of 338 metres 'but it is considerably out of true and few of the stones actually touch the circumference of the circle described on the plan. The most accurately placed stones were in the NW and SE quadrants. There is much flattening (inwards) on the SW, a short flattening on the N, and a decided outward bulge on the NE.'[24]

It is from his excavations that one obtains an appreciation of the labours of the builders of Avebury. Statistics are dull but not when it is estimated that from the ditch these people removed over ninety thousand cubic metres of chalk. This was enough to build a pyramid with a seventy metre base and a height of forty-six metres. Indeed, the average volume of the seven pyramids of the Vth Dynasty, put up between 2560 and 2420 BC around the same time as Avebury, is about the same as the contents of this massive ditch.[25]

In 1922 Passmore had suggested that Avebury's ditch had been intended as a moat,[26] a belief repeated recently:

We can be sure that whenever there was water at the confluence, there was water in the huge moat . . . The monument at Avebury, or Aubury as it was known in the seventeenth century, was built to create New Water, and in the oldest European language, the Neolithic Basque tongue, Urberri means New Water! True to the cyclical nature of mythical reality, the Aubury water was new not only in 2600 BC but every spring![27]

However attractive this may be as a theory, overlooking the dubious place-name derivation, there are many sensible reasons for disbelieving that Avebury's ditch held water. Gray himself remarked that water would have left a sediment of mud and fine silt in the bottom and would have stained the chalk walls. His argument is strengthened by the excavation of a related earthwork at Waulud's Bank near Luton where the ditch had been waterlogged and did contain a silt forty-eight centimetres deep 'showing signs of having been under water for a long time'. A little above it was another layer of chalk 'with much pure white water-logged clay'.[28] At Avebury there was neither silt nor staining.

At Marden earthwork just seven miles south of Avebury and of the same period the present water-table reaches as high as the ditch-bottom and there were clear traces of waterlogging. The excavators in 1966 and 1967 wrote, 'The level of the water table early in the 2nd millennium bc [c. 2500 BC] cannot be ascertained, but it was probably *lower* [my italics] than at present, or else the excavation of the ditch . . . would have presented considerable difficulties.'[29] From Gray's survey he demonstrated that parts of Avebury's ditch were as much as 2.4 metres above the present level of the River Kennet[30] and so, presumably, even higher above the prehistoric level. The evidence from Marden, so close to Avebury, the silting at Waulud's Bank, and the absence of waterlogging at Avebury all argue against the theory that its ditch had ever been a moat, and an alternative explanation must be sought for its depth.

To understand Avebury factual evidence is needed ranging from the size and architecture of the monument to the efforts of the builders and to the objects they left behind them. The significance of the pottery and the flints will be considered later. What has to be emphasised here is the quantity of human bones discovered by Gray. Smith had found none in his 1865 excavation inside the circles but Gray recovered at least twenty from the ditches: six jaw-bones; eight arm- and leg-bones; three pieces of skull and three other fragments, none from a burial, just scattered bones lying in the chalk above the rubble. Yet not one-twentieth of the ditch had been excavated and even allowing for a greater concentration of bones near the entrances it seems likely that upwards of three hundred human bones still lie buried. Like the antlers, the flints and the pottery their presence must be explained.

During the time Gray had been at Avebury other work had gone on nearby. After 'Adam', the one surviving stone of the Beckhampton Cove, tumbled down in 1911 Maud Pegge Cunnington and her husband, Benjamin, great-grandson of William Cunnington I, supervised its re-erection the following summer.[31] The difficulty they had in lifting the stone even though using powerful machinery, creates an even greater respect for the prehistoric engineers who raised this sarsen with only simple levers and their own muscles.

Stukeley had miscalculated the stone's weight as sixty-two tons but even though it weighed only about half that it took the Cunningtons and two labourers four weeks to erect it. Their first attempt was made with two forty-ton and one fifty-ton jacks (borrowed from the Great Western Railway). They intended to raise the stone a little and then pull it upright 'by means of two traction engines. The plan was found not to be satisfactory, the only result being the breaking of the wire ropes, tested to a strain of 50 tons, without moving the stone at all.' Finally they had to resort almost to prehistoric methods, inching the stone up with the jacks, and supporting it day by day with timbers and wedges. Almost inevitably the work was delayed by rain.

Stukeley had recorded the discovery of human bones by the second of the Cove stones, and by the inner face of their own stone the Cunningtons unearthed another skeleton, a middle-aged man lying crouched in a shallow grave, the plough-smashed sherds of a beaker near him.[32] This bright-red pot which can be dated to about 2300 BC had been made by people who came to Avebury some time after the circles had been put up.

As well as the Cove stone the Cunningtons raised another stone in 1912, one in the Kennet Avenue that had fallen about twenty years before.[33] They embedded its base in concrete as they had done with Adam but, unfortunately, not only sited it wrongly but also put it upside down so that it had to be repositioned by Keiller during his restoration of the avenue. In 1913, the Cunningtons reported the discovery of a buried stone in the avenue.[34] Fragments of arm- and leg-bones showed that there had been a burial here also but as the stone was too heavy to raise without great expense there was no further investigation.

Alexander Keiller himself started digging in the Avebury district as early as 1925 shortly after he and others had averted the threatened building of a Marconi wireless station and tower there. Between 1925 and 1929, at first assisted by St George Gray, he excavated at the causewayed enclosure of Windmill Hill just north-west of Avebury, a tantalising Neolithic site that holds some of the clues to the mystery of Avebury. In 1934 Keiller turned to Avebury. Before then Flinders Petrie, the famous Egyptologist, had dug two more trenches into Silbury Hill. Kendall had proved the enclosures on Windmill Hill to be Neolithic. In 1930 the Cunningtons rediscovered and then excavated the site of the Sanctuary on Overton Hill[35], the concentric stone circle whose destruction had so grieved Stukeley. The finding of beakers and earlier pottery proved its contemporaneity with Avebury.

The clues were being assembled. Once Keiller had acquired most of the land on which Avebury stood he moved from London, transferring his library, equipment and museum to Avebury, and founding the Morven Institute of Archaeological Research, named after his Scottish estate. From 1934 up to the outbreak of war he excavated methodically first along the line of the Kennet Avenue, later within the earthwork itself. On one occasion he spoke to an old man who had dug with Gray. 'Well, zur, we did find God's amount of antelope.' The possibility of Avebury having been a prehistoric zoo has not been accepted by archaeologists.

Most of the avenue stones had been buried in mediaeval times but one by one their positions were located along the northern third of the part that Keiller had bought, and where the stones survived they were re-erected. If a stone had been smashed its debris and soil-filled stonehole showed where it had stood and its position was marked. Sometimes a stone had laid concealed since the fourteenth century and its chalk-filled pit was almost unnoticeable. Only sensitive trowelling could detect the softer texture of the filling against the hard, untouched edge of its pit.

In an experiment using prehistoric equipment, but with the security of steel cables, twelve men under the direction of an experienced foreman, managed to put up a smallish sarsen of about eight tons in five days. As nearly all the stones at Avebury weigh much more than this and are of awkward shape and bulk, and as originally in the circles and the avenues there were some six hundred of these sarsens, we are once again given a glimpse of the appalling demands this monument made upon the primitive society that constructed it.

Only quite shallow holes had been dug for the avenue stones and they were held upright chiefly by the packing of sarsens and blocks of chalk around their bases. Some of this chalk had been dug from the lowest reaches of the ditch indicating that the earthwork and the Kennet Avenue were probably being put up at the same time. Keiller and his associate, Stuart Piggott, noticed the way in which posts and stakes had been used in the erection of these stones. They also observed that the avenue, laid out not in sinuous, dragonlike curves but in a succession of straight lengths, narrowed as it got nearer the entrance, decreasing from an average width of fifteen metres down to ten metres while the stones themselves increased dramatically in height as John Aubrey's comment about 'the great stone at Aubury's towne's end, where this Walke begins' appears to confirm. The funnelling effect of these taller stones must have made the approach towards the bank all the more spectacular.

Sarsen occurs naturally in two shapes, a long thin pillar and a broader diamond, called by Keiller and Piggott, Types A and B. It seemed significant that along the parallel rows of the avenue not only were Type A stones set opposite Type B but that the types alternated along each row so that whether one looked across the row or along it there was always a contrasting shape.[36] Keiller speculated that the avenue might have been not only a processional way but also a representation in stone of a vital aspect of the activities that took place in the circles, the stones symbolising male and female sexual organs. 'If the A and B stones in the Circles and Avenue do indeed represent male and female symbols, the implication must be that the monuments were dedicated to a fertility cult.'[37] This surmise, based on the physical appearance of the sarsens, was one of the first objective interpretations of what Avebury might have been used for.

Half a mile outside the southern entrance on the line of the avenue Keiller's workforce found an apparent prehistoric occupation site with the remains of hearths, pits, flints, broken pots, animal bones but no traces of huts. And by four of the stones, as in the case of the graves recorded by Stukeley and Maud Cunnington alongside the Beckhampton Cove, they dug up burials, two of the skeletons with beakers. The grave of one was actually part of the stonehole and the body must have been interred before the stone was fully raised, 'a proceeding which, incidentally, had been responsible for some degree of damage, through crushing, to the skull'.[38] The dating of this beaker between about 2300 and 2150 BC and the discovery of beaker sherds in other stoneholes was further evidence of the age of the earthwork and the Kennet Avenue. Altogether eight beakers, either whole or in fragments, have been discovered within the Avebury complex: from the Sanctuary, the Kennet Avenue, the Beckhampton Avenue, and the ditch of Avebury itself, and although the earliest and latest possible dates for their manufacture range from about 2520 to 2035 BC the great majority of them might well have been made within a few decades of 2300 BC, giving much more precision to the conclusion that Avebury was built in 'the Neolithic–Bronze Age transition period', at a time just before the makers of beakers arrived in North Wiltshire.[39]

33. A pair of Kennet Avenue stones. Stone 26b, the 'female' lozenge, Type B, is on the left, facing the Type A pillar.

In 1937 Keiller, with the help of the Ministry of Works, turned to the bank and ditch and stone circles. He was disgusted with the indescribable squalor of the side nearer the village, a metre-high heap of tins and bottles by two stones, rusting pig-wire in the grass, the ditch foul with rubbish, the bank hidden in a jungle of undergrowth and trees. All this had to be cleared and the tedious business of finding the buried stones started, all the more difficult because of the depth at which some of them lay, two just north of the west entrance, numbers 30 and 31,[40] being nearly two and a half metres below the surface. Even so, eight stones were unearthed, some of which Stukeley had thought destroyed, and the situations of five others were marked by curious obelisks, intentionally moulded in concrete to distinguish them from the prehistoric sarsens. Surprisingly the gap in the bank at the north, long believed to be an historic gap made for the Swindon road, proved to be a genuine entrance with a causeway of undisturbed chalk. Even more unexpected to the workers trowelling around the entrance was the discovery of three totally unrecorded stoneholes, one far too close to the colossal Swindon Stone for its stone to have stood alongside it. Markers by the ditch at the North Entrance show where these stoneholes were, eleven metres apart on the arc of a circle about 103 metres in diameter, much the same as the known North and South inner circles whose stones were also spaced about eleven metres apart. The centre of this third 'circle' was on

71

the same north–north–west to south–south–east axis as the others and Keiller concluded that 'it seems impossible therefore not to conclude that what one may term
"Avebury I" consisted of three settings of stones . . . unaccompanied by banks or
ditches'.[41] Because there was no sign of the three stones having been destroyed it was
assumed 'that these stones were taken down in some way and used again in the
construction of the new Outer Circle'.[42] The idea that Avebury might have had
several phases, the first of unenclosed stone circles, had not been considered by any
previous worker. It was a stimulating possibility.

Keiller was also able to provide a matter-of-fact explanation for a sarsen that,
because its face angled not in line but obliquely to the arc of stones, had caused all
manner of theorising, 'much of it of a fanciful and far-fetched nature'. Its axis,
however, had not been deliberately aligned on the midsummer sunset nor was there
any other esoteric reason for its unusual setting. Quite simply, it had slipped during
erection, just as another stone had done, and twisted sideways in its hole. No one had
bothered to put it right.

The following year Keiller had the south-west quadrant restored, at that time a
field of rough grazing with only one standing stone. At the break in the bank at the
west through which the village street descends there was another causeway across
the ditch proving that this, like the south and the north, was a prehistoric entrance.
Only the eastern gap remains untested. Two derelict cottages mouldered at the West
Entrance and these and their outbuildings were demolished by Keiller with all the
zeal of the mediaeval priest who overthrew the stone circles. Underneath was a
filled-in pond containing the shattered bits of a sarsen. Other parts had been built
into a wall. Most of this stone was reassembled, one lump like an afterthought stuck
uneasily on top, and it is now the first pillar one comes to from the street with the
splendid curve of sarsens, most of them disinterred and re-erected by Keiller,
bending away towards the South Entrance. It was under one of them that the
barber–surgeon had been discovered.

A cutting halfway along this quadrant revealed that contrary to the belief that the
bank had been designed as an evenly topped terrace on which spectators might sit
the builders had taken little bother to level it off. A little away from the ditch they
had constructed a rough wall of chalk blocks to prevent rubble slipping back and
had then piled up turf and soil and chalk in a series of dumps all round the
circumference. They did make an attempt to fill the intervening hollows with finer
rubble but had not rammed it down and the heaps ultimately weathered together
into the undulating crest of the bank that is visible today.

Little was found in the bank, a piece of bone and, on the prehistoric landsurface,
some worn-down sherds of Neolithic pottery and a couple of stakeholes near a
hollow where people may have squatted. These finds and others from Avebury
were placed in the museum by the manor-house, opened by Keiller in 1938.

Keiller's one small section into the ditch did not produce anything informative
and in 1939 he started work on the South Entrance where a posthole large enough for
a big tree-trunk was discovered alongside a stonehole on the causeway. The modern
road covers the other side of the entrance and it may be that a corresponding
posthole is buried there, one of a pair of vast posts similar to the portal stones that

34. The repaired stone by Avebury's western entrance.

once towered at the entrance to Stonehenge and other Neolithic henges.[43]

Just before the beginning of the Second World War about a quarter of the South inner circle was excavated, locating the precise position of the large centre stone named the Obelisk by Stukeley, discovering the stump of the Ring Stone just outside the circumference, and bringing to light a peculiar row of smallish sarsens buried to the west of the Obelisk. These sarsens, or Z-Stones as they are called, were re-erected as were three stones of the circle itself but no trace of an inner ring was found and it seems that Stukeley was wrong in thinking that the South Circle had been concentric like the North ring. It was also noticed that the Z-Stones had been supported by blocks of chalk from the ditch, just like the pillars of the Kennet Avenue so that they also had to be contemporary with the construction of the earthwork. The Z-Stone setting remains unexplained because 'unfortunately our work on this feature was interrupted by the outbreak of war, and we cannot attempt to interpret its meaning until that work has been completed'.[44] To date no further investigation has been made here.

Keiller never did complete his work. Ill health after the war prevented any further excavation and he died in 1955. His excavations both at Avebury and at Windmill Hill were published in a definitive and finely edited volume,[45] and every visitor walking across the trimmed grass, sauntering round the edges of the cleared ditch, by the standing sarsens that tell nothing of their centuries below the soil, every visitor to the museum with its attractive display of finds from his excavations, all of us by our pleasure acknowledge our gratitude to the man who did so much to change Avebury's untidy neglect into its present majestic state worthy of its magnitude and importance.

His efforts had transformed Avebury, resurrecting the Kennet Avenue and the western half of the earthwork so that the site now has a semblance of what it had been like before the depredations of the fourteenth century. Keiller's work had introduced the possibility that fertility rituals had been part of the ceremonies here. What he was unable to do was to prove or disprove the existence of Stukeley's Beckhampton Avenue and he was inclined to believe that if there had been any such feature it was part of an entirely separate monument. Since the war, however, W. E. V. Young, who had worked for so long with Keiller, disinterred the skeleton of a child at Beckhampton.[46] It lay by a buried sarsen and with it were the bones of a young ox, a piece of chalk with grooves deeply cut into it, and a beaker, broken and repaired, of about the same period as the similar pot found by Keiller and Piggott in the Kennet Avenue. The discovery of the Beckhampton beaker was accidental, made when a plough struck the stone which must have stood exactly on the line where Stukeley said the Beckhampton Avenue ran. Since 1968 the burning-pit of another stone has been unearthed in Avebury's main street, and a further buried stone revealed near the present Beckhampton traffic island. It would seem, therefore, that this avenue did follow the course that Stukeley claimed for it.[47]

The last quarter of a century has seen much archaeological activity around Avebury. Long burial mounds of the New Stone Age have been excavated near Windmill Hill, at Beckhampton and Avebury South Street. Silbury Hill has been explored yet again. The megalithic tombs at West Kennet and Manton have been investigated as well as Wayland's Smithy some miles to the east. The introduction of radio-carbon analysis has provided archaeologists with a far more accurate method of dating than ever we had before and although no carbon assay has yet been obtained from Avebury determinations from other excavations enable us to pinpoint dates much more precisely. Even though the Carbon-14 process needs some adjustment the fact remains that it is now feasible to speak of centuries, even of decades, instead of broad periods such as the 'Late Neolithic' or the 'Early Bronze Age'.

Many problems remain. Excavations by Stuart Piggott in 1960 discovered no extra stoneholes for Avebury's hypothetical third circle and its existence is now doubted.[48] Other excavations by Major and Mrs Vatcher on Avebury's bank near the West Entrance showed that, just as Leslie had recorded in the Meux cutting on the opposite side of the earthwork, there had been a primary turf core at the heart of the bank with layers of rock and soil above it.[49] This could have been an earlier bank but as it was set so far back from its little ditch with an unnecessarily wide stretch of ground between them it was more probably put up as a guideline for the people who later heaped the huge bank-dumps over it.[50] This would have taken years. Much of the marker-bank would have become grass-grown over the generation or so before it was covered but if the imposing North and South Entrances were constructed first this would explain why Gray's bank-cutting near the entrance had no trace of an internal turf-line. Grass would not have had time to grow before the ditch was deepened and the final bank built. If this interpretation is correct then it follows that the design of Avebury was based not on the shape of the megalithic rings or of the present ditch but on the inner, concealed core of the bank.

A hundred years of excavation at Avebury have extended our understanding of it. Besides its architecture we now know much more about the way in which it was built. The discovery of native pottery and flints show that it was constructed by local people before makers of the finely burnished beakers came to North Wiltshire, some time in the Late Neolithic around 2600 BC. The presence of the domestic pottery, moreover, and the general lack of weapons suggests that Avebury was used for some ceremonial purpose. This seems to be confirmed by the burials by several standing stones, by the antlers in the bottom of the ditch, by the isolated human bones higher up. Excavations on earthworks like Avebury at Durrington Walls, Marden and Mount Pleasant, all in Wessex, and at Waulud's Bank, can be interpreted in the same way. What is known of other stone circles tells the same story of mysterious rituals in sacred rings during this period of British prehistory.[51]

Yet much is unexplained. Despite the digging by Smith, Meux, Gray, Keiller and Piggott virtually none of the ground between the Outer and Inner Circles has been explored. Indeed, the whole of the excavations covers less than two acres, mainly in the vicinity of the ditch, leaving ninety-four per cent of the interior untouched.

But more extensive excavation will not necessarily provide vital information. What is needed now is to put Avebury into its cultural background, looking at the customs of the people who built it to see if its use arose from their long-held beliefs or whether it was created from some sudden change introduced by new people, perhaps conquerors, who found no value or beauty in the older ways. Is it true that 'the earth goddess of phallic fertility rites which preoccupied the mind of Neolithic man . . . lost their hold. There was a shift of interest from the earth and the womb upwards to the sun and the heavens—well symbolised by the change from the dark, closed tomb to the open sun-orientated temple.'[52] To test this we must look at the people themselves.

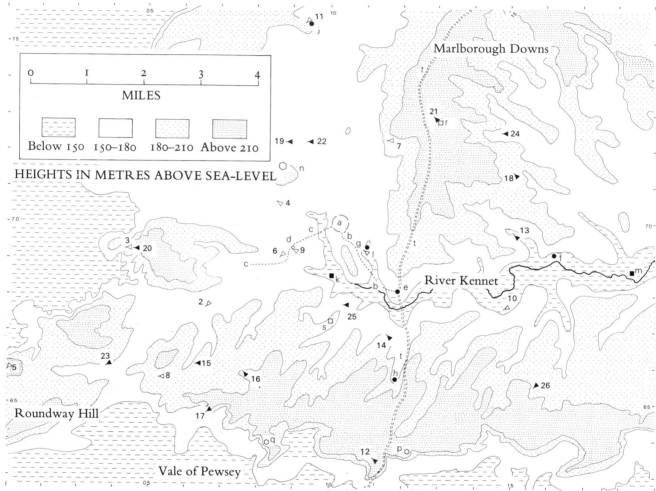

Fig. 2. The Avebury Region.

Earthen Long Barrows: 1 Avebury 21, 2 Beckhampton, 3 Calne Without, 4 Horslip, 5 King's Play Down, 6 Longstone, 7 Monkton Down, 8 Roughridge Hill, 9 South Street, 10 West Overton 24, 11 Winterbourne Bassett. *Megalithic Tombs:* 12 Adam's Grave, 13 Devil's Den, 14 East Kennet, 15 Easton Down, 16 Horton Down, 17 Kitchen Barrow, 18 Manton Down, 19 Mill Barrow, 20 Oldbury Hill, 21 Old Chapel, 22 Shelving Stones, 23 Shepherd's Shore, 24 Temple Bottom, 25 West Kennet, 26 West Woods. *Avebury:* a Avebury circles and earthwork, b Kennet Avenue, c Beckhampton Avenue, d Beckhampton Cove. *Other Stone Circles:* e Sanctuary, f Clatford (Broadstones), g Falkner's Circle, h Langdean Bottom, j Winterbourne Bassett. *Round Mounds:* k Silbury Hill, m Marlborough Mound. *Causewayed Enclosures:* n Windmill Hill, p Knap Hill, q Rybury. *Rectangular Mortuary (?) Enclosures:* r Old Chapel, s Huish Hill. t is the Ridgeway.

CHAPTER FOUR

Avebury before Avebury

We may be assured that this whole country was well inhabited by the ancient Britons.
William Stukeley. *Itinerarium Curiosum* 1, 5.

AROUND the time, six thousand years ago, when Ur was an important town in Sumer, long before the pyramids, when across the Atlantic villages of hunters and food-gatherers were subsisting on shellfish in the Tennessee and Ohio valleys, farmers first settled in the forested wildernesses of Avebury.

The countryside seemed peaceful. On the low ground the gloom of trees buried the land down to the riversides, pathless, untravelled, with alders by the streams, hazels under the forest canopy, elms, oaks heavy and twisted and dark with ivy. Yet apart from the birds there was no movement. No smoke curled and drifted above the trees. In the deeper valleys thorn and bramble clawed between the trunks but on the higher chalk of the downs the trees thinned. A few oak copses grew on the patches of clay. Otherwise these sarsen-littered plains were bare of anything but grass and lonely thorn-bushes, and from the bleak heights the treetops of the lowlands could be seen thickening to the west and north as they reached the heavier soils of the Severn Estuary and the Oxford plain. To the south long-billed curlews flew over the marshes of the Vale of Pewsey. Further south still, on the horizon, was the escarpment of Salisbury Plain on which people were already clearing trees and planting crops.

In the slightly warmer, slightly drier climate of six thousand years ago the gentle slopes and light chalk soils of the downs must have seemed ideal country for Neolithic farmers. The forests provided timber for their homes, fodder for the pigs. The rivers watered their cattle. Perhaps forced from the European mainland by competition for land, bands of these agriculturalists crossed the Channel, settled along the eastern and southern coasts of Britain, communities of a few score people that split up into family groups to work the land for a few years until it was exhausted, moving inland along the rivers and the hill-ridges, to the austerity of Salisbury Plain and, ultimately, further still to the woodlands around Avebury.

Already earlier Mesolithic hunters and food-gatherers had made clearings in the forest by fire. In Dorset and around Bristol and along the Kennet Valley they had hunted the woods for deer, wandering along riversides fishing, and a few of them settled for a while near a stream at Cherhill four miles west of Avebury's tree-covered hillock. They were skilful enough to trap beaver, adventurous enough to kill the wild ox. They shaped the local flint into delicate flakes for their weapons but also used other coloured flint, sandstone, red ochre, limestone, all stones foreign to the Avebury district, working fine chert from Portland seventy miles of forest away, showing how far they travelled in their search for food. Two thousand years before the farmers these Middle Stone Age nomads lingered here before their campsite was flooded and they moved away.[1] Perhaps they were the only people in the region. It has been thought that the whole of Salisbury Plain, some 120 square miles, might have supported one hunting band of about fifteen people,[2] and if this is true large parts of Wiltshire must have remained unvisited for years by human beings.

Then, in the centuries around 4200 BC, a band of farmers, maybe three or four families, men, women, grandparents, children, reached the Avebury region, perhaps coming from the north-west corner of Salisbury Plain where long burial mounds at Edington, Wilsford and Tilshead show where other Neolithic people once farmed. If this was their origin then the colonists may have descended from the plain near Lavington, crossing the few miles of forest and swamp before walking thankfully up the slopes of Roundway Hill to the safety of more open country. Once there they broke up again into families, each searching out and claiming its own territory of a few square miles.

From what is known of early Neolithic houses elsewhere in Britain it is likely that these people lived in well-built timber homes, log cabins about the size of a large cottage and quite big enough to accommodate a large family. Almost all remains of these buildings have gone. Traces of a possible dwelling and its hearth were uncovered by Keiller on the eastern side of Windmill Hill,[3] charcoals of hazel, elder and blackthorn, all hedgerow trees, suggesting it had been built at the edges of a clearing in the forest.

Otherwise, no structures are known in the region. If these first farmers chose to live near water in the valley-bottoms their homes may lie under today's villages. Occasionally on the uninhabited downs archaeologists chance upon the remains of open-air summer sites occupied while the herds grazed on the uplands, isolated shallow pits for cooking and fires, scatters of broken pottery, animal bones, flints marking places lived in for a month or two before colder weather forced the herdsmen down from the hills. Within a few miles of Avebury are several camps: on Overton Hill, at Hemp Knoll, Bishops Cannings Down, Hackpen Ridge, on Roughridge Hill, on Avebury Down, even on Waden Hill overlooking Avebury where a pit was filled with black earth, charcoal, fragments of coarse pottery, flints and the broken bones of sheep, pig and oxen.[4]

The cattle may have been stalled for most of the year, fed upon ivy and elm leaves. The space needed for grazing meant that a large herd would have been impossible in the forests of the early Neolithic. At first the people must have relied mainly on crops for subsistence, year by year felling trees around their clearing, laboriously cutting through the turf with ards, digging the soil, sowing the wheat.[5] Pollens from weeds like ribwort and plantain that flourish among cereals survive to tell us where these patches of ground were cultivated. Gradually the soil would lose its richness and within twenty years or so the people would have to move a few miles to another clearing, raise another cabin, sow, harvest, move a short way again until, maybe a century later, their descendants returned to the first decayed, overgrown settlement. Always inside the group's territory the cycle might continue for centuries until either the family became too large and had to break up or else died out leaving the area deserted.[6]

35. Windmill Hill ware. Made of local clays by native women, these were some of the earliest forms of pottery in Britain.

Over the years as the forest clearances extended more cattle could be kept, and pigs, some sheep, a farming economy in which hunting played only a small part although the existence of leaf-shaped flint arrowheads, skeletons of hunting dogs, and the discovery of antlers and deer bones show that wild animals, even the wolf and boar, might occasionally be killed. Each family must have been almost self-sufficient. Wood and bone for tools were easily obtained. Good flint could be found in Wiltshire and Sussex. Some stone suitable for shaping was available for axes and adzes and grinding-stones. The fine handmade pottery, round-based for resting on the uneven ground, was made from local clays. The crops and the animals were enough to feed the people and could be supplemented by berries, fruits and nuts from the forests. Clothing came from the hides of flayed beasts. The women scraped off the fat with flints and combed out the coarse hairs after soaking the leather in urine. Then they suspended the pelt in cattle dung to make it swell, steeped it in an infusion of oak-wood for tanning and softened it by rubbing in animal brains. The resulting pale, supple leather could be shaped into garments and stitched together with thonging.[7]

It was a time when there were no months or weeks, only day and night and the blurred changing of the seasons, when the rhythms of life were the rhythms of agriculture, an age when each family was independent and yet linked by kinship to the few other families in the locality. Decisions were made within the family, usually

79

by the man as head of the household because the growing of crops was slow, tedious, without instant reward, demanding patient acceptance of conventional methods long-tried and successful. Innovations could be dangerous and were discouraged. Young men were expected to learn by example. It was the collective experience of the older farmers that was respected. Problems of husbandry, social change, religion were decided by reference to long-held beliefs. It was a social state in which tradition was binding, sometimes so constricting that it developed into fatalism, a belief that things were ordained beyond the powers of human beings to alter. Nor were there many outside contacts to modify this conservatism. There was not much to trade and, in any case, travel was hazardous once one passed beyond the familiar, secure limits of the homeland. Each family was almost a prisoner inside its own territory. Neither house nor crops could be moved. Corn-grinding stones, axes, pottery, were heavy and awkward to move. Territories were too precious and scarce to be abandoned. Customs became fixed, patterns of living remained undisturbed across the generations.[8]

How many of these family groups there were in the countryside around Avebury can never be known although it is unlikely that at first there were more than a few-score people altogether. What is probable is that these families would have had to meet at least annually, for the men to reaffirm their agreements about the rights to watering-places, the size of territories, boundaries, ownership of strayed cattle, to settle quarrels between families, everything done by precedent, each opinion listened to until agreement was reached.

On the occasion of communal meetings young girls may have been married out into other families, an exogamous practice that resulted, archaeologically, in the near-uniformity of pottery styles over wide areas and, much more important socially, helped to strengthen the bonds between the groups. In the thirty square miles of countryside around Avebury even if there had been as many as ten families, one to two hundred people, then within a few generations of intermarriage every family would have had relatives in the others, parents, sisters and brothers, aunts and uncles, cousins, nieces, nephews, a mesh of blood-ties that inevitably led to the growth of lineages in which these families looked back through the generations to mutual heroic ancestors whose powerful spirits would, if treated with respect, safeguard the living.

The living needed safeguards. These were sinewy, gracile people, slender, long-headed, the men about 1.7 metres in average height, the women 1.4 metres, shorter than today's western Europeans, but it was not their physique but the rigours of their existence that endangered them. Superficially their existence seems idyllic.

They were apparently a healthy, moderately prosperous and generally peaceful people, earning their living from the soil without too much strain and with ample time left over for constructing monuments and taking part in ceremonies around them . . . The climate was salubrious, the land was fertile. The hardy herds of cattle and swine more or less took care of themselves. If crops occasionally failed, wild game was always within reach, and edible herbs and berries grew wild in the forest clearings. If a house burned down, a new one could be put up with the aid of friendly neighbours.[9]

The truth is a long way from this vision of paradise. From the burials of these early farmers emerges a stark picture of their health. Arm fractures and wounds were not uncommon amongst the men. Spina bifida was known amongst the women. Most adults suffered from arthritis. Bad mouth hygiene caused inflamed gums and 'dirt' pyorrhoea, abscesses and tooth loss. Amongst the children the defective diet and malnutrition led to rickets and often to death. Some people suffered from polio, sinusitis, tetanus, tuberculosis; and to this dreadful list must almost certainly be added plague and malaria.

Death came early. Many men were dead by thirty-six, women by thirty, and although some endured in life to the great age of seventy perhaps as many as half the children died before they were three years of age. Four people in ten died before they were twenty.[10] 'It is no surprise that men of those times, unlettered, unable to know anything of the world beyond their senses, except for what old men and bards told of past days and far lands, were so filled with fatalism and superstition.'

For people like these, intelligent, skilful in crafts and husbandry and the lore of the countryside, it was not the inability to think but a mode of thinking quite different from ours, even alien to ours, that led them to respond differently to the dangers and mysteries that filled their existence. Danger was everywhere and each family had only itself for protection. Some perils were feared but understood. At the edges of the forest gaily-coloured and poisonous flowers, the pink-purple foxglove growing high in summer, the autumn crocus, the black cherries of the nightshade tempted the children accustomed to searching for nuts and berries with their mothers. By streams the tall white hemlock was as deadly. On open land there was henbane with its nutlike seeds. All these were known and children could be taught to avoid them.

Accidents always threatened the men as they cut down the trees, hauled logs, and although fractures could be splinted there were times when an injured man meant starvation for the family. In the dangerous forest the aurochs trampled, the giant ox with its terrible goring horns. Packs of wolves might break into the cattle-stalls. No child could be allowed in the forest alone. Even men stayed at home at night. During the day the viper slept among the rocks, half a metre long. Despite the coiled beauty of its dark, zigzagged back its bite brought pain, swelling, listlessness, vomiting, death within hours. Brown bears were to be seen on the higher slopes. Worst of all was the wild boar, most vicious at night, its tusks honed razor-sharp by the grinding of its lower canines, too fast and powerful for one human to resist.

Most deadly of all was man. It is sometimes implied that Neolithic people lived together in peaceful co-existence, tending crops in a mild climate, leading calm, congenial lives, but this is a mistaken view. It is rarely possible to identify the cause of lesions noticed on skeletons and it is likely that many of them were the results of day-to-day accidents but in some cases less humdrum explanations are required.

In the long mound of Wor Barrow a few miles south-west of Salisbury the skeleton of a grown man was found, a leaf-shaped flint arrowhead in his side. At Crichel Down nearby another skeleton had an arrowhead by its ribs, presumably where it had dropped as the flesh rotted. In a large grave at Fengate near Peterborough the skeleton of a youngish man lay on its right-hand side. There was an arrowhead in its rib-cage. In the long chambered tomb of Ascott-under-

Wychwood on the edge of the Cotswolds in which over a score of people were interred one man had been killed by an arrow that had penetrated his right side from below, embedding itself in his backbone. In an adjacent compartment another adult had a flint arrowhead by his chest. Far to the north at Tulloch of Assery in Caithness there were similar signs of violence. Heaped up in the tomb's chamber were the remains of an elderly man, his shattered skull on top of the bones, his teeth worn down and infected. He had been killed by an arrow that had hit him in the back, part of the flint head breaking off in his spine. Even within a mile of Avebury the old man in the north-east chamber of West Kennet long barrow had a wound in his left arm and an arrowhead near his throat. When one adds to these instances the many human skeletons in which the cause of death is no longer determinable, the lacerations, cuts, haemorrhages decomposed, it is probable that there were many more killings in the New Stone Age than is usually acknowledged. Quarrels over livestock and land, suspicion of strangers, robbery, chance encounters with a band of Mesolithic hunters, even warfare may have been well known amongst these people.[11]

The insecurities of such primitive societies were many. People could be lost in the trail-less forests, trapped in swamps, drowned in fast-flowing rivers, attacked by wild animals and there were few people to assist each other. Far worse than the everyday dangers, however saddening, were the disasters that were not understood and could not be coped with, drought, blizzards, storms, disease. Again, skeletons tell only part of the story but in the bones of these people is the testimony of their suffering, of injuries and of illnesses. Some of these early farming people must have lived in pain, their fellows helpless to relieve them, wondering what caused the agony, what unknown power had been offended. Just as perplexing and fearsome were the forest fires, gales, epidemics. Cattle wasted, weakened, died. Crops grew black fungus, withered and failed. Against these disasters the people were powerless, for their science and knowledge did not reach so far. In this futility it was religion that protected their minds.

It is not true that the thinking of primitive people is illogical or subnormal. Any society that is to survive has to have a healthy body of common sense. But the thinking of people ignorant of physics, chemistry, meteorology, astronomy is often allusive and symbolic. Just as they find it difficult to follow our reasoning so we, in turn, cannot easily understand the poetic images that 'explain' the man–animal–thing world in which they live.

Primitive people construct belief-systems to help them cope with strains and frustrations against which they have no other defence. Man's intelligence enables him to foresee danger and the inevitability of death. Against these fears he creates beliefs through which he can attempt to manipulate 'spiritual' forces that will give him safety.

Sometimes witch-doctors or diviners were used to decide who or what was responsible for their troubles. Sometimes inanimate objects and places were given semi-human attributes so that people could enter into contact with them and by invocations or sacrifices avert an anticipated threat. It is easy, even for us, to perceive how a belief in ghosts and spirits might come about from an echo, a reflection in rippling water, distant thunder, a half-glimpsed shadow on a rock, all of them

82

seeming to be brief, unclear images of other forces within the dark world of which man was a part.

To him there was no distinction between the natural and the supernatural world. A rain-making ceremony was not a medical prescription which, if performed properly, would bring rain. It was part of the-thing-called-rain and not separate from it. Birket –Smith observed how a child will hit the chair it has stubbed its toe against. A primitive has the same personalised relationship with natural objects. The water-hole, the grotesque rock, clouds, wind swirling up cones of dust, these were not 'spirit' manifestations but ordinary phenomena endowed with personalities that enabled man to communicate with them.

Evidence from monuments near Avebury, the long burial mounds, Windmill Hill, pits along the Kennet Avenue, suggests rites of homeopathic magic miming what was desired just as witches were supposed to impale wax models of their victims to bring about death.

To understand the remote people of Avebury it is necessary to understand their society and such a society has to be reconstructed from its remnants. Information from recent primitive communities helps to make analogies between them and the way people lived in prehistory. It might be thought, indeed some archaeologists and social anthropologists have claimed it as fact, that between the meaningless litter of antiquity and the impenetrable thinking of modern primitives there is no means for us to reach back into the past. At its strictest this is true. We could never be certain that our analogies were wisely chosen or properly comprehended or were even the most appropriate. It is probable, moreover, that there is no utterly relevant comparison. Tribesmen in the New Hebrides, the Pawnee Indians of North America, Gambian Negroes are unlikely to have had a life-style and religious symbolism identical with that of the people of Avebury.

There are nevertheless some remarkable parallels between the monuments and artefacts around Avebury and the history of the Woodland Indians of temperate North America between about 1250 BC and AD 1000. Both peoples lived through periods of climatic change, both used simple agricultural methods, both evolved from a mosaic of family groups into large communities with extensive trading networks. Their practice of burying the dead developed into almost obsessive cult practices. Metal gradually replaced stone and flint. Both cultures used enclosures and 'sacred' circles for their later ceremonies and both incorporated astronomical events like the rising or setting of the sun into their rituals. In their final stages the Indian societies were encountered by Europeans whose narratives survive to enrich the archaeological material. In the same way anthropologists such as Deacon and Layard described the rites on Malekula in the Pacific where islanders seeking to improve their social rank raised stone circles and avenues and sacrificed wild boars at 'degree-taking' ceremonies.[12] Used cautiously descriptions of these distant groups may uncover some of Avebury's mystery.

The religion of early Neolithic agriculturalists probably included some practices that are widespread among primitive crop-growers. 'It must be remembered what a close connection there is between woman and sexuality on one hand and tilling and the fertility of the soil on the other.'[13] Anxious for a good harvest but ignorant of what caused capricious weather, crop disease and soil exhaustion the Neolithic farmer thought by analogy of other examples of fertility and integrated them into his ploughing, sowing and reaping. 'There is one custom whereby naked maidens must mark out the first furrows with the plough',[14] obviously related to those spring festivals when 'ritual marriages' sometimes accompanied the first appearance of the germinating shoots in the belief that the mating of human beings in the fields would give fruitfulness to the earth.[15] 'To the "primitive" agriculture is no merely profane skill. Because it deals with life, and its object is the marvellous growth of that life dwelling in seed, furrow, rain and the spirits of vegetation, it is therefore first and foremost a ritual.'[16] Some activities were necessary when sowing, others at harvesting when the last sheaf might reverently be offered back to Earth who had been robbed of her offspring. In some areas strangers were killed at harvest time and their blood sprinkled on the stubbled ground to bring life back to it. The Pawnees sacrificed a captured maiden at their Morning Star agricultural festival.[17] To the primitive mind any interference with the rhythms of the world had to be balanced by an offering or some act of propitiation.

The dead were not excluded from this vision of the world. To the contrary, they were intimately coupled with rebirth through their bondage to the soil. While the seeds grew into food-giving plants the spirits of the dead protected them. In return, in some societies, gifts were offered to these ancestral guardians, often at the blackest time of year at the midwinter solstice when night was longest and men feared that summer might never come back and that the crop-bearing Earth had become sterile. It was a time when reassurance was most needed.

In these ways the fertility of the ground, the fecundity of women, the spirits of forebears that interceded with Nature on behalf of the living, the cold winter sunset and joyful summer sunrise, all these merged together in the animistic minds of these early farmers.

> The major feasts of agriculture or fertility came to coincide with the feasts in honour of the dead. At one time Michaelmas (September 29) was the feast both of the dead and of the harvest all over north and central Europe. And the funerary cult came to have more and more influence upon fertility cults, absorbing their rites and turning them into offerings or sacrifices to the souls of ancestors. The dead are 'those who dwell under the earth', and their goodwill must be won . . . Reconciled, fed, their goodwill sought after, they protect and increase the crops. The 'Old Man' or 'Old Woman', whom peasants look upon as the personification of the 'powers' and fertility of the soil, come to have a sharper outline under the influence of beliefs concerning the dead; such figures take on the nature and characteristics of the 'ancestors', the spirits of the dead.[18]

In this insecure existence of fear and superstition among the harsh forests, hills and rivers the dead were respected and received much attention. It is likely that the first pioneers had no time to spend on formal burials and let corpses decay in the open air, perhaps taking away a skull or a long bone as a link with their ancestors, but as the woodland clearances extended year by year and the countryside became easier to manage so the farmers had leisure to put up massive long mounds of chalk, the

84

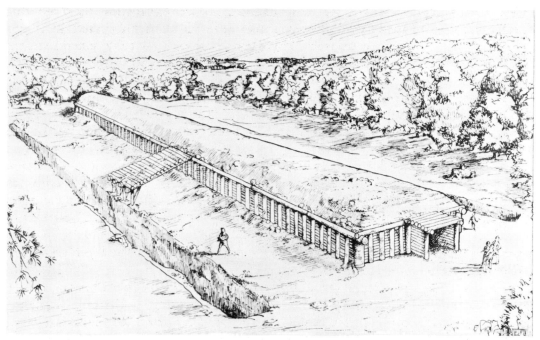

36. Reconstruction of the Fussell's Lodge earthen long barrow, Wiltshire.

earthen long barrows of lowland Britain with clusters of human bones under their higher eastern ends.

Even after a couple of centuries there cannot have been many of these around Avebury, perhaps only two or three in the most central district: Horslip on the mild southern slope of Windmill Hill or South Street now ploughed down into an indistinct hump, both on the best and earliest cleared land, monuments intended as family burial places. Such long barrows are to be seen all over Wessex in six great regions: Dorset, Cranbourne Chase, the Hampshire Uplands, Salisbury Plain East and West, and the Marlborough Downs;[19] grass-grown banks up to sixty metres long that persistently perplexed nineteenth-century excavators like William Cunnington I and Thurnam who believed that Neolithic people had laid corpses on a low platform of flints and then piled chalk from long side-ditches over them. The facts were much more complex.

The stained surfaces of many bones and the incompleteness of skeletons show that dead bodies had not been brought straight to the site but had been left to rot in a large open stockade, like a ditch on Windmill Hill that ran round the four sides of a square and which had held a substantial palisade with a western entrance. Bodies may have been laid inside such protective corrals. Sometimes a corpse had actually been buried and it was not until the flesh had decomposed that the bones were dug up and transferred to a small, plank-roofed structure nearby. Skeletons were laid on their sides, crouched as though in sleep, but often finger- and toe-bones were left behind if the ligaments holding joints together had disintegrated and the people had to carry armsful of long bones to the mortuary house, setting them down neatly

37. Catlin's painting of the mortuary scaffolds of the Mandan Indians. (Thomas Gilcrease Institute of American History and Art, Tulsa, Oklahoma.)

inside, the skull near others, arm- and leg-bones stacked tidily in a convenient corner. For years dry bones may have been put inside until it was decided to erect the great long barrow, a mound that not only enveloped the charnel-house but also covered untouched grassland for many metres beyond the place where the bones lay. Gradually the wood deteriorated and the building collapsed bringing blocks of chalk crashing down, breaking and disturbing the bones to the confusion of excavators five thousand years later.

The practice of excarnation, of defleshing corpses so that the spirit may be freed from the presence of its carcase, is known from many parts and periods of the world. It was widely employed in Neolithic Britain. At Catal Hüyük in Turkey, one of Europe's earliest towns dating back long before the Avebury burials, bodies were left out on platforms for vultures to tear and when the ancestral bones were finally interred under the places where the living slept the walls of the bedrooms were painted with friezes of those birds hovering over the headless torsoes of the dead.[20]

Even more relevant as a social analogy to the early Avebury people were the agricultural Indians of North America. In the late sixteenth century the Elizabethan artist John White made a series of brilliant water-colours of Virginian Indians, some of whom flayed corpses, removed the bowels, dried the flesh in the sun and placed the skeleton, wrapped in its skin, on a high roofed platform beneath which a priest lodged.[21] As late as the nineteenth century Sioux Indians exposed their dead on platforms until the fleshless bones could be deposited in a rock crevice. In 1833 the painter George Catlin visited the Mandans of North Dakota who placed their dead on scaffolds with the feet towards the rising sun. 'When the scaffold on which the body rests, decays and falls to the ground, the nearest relative, having buried the rest of the bones, takes the skull . . . and places it with others in circles of a hundred or more on the prairie.'[22] The Choctaws of Mississippi wrapped corpses in skins until the dried remains could be cleaned by a priest and buried in a mound.

More similar still to the Avebury culture was that of the east American Woodland Tradition, the Adenas of Ohio who, like the Neolithic farmers of the British Isles, were the first people in North America to combine the cultivation of crops with the manufacture of pottery and the building of large burial mounds. Scattered along the fertile and wooded river-valleys in hamlets of no more than four or five small houses and organised, as the Avebury communities seem to have been, in family groups, these crop-growers buried their important dead in long, rectangular tombs of logs having first reduced the bodies to skeletons. The fact that the dead person was sometimes represented only by his skull hints at a cult of the dead that is strangely paralleled in the Avebury long mounds,[23] especially as in both cultures there is a noticeable lack of grave-goods as though the dead were not expected to go on any journey but were to remain in the vicinity of their former homeland. From their earliest period, Burial Mound I, between about 1250 and 400 BC these hunter–farmers closed their mortuary houses by heaping earth over them, one of the largest, the Grave Creek Mound in West Virginia, being over twenty metres high. The result was the same as in Britain: 'later the rotting timbers collapsed under the weight of earth, leaving a complicated mélange for the archaeologist to sort out on his excavations'.[24]

In time this Adena culture developed into the famous Hopewell Mound Building tradition with its elaborate earthworks, a society whose economy and ritual customs were, as will be seen, very similar to what can be deduced from the surviving material at Windmill Hill and Avebury.

Many of the Avebury long barrows were evenly distributed about the countryside around the outskirts of the region as might be expected if each lay in the territory of an individual family. They did, moreover, resemble the rectangular houses of the Neolithic albeit much enlarged and may have been intentionally designed as symbolic dwellings for the dead whose spirits would watch over the living family and its land. There are several reasons for believing the function of these barrows was to harbour powerful forces rather than merely to contain the respected but lifeless bones of the family's forebears, not least of which was the unnecessary labour put into building them if they were to be no more than tombs. The average barrow was about forty-five metres long, eighteen metres wide and

Millbarrow.

The length of this monument is ···· perches;
it lies between Mounkton and Aubury: some yeares
since a Windmill stood on it: from whence it hath its
denomination. the Barrow is a yard high, at least.

On ··· Downe, about a mile westward from
Marleborough, towards Hakpin, is this ancient
monument fowre perches long: the Barrow, or
tumulus, is not above halfe a foot high.

On the Brow of the hill, south from wᵗ Kynnet,
is this monument, but without any name: it is about
the length of the former: but at the end, only rude
grey weather-stones tumbled together: the Barrow
is above halfe a yard high.

38. John Aubrey's sketches of three long chambered tombs near Avebury. Mill Barrow is destroyed. So is Manton in the centre. The bottom drawing may be of West Kennet.

two metres high and, even allowing for the expansion of broken chalk, was well over 1,000 cubic metres in volume. Quarrying with levers and picks of antlers, scraping up the chalk with ox shoulder-blades, carrying it up from the ditch in wickerwork baskets, this must have involved at least 4,000 man-hours of work, perhaps six continuous weeks of labour for the ten or so able-bodied persons of a normal group, a stretch of time not easily spared in those demanding days and surely only given to a monument whose purpose was more than that of a mausoleum for the dead. The titanic Longstone Barrow, 'a vast body of earth' still to be seen near Beckhampton on a natural shelf that accentuates its height despite the shrubs, cornflowers, elders and cowslips that blur it, must almost have disrupted the working-year of the people who heaved up the thousands of basketloads that made up its bulk. It is when one regards such earthworks that one senses the compulsions and dreads that drove people to these efforts.

Perhaps some while after the earliest of these long barrows people also began building long megalithic tombs around Avebury, mounds that covered stone-built chambers. Many survive in the Cotswold Hills to the west and it may have been from here that the first 'big-stone' builders came in their continuous search for land. One of the most rewarding to visit of these Cotswold–Severn tombs, the reconstructed Stoney Littleton with an ammonite the size of a car tyre fossilised in an entrance stone, was only twenty-three miles from Avebury just where the valley forests narrowed to barely a mile wide near Frome. To the north were the beechlands of the Cotswolds. To the south were the overgrown, rainy hills of the Mendips. But from the rich limestone of the Bristol region to Avebury was less than thirty miles, half of it across unattractive, badly drained clays. No long mounds were built there. The Cotswold settlers did not linger in that wasteland but moved onto the chalk uplands where one group put a sarsen-chambered barrow over the diminutive earthen long mound of Waylands Smithy. From the early Neolithic onwards there were continuous contacts between the Avebury and Severn regions perhaps because of the kinship ties of these migrating megalith builders.

Such monuments had the advantage of durability although the weight of the stones asked for even more effort on the part of the builders. It is likely that several families banded together to put up each other's sites. And unlike the timber mortuary houses these stone tombs were not closed off once the long mound was erected. They could be entered time and time again.

Already the Avebury region was developing an individuality. In the rest of Wessex over 130 long barrows have been recorded but only four had stone-built chambers whereas nearly sixty per cent of the Marlborough long mounds contained megalithic structures.[25] Many of these were simple box-like rooms at the extreme eastern end. These terminal-chambered barrows may have been the earliest of the megalithic tombs here and one or two like Mill Barrow and the Shelving Stones were built near the central areas.

The history of Mill Barrow, once sixty-six metres long, reveals the fate of many of these great mounds. John Aubrey drew it, adding that 'some yeares since a Windmill stood on it'. Stukeley also sketched it, 'a most magnificent sepulchre', although his illustration seems to have been reversed and the high eastern end with its stone chamber is shown at the west. During the eighteenth century farmers ploughed it and by Colt Hoare's time it was almost levelled. Eventually it was destroyed. In 1849 Merewether 'saw the man who was employed in the profanation. It contained "a sort of room built up wi' big sarsens put together like, as well as a mason could set them; in the room was a sight of black stuff, and it did smill nation bad" '. Today only one great stone in the hedge shows where this once 'large and flat long barrow, set round with stones' stood.

By about 3600 BC most fertile stretches of the landscape must have been settled and cleared. It has been reckoned that one family might remove up to half a square mile of forest in a century.[26] The Marlborough Downs have well-defined edges, a plateau of chalk steep-sided to north-west and north-east with high hills towards the south where Martinsell, 'one of the steepest and shapeliest of all chalk hills' overlooked the Pewsey marshes. From Marlborough in the east to Windmill Hill in the west, from Winterbourne Bassett in the north to Adam's Grave in the south, the region is confined within some thirty square miles, an area that in six hundred years could quite easily have been deforested and cultivated by ten or twelve family groups.

All around Avebury are the remains of their long barrows, the earthen ones in the centre and to the west on low land where stone was scarcer, the megalithic tombs high among the sarsens of the downs, many built on the middle slopes of the chalk where the mantle of characteristically well-drained black loam provided good tillage. Some are discernible only as the merest bump in a ploughed field. Others are more conspicuous. The stones of the Devil's Den have been stripped of their mound and stand naked in a wide, dry combe. Some like Kings Play Down were built near hilltops and are vivid against the skyline, Adam's Grave 'a crouching bison-like monster with its head sunk down, for ever looking to the east', and East Kennet planted with trees and bristling like a defensive porcupine against the horizon.

It is tempting to think of these barrows as family vaults, each group having a funerary monument inside a territory of about two square miles. John Aubrey perceptively wrote, 'in those times they chose to lye drye upon such hilly ground: and those of the same familie would desire to lie neer one another'. The mounds, however, were not just cemeteries. Although they took so long to erect they hold, on average, only six people—men, women and children—in the timber versions, fifteen in the megalithic tombs. On the basis of mortality rates amongst modern primitives it can be assumed that about forty people out of every thousand would have died annually[27] and in a family group of twenty to thirty persons one death could have been expected each year. If every member had been buried in one of these barrows, it would have been filled inside six to fifteen years. Either only selected people were placed in these monuments; or the mortuary houses and stone chambers were used for only a few years; or the living deliberately took bones from these places leaving only a misleading proportion behind.

All these alternatives may be correct because customs were not static and over hundreds of years they slowly changed. What had begun as ordinary burial rites

IV. (*right*) Stones of the south-west arc, looking north-west.
V. (*over page*) The south-west arc, seen from the top of the bank, looking north.

developed into a cult of the dead as the population grew and families intermarried. After a score of generations it would not have been possible for these groups to have remained independent. As in other primitive communities they had become bonded by blood-ties into kin-units or 'clans' in which people had loyalties beyond their immediate family because all clan-members shared ancestors in common whose ghosts could be expected to watch over the welfare of the living.

In this increasingly complex society the family retained its individuality through its territory and the long barrow where these ancestors rested. The mounds became more than houses of the dead. Their presence announced that the land had been claimed and the conspicuous siting of many may have been intended for this purpose, located not at the centre but in the upland areas of the land where they might most easily be seen. Within them the spirits of the dead could be reached and could help the living converse with the Other-World whose terrors reached to every part of the universe.

The barrows were shrines and temples rather than tombs. Their sacred nature is confirmed by the absence of grave-goods; by the great length of the mound, far longer than the restricted space of the burials, demonstrating how essential length and bulk were to the builders; and by the fact that the mounds seem to have been aligned towards the sunrise or extreme moonrise.

At midsummer the sun comes up in the north-east and over the next six months rises progressively further towards the south, by September lifting above the horizon at the east and by the midwinter solstice in December appearing far down the skyline at the south-east. By the spring equinox in March it is rising again at the east and moves day by day nearer to the June midsummer solstice at the north-east. The moon has a similar although more complicated cycle and never rises beyond north-north-east or south-south-east. The sun and moon never come up farther to north or south than these limits in southern England and the axis of every one of the thirty-one long tombs around Avebury whose orientation is known also lies between these points, the higher end covering the burials always being here, never to north or south or west. The earthen long barrows have directions evenly spread between north-east and south-south-east. The megalithic tombs have entrances rather more between east and south-south-east as though the builders had favoured a time late in the year for putting up their monuments, especially noticeable amongst the stone-built mounds on the downs: Old Chapel, Temple Bottom, Manton, the Devil's Den; whereas many of the barrows along the Beckhampton valley pointed towards the summer and autumn risings. Because of the shortness and width of the megalithic passages, these orientations pointed only in the most general way to any particular position on the horizon and must have been designed to 'catch' the sun or moon as an act of symbolism. They were far too imprecise ever to have been used for a scientific and astronomical purpose.

Perhaps in the autumn months when farming was slackest people who intended to build a long barrow watched the sunrise and aligned their sacred place towards it just as the Mandan Indians pointed their mortuary scaffolds towards the rising sun,

VI. (*left*) The South Circle, looking north.

39. The Devil's Den.

blending the sun itself into a cosmology of shrine, guardian ancestors, death, fertility and human bone that would protect them from harm.

There is no evidence of a national unit of length being used in the design of these monuments. For the stone circles and rows of the Late Neolithic and Early Bronze Age in Britain Professor Alexander Thom has suggested that a measure, the megalithic Yard of 2.72 feet or 0.829 metre was employed all over the country and has presented a corpus of data to support this thesis.[28] This hypothesis has not been accepted wholeheartedly by archaeologists.

	NNE	NE	ENE	E	ESE	SE	SSE
Earthen Long Barrows	0	2	1	3	1	3	2
Megalithic Tombs	0	1	3	7	0	5	3
Totals	0	3	4	10	1	8	5

Table 2. Orientations of Long Barrows in the Avebury District.

For earthen long barrows whose banks are weathered and spread there are few indisputable lengths available to test the theory of the 'Megalithic Yard', perhaps only the length and width of the mortuary structures under Fussells Lodge and the first barrow at Waylands Smithy. From megalithic tombs there are more definite plans of the stone-built chambers. The excavators of the superbly constructed West Kennet noticed that the transepted chambers appeared to have been arranged inside a perfect isosceles triangle whose height was twice the length of the base and which had been laid out 'presumably to definite units of measurement'.[29] There is, however, only a poor correlation between the measurements of these Wessex sites even though they are less than thirty miles apart. The burials at Waylands Smithy were placed on a platform 4.9 × 1.5 metres under a stone-edged mound 16.5 × 11.5 metres wide. The mortuary structure at Fussells Lodge was 19.8 × 7.3 metres.[30] The 'triangle' at West Kennet had a base of 9.8 metres. Not one of these lengths is an exact multiple of the Megalithic Yard but they could easily be subdivided into multiples of the flexible 'body-yard' measured from the nose to the tip of the outstretched arm. Hicks has suggested this as a plausible alternative to the improbably rigid Megalithic Yard, each community using this method and each local measure being slightly different from its neighbour because of the varying heights of headmen. Maria Reiche has inferred that a 'fathom' of 1.35 metres, the distance between outstretched arms, was used by the designers of the Peruvian animal drawings in the Nazca desert.[31] The word derives from the Old English *faedm*, a length of about six feet, and is of great antiquity as a quotation from the eighth-century AD poem, *The Phoenix*, shows:

> *Is paet torhte lond   twelfum horra*
> *folde faedmrimes   swaus gefreogun gleawe*
> *witgan purh wisdom   on gewritum cypad*

('That radiant land is twelve fathoms higher, so wise sages in their wisdom tell us in their writings from hearsay.') A 'yard' of about 0.81 metre or a 'fathom' of 1.6 metres would fit comfortably into the lengths cited above, especially as the prehistoric people of Wessex had counting-systems not of decimal tens but of fours, sixes or threes.[32] 'Very similar sets of body-based measurements have been found . . . to be used not only in Europe . . . but also throughout much of the world, including Melanesia and among the American Indians. This suggests either their very great antiquity or their obviousness.'[33]

The time for building was also the time for feasting. Whether putting up a megalithic barrow and its chambers or adding a long mound to an old mortuary house it was the custom to mark out the axis by a series of soil-dumps, the earth and turf coming from the tops of the side-ditches. Having set out their monument the people celebrated with the rare delight of meat. In a black layer left on the prehistoric land surface by these compressed heaps of soil excavators have found cattle bones split for their marrow, the inedible hoofs and skulls thrown casually onto the dumps. Oxen were popular in Wessex. Pigs were eaten in Yorkshire. A whole goose was discovered in a barrow at Amesbury near Stonehenge. Such a bird raises the possibility that there were totem animals amongst the clans of Neolithic Britain.

THE LIBRARY

🌳 THE SURREY INSTITUTE OF ART & DESIGN

Farnham Campus, Falkner Road, Farnham, Surrey GU9 7DS

40. The tree-covered mound of East Kennet conspicuous on the skyline.

At Sherrington earthen long barrow, people living within ten miles of the place where Stonehenge would be built had very carefully buried an ox skull and a deer antler in a cist of chalk blocks beneath the barrow. There is a similar example from the Marlborough Downs. The sarsen-faced tomb of Manton had a shallow forecourt that gave access to the terminal chamber. Its users had dug a pit immediately in front of the entrance and deposited an ox skull in it. The animal had been pole-axed. Even nearer to Avebury the long barrow of Beckhampton covered no human bones but three ox skulls had been neatly set on the grass along the axis of the mound.

These, like the goose from Amesbury, may have been totem animals. In front of Hetty Pegler's Tump, a megalithic tomb in the Cotswolds, two human skeletons and the lower jaws of several wild boars were discovered. Far to the north in Yorkshire the long barrow of Hanging Grimston was opened in 1868 and the excavator, Mortimer, came upon 'three somewhat scattered heaps of bones, consisting of the upper and lower jaws of pigs . . . in all there were jaws of at least twenty pigs, and it was curious to notice that small portions of most of the tusks had been broken off before interment'.[34]

The carefully buried ox skulls, oxen being castrated bulls, could be the relics of a cult amongst these early farmers. There have been many societies in which the bull has been venerated as a source of strength. It pulls the plough. It increases the herd. Its horns have been portrayed as symbols of power. The bull could be both cult-object

98

and totem, symbolising the clan while also protecting it. In the prehistoric town of Alaca Hüyük in Turkey where both bulls and stags were holy animals the roofed burial-pits had ox hides, head and hoofs still attached, stretched over them, guarding the dead.[35] Contemporary with the long barrows of Avebury and only a few miles south of them the mortuary house that preceded the Fussells Lodge long mound had an ox skull lying in front of it, the hoofs on the ground on either side of the walls, presumably falling there when the hide that had been draped over the wooden chamber, ox head over the entrance, decayed.

The 'tombs', then, even if the earliest had been burial places, are probably best regarded as cult centres for the protection of the living. Within them ritual activities became more important. Leaf-shaped flint arrowheads with tips broken off were discovered at the Giant's Grave, at Adam's Grave, at Waylands Smithy where three lay by the pelvises of human skeletons. That the breakages were not accidental was shown at Rodmarton where two broken arrowheads were in the north chamber and the tip of one was found later in the south cell. To the allusive, primitive mind such mutilation could have signified death, the deliberate killing of an object. The arrowheads may have been offerings.

Offerings in the barrows could be expected if these mounds were to be used to commune with the dead and with powerful, invisible spirits. It is even possible that at the worst times when the group was threatened with starvation or disease human beings were sacrificed.

Deaths caused by arrow-wounds may represent nothing more than human aggression. But it has been claimed that the skulls of many skeletons had been dealt heavy blows before death and, if correct, these could be the bodies of persons deliberately killed in an act of propitiation or supplication. Sometimes these fractures were caused when timber rotted and the roof fell in or when stones toppled but Thurnam who cited many instances of 'cleft skulls' in the Avebury barrows was a practising doctor of medicine and well qualified to recognise the cause of the breaks. In 1865 he collaborated in the writing of a book about ancient skulls, the *Crania Britannica* which is still highly regarded.

At the Giant's Grave, an earthen long barrow on the southern slopes of the Vale of Pewsey, he reported that one of the skulls 'had been forcibly cleft before burial'. At Rodmarton less than twenty miles north-west of Avebury 'four of the skulls present numerous deep clefts and gashes inflicted apparently during life, and probably the death wounds . . . the edges of the [first] cleft are sharp and stained brown'. According to Sir Arthur Keith such staining is the only proper confirmation for pre-mortem injuries. At West Kennet on its wind-blown ridge near Avebury Thurnam wrote that 'two of the skulls were remarkable for distinct traces of fracture, unequivocally inflicted before death'. At Belas Knap, another Cotswold–Severn tomb, many miles away, several skulls had been fractured 'while the bones were still green', implying that the people had been killed. When William Cunnington I opened a long barrow on Oxendean Down in 1802 he found the skull 'literally beat into pieces previous to interment'. According to Thurnam so sharp was the cut through a neck vertebra of one of the skeletons in Boles Barrow that the person must have been beheaded. The evidence is certainly not indisputable and must be treated with caution but it could indicate that human sacrifices were made on occasion at times of crisis.

It was a countryside of contrasts, of cultivated wheat-sown patches, of scrubland, thickets of trees, long mounds black against the sky, abandoned and tumbling cabins, cattle grazing on the fallow grassland, young lightly built people striving to keep their shifting world in balance. All the best land had been taken. Population was increasing. Taking advantage of the demand for good stone, traders brought roughly fashioned axes from the Lake District, from North Wales, from Cornwall to barter with the natives of Wessex. Travelling a hundred miles or more they discovered the safest routes, the rivers, the hill ranges above the forests and the swamps, and they were already trampling out the most famous of all prehistoric ways, the Ridgeway southwards over the western shoulder of the Marlborough Downs, descending to the river and climbing past the mass of the East Kennet barrow before wandering down again to the unhealthy reeds and mud of Pewsey.

Some of their axes are so beautifully finished and of such exotic stone like jadeite that they may have been carried as regalia rather than tools, fine objects to be carried by a headman, the person who had the power to order work done. Just as some women proudly wore necklaces of wolves' teeth or boars' tusks that showed the hunting skill of their men, so the axe, the striker of sparks of fire, the feller of trees, might have come to represent authority. The axe certainly had a significance beyond that of a mere woodworking implement. In Brittany miniature perforated versions in rare stone were hung as pendants around the neck. Chalk 'axes' were buried at Woodhenge and Stonehenge. Shapes of axes were sometimes carved on slabs covering the dead. That special axes should have been held by the head of the family or of the clan is not at all unlikely and may have marked the beginnings of a chieftain society.

With trade introducing rare desirable objects into people's possessions, with more people, with less land uncultivated, life became even less secure. It was hardly possible for this relatively small region to support more than about five hundred persons and any attempt by newcomers to claim a few acres for themselves would

41. The steep southern escarpment of the Marlborough Downs overlooking the Vale of Pewsey.

have been resisted by the natives who now regarded all the region as clan-soil.[36] In response to the threat they piled up earthworks known as causewayed enclosures because their ditches were not continuous but were dug in a series of long trenches with gaps between.

Perched high on the scarp where the Ridgeway twists down to the Vale of Pewsey the camp at Knap Hill retains a formidable appearance even today with its bank smoothed and its ditch half filled. Its flat-bottomed ditch, four metres wide and two deep, the bank behind it as high as a man, must have presented a daunting obstacle to anyone attempting to scramble past it. Little has been discovered here, just a few Neolithic sherds under the bank, some local, some from the Cotswolds, flints, some antlers dated to about 3550 BC, one or two animal bones, and it seems that the camp was not occupied for long, maybe was not even finished.[37] Yet for people to have enclosed four acres of this exposed and waterless hilltop with such a ditch implies a need for defence that had not been necessary before. Half a mile to the west, on a hill opposite, the chambered tomb called Adam's Grave crouches over the other side of the Ridgeway like a watchful hound.

Three miles farther west is the strangely named Kitchen Barrow with oolitic limestone in its façade, stone that must have been imported from the distant Frome region. 'Kitchen' is a corruption of the Anglo-Saxon 'crechen' or 'summit', descriptive of the barrow's position on a spur above the valley. Less than a mile south-east are the traces of another camp at Rybury, again at the crest of a steep slope overlooking the Pewsey marshes, its flat-bottomed ditch as deep as Knap Hill's. There are further ditches on the adjacent Cliffords Hill. Heavy-rimmed pottery from Rybury shows that it too was Neolithic.[38] With the fearsome man-sized yew bows of the time the narrow passes between these hills could have been watched over from these camps.[39] Their presence at the edge of the downs indicates that it was from the south that the defenders anticipated the threat. That such dangers were real is demonstrated from another of these causewayed enclosures at Crickley Hill thirty-four miles north-north-west of Avebury on the far side of the Cotswolds. Alongside a fenced trackway leading into the defensive earthwork were the remains of a rectangular Neolithic house. It had been burned down.[40] Nearly two hundred leaf-shaped arrowheads lay around the ruins in a scene more reminiscent of a Red Indian war party than of the farmers of the 'peaceful' British New Stone Age.

Chambered tombs were still being erected in 3600 BC, perhaps now by all the families in a clan and so with several chambers. Designs varied. Sometimes there was an entrance passage with transepted cells on either side of it. But at Lanhill, a dozen miles west of Avebury, at least three 'boxes' stood quite separately in the sides of a long mound whose eastern 'entrance' was a big facing stone with only solid earth behind it. The similarities between the bones in the north-west chamber suggested they might have come from members of the same family.[41] Lugbury nearby also has a blind entrance, 'a great Table stone of bastard freestone leaning on two piched perpendicular stones' wrote Aubrey whose home was only three miles away. Four separate chambers along the south side may have been family vaults. Other chambered mounds like Ascott-under-Wychwood with several cists or cells may also have been designed for clan use. The robust male skeletons from three of the transepted chambers of West Kennet had quite a different build from the slender man and woman in the north-east compartment.[42] Here again, up to five families may have been sharing the same monument. 'Three of the male skulls obtained by Thurnam from the west chamber resemble each other very closely.' If society had indeed grown from the first scatter of families into a more tightly connected clan system then some of the later long mounds might be expected to reflect this change in their more complex architecture. It is not possible to prove this archaeologically and it must remain a matter of anthropological speculation.[43]

Certainly the one hundred-metre long mound of West Kennet with its geometrically designed side-cells gives every indication of being a development from smaller and simpler tombs, its very magnitude and the size of sarsens like the north-east capstone weighing some seven tons suggesting that it must have been put up by a great number of people. In this respect, it is noteworthy that the three possible transepted mounds in the Avebury region: West Kennet, East Kennet and Waylands Smithy II; with an average length of ninety metres are nearly three times as long as an ordinary single-chambered tomb there.

The heavy sarsens that make up the five chambers of West Kennet all came from the nearby Marlborough Downs as did the smaller stones that formed the core of the mound but the delicate drystone walling between the standing stones of its façade, either of oolitic limestone or Forest Marble, was stone which cannot be found closer than Frome twenty-five miles to the west. Well over a ton of this 'foreign' stone was fetched from there for the building of West Kennet, and more was used in Adam's Grave, Kitchen Barrow, Shepherds Shore and Easton Down, even in the earthen long barrow of South Street. The limestone may have been regarded as magical or may have reminded the builders of their Cotswold origins where drystone walling was common and for which the Avebury sarsen was quite unsuitable. Its presence shows that contacts between Avebury and the Bristol region remained strong.

Laboriously built on grassland from which woodland had been cleared the incredibly long mound of West Kennet extends spectacularly along its hillcrest, a fitting place for the dead to rest. From its chambers the remains of well over forty bodies were recovered, half of them adults all of whom had suffered from severe arthritis, 'the plague of this community', reminding us once more of the ill health of these Neolithic people. Some children's and infants' bones had been pushed into niches between the stones. The adult bones lay on the floors and some had been scorched by having burning charcoal thrown on them in the 'widespread belief . . . that the ultimate departure of the soul from the body did not take place until the bones were completely dry'.[44]

Stranger still, although in some chambers the long bones had been meticulously stacked against the walls, many of the skulls and jaw-bones were missing. Even if the bodies had been brought as skeletons from elsewhere these bones would not have been left behind and it has to be assumed that they had been intentionally removed from the tomb. This would explain the irreverent jumble in the south-east chamber. 'It is possible . . . to compose the ghoulish picture of a visitor to the barrow picking up a partly decomposed arm, detaching the humerus and flinging the other bones into a dark corner.'[45] Given the circumstances of a cult of the dead there is nothing

42. The passage and side chambers of West Kennet.

improbable in the taking of important parts of the skeleton for rituals elsewhere. It is another example of the dead being used by the living. It also implies that some ceremonies, however humble, were taking place outside the 'tomb'.

This is implied by the monumental appearance of some of the façades which were surely designed to attract attention. At Waylands Smithy the front of the barrow is dominated by six towering sarsens that dwarf the low mound and chambers behind them. Stones almost as high at West Kennet curve outwards on either side of the entrance, marking out a shallow forecourt where rites may have been held. A crescent-shaped forecourt may also have existed at the ruined Devil's Den and, if Stukeley's reconstruction of the destroyed Old Chapel is correct, that tomb had a very deep forecourt with no means of reaching the chamber behind as if the semicircle of great stones had become more important than the burial-place. It is even possible that it was added to an existing small tomb.

Such forecourts were not usual amongst the builders either of earthen or

43. The long mound of West Kennet from the north.

megalithic mounds around Avebury. The nearest stone-built long barrows with concave façades are the Bridestones over a hundred miles north-west in Cheshire or the charmingly named Grey Mare and Her Colts near the south coast. But on the Yorkshire Wolds there were many earthen long barrows whose crescent-shaped forecourts were constructed of tree-trunks. With the reaching out of trade it is possible that people from distant areas were travelling along the hill ridges known as the Jurassic Way, meeting other people from North Wiltshire, exchanging gifts, spreading new ideas. There is a little evidence.

From a stonehole at West Kennet came a broken pot whose sharply formed shoulder is like many Yorkshire carinated bowls. In a later layer a beaver tooth and a worked boar's tusk lay together in an association very similar to those from two Yorkshire round barrows, one of oolite at Langton, the other the giant Duggleby Howe once nearly ten metres high.[46] Duggleby Howe will be mentioned again. Here it is sufficient to point out the contacts that were being made between these remote peoples.

To meet and to trade in the land of strangers, incomers needed a place of safety, often at the very edge of the foreign territory. Whether it was because of this or because of their continuing fear of attack the Avebury communities started to dig out a vast causewayed enclosure on Windmill Hill, an earthwork so big that the outermost of its three concentric ditches was almost three-quarters of a mile long and enclosed 8.5 hectares, about twenty-one acres.

104

44. The spectacular façade of Waylands Smithy.   45. The long mound of Waylands Smithy. It was deliberately built on top of a small earthen long barrow of which no trace can now be seen.

Unlike the long mounds which invariably had been erected on grassland long cleared of forest this low hill seems still to have had a few trees and brush growing on it,[47] suggesting that the people's need was great enough to justify the extra effort of removing this undergrowth. They must also have had some organisation because from the outer ditch alone over 7,000 cubic metres of chalk were quarried, about 13,000 tons hacked out of a ring of irregular trenches anything from four to seventeen metres long, perhaps each one the task of an individual family. It is doubtful whether such an enterprise could have been completed without overseers and the Windmill Hill project may be an indication that the clans themselves were banding together into a loosely structured tribe with an accepted leader or chief.

There are many other causewayed enclosures known from this period in southern and eastern England. On the Marlborough Downs as well as Knap Hill and Rybury there may have been others at Cherhill and Overton Hill.[48] It is unlikely that all these enclosures had the same purpose. They have been interpreted as camps, as cattle-kraals, as ritual centres and fairs, as mortuary enclosures. Windmill Hill is amongst the largest, rivalled only by the Dorset sites of Maiden Castle and Hambledon Hill and like those may have been intended as a defensive refuge or even permanent settlement. This view has not been favoured in recent years but the size of the outer ditch five metres wide and over two metres deep with a high steep-faced bank behind it would, like Knap Hill, have formed a considerable barrier. The bank has been ploughed into extinction but like Avebury it was first marked out by a run of small turf and earth dumps around the perimeter over which the deeper chalk was piled.[49] From computations based on the volume of chalk removed from the three ditches of which the outer was by far the most substantial, it can be estimated that the enclosure would have taken about 65,000 man-hours to complete. Had as many as twenty families combined, each with ten able-bodied persons, the two hundred workers might have finished the work in sixty to seventy days. This would have involved perhaps the whole population of the area in continuous digging for a couple of months and however the calculations are manipulated the undertaking obviously engaged the efforts and zeal of many people for a long period.

Related earthworks like Hienheim in Germany have signs of settlement or occupation within them and the discovery of animal bones including complete skeletons of pigs and goats and skulls of oxen in the ditches at Windmill Hill may be signs that people once lived inside the enclosure. At Abingdon only thirty miles north-east an earthwork had been built on a small gravel peninsula between two streams that provided some protection. The third side was guarded by marshland and the fourth had a ditch and bank running across it. Storage pits, hearths and stone axes all bear witness to the occupation that had gone on there. At Hambledon Hill an enormous defensive ditch ran round the entire hill. When the ditches at Windmill Hill were silting up people recut them to restore their depth and steepness, something not undertaken unless there were some real compulsion.

It may be that such enclosures were not occupied all year round but were intended partly as places of retreat when danger threatened, partly as meeting-places at special times of the year. From the radio-carbon dates available they seem to have been built within a few decades of each other around 3600–3500 BC,[50] and this must surely reflect a reaction to changing conditions in southern Britain.

Life was certainly no more peaceful. Human bones from Windmill Hill's ditches tell the familiar story of stress and danger, a leg-bone with two marks made before death; a man's femur with the healed traces of an old injury; another femur from a very short man, this bone with a shallow cut in it 'caused during life by a blow which grazed along the bone'.[51] It is not difficult to imagine how in times of increasing disturbance people would band together to throw up an earthwork that would be refuge, a centre for trade and a focus for the ever-more elaborate symbolism of their religion.

The ditches contain the remains of feasts made perhaps at autumn when relatives from far-off districts assembled here as they had always met, to gossip, to marry, to trade, to settle disputes, to celebrate. From the ditches has come domestic equipment, heavy querns for grinding wheat and not likely to have been carried far, local flint-gritted pottery, flint tools, antler picks. There is also finer pottery with grains of oolite from the Cotswolds, brought either by traders or by people visiting from there. There are stone axes from mountains and outcrops hundreds of miles away, tough sharp stone not to be equalled by the hard but dull sarsen of the downs. Many of these axes may have been brought directly from their source, laden in canoes and paddled along the rivers near which many of these enclosures were situated, but the fine axes from the Lake District may have been taken in bulk across to the Yorkshire Wolds and redistributed from there.

At Windmill Hill there is pottery from Cornwall, fine elegant pots that might have been bartered here for their quality or else imported because of their now-unknown contents. There are limpet and whelk shells, perhaps even oyster, from the west coast. 'Foreign' stone also occurs in pits and in the ditches: an arrowhead of Portland chert; thirty-five bits of oolitic limestone; a score of Forest marble fragments, perhaps left over when megalithic tombs like West Kennet were built; red sandstone from the Mendips; slate from Oxfordshire or the Cotswolds. 'Many of these rocks are simply pebbles or fragments which do not appear to have been put to any practical use.'[52] That people had bothered to bring them so far suggests a different and possibly mystical intention. Oolitic limestone has been recovered not only from the chambered tombs but also from a pit inside the square enclosure on Windmill Hill, supposedly used for the exposure of corpses.

In this bustle of trading activity and in their building of enclosures the Avebury people again parallel the developments suspected for the Adena Indians of North America. By the Middle Woodland period between 400 BC and AD 500—or Burial Mound II as it is dispassionately called—the Hopewell culture that succeeded the Adena was flourishing, most of the people still living in small, semi-permanent villages but going for their trading occasions and ceremonies to great earthworks alongside the rivers of Ohio. Although the family was still important these Hopewellians had a highly developed social organisation with inherited leaders, with specialist craftsmen, a complex system of religious beliefs and a tradition of co-operative labour. The broken artefacts from West Kennet and Windmill Hill do not enable us to be so definite about these British societies but they are not incompatible with the idea that a society comparable to the Hopewell might have existed around Avebury in the middle of the fourth millennium BC.

The Hopewellian trade-system with its emphasis on exotic objects vitalises the picture. From the Great Lakes these Indians obtained copper, mica from the Appalachians, conch shells and bear teeth from Mississippi, obsidian from Wyoming, trading their own fine flint and pipe-stone in exchange. In the autumn, their faces painted with motifs of peace, a group would set out in a canoe laden with goods, travelling along the forested rivers to the agreed enclosure to which other people might have come from hundreds of miles away. It was an area of truce. Enmities were ignored. Difficulties of language were overcome. It may not have been trade as we know it but more probably hundreds of exchanges of gifts between people of different groups who established bonds of friendship and partnership that frequently were strengthened by the marrying out of the women.[53]

An analogous mixing of societies seems to have occurred at Windmill Hill. As well as the local pottery and the finer wares from the Cotswolds there are also some shell-gritted bowls with thick, rolled-over rims. These heavy Abingdon pots decorated with strokes or dots were first made in the Upper Thames Valley where stretches of fairly open country lay between low, wooded hills and waterlogged, marshy tracts that no one except the fowler visited. There were good routes between the Upper Thames and Marlborough and it is forms of Abingdon ware that are often found in the megalithic Cotswold–Severn tombs. A bowl was present at West Kennet. The east-west distribution of this pottery contrasts with the more southerly concentration of Windmill Hill ware that was made all over Salisbury Plain as well as the Marlborough Downs. The discovery of Abingdon pottery indicates the widening contacts of the people, mixing with those to the west around the Cotswolds, to the east along the Thames Valley, even to the north towards Yorkshire.

Windmill Hill, however, was more than an annual trade centre, more than a defensive earthwork. Less than one-third of its ditches have been excavated but from them have come not only over a score of human bones but the complete skeletons of two very young children, both in the outer ditch, lying on their right sides with their heads towards the east and the sunrise. These may have been burials but the other bones, fragments of children's skulls, adult femurs, arm-bones, broken by burrowing rodents but already 'old and dry when the damage occurred', were too scattered to be disturbed burials. They may be the relics of corpses left on scaffolds or on the ground inside the earthwork until the flesh decomposed, some of the bones slung into the ditch. This was the explanation for the two or three burials and some casually lost bones at the Offham Hill enclosure in Sussex[54] and it might also account for the many carefully buried human skulls in the ditches of Hambledon Hill if that site had been an enormous hill of the dead. Such an interpretation would not contradict the idea that some of these causewayed enclosures were semi-permanent settlements occupied by the living who exposed corpses of their relatives around the edges of their enclosure. It seems just as likely, however, that some of the bones were deliberately brought to Windmill Hill for magico-religious rites, having been abstracted from tombs like West Kennet and then reburied when they had been used, bones specially selected for the purpose because 'the finds consist only of skull and long-bones fragments'.[55]

That ritual activity did take place at Windmill Hill seems indisputable from the discovery there of artificially carved chalk objects, some of them fashioned like little cups but far too small and easily broken even to be lamps for oil. Nor are any scorched or sooted as lamps would have been. The pieces are never more than about ten centimetres across and the neatly gouged hollows are tiny, two to three centimetres across and deep. It was these 'cupmarks' that were significant. The rest of the chalk is often unworked.

These peculiar objects have been found at other causewayed enclosures and at Stonehenge and they have been considered to belong with 'those other unexplained things with which Neolithic tribesmen attempted to make their corn grow, their cattle multiply, and their trade thrive'.[56] More puzzling are the chalk plaques with incised lines. So are the stone discs with shaped edges, five to six centimetres in diameter, of which eleven were found at Windmill Hill. But like the 'cups' these too were objects that their makers associated with death for one was found in the forecourt of West Kennet, others in chambered tombs in Wales and Scotland, with human cremations at the later northern stone circles of Moseley Height and the Druids Temple in Lancashire, even in round barrows of the Bronze Age like

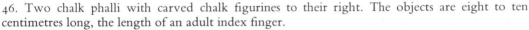

46. Two chalk phalli with carved chalk figurines to their right. The objects are eight to ten centimetres long, the length of an adult index finger.

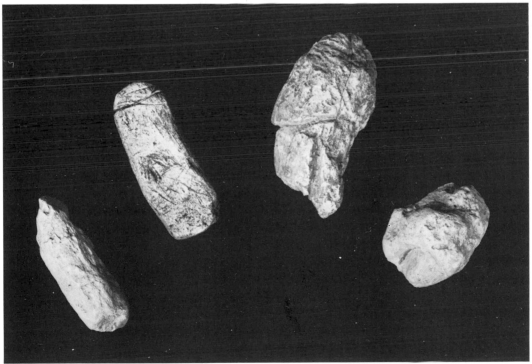

Charleton Horethorn in Somerset where a 'chipped flint disc' lay in the ashes of the pyre underneath the cremation.[57]

Such objects show how death, the sun, fertility, sexuality were perceived symbolically in the minds of the prehistoric farmers. So do other 'non-functional' carved pieces, roughly-shaped chalk figurines without head or arms but with a 'deep vertical groove [that] defines the division between the thighs in each instance'.[58] These and other perforated slabs were probably made for fertility–death ceremonies of magic for which most evidence has disappeared. The thirty carved balls of chalk from Windmill Hill, about five to six centimetres in size, may have been representations of male organs, particularly as many were found not singly but in pairs in a pit or in separate segments of the middle ditch. Least equivocal of all are the four chalk phalli. In that uncircumcised age these could hardly be more explicit, the exposed glans showing that the penis was supposed to be in a state of erection. Similar replicas have come from the long barrows of Winterbourne Stoke and Thickthorn on Salisbury Plain.

Carvings like this were probably used in imitative activities to ensure the fecundity of the world and when they are found in places of the dead we must assume not that they were meant for the dead but that the dead were to be used together with the carvings for the benefit of the living. All the superficially disparate chalk objects from Windmill Hill can be integrated into one picture of fertility rites because, fortunately, they have in one instance been found together in an undisturbed setting whose interpretation seems clear.

Far away from Avebury, near the east coast, prehistoric people had mined for good flint under the thick layers of sand and clay in Norfolk. At Grimes Graves hundreds of deep pits were dug down to the best levels. Radiating galleries at the bottom show where more flint was prised out. Pit 15, seven metres deep and with eight low galleries had not yielded as much as the miners had expected. In their disappointment and dismay the workmen revealed how their minds perceived life in all things, believing by the human performance of a fertility ritual the Earth could be stirred to produce more of the flint in her body.

On a ledge just above the floor they placed a crude chalk carving of a childbearing woman. Near her and undoubtedly related was a chalk phallus and a number of chalk balls signifying, surely, that just as acts of generation bring forth children so Earth too might be impregnated and bring forth good flint. In front of this sexual tableau was a triangular pile of mined flint as a statement of what was needed. On top were seven red deer antlers, and at the apex of the triangle was a little chalk 'cup' like those enigmatic objects from Windmill Hill and which may have held some drops of liquid as a further libation.

It would be futile and misleading to attempt a more detailed analysis of the rite at Grimes Graves. Its outline is clear enough. What must be stated is that fertility cults like this must often have involved mimes of sexual intercourse, even intercourse itself at the time of sowing or harvest, not in pornographic bestiality but in the belief that man and the world that enveloped him were one and the same and could influence each other. 'It constitutes one of the most dramatic documents of primitive religion in prehistoric Britain.'[59]

47. Alan Sorrell's reconstruction of the scene at Grimes Graves.

During his stay with the Mandan Indians Catlin watched their Buffalo Dance and though for reasons of modesty he omitted any account of it from his books he did describe privately what he had seen. An almost naked warrior, painted black with jagged white canine teeth drawn on his face, represented *O-Kee-Hee-De*, the Evil Spirit. This figure who

> entered the area of the buffalo dancers to the terror of the women and children, had a small thong encircling his waist, a buffalo's tail behind; and from under a bunch of buffalo hair covering the pelvis, an artificial penis, ingeniously (and naturally) carved in wood of colossal dimensions, pendulous as he ran, and extending somewhat below his knees. This was, as his body, painted jet black, with the exception of the glans, which was a glaring vermilion.

He advanced towards the alarmed women, raising his wand and

> there was a corresponding rising of the penis, probably caused by some invisible thong connecting the two together . . . and placing himself in the attitude of a buffalo bull in the rutting season . . . he mounted on to one of the dancing buffalos . . . He approached and leaped upon four of the eight, in succession . . . producing the highest excitement and amusement in the crowd.[60]

Although there is no reason to believe that any ceremony like this took place at Windmill Hill there are reasons for believing that the allusive thinking behind such imitative magic is common to many primitive societies. It has even been thought that the forecourts of some megalithic tombs had 'male' and 'female' stones built into them as symbols of the link between fertility and death.[61] At Waylands Smithy the 'phallic' stone to the right of the entrance is tall and pointed, the one on the left, the 'vulva', is flat-topped. At the Bridestones in Cheshire the high south stone is pointed as is another to the north whereas the portal stone is flat and has a groove in it. The validity of the interpretation remains questionable but the symbolism implicit in it is entirely relevant to these ancient people and their ceremonies.

Yet it could be that even as the ceremonies to ensure the unbroken goodness of life were being practised the people themselves had broken the cycle by their own over-exploitation of the soil. In many regions of the British Isles there are signs that where forest had been cleared in the early Neolithic it was regenerating by the later fourth millennium BC. On the chalklands cultivation lessened and grass was growing over the fields. Perhaps the easily worked soils had been used too hard for too long and now the land could not support the increasing population. A change in the climate would have aggravated this. People had to turn to the less productive uplands, the damper valleys. Here and there trees were allowed to spread, at the Horslip long barrow, at South Street, at Waylands Smithy as though people could no longer keep the ground clear. After a thousand years of cultivation the settled way of life was interrupted. 'The conditions for an actual reduction in human numbers, either through famine or enforced changes in the patterns of fertility, seem thus to be provided.'[62]

Whether there was an epidemic, starvation, whether with difficulty people adjusted to even greater hardship, these are questions archaeology cannot answer definitely. But the building of the long mounds seems to have stopped around 3100 BC. Against the fifteen sites with dates before then only one, at Alfriston in Sussex, is later and that by only fifty or sixty years. Even here dense vegetation had grown over the mound shortly after it was built.[63] Although the people, maybe the survivors of a calamity, continued to use some of those in existence no new barrows or enclosures were built. West Kennet was abandoned. Drystone walling tumbled in over the bones and it was not for 'some further interval' that people returned to restore it.[64]

If societies do follow cycles of settlement, maturity and decay it is not only a coincidence that the Hopewell culture also declined. By AD 500 no more of the earthworks were erected. Grave-goods for the chieftains became sparse. Maybe the inevitable growth of population had disrupted trade routes and spoiled the agreements. With a change in climate people in outlying areas were forced to change their way of life and no longer brought goods to barter in the central markets.[65] Networks collapsed. 'The questions that arise are whether or not agriculture had regressed and if so, was this subsistence failure responsible for the Ohio Hopewell . . . decline in the northern sub-areas of the Eastern Woodlands?'[66] Whatever the cause new cultures would develop in time owing something to their Hopewell antecedents but with new vigour and with new ways of living. The same was to happen at Avebury.

At some time after 3000 BC people put up a sturdy timber hut on the hillside where the Ridgeway sloped down to the Kennet stream. The building was not very big, less than ten metres across, but it was different from the previous Neolithic houses in the region. It was circular. This hut on Overton Hill was the first of several structures on the site. It was possibly a mortuary house alongside the prehistoric trackway and it was put up near the time when the temples of Avebury themselves were to be erected. It came to be known as the Sanctuary.

CHAPTER FIVE

The Time of Avebury

Thus the Druids contented themselves to live in huts and caves, whilst they employ'd thousands of men, a whole county, to labour at these publick structures.

William Stukeley. *Stonehenge*, 30.

THE YEARS between about 3250 and 2650 BC constitute a 'Dark Age' in the prehistory of southern Britain, an obscure time from which little has survived. During these centuries the slow creeping back of the forests, the grass encroaching upon cultivated land turning it into prairie, the absence of new ceremonial centres, the silence of the landscape show how critically Neolithic society had been affected. In the lowlands of Britain only the opening up of flint mines in East Anglia and the continued building of wooden trackways across the fens of Somerset contradict the picture of a decline in the vitality of the people.

The evidence obtained from articles that can be securely dated by the Carbon-14 process graphically illustrates this decline. Excluding for the moment the disproportionate number of dates from the Grimes Graves flint mines and the Somerset trackways we find that the evidence of steadily growing activity in southern and eastern England from the earliest Neolithic onwards, around 4450 BC, suddenly and dramatically declines between 3100 and 2850 BC, before recovering its steady rise as population and output began once again to increase. (Fig. 3)

What had happened is uncertain. Around the fens of Somerset less than fifty miles west-south-west of Avebury people since early times had been farming on sandy uplands in an area of wide marshes and forest, travelling in canoes across the flooded plain to their islands. In this difficult terrain people were fewer and exploitation was slower, perhaps continuing longer than on the easily worked chalky soils of the Downs. Yet even here the factor that may have caused problems in Wessex affected these farmers. The climate was altering with less rainfall and the waters were draining away leaving muddy expanses of raised bog impassable by foot or boat. Almost from the beginning the settlers had to lay out great lengths of hurdles across the soft ground, building new trackways as the old deteriorated or as new land was cultivated.

Like the miners of Grimes Graves the people left glimpses of their beliefs. Between two low hillocks a flimsy track had been inadequate for the intervening swamp and a sturdier causeway was constructed. Before it was laid down someone had roughed out a hand-sized bisexual figurine with breasts and extended penis, burying this freshly carved ashwood 'god-dolly' upside down in the mud. This repetition of male and female organs shows how sexuality was thought to be potent magic to ensure the success of the second trackway.

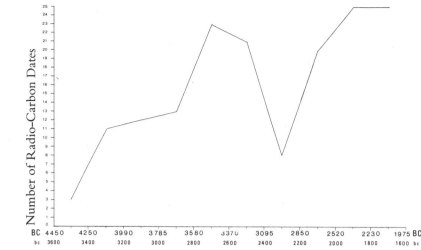

Fig. 3. Graph to show the fall in the number of radio-carbon dates between about 3250 and 2650 BC.
Dates in the larger numbers have been corrected into 'real' years BC.
Dates in smaller numbers on the line below are in uncorrected radio-carbon years bc.

48. The 'god-dolly' from the Bell trackway, Somerset. It is about sixteen centimetres high, about the length of an adult's hand.

Even in Somerset the clearances of birch and elm and lime were followed by 'a regeneration of some of the components of the mixed-oak forest' and a decline in agriculture.[1] Centuries of drier weather combined with over-grazing and planting led to the impoverishment of previously good soil, a disaster that may have been aggravated by high winds blowing away storms of topsoil after a series of hot summers. It was against just such adversities that the Neolithic farmer must have felt most helpless.

At Avebury itself, it has been reckoned that after some early years of cultivation the land had been allowed to revert to grass, the same sort of evidence that emerges from a study of the environments of the Beckhampton and South Street earthen long barrows nearby.[2]

Of the few dates that are available for this hiatus in the story of Avebury a majority come from either North Wiltshire or more particularly from eastern England, especially if those from Grimes Graves are taken into account[3] and it could be that it was from the east, from the Thames Valley, East Anglia and even from the Yorkshire Wolds that bands drifted in to settle on deserted, grass-infested tracts amongst the patchwork of land still being cultivated on the Marlborough Downs. They too may have been forced to move for the same reasons of misfortune and bad husbandry. An early agricultural phase at the settlement of Broome Heath in Norfolk was followed by a period of pastoralism during which the soil was ravaged and wind-blown by over-grazing[4] and if such a pattern of disruption was widespread in the fertile lowlands of the south and east many people may have been forced to seek new territories.

To avoid total destruction of the soil fewer crops may have been grown, more animals herded. In Somerset some of the first narrow walkways for human beings were replaced by wider, heavier tracks such as the Abbot's Way 'and cattle might be

114

held responsible for worn areas of roadway'[5] showing that here too people may have turned to herding.

The regrowth of forests does suggest that agriculture was less important during the Late Neolithic period. An increase in the number of pigs which are woodland animals indicates some loss of open land. Hunting implies the same. Traditional leaf-shaped flint arrowheads were supplanted by chisel-ended forms which did not penetrate but sliced across muscles and caused haemorrhaging, ideal for fowling and the hunting of small creatures in the woods by people who did not rely entirely on crops for subsistence. At the Sanctuary on Overton Hill the round hut was built of stout oak posts from local forests and put up in an area of scrub and ungrazed

Fig. 4. Important related sites to the north and east of Avebury.

1	Duggleby Howe	4	Callis Wold	7	Whiteleaf Hill
2	Wold Newton	5	Arbor Low	8	Waylands Smithy
3	Willy Howe	6	Grimes Graves	9	Avebury

grasslands. Snail-shells show there was marshy land nearby.[6] And from West Kennet, nearby, came the bones of foxes, badgers and polecats, nocturnal predators that padded between the quiet trees in search of prey.

Native people still lived here, for their pottery appears in the weathered ditches of the long mounds and around 3100 BC only three miles west of the Sanctuary at Beckhampton they were erecting perhaps the last of these long barrows. Unlike earlier monuments this was put up not on ploughed soil but on open grassland. Nor were there any burials under it, or a mortuary house. All that has been found are a few sherds of Windmill Hill ware, perhaps a rim from an Abingdon bowl, and three ox skulls spaced along the axis. Like South Street two miles nearer to Avebury this was a solid mound that covered no bodies but did contain an elaborate framework of

Fig. 5. Neolithic 'Rectangular' Enclosures.
(A) Dorchester I, Oxfordshire (after Atkinson, Piggott and Sandars, 1951); (B) Barford, E, Warwickshire (after Oswald, 1969); (C) Windmill Hill, Wiltshire (after Smith I. F., 1965); (D) Fengate, Peterborough (after Pryor, 1974).

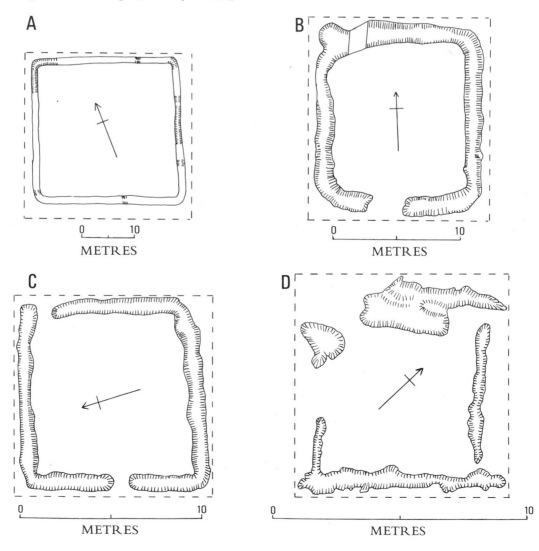

wickerwork partitions which held alternate layers of white chalk and black earth.

Several features reveal the indifference of these long barrow builders to any exact planning. Each barrow had a regular quarry-ditch along its south side, and a more erratic one along the north, carelessly measured off at intervals from the first. Use of this imprecise method was noticed at the Fussells Lodge long barrow and in the line baffling six-mile-long double banks and ditches of the Dorset Cursus.[7] Such a practice would nearly always result in untrue corners and sides of varying lengths. Plans of Neolithic 'square' enclosures and houses prove this. The so-called square was good enough to enable walls to fit together but no real effort was made to set out four right-angled corners. Modern attempts to transform these peasants into meticulous surveyors are not always based on observation of archaeological facts.[8]

It is noticeable that the 'body-measurements' at South Street and Beckhampton are somewhat different, about 1.6 and 1.56 metres respectively, not surprising if they were determined by the outstretched arms of people living four hundred years apart. Three radio-carbon dates from the ditch at South Street averaged 3485 BC, two from antlers on the prehistoric ground under the Beckhampton barrow having a mean of 3110 BC. Yet in both instances the builders seem to have had a counting-base of three. At South Street there were twenty-one hurdle-bays, each about a fathom wide and six long. At Beckhampton the mound was some twenty-seven fathoms long, the south ditch about thirty long, and there may have been twenty-one bays with an overall length of twenty-one fathoms. The combination of numbers divisible by three: 6, 21, 27 and 30 seems to indicate an elementary numeracy on the part of the builders. It will be remembered that three skulls of oxen lay under the Beckhampton mound. The builders of West Kennet two miles away may also have counted in threes, a 'body-fathom' of 1.63 metres being used to lay out the triangular chamber area, six units for the 9.8 metre-long base, twelve for the height of the triangle.

Most primitive societies have had very simple counting-bases such as three or four or five. People would count: 1, 2, 3, 3 + 1, 3 + 2, 3 + 3, 3 + 3 + 1 and so on, a method easy to learn and not at all inconvenient when the things to be counted, cattle and calves, were not numerous. Because people needed to count their possessions, elementary numeracy preceded literacy and it was not until the complexity of large numbers of trade-goods demanded recording systems that counting-bases larger than seven became necessary. If the Neolithic people around Avebury did have a counting-base or radix of three this tells us something about the limited 'scientific' concepts of the builders of the Beckhampton mound.[9]

If this long barrow was erected as late as the Carbon-14 assays suggest then the absence of human bodies may mean only that some long mounds were no longer regarded as tombs but as ceremonial centres that needed no bones except perhaps a totem skull to symbolise the strength of the clan. Over the years religious beliefs would in any case have changed but a climatic disaster would have hurried the change, partly because to the survivors the old ways would seem to have failed, partly because new people coming into the region would bring different beliefs with them. As long as these infiltrations were peaceful the same processes of intermarriage would eventually result in new creeds. Such co-existence is suspected in the earlier part of the Neolithic from the presence together in the Marlborough region of local pottery, of 'Cotswold' wares and of 'Abingdon' bowls from the Thames Valley. In the Late Neolithic Age native women on the Marlborough Downs were still making their traditional flint-gritted pots, but broken sherds of this Windmill Hill style were often found intermingled not only with Cotswold and Abingdon sherds but also with pieces of 'Peterborough' pottery whose early 'Ebbsfleet' style had, by 2850 BC, been succeeded by heavily decorated 'Mortlake' ware. It was users of Mortlake vessels who were the builders of Avebury.

In that age of flux circular timber huts slowly replaced the customary rectangular houses. Some of them may have been no more than ramshackle tinkers' shelters to be huddled in through the rains and winds of a couple of winters. Some were the temporary homes of semi-nomadic herdsmen. Still others were solid, spacious and permanent houses that, here and there, have been discovered inside gigantic earthwork enclosures constructed around 2500 BC. Earthworks like those at Waulud's Bank, Durrington Walls, Marden, Mount Pleasant, all in southern England, seem to have been put up on the sites of earlier unenclosed settlements of the middle Neolithic once occupied by the users of Windmill Hill pottery. Forest clearance and crop-growing had been followed by a long cessation of cultivation before the earthworks were thrown up as many as five centuries later. In every one of these enclosures 'Grooved Ware' has been found.

This flat-based coarse pottery, far inferior to previous Neolithic ware, may, like Peterborough pottery, have had an eastern origin, deriving its flowerpot shape and lined decoration from the interwoven strands of native basketwork. The entire absence of impressions of cereal grains from the hundreds of sherds found in Wessex has led to the conclusion that its makers were cattle and pig breeders, following their herds from one grazing-ground to another, claiming rights to watering-places until the grasslands of the south were taken over and portioned out by these aggressive herdsmen. Living on the chalk plains, always near forests, they were expert at the digging of ditches, the raising of banks, were excellent carpenters, and it is not surprising that their pottery is almost invariably found in the ceremonial henges of Salisbury Plain and Dorset: at Woodhenge, Stonehenge, Maumbury Rings, in the stone-free areas of slow rivers ideal for cattle. Sometimes they mingled for a while with other people. At Stacey Bushes near the Upper Ouse they shared an autumn grazing site with people using a Yorkshire style of pottery, perhaps exchanging some cattle for grain.

Yet at the beginning of the Late Neolithic very little Grooved Ware seems to have been made around Avebury. This was a stone-building region and its occupants held their allegiances not so much with the south where marshes inhibited travel to Salisbury Plain but with the Cotswolds to the west and with the Thames Valley to the east. What little Grooved Ware there was came from that direction, and it was from there that people making Peterborough ware came.

This pottery is often found near water, in pits by rivers, and the bones of small animals and birds with which the decorative patterns all over the bowls were made suggest that the dynamic people whose vessels are discovered from Yorkshire down to the south coast may have relied partly on fishing, trapping and fowling for a living. Paradoxically, no consistent set of flint and stone tools can be linked with the

118

49. A reassembled Grooved Ware vessel.

50. A Mortlake bowl with its characteristic impressed decoration, heavy rim and deep collar. These were the pots used by the builders of Avebury.

pots as should be the case had the people kept themselves to themselves, nor can they be associated with monuments exclusive to their 'culture', and the distribution of this pottery could reflect the marrying out of women from the region of the Thames Valley. In this way new beliefs would be spread, introducing into Wessex 'traditions which women founded, maintained and could distribute outside their own group as brides (if the word may pass) never affecting the menfolk's tools and flintwork, which vary little if at all'.[10] The revival of trade, the exchanging of women to form kinship ties between distant groups, the wandering of families in search of territories would all encourage the spread of ideas in a world uncertain of its old values. What would be accepted, what rejected, would differ from region to region. Thus cremation which was quite widely practised in Yorkshire and East Anglia was sporadically taken up on Salisbury Plain but hardly at all on the Marlborough Downs where inhumation remained the custom. Yet both regions took up the novel idea of holding open-air ceremonies inside circular banks and ditches.

It was in eastern England that well before 3000 BC people had started the construction of circular ceremonial earthworks known as henges in which the bank surrounded a spacious central plateau for communal activities. Sites like Arminghall in Norfolk, Barford in Warwickshire, Llandegai on the north coast of Wales were all probably put up before 3200 BC. With their low-lying situations near rivers and with single entrances that may have been astronomically aligned these seem to be monuments for an open-air cult in which water was important. Sometimes round barrows were put up inside them, linking the dead with the living. Sometimes two henges were put up alongside each other, three at Thornborough in Yorkshire, even four in line at Priddy on the Mendip Hills of Somerset.

The earthwork enclosures appear to be ceremonial constructions rather than defence works. Many are almost perfectly circular. These 'sacred circles' average 100 metres in diameter and are enclosed by low embankments with the 'moats' for these embankments within rather than outside the circle. Gateways open through the embankments. Burial mounds sometimes have been found inside the circles, and there are instances where several such circles were constructed together at a single site.[11]

This is a description not of the early English henges but of the enclosures put up by the Adena Indians in Ohio sometime before 400 BC. With such banked rings and with their conical burial mounds they resemble quite closely the middle Neolithic societies of eastern England where round barrows were already being built. It is this turning to circular forms, perhaps in imitation of round timber houses, even of wigwams, that distinguishes the easterners from the people of Wessex. On the Yorkshire Wolds huge round barrows like Duggleby Howe, Willy Howe and Wold Newton lie in a straight line six miles long along the bottom of a chalk valley. Another at Callis Wold to the west was encircled by a great V-shaped ditch over a metre deep. In the central space a mortuary house had stood. Inside was a rectangular platform of Lias stones which had been brought from at least two miles away. On it were the cramped skeletons of ten adults, one with an infant's skull under its hip. Like Waylands Smithy three flint arrowheads, two with broken tips, lay near the bodies.[12] How long this east-facing structure with its human bones stood in the open air, separated from the ordinary world by the ditch, is not certain but eventually it was covered by a small round heap of rubbly chalk in which animal bones, sherds and over eighty flints were mixed. Two slingstones also were found. This first little mound was soon covered by a layer of turves and then by larger tips of clay and soil.

Far closer, within fifty miles of Avebury, people using early Peterborough and Abingdon pottery had buried one of their dead on Whiteleaf Hill after lengthy and intricate rites. They dug a circular ditch to mark out a 'sacred' precinct in a damp woodland high on the Chiltern Hills. Inside this ring they put up a timber vault, open to the sunrise at the east-north-east, and to it they brought the skeleton of a middle-aged man. His body must have been buried elsewhere for a long time because the bones were very brittle, 'more than would normally be found in bones that had been in the earth for so short a time as a few decades'.[13]

This man, obviously someone of importance, had suffered severely from arthritis of the spine, ribs, hands and feet, and his teeth, some of them worn down to the roots, had several abscess cavities. Life was no easier in the middle than in the early New Stone Age.

His might have been the remains of a respected ancestor whose bones were needed to invest the new ritual centre with potency. They may even have been taken from an abandoned 'shrine' when the people wandered away. And maybe because the earliest Neolithic 'temples' had been tombs, the structure on Whiteleaf Hill also was designed like a mortuary house but one which was used symbolically at the centre of the ritual circle. The bones may have been placed in the 'mortuary house' in the accustomed manner to be taken out for later ceremonies that involved a fire in a little pit. A deeper pit surrounded by small posts lay nearby. Nothing was found in it. Whatever had happened, only the bones of the man's left foot lay inside the building. The rest were strewn outside.

51. Callis Wold, Yorkshire. The excavation shows the deep outer ditch. The U-shaped and straight slots at the centre of the monument were the foundation-trenches for the ends of the mortuary house.

After years of ritual the people finally congregated here bringing with them sherds from scores of roughly made pots broken 'just before the barrow-building ceremony'. Some had impressions of wheat in them. One rim had patterns of incised lines whitened to bring out the decoration. The people also brought charcoal, hundreds of flint flakes, a bone pin, pig bones and bones of other animals: oxen, sheep, beaver, red and roe deer, even a bird, the collection farmers and hunters in a forested landscape might be expected to gather together. Now that the dead person was to be sent to his rest this 'rubbish' may have been spirit-offerings representing the riches of the living world to enhance the world of death. Flints and bones were intermingled in the first mound at Callis Wold. Greenwell recorded deposits of flints and sherds in Yorkshire barrows. It was a widespread practice to include such domestic refuse in these mounds, particularly in northern and eastern England.[14] At Whiteleaf Hill it was mixed with the earth and clay that was heaped over the mortuary house. In turn this primary core had a kidney-shaped barrow of chalk and rubble heaped over it sealing off the human bones and its belongings from the living world.

The original purpose of placing apparently useless pot sherds with the dead was to provide the departed tribesman with the spiritual utensils thus represented, the spirit-forms having been liberated by the breaking of the vessels. Similarly, the charcoal, the calcined pebbles, or 'pot-boilers', and the few scraps of flint, would supply him with fire, first material, afterwards spiritual. Thus he had the means of making a fire, and of carrying water and hot embers.[15]

121

The association of sunrise and death at Callis Wold and Whiteleaf Hill, the use of human bones, the poetic symbolism of the broken pottery, the flint, the animal bones, to make up a complete 'world', show that these Neolithic peasants were not modern men dressed up in shabby leather but people whose thoughts and values were very different from our own.

The Whiteleaf barrow is interesting because it is Neolithic, far earlier than the more common Bronze Age round barrows, and because the activities there took place inside a circle. The barrow itself is only the closing off of the area. Like Callis Wold it was the ring-ditch that was important, a circle that demarcated the space for as long as people wanted to use the mortuary house at its centre. With these early round barrows it is possible to detect the beginning of a tradition in which fertility ceremonies connected with death would take place in a circular enclosure, sometimes with replicas of mortuary structures inside them.

Parallel with this was another custom, perhaps deriving from the same source, whereby people raised huge round barrows, often without burials in them, near water, apparently as symbols to show that the fertile land had been claimed by the clan or tribe. By 3000 BC in the Late Neolithic, people were once more banding together, with leaders, perhaps priests or medicine-men, and were meeting at central places for rituals still very much infused with death but more elaborate and more formal. Some of the great round barrows with their sealed-off bones became temples rather than tombs. Indeed, some, built in the Late Neolithic itself, had no central grave and if there were any bodies they were disposed around the important feature, the small mound at the barrow's heart. Frequently the people chose clay for this core, maybe because it contained the precious, fire-making flint. Fire and water, the elements of primitive existence, came together, for the peasants often selected low-lying places for these barrows, in hollows or valleys near a river or a spring. To its makers such a simulated burial mound may have combined the traditional tomb, the power of dead ancestors, the fertility of the earth, all expressed in a massive symbol of the group just as long barrows earlier had represented the individual family.

The exceptionally large round barrows of Duggleby Howe, Wold Newton and Willy Howe, built along a low valley in Yorkshire, illustrate this. Only the first contained a central burial.[16] As many as fifty men and women laboured here, heaping a clay core over the grave, eating foxes in a funeral feast before piling grit over the clay. Like other primitive people their leg-bones showed that they had persistently squatted on their heels when relaxing.[17]

At Wold Newton there was no central interment, only a 'spirit' collection of flints and broken pottery.[18] Nor was a burial found at Willy Howe. And at Gib Hill near Arbor Low in the Peak District the barrow was built over four small clay mounds containing hazel, charcoal, animal bones and burnt flints.[19] The analogous barrows without burials in Wessex show how far new customs were spreading.

Over the early centuries of the third millennium BC the movement of people continued, settling on deserted land, slowly repopulating the countryside, families mixing. An abandoned site halfway down West Kennet's hillside was reoccupied by users of Peterborough pottery who took over this sheltered woodland spot. The forest had never been cleared in contrast to the adjacent expanse of grass round the tomb where the trees had been felled in earlier times. The camp was not large but the availability of timber, water, grazing land made it an attractive spot for a family and it was used several times. Windmill Hill pottery, Peterborough ware, Grooved Ware, beakers, all have been found here, indicating a sporadic settlement pattern that must have spanned many centuries. Less than a mile to the north and right alongside the Ridgeway another open-air site, first used at the time that the Windmill Hill causewayed enclosure was being built, was later taken over by people with Ebbsfleet pots, cleaning animal skins with flints, cooking at open fires. Later still a group of Grooved Ware people left many of their broken pots scattered about the place. They had come from the east as the sherds indicated. 'The greater part of the comparative material comes from Essex and Yorkshire', and one has the impression of wandering groups, staying for a while, grazing their small herds, moving on again until at last they found a permanent home with water and shelter, settling there to mix with other families in a confused blending of traditions.[20] Similar sites testify to the refilling of the landscape during the beginning of the Late Neolithic period.

If it was women who made the pottery and if they were married out to groups with differing burial customs it is understandable why Peterborough pots occur in a variety of tombs. They have been found with many bodies in caves, in circular family cemeteries in Oxfordshire where the dead were cremated, even in megalithic barrows like West Kennet where it was the major ware, entirely supplanting the older, native pottery. When the long mound was tidied up after maybe a hundred years or more of neglect no more Windmill Hill ware was brought to it though this pottery continued to be made on the Marlborough Downs. Now it was the eastern styles that were common. Significantly, the few Grooved Ware pots at West Kennet were like distant East Anglian vessels even though, much closer on Salisbury Plain to the south, there were other styles of this pottery.

Although traditions continued, others were added. Bones were still taken from West Kennet. A man's femur in the forecourt probably came from a skeleton in the south-east chamber. But the cremations of a man and woman in the opposite cell suggest that new customs were being introduced. Novel objects appeared. Six ox phalanges or footbones were found. These finger-long bones had off-centre perforations the thickness of a pencil through them. They may have been whistles to summon up the dead or to comfort them, or perhaps symbolic figurines of Death herself.[21]

Whatever the imagery behind them carved bones have come from other British tombs. At Nympsfield, thirty miles north-west of Avebury, there was 'a piece of bone carved perhaps in the shape of a human figure'. In the same barrow, reminding us of the barbarous nature of these early societies, there was red ochre especially carried from a dozen miles away 'to colour bodies placed within the chamber' just as the Adena Indians would pour basketloads of this red pigment over skeletons. Also inside Nympsfield were three quartz pebbles and the perforated shell of a dog-whelk.[22] Another came from West Kennet together with holed limpet and periwinkle shells like amulets to be worn around the neck as protection against evil, shells traded from the shores of the Bristol Channel and the Severn Estuary.

Strange graves with no mound over them could be other Peterborough burial-places near Windmill Hill. One, nearly three metres across, near Mill Barrow had a paved circular pit into which four or five skeletons had been jammed with lots of stones on top. The soil thrown over the stones had 'solid masses of black unctuous kind of earth' in it and contained 'small pieces of flint and charcoal' like the Yorkshire and Thames Valley round barrows.[23] Over this, a massive sarsen weighing over twenty tons had been heaved. Another vast cist had twenty-two skeletons in it, very unlike the later custom of single burial practised by the makers of beaker pottery, and this mass-grave may have been a cemetery of Ebbsfleet and Mortlake people whose 'rude hard black pottery'[24] was found with the skeletons together with a sarsen grindstone and the bones of dogs, pigs, sheep and oxen. Three men's skulls had 'remarkable clefts' in them. 'The cuts are of great length, extending from front to back, with very sharp edges having a slightly brown discoloration',[25] evidence of blood-staining that implies that these men had been killed.

In the farthest and presumably latest pit was the sole skeleton of a man with some jet ornaments and two beaker pots made some time between about 2250 and 2050 BC.[26] Probably the other great sarsen-covered pits with their multiple burials belonged to previous centuries when long barrows were no longer being built but when collective burials were still fashionable. It is this mixing of traditions that was responsible for several splendid monuments in the district culminating in the Avebury circles.

One of these was the Sanctuary, now an unimpressive collection of rings of drab concrete cylinders and slabs overwhelmed by the noise of hill-climbing lorries on the main road but once a lovely stone circle that itself was the successor to a series of round wooden structures whose history is impossible to dissect with certainty. After the destruction of the stones the site was forgotten and when Maud Cunnington decided, in 1930, that it should be excavated she was able to locate it only from Stukeley's statement that it could be seen from the end of the Beckhampton Avenue 'near a fine group of barrows under Cherhill-hill . . . And in this very point only you can see the temple on Overton-hill, on the south side of Silbury-hill.' From that spot Mrs Cunnington could make out the triangle of Mill Field and by counting the number of telegraph poles along the road two and a half miles away she was able to discover just where the Sanctuary had stood.

There is an unverifiable rumour that she used her umbrella as a measuring-rod when excavating Woodhenge but her excavating methods need not be discussed here. At some time around 2900 BC people had erected a round hut alongside the Ridgeway, probably a roofed building some ten metres across whose outer wall was constructed of twelve thick oak posts set deeply in the ground and with an inner ring of eight huge posts to support the thatched roof. Although it would soon have been affected by rising damp it was so strongly built that it could have stood for as long as two hundred years before it was replaced by another, rather larger hut, which itself might have lasted until as late as 2500 BC.[27] Archaeologists have called these two phases Sanctuary IA and Sanctuary IB.

About six hundred years passed between this first and the last rebuilding of the Sanctuary around 2300 BC. During all that time the people who built the monuments appear to have counted in fours and this apparently trivial fact is a vital clue to one aspect of their society. That it is a fact seems certain. In phase after phase the number of posts or stones was a multiple or a half of 4: 8 and 12 (twice); 8 and 34; 6 and 16; 16 and 42; far too consistent arithmetically for accident.

A counting-base of four was, of course, different from the radix of three already noticed amongst the builders of long barrows but as the circularity of the Sanctuary implies that its builders had a cultural background different from the first Neolithic people in the area with their rectangular burial mounds such a difference could be expected.

Counting in fours would surely not have been restricted to the number of posts but would also have been used in measuring the diameter of each ring. Had this been based on the arm-lengths of the headman living at the time a new building was put up then a variety of 'fathoms' could be expected, almost irrecoverable today. It has been claimed, however, that like everyone in Britain the Sanctuary designers adopted the Megalithic Yard of 0.829 metre, a supposition that demands a reappraisal of prehistoric societies many archaeologists find hard to accept.

The Sanctuary with its seven concentric circles offers a unique opportunity to examine the validity of this 'yardstick' because consistency could be expected in the counting and measuring of these closely related rings. Yet, although a counting-base of four is manifest here from the number of posts in each ring, four is never used in the number of Megalithic Yards supposedly making up each diameter. Nor is any diameter an exact multiple of this Yard. Instead of a logical progression of 4 Megalithic Yards, 8, 12 and so on, one finds an unconvincing mixture of 4.4 Megalithic Yards, 5.0, 7.1, 11.4, 12.6, 17.2 and 23.8 Megalithic Yards.

Fig. 6. Plans of the postholes of Sanctuary 1A and its rebuilding, Sanctuary 1B. (After Cunnington M. E., 1931).
The postholes of D2 in many cases cut into those of D1 proving they were later. The gap at the north-west indicates the possible entrance. There were finds from several postholes of Sanctuary IA: (a) 50 Windmill Hill sherds and an ox bone; (b) Windmill Hill sherds; (c) pig leg-bone; (d) horse bone.

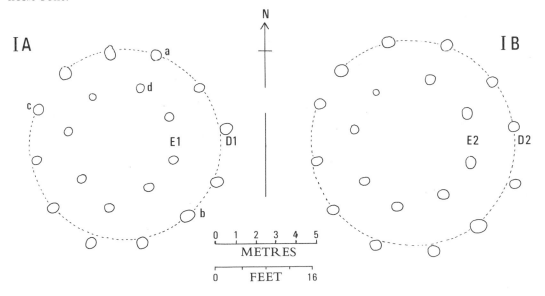

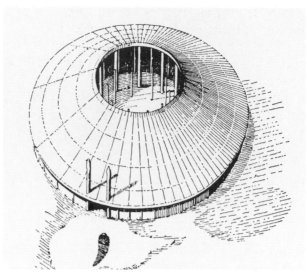

52. A possible reconstruction of the timber building at Durrington Walls. The Sanctuary may have been similar.

Such random multiples are incompatible with the precision claimed for the astronomers of Thom's Megalithic Britain who, at the Sanctuary, apparently could neither measure nor count. The paradox can be resolved by recognising that there were slight variations in the units of measurement. The theoretical seventeen Megalithic Yards diameter of Sanctuary III's inner ring with an error of 0.17 metre according to Thom could, in reality, have been eight body-fathoms of 1.78 metres or sixteen body-yards from nose to outstretched fingers of 0.89 metre. Similarly the thirteen Megalithic Yards of Sanctuary IB (error −0.3 metre) may originally have been made up of twelve body-yards of 0.87 metre, an interpretation quite consistent with the work of sub-numerate peasant craftsmen living in prehistoric Britain who were not much concerned with nice measurements as long as their buildings were solidly constructed.

It is fair to add that impartial statistical tests have already shown that the Megalithic Yard, if it ever existed anywhere, had many competitors but the tests are so mathematically involved that they convince the layman only by their cabalistic appearance.[28]

The Sanctuary has been described as a house or observatory for an astronomer–priest. It was far more probably a charnel-house for dead bodies. A lot of Windmill Hill sherds and a Mortlake rim were found at the bottom of a posthole in the outer ring but the general lack of domestic rubbish, waste flakes from flint-working, hearths and middens suggest that this was never an ordinary dwelling-place. In earlier centuries dead bodies must have been either buried or exposed inside large rectangular stockades before being taken to a long barrow. Mortuary enclosures like this have been discovered at Normanton near Stonehenge and probably on Windmill Hill. It is possible that Stukeley saw the remains of one when he sketched the ruins of the stone-lined rectangle directly outside the deep forecourt of Old Chapel megalithic tomb on the high downs three miles north of the Sanctuary and alongside the same trackway. There may have been another half a mile south-west of West Kennet and described by Stukeley as 'a very large oblong work, like a long barrow, made of stones pitch'd in the ground, no tumulus', an enclosure nearly eighty metres long.[29]

With the growing Late Neolithic preference for round houses and for rituals of the dead associated with water the Sanctuary could have been erected as a circular mortuary house in which some dead were stored until their bones could be washed clean and taken away for ceremonies or for burial. Bodies certainly have been found nearby. John Aubrey wrote, 'About 80 yards from this monument, in an exact plain round it, there were some years ago great quantities of humane bones and skeletons dug up.' These bones, extracted by Dr Toope for his elixirs, may have been the relics of the battle of Kennet in AD 1006. Yet Toope himself remarked on the 'Teeth extreme & wonderfully white, hard and sound. (No Tobaco taken in those daies)', a condition nearer to the state of Neolithic than Saxon teeth. Hoare and Cunnington noticed how undecayed the teeth were in the excavations of prehistoric barrows. Despite tooth loss and abscesses, there was little sign of dental caries at West Kennet.[30]

There were dozens of bodies buried around the Sanctuary, 'soe close one by another that scul toucheth scul . . . I really believe the whole plaine, on that even ground, is full of dead bodies', wrote Toope who also hacked at West Kennet to the disgust of Stukeley. 'Dr. Took has miserably defaced South Long Barrow by digging half the length of it.' Stukeley also recorded something about the Sanctuary burials which suggests they were indeed prehistoric. 'Mr. Aubrey says, sharp and form'd flints were found among them; arguments of great antiquity. They were of the lower class of Britons.'[31]

Because it was lost and forgotten for so long the Sanctuary has had few theories attached to it. One recent suggestion is that it was a building used for the puberty rites of young girls. 'The serpentine maze aspect of the Sanctuary ground plan also points to the female sex' with the hut and stone circles shaped to 'match the greatest womb in the world, Silbury Hill'.[32] The argument depends partly on the Sanctuary being a one-phase, unrepaired structure, something which the intersections of many postholes belie, with an outer wall capable of supporting the weight of a heavy roof.

53 and 54. Stukeley's sketch of Old Chapel chambered tomb as he saw it and his reconstruction. There may have been a large rectangular mortuary enclosure alongside the tomb which has a Cove-like setting at its rear. Nothing remains of these structures.

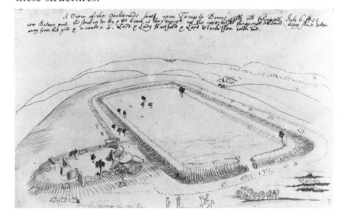

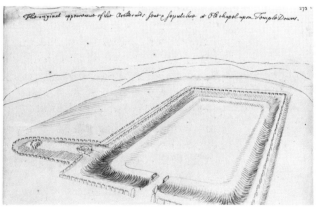

As the real posts were probably not more than twenty centimetres thick they seem unsuited to this purpose. It is, moreover, difficult to reconcile initiation ceremonies for maidens with the discovery of human jaw-bones at the Sanctuary. Rituals connected with death seem more likely.

Here at the Sanctuary in the years around 2900 BC the dead may have been brought, some, the most important, laid inside the charnel-house, perhaps to be attended by a medicine-man or witch-doctor just as priests squatted under the mortuary platforms of Virginian Indian chiefs while the corpses shrivelled. On Malekula in the New Hebrides, on the opposite side of the world from Avebury, where stone circles were still being erected in the nineteenth century ordinary men were buried but chiefs were exposed on a scaffold, their bodies continually washed to hasten corruption. At a fixed time all the villagers bathed to prevent the sickness of death spreading amongst them, and a few days later there was a feast to celebrate the lower jaw dropping from the skull. Similar processes of decay may have been watched over at the Sanctuary by holy men. 'Perhaps at this angular Turning might be the Celle (or Convent) of the Priests belonging to these Temples.''[33]

If then heated stones and charcoal were piled over the skeletons it would explain why lumps of burnt sarsen were discovered in the postholes. It is improbable that they came from the stone-burning that Stukeley witnessed because by then these deep postholes had been earth-filled for thousands of years.

At West Kennet bones of the later bodies had quite often been charred but there was 'never any indication that burning had taken place *in situ* within the chambers or passage',[34] and with the Sanctuary less than a mile to the east—and the same distance north of the great East Kennet barrow—it may have been there that when bodies had lost their flesh the last moisture in the bones was evaporated by heat. Scorched bones are known in many southern tombs: at Belas Knap, Tinkinswood, Nympsfield, Randwick, Rodmarton, Stoney Littleton, at Temple Bottom just north-east of Avebury. At Tinkinswood the bones had been burned 'long after the flesh had perished from them'.[35] It was a widespread Neolithic practice, perhaps to remove all the liquid of life, perhaps because in the same way that they parched wheat to preserve its goodness so in their metaphoric, analogistic thinking the people believed the spirit of the dead man might be preserved once it was released from the corruption of its body.[36]

None of the early skeletons at West Kennet was burned and the introduction of half-charred bones and of two complete cremations coincided with the construction of the Sanctuary with its fire-crackled stones. If it were indeed a mortuary house from which charred bones were eventually removed it would explain the comparative scarcity of human bones there. It might also explain something of the enigma of Silbury Hill a mile to the west on low ground by the modern-day Swallowhead spring. This stupendous circular mound was considered to be the burial-place of an important chief or priest but even the recent, vigilant excavation by Professor Richard Atkinson failed to find any body.

John Aubrey recorded that 'the tradition only is, that King Sil or Zel, as the countrey folke pronounce, was buried here on horseback', the beginning of a legend that a golden horseman was to be found at the centre of the mound. The meaning of

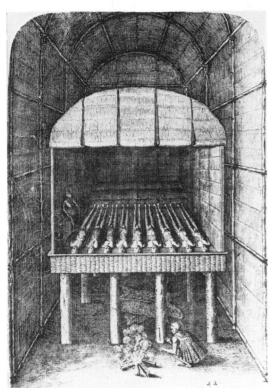

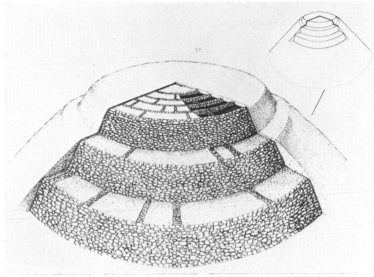

55. John White's drawing of a priest inside the mortuary lodge of Virginia Indian chiefs.

56. The structure of Silbury Hill.

Silbury is obscure, perhaps 'the mound where willows grow', not unlikely considering the wet surroundings of the hill. Stukeley, also struggling with the problem of place-names like Kennet and Cunetio, the Roman name for Marlborough, suggested that a prehistoric King Kunedha 'lived at Marlborough, was buried in Silbury, was the founder of Abury'. This was a reasonable guess and shames a more recent, preposterous theory that the Hill was the pyramid of the leader of an Egyptian scientific expedition who set up an astronomical centre at Stonehenge, lived at Avebury and was interred in Silbury, doubtless exhausted by the daily twenty-mile walk to his observatory on Salisbury Plain. This obsession with what Professor Glyn Daniel described as 'a set attitude of mind with regard to the Egyptian origin of all culture' has been defined as 'pyram-idiocy'.[37]

Around 2750 BC in the heat of a late summer, ants flying in the sultry air, people assembled at a low terrace of chalk jutting into the plain of silts and gravels where the Swallowhead spring now rises. Here they would build one of the wonders of the world, the largest man-made mound in Europe. 'Silbury indeed is a most astonishing collection of earth, artifically rais'd, worthy of Abury.' Stukeley's words are true. The Hill is a mass domineering the landscape, its flat top visible far along the Ridgeway.

Figures mean little. Forty metres high, a base with a diameter of 165 metres, covering 21,000 square metres, a flat top thirty metres across, these are mere numbers. But another, that the hill contains a quarter of a million cubic metres of chalk, does have meaning because it signifies some 35,000,000 basket-loads of rubble to be passed around the rising sides of the mound from person to person in a long, spiralling chain. John Aubrey noted the folk-story that Silbury 'was raysed whilst a

129

posset of Milke was seething' but it took much longer. He was told by Sir Jonas Moore, Surveyor of the King's Ordnance, who cured his own sciatica by 'boyling his Buttock', that the seventeenth-century cost of building Silbury 'according to the Rate of worke for Labourers in the Tower' would be 'threescore or rather (I thinke) fourscore thousand pounds' but it cost much more. To finish it demanded more of the resources of the people than a modern space programme in time, in effort and in wealth. People who were young when the project began were dead long before it was ended. It was, moreover, not a simple pile of chalk. To the contrary, it was designed by people with a good working knowledge of soil mechanics and by people whose society was large, rich, and with leaders who had the power and compulsion to organise the enterprise. 'We cannot but make this general reflexion . . . that this temple . . . when in perfection, must have been the work of a very great and learned people.'[38]

It did not begin so stupefyingly. In that first summer the people erected a circular hurdle work fence of widely spaced stakes. At the centre of this enclosure on the undisturbed grass they heaped up a mound of clay-with-flints specially brought to this spur, very like the clay cores of the great round barrows of eastern England with their flints, animal bones and nearness to water. Each of these features is shared by Silbury. The core, so often associated with burials in the other barrows, suggests that the activities at Silbury also were related to death. Fragments of hazel and other plants preserved in the core were dated to about 2750 BC.[39]

The builders covered this mound with a stack of turves dug with wooden spades from outside the fence, then piled topsoil over this, 'a black peaty substance, composed of sods of turf piled together, containing great quantities of moss still in a state of comparative freshness'.[40] A few sarsen boulders were scattered randomly around the base. 'On top of some of these were observed fragments of bone, and small sticks, as of bushes, and . . . of mistletoe . . . and two or three pieces of the ribs of either the ox or red deer, in a sound and unusually compact state, and also the tine of a stag's antler in the same condition. It is not improbable that it may have been specially regarded.'[41] Other antler fragments were found during an 1867 excavation. These relics, like the 'rubbish' at Whiteleaf Hill, Wold Newton and Gib Hill, may have been the 'spirit' representations of the fecund world desired by these early farmers, a gathering together of fertile earth, vegetation, edible animals, flint and stone, a concentration of richness sealed under the great mound close to life-giving water.

Four more layers were added of gravel and soil from the flood plain, doubling the size of the round barrow and completely hiding the fence. Beetle wing-cases, ant wings, plants, ox or deer vertebrae, a piece of oak, all were perfectly preserved in the 'dense accumulation of black earth, emitting a peculiar smell, in which were embedded fragments of small branches of bushes' that had been transformed 'into a beautiful cobalt-coloured blue' within this rather irregular mound. Merewether thought he had found some pieces of grass string 'about the size of whipcord' but it is more probable, in Professor Atkinson's words, that this was 'slightly twisted, fibrous plant stem, mainly of nettle, which did superficially resemble rather loosely twisted string'.[42]

Despite the shaft down its centre in 1776, the tunnel into its core in 1849, another cutting in 1867 and two more trenches in 1922 no burial has been discovered although the more thorough investigations of 1967–70 did come upon hints of a central deposit destroyed by the Duke of Northumberland's excavation in 1776. The moss, the bushes, the hundreds of freshwater shells, the proximity of the Winterbourne stream that today meanders past Silbury show that the plant-laden material from the upper layers had been selected intentionally and purposely brought from the damp water-meadows rather than from the drier, higher chalklands to the south.[43] Water and the rich alluvial soil were clearly important.

This barrow did not stand long on its chalk platform before it was enveloped in the colossal cone of Silbury Hill and its sides never became weathered. Professor Atkinson observed that there was 'no evidence for any significant lapse between the successive stages of construction'.[44]

A great ditch was gouged out, as deep and wide as Avebury's, to provide the chalk blocks for a stack of gigantic drums, each laid out in a honeycomb of cells into which rubble was tipped before the next, smaller drum was built on top up to five metres high, the white walls rising like the iced tiers of a wedding cake. The 'cells' of chalk blocks made the mound very stable. It was a technique long known to builders of Cotswold–Severn tombs who incorporated internal walls in their structures, and its adoption at Silbury shows that it was natives who raised the mound.

Through the dust and crumbling chalk the labourers scrambled, hauling themselves up ladders, dumping the chalk, swarming along the hoar-white walls that extended like a frozen spider's web against the green of the autumn landscape behind it. This mound, over a hundred metres across its base, was not big enough. The ditch was filled in and an even bigger one begun, 160 metres from rim to rim. A lake-sized extension to the west provided more chalk. Two causeways to the south where the ditch was narrowest gave access to the uplands. Here the ditch was cliff-like. It must surely have been dry at its bottom or the difficulties of digging into rock-hard chalk while up to the ankles or knees in sludge would have been insuperable. After a long dry spell in September 1886, A. C. Pass sank ten deep shafts at the western foot of Silbury and, noting that the pits constantly had almost three metres of water in them, decided that the ditch had probably been a moat for defence. He had failed to take into account the change since prehistoric times when the water-level must have been at least ten metres lower than today.[45]

When the seventh and final drum was finished the steps of all the terraces but the topmost were filled in giving the monument the smooth, sloping sides that, apart from their grass, have altered very little between then and now, a truncated cone that rested like an upturned cup in its saucer whose rim was the level horizon. Seen from the flat top only a chip at the west and a slight imperfection to the north spoiled the symmetry of the skyline and it may have been the desire for this that caused the people to build so high. The seemingly thoughtless choice of a skewed hillside for the site of the first Stonehenge has been explained by the builders' wish for a horizon level all round.[46] Silbury, however, would have been a most inconvenient viewing-platform for astronomer–priests. It was not intelligently placed as an observatory and, seen from its top, the extreme positions of the sun and moon did not coincide

57. Silbury Hill from West Kennet to its south.

with any noticeable landmark. The midwinter sun did not rise over West Kennet nor did the moon set over Tan Hill, the scene of later pagan rites.[47] Yet alternative sites could easily have been chosen. Just a few hundred metres east of Overton Hill an elevated observer could have seen the midsummer sunset over Windmill Hill, and a dozen other situations could have been found for whatever the 'priests' demanded. Perhaps the most cogent argument against any astronomical theory is the low-lying location of Silbury had the people wished to build a viewing tower. The place, surely, was specifically picked for the very reason that it was low-lying, damp and fertile. Comparable barrows had the same relationship to water.

Moses Cotsworth claimed that Silbury had originally been topped with a twenty-nine metre-high post for casting a shadow onto the flat land below where the world's biggest sundial had been laid out. There are three objections. Some trees might just have grown to this sort of height but would have been gnarled and distorted, and any jointing of several trunks would have grossly weakened this wind-quivered pole. Secondly, it would have weighed over twenty tons. Manipulating nearly thirty metres of ponderous, sagging wood up the slopes of Silbury would have been awkward and putting it up on the top impossible. Of course, an even longer post could have been erected first and the mound built up around it but the timber would have rotted before the mound was finished. Thirdly, its creators would have discovered that even on those days when the sun shone the pole would normally cast only a broad, diffused shadow without definition, rendering their prehistoric almanac useless.[48]

How long it had taken to build Silbury remains in doubt. We cannot be certain how many people were involved or how long they laboured each year, whether there were interruptions, or even what the construction methods were. Starting from an assumption that there were, at most, twenty-five long barrows on the Marlborough Downs each for a family of some twenty people occupying a territory of one and a half square miles, this would give an overall population of about five hundred in the early and middle Neolithic period, quite a high figure when it is realised that even today, excluding the busy town of Marlborough, hardly more than two thousand people inhabit the downs.

By the Late Neolithic the countryside could once again have been providing food for four to five hundred people of whom about half worked at Silbury, the others, the aged, children, cripples, unable to participate. It has been calculated that Silbury took 18,000,000 man-hours to build. If each able-bodied person worked for ten hours a day for two months in the early autumn the project would have gone on for as long as a hundred and fifty years. With the same workforce but taking a different calculation that one person might shift up to ten hundredweights of rubble daily, something in the region of forty basketloads, allowing fifteen minutes or less to get the pannier filled, passed from hand to hand along the ditch, up the slopes and ladders, emptied and returned to the miners in the quarry-ditch, this would allow Silbury's 250,000 cubic metres of chalk to be extracted, carried and heaped up in about a hundred years. Even with the most concentrated and unlikely programme employing every person in the district on full-time navvying with only the aged to tend the beasts and the fields, ten years would pass before the hill was completed. This great length of time between the beginning and end of the work would explain the seeming discrepancy between the earliest and latest of the Carbon-14 determinations.[49]

That people other than the natives of the downs laboured here is made rather less probable by the two other huge round barrows that were put up within seven miles of Silbury, the Hatfield Barrow at Marden and the Marlborough Mound, neither as big as Silbury but both large enough to demand the efforts of local people for long periods. Their existence suggests that one purpose of these giant barrows in North Wiltshire was indeed to act as territorial markers, stamping the earth with the presence of the people, each group living within its own boundaries.

Neither of these gigantic tumuli is well known because the Marlborough Mound is overgrown with trees and concealed by buildings of the famous College, and the collapsed remains of the Hatfield Barrow in the Vale of Pewsey were entirely levelled before 1818, its precise location only recently determined by geo-physical detection. This 'Giant of Marden' had stood inside an irregular U-shaped earthwork maybe put up long after the barrow which, predictably, was very close to the drifting waters of the Avon at the edge of a flood plain. William Cunnington I excavated the sandy mound in 1807, sinking a great conical pit from its top but not unexpectedly failing to find a central burial. What his eight labourers did discover was charred wood, some sherds, and the bones of red deer, pig and a large bird,

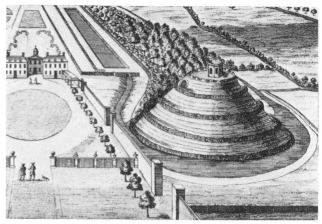

58. The Marlborough Mound, overgrown with trees and supporting a water-tank.

59. Stukeley's sketch of the Marlborough Mound after its conversion into a terraced walk with a summerhouse on top.

remains like those from other grave-free round barrows, placed at the core before the final capping was heaped over it. Two human cremations like those from Duggleby Howe were found. On the prehistoric land surface a mass of burned wood and some flecks of bone led Cunnington to think he had discovered a pyre. He had not. Like many other of the great mounds no grave had been dug here before the barrow was started and a different interpretation must be given for its construction. 'I am therefore inclined to think that this barrow was designed for an hill altar, or a place of general assembly, not a sepulchre', wrote Hoare.[50] Now it is gone. Almost immediately after the disappointed Cunnington called his workers out of the pit the sides fell and the mound caved in leaving an untidy heap that a Mr Perry shovelled into the earthwork ditch a few years later.

Aubrey mistakenly described it as 'the largest barrow in these parts, except Silbury, together with a tradition of a fight, and of some great man's being bury'd under the barrow' but it was, in fact, only one fifth the size of the Marlborough Mound five miles east of Silbury, perhaps the third biggest prehistoric barrow in the British Isles.[51] That two such monsters were constructed so close to each other is perplexing until one realises that prehistoric distances should be reckoned not in miles but in hours. Today a relaxed drive of nine or ten minutes takes one from Marlborough to Silbury and it is easy to forget that to Neolithic people these places were separated by as much as an hour and a half's walk alongside the river or a more energetic striding across the hills and valleys of the downs. Marden was two hours away. The times are long enough, the communities small enough to support the belief that these great barrows were in some sense territorial markers, a tradition not generally taken up on Salisbury Plain. No giant barrow rises near Stonehenge or Durrington Walls and presumably the distinctions between north and central Wiltshire were becoming sharper. One exception may be at Silk Hill five miles north-east of Stonehenge where another of Hoare's 'hill-altars' stands in a wide circular ditch near a fine group of Bronze Age round barrows. 'We made a very large section in its centre, and discovered only a few animal bones of deer etc., and no symptoms whatever of cremation'.[52]

For a long time the antiquity of the Marlborough Mound remained in doubt. Some thought it to be a castle mound put up by the Normans, redesigned in 1650 as a hill of pleasure with a grotto and a spiral pathway. Nowadays with a huge water-tank and a brick chimney on its flat top, with a flight of rough concrete steps up it, with trees choking its mauled sides, it lacks the austere remoteness of Silbury. But it is clearly pre-Norman. The Saxon name of Marlborough, Maerle-beorg, Maerla's hill, probably refers to this mound. John Aubrey mentioned that Roman coins had been dug up when the Hartford family reshaped it. Antler picks used by its prehistoric builders were unearthed in the late nineteenth century and again in 1912 when a trench was cut for the flue of a new engine-house chimney. About halfway up 'a pocket of red deer antlers was found from two to three feet within the mound'. 'Prolonged contact with the chalk of the mound had thoroughly impregnated them and rendered them very brittle.'[53] It was a cache very like that discovered by the Meux excavation at Avebury. This evidence, together with the Roman coins, makes a prehistoric origin for the mound likely.

This massive heap of chalk, nearly a hundred metres across and eighteen high but not a quarter the volume of Silbury, stands in a bend of the Kennet with a suspected western causeway and is reputed to have a spring underneath it. 'There is a spring in the ditch', wrote Stukeley who remarked that Merlin the magician was supposed to be buried there but that such monuments were 'incomparably older than Merlin's time . . . And the archdruid who . . . was the projector and executor of the stupendous work of Abury, was buried at Marlborough.'[54]

There have been many attempts to explain what Silbury was. Most archaeologists believed it to be an excessive version of a round barrow under which an important chief lay buried but excavations seem to have disproved that. The mound does not appear to be sensible astronomically nor was it well placed to be a watch-tower. Less probable still is the suggestion that 'sacrifices of human victims [were] made by the Druids on the platform of Silbury' whose hill was as grim and blood-stained as an Aztec pyramid.[55]

What can be observed is that Silbury was unlike any earlier 'ritual' monument in the Avebury district, most of which were low, long and rectangular. The prototypes for this great hill were in the north-east, in large Yorkshire mounds like Duggleby Howe, Wold Newton and Willy Howe. Silbury may have been raised just because it was so novel to the natives of the Marlborough Downs, suggesting the introduction of a new cult structure by people from the east who were becoming dominant in this part of the downs. The two other great mounds were not built at the heart of the region but at its edges, the smaller Hatfield Barrow to its south, the Marlborough Mound to the east. The Late Neolithic pottery found at the Sanctuary and in the later layers of West Kennet had strong links with eastern England. It is possible, then, that this Kennet district, so easily reached from the Thames valley, was an area settled by easterners whose power was increasing and whose building of Silbury, long after the modest Sanctuary, was a confident proclamation of their own faith.

Such a massive construction could only have been achieved by a unified people who were prepared to work alongside each other year after year. It was big because the community was big but, paradoxically, because the community was a mosaic of small groups only an enterprise like the building of Silbury could fuse them together. The 'project was creating a type of community which had never existed before. Tribal villages were welded by common work into people with the consciousness of nationhood . . . Working together under one administration, their differences and mutual suspicions were bound to lessen.'[56] Written about the building of Egyptian pyramids these words, by a quirk of prehistory, might be applied to the pyramid-like Silbury.

What seems unarguable is that by the Late Neolithic people around the Marlborough Downs were numerous and socially stratified with at least one leader, perhaps with 'princelings' in outlying districts. Communal efforts without careful planning and direction would not have permitted the involved design of Silbury to have been maintained over so long a time. Nor would full-time agriculture. A largely pastoral way of life would have allowed time for such ventures while the mature herds were safely feeding on the autumn pastures watched over by boys. The fact that Silbury was started around the beginning of August points to many of its builders being pastoralists free to range the grasslands, not entirely dependent on crops, not restricted by the demands of harvest. Some agriculture, more animals, a sporadic movement of families living in spacious leather tents that were easily dismantled, lashed to poles, dragged along after the cattle and the flocks, on the high land in the warmer weather, down in the valleys in the icy bitterness of a chalk winter. There were still briefly occupied summer camps, and perhaps some longer-lasting homesteads dispersed about the countryside. Whether there were larger and permanent settlements is not known. There is some evidence that people may already have been living at Avebury itself.

Many years before Silbury the dense forest by the present Winterbourne stream had been cut back and the soil of Avebury's gentle hillock was ploughed. It never returned to woodland. Instead the grass was allowed to grow over the cultivated earth and cattle may have grazed here year after year down to the time that the great barrows were built.[57] Before Avebury's bank was put up people had been here. Burnt animal bones were found at ground level when Lord Stawell had part of the bank demolished, though these may have come from a workers' camp. Traces of hearths, a posthole or two, rain-worn sherds that had been left lying in the open have been recorded from later, better excavations. Perhaps these are the only known traces of an unenclosed settlement like those elsewhere in Wiltshire, Marden and Durrington Walls amongst them, hamlets of round timber huts like African kraals with the stench of rubbish-tips, cattle hoof-deep in a muddy stream, the chatter of people by their homes, little centres of life in the wide countryside.

If there were such a village at Avebury then it was its occupants who were to erect the splendid stone circles.

CHAPTER SIX

The Building of Avebury

We may well wonder how these people could bring together so many of these great stones and set them up so exactly.

William Stukeley. *Abury*, 30.

EVEN before there were any stone circles at Avebury people put up at least one free-standing megalithic structure nearby, the Devil's Quoits Cove, a three-sided setting of sarsen slabs at the entrance to the Beckhampton valley. Although it has never been dated it was probably erected when long mounds were no longer being built but when Late Neolithic natives still used human bones in their ceremonies, taking them to monumental versions of the forecourts and entrances to megalithic long barrows. A mile north of Avebury was the Shelving Stones chambered tomb. This has long since been destroyed but sketches by Aubrey and Stukeley show how similar its box-like end-chamber was to a Cove. Formerly people had carried the dry bones of their ancestors to such cells for burial, and it may have been to replicas of them that later people brought skulls and long-bones not just for burials but for more elaborate fertility rites, families bringing their human relics in the thin winter dawn to Coves like the Devil's Quoits.

Here, a mile south-west from Avebury, a hundred or more men and women heaved up a thirty-three-ton slab, two other enormous sarsens splaying out from it, their unweathered, smoother sides facing inwards, towering over the people, looking very like the first stages of a megalithic tomb before the mound was added. Years later Beaker people incorporated the Cove into the Beckhampton Avenue much as they dug an earth avenue on either side of Stonehenge's Heel Stone. Four thousand years later still Richard Fowler of the Hare and Hounds burned and smashed the west pillar. The back stone had already fallen. Today only Adam, the huge eastern stone, remains, set in concrete by Mrs Cunnington, with Eve, the one survivor of the avenue standing diminutively to its east.

The Beckhampton Cove must originally have stood alone 'upon an eminence, the highest ground which the Avenue passes over'[1] but it was not unique. One just as isolated still exists on a terrace well to the west of Stanton Drew's great circle. That such coves were used for funerary ritual is implied not only by their likeness to Neolithic chambered tombs but by their orientations. Just as the tombs faced the morning sun so the Beckhampton Cove was aligned towards the midwinter sunrise.[2] In later years when Beaker people came to Avebury they obviously understood that the stones of the avenues and the Cove were associated with death because they buried several of their fellows by the sarsen pillars, two inside the cove itself. Neolithic people had not done this. They may have brought skulls, jaws, arm- and leg-bones here but they buried them elsewhere, perhaps in the stone-covered pits with their jumbles of bodies.

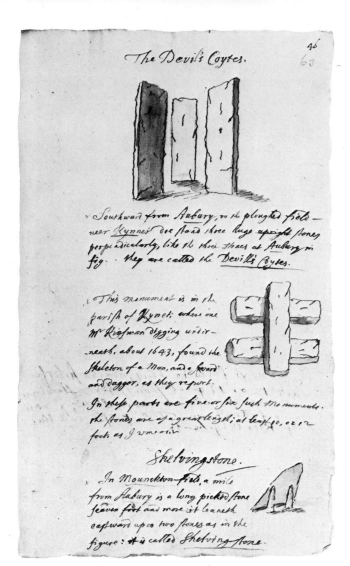

The Devil's Coytes.

Southward from Aubury, in the ploughed field neer Kynnet doe stand three huge upright stones perpendicularly, like the three stones at Aubury in fig. they are called the Devills Coytes.

This monument is in the parish of Kynet; where one Mr Ráusman digging underneath, about 1643, found the Skeleton of a Man, and a sword and dagger, as they report.

In these parts are five or six such Monuments. the stones are of a great length; at least 10, or 12 foot as I ween or.

Shelvingstone.

In Mouneckton field, a mile from Habury is a long picked Stone seaven foot and more it leaneth eastward upon two stones as in the figure: it is called Shelving Stone

60. For his *Monumenta Britannica* John Aubrey made this sketch of a Cove he called the Devil's Coytes. This may have stood in the Beckhampton Avenue but Aubrey's stones do not resemble Adam, the survivor of that structure. The bottom drawing is of the Shelving Stones, a destroyed chambered tomb that stood near Mill Barrow.

61. Stukeley's drawing of the ruined Shelving Stones with its boxlike entrance.

There is something of a mystery. During his visits to Avebury John Aubrey saw a cove and wrote that it was called 'the Devill's Coytes'. This is presumed to refer to the Beckhampton Cove. Yet Aubrey never mentioned the avenue there even though in the seventeenth century many of its stones still stood right alongside the cove. Nor does a sketch of his resemble the cove whose ruins Stukeley saw though this may not be important as Aubrey was not always accurate in his drawings. But it is strange that he located the Devil's Quoits not to the west but 'southward from Aubury, in the ploughed field—neer Kynnet', a direction that is repeated in Camden's *Britannia*.[3] By the time that volume appeared Aubrey was an old man, his fieldwork long finished, and his memory may simply have failed him as it did over several matters.

Stukeley, however, took the report seriously enough to search out a spot on the Kennet Avenue which he thought might be where another cove had stood. 'As soon as I saw longston cove [at Beckhampton] and found it the interval of 50 stones from Aubury I conjectured there must have been another at Kennet avenue and measuring with nicety I found at the 50th stone an entire vacancy that its upon an eminence . . . there was a cove here too.'[4]

The number of avenue stones is irrelevant as they were only added later but it is just possible that before Avebury's stone circles were erected there was one Cove to the west, another at the head of the first little rise slightly south of where the present Kennet Avenue ends. The area has never been excavated. Nearby was an earthen long barrow, Avebury 21. A small stone circle was to be put up close by. It is fair to add that Stukeley changed his mind and omitted all reference to the Kennet 'Cove' in his book, and the probability is that Aubrey's memory was faulty. Yet the former presence of a Cove might explain the irregular path of the avenue and the existence of the avenue itself, designed as a means of linking an ancient holy place with the grandiose megalithic complex of Avebury itself.

62. Stukeley's imaginative reconstruction of the Beckhampton Cove. Stone A is Adam and E is Eve. Windmill Hill is in the background.

63. (*bottom*) Stukeley's drawing of the 'Kennet Cove', the gap between the stones showing where he thought John Aubrey's Devil's Coytes may have stood.

In other parts of the British Isles people were already putting up great stone circles for their ceremonies. At Stenness in the Orkneys twelve steepling columns stood in a ring defined by a jagged ditch obsessively quarried from the bedrock. In Ireland the chambered round cairn of New Grange with its quartz walls and with a passage aligned towards the midwinter sunrise was placed inside a circle of over thirty massive blocks of stone. In the Lake District, source of many stone axes, people were going to splendid stone circles with names that peal like a prehistoric roll of honour: Long Meg and Her Daughters, the Carles at Castlerigg, Sunken Kirk, the Grey Horses. Rites inside these sacred rings differed but in every region where there was a fair-sized population circular enclosures were the foci of ceremonies, megalithic rings in the north and west, henges of earth or chalk in the stoneless areas of lowland Britain.[5]

The ever-widening trade in stone axes probably hastened the spread of ideas with the people of the east dominating the distribution of these essential tools, bringing Lake District implements into Yorkshire and bartering them from there along the rivers and tracks of the midlands and south. From Land's End came Cornish axes, transported by water round the south coast to East Anglia where they may have been traded from the eastern henges with their characteristic double ditches and intermediate bank.[6] Ideas are disseminated by people and it was not just the traders, the flint miners, the stone workers who travelled but the chiefs and their young men, canoes twisting along the dark rivers, parties tramping the ridgeways, their packs heavy with gifts to exchange inside the henges and the megalithic circles just like the Hopewell Indians of Ohio setting out for the ceremonial centres many cautious miles from their own settlements.

Soon after Silbury Hill was finished some leader, impressed by the awesome rings of standing stones, must have decided that a stone circle should be erected at Avebury but one in keeping with the other monuments there, larger, heavier, grander than anywhere else. Situated at the junction of waterways to west and east, alongside the Ridgeway that passed to north and south, already so populous and prestigious an area that it drew trade to it, Avebury became almost a metropolitan centre to which people came from miles around to trade, to settle disputes and to worship in the marvellous stone rings that expressed the barbaric pride of the natives.

Regions were more clearly defined by now in Wessex, tribal territories jealously held by their inhabitants whether in Dorset, Salisbury Plain or on the Marlborough Downs. Increases in population were partly the cause. Land had to be safeguarded from strangers. It was necessary to avoid quarrels within the homeland, necessary to come to understandings with other families and with other clans about boundaries, watering-places, the grazing rights of cattle. As some families acquired wealth through the possession of better land, or through good fortune or a productive herd they also gained respect. Leaders emerged to order the affairs of the many families within the territory, people needing agreements between each other and having to have someone to enforce sanctions against dissidents. An increase in population could transform the loose clan-bonds into a tight tribal unity with a common culture, language and territory. Threats from outside could also cause individuals to forego some privileges for the benefits of protection. All these may apply to the society that built the stone circles of Avebury.[7]

Sharing of property is rare amongst farmers who prefer to keep possessions within the family, but co-operation, particularly at times of sowing and harvesting, is highly esteemed, and the organisation of increasingly complicated clan-rights must itself have stimulated the creation of organisers and chieftains. Slowly over the centuries these farmers, hostile and suspicious of neighbouring regions where they had no close blood-ties, bound to each other by common ancestors, meeting for communal activities at certain times of the year, anxious to preserve their kinship links 'so that relations between the groups [would] include the exchange of spouses among them',[8] given to fantasy, these farming families melded into tribal groups with leaders and with great religious ceremonies.

Evidence for chiefs comes not merely from the fact that Silbury Hill and Avebury could not have been built without their direction but from the survival of articles of regalia, not rich but novel and personal, items such as large 'maceheads' perforated for a wooden handle and to be held swaggeringly as a symbol of authority akin to the Kenyan fly-swatter. Two stone maceheads, one from North Wales, were found in Late Neolithic layers at Windmill Hill. What looked like a very big one of sandstone came from a stonehole at Avebury itself. Another of flint lay in the Kennet Avenue. At West Kennet someone had tried to make one out of chalk, had broken it while drilling the hole and reshaped it as a pendant ultimately buried with its owner in the tomb.[9]

In their forest-bounded lands the people of Avebury were already acquiring a distinctive personality. Thousands of years later John Aubrey contrasted the strong, hard-working shepherds of Salisbury Plain with the 'Aborigines' of North Wiltshire, their

> Skins pale and livid; slow, and dull, heavy of Spirit: here about is but little Tillage, or hard labour, they only milk the Cowes and make Cheese. They feed chiefly on

64. A stone macehead.

Milke meates, which cooles their Braines too much, and hurts their Inventions. These Circumstances make them Melancholy, contemplative, and malicious . . . And by the same reason they are generally more apt to be Fanatiques.

A degree of fanaticism must be allowed to their prehistoric forebears when the sheer size of the Avebury monuments is considered though whether this was because of pastoralism and lack of hard work in the fields is questionable. Not to be questioned are their 'Inventions'. Those slightly-built men and women put up a succession of stone circles, avenues, ditches and banks unmatched elsewhere in the British Isles. Their kinsmen thirty miles to the west built a comparable but lesser complex of megalithic rings at Stanton Drew. In the south the earthwork enclosures of Marden and Durrington Walls are of a size with Avebury. But nowhere else did stone circle and earthwork combine so massively. Within them, grown from earlier customs, rites of sexuality stated the need for fertile land, and magical performances captured the image of the sun, human bones maintained ancestor cults, offerings were still made to the dead, broken pottery, broken arrowheads, broken twigs formed a 'spirit' world in the fearful and imaginative minds of the people. Performed within circular enclosures the rituals and ceremonies were echoed in the architecture of the rings and the rows.

Every one of these things came from older traditions and today's reader has no need for escapist explanations of what Avebury was. It is simply not true that the countryside around had been laid out like the precincts of an Egyptian temple with the varied monuments arranged in astrological order[10] as the wide differences in their dates of construction show. The same, sensible objection applies to the suggestion that the long barrows, causewayed enclosures, Silbury Hill and stone circles were deployed 'around the periphery of [a] topographical squatting goddess'[11] with a deformed head and sadly unemphasised breasts, the landscape modelled into the shape of a prostrate woman, the fecund Earth Mother, her outline marked out by the addition of man-made mounds and stones. Despite the warning that 'English archaeologists who deny this in the name of knowledge should watch more television' it is difficult to find such a panorama credible when the left thigh at Horslip was five hundred years earlier than the left hip at South Street long barrow, with the groin, indispensable for this fertile Earth Mother, added a thousand years later, a remarkably long approach to pubescence.

Nor is there good reason to accept that Avebury was one of the places like the Gateway of the Sun at Tiahuanaco in Bolivia chosen because it was a centre of high magnetic energy related to others by lines of kinetic telepathy called 'Leys' or 'Dragon Paths', Silbury Hill being moulded when 'the Sky People came down and instructed earth man'.[12]

Avebury was designed and built by prehistoric people whose beliefs were different from our own, whose lives were hard and who had a fierce desire to survive in their harsh, gaunt world. At the time that the stone circles were put up the population was no healthier. This was the time of the old man from West Kennet, a slender, not especially muscular person, with a broken arm and misformed spine. It was the time of the two cremations at West Kennet, a man and a woman both of whom had died young, one with a tooth abscess in the lower jaw. It was these people and their relatives who were to erect the enormous and heavy stone circles. A warning must be given. Avebury is a site with many architectural features and it is unlikely that they were all built at the same time. Today, the sequence of construction remains conjectural. There is evidence from pottery, artefacts and packing material in the stoneholes that certain parts of the complex were put up before others. Comparisons with similar circles in other areas of Britain also provide clues. But it must be stated that however serious and objective the speculation about the successive stages of Avebury it is still speculation and not a definitive conclusion.

The site was a low dome of chalk a few hundred metres east of the present Winterbourne stream and may have been chosen because it was clear of trees and because there was already a scatter of huts nearby. The knoll was not pronounced but it did dip down gently, especially to the west, and only to the south was there a fairly level plateau of about six acres or 2.5 hectares. 'The situation of Abury is finely chosen for the purpose it was destin'd to, being the more elevated part of a plain; from whence there is an almost imperceptible descent every way', wrote the observant Stukeley.[13] Yet it was not close to a source of stones and it was over a mile from the Ridgeway. The decision to build Avebury below the downs probably stemmed from the existence of a settlement nearby, the availability of water, and the presence of trees to give shelter during the snow-deep winters in those dry centuries of declining warmth.[14]

Just to the south of Avebury by Waden Hill in the valley where the Kennet Avenue was to wind trees were dense and hawthorns, hazels, blackthorns grew along the sunlit edges of the forest. To the east was the rim of the downs with the Ridgeway on its shoulder and beyond that, on Burton and Overton and Fyfield Downs, were thousands of sarsen boulders like carcases of sheep covering the wastelands. Even today after many have been broken and dragged away they can still be seen, radiating in spokes down the long valleys, and at Lockeridge Dene a whole stream of these grey stones is preserved in a National Trust plantation.

Most of the biggest stones have been smashed for building purposes but those that remain are up to two or three metres long, heavier than a ton, some coarsely pebbled, others a cool grey or red, 'some dusky white; some blew like deep blew marble; some of a kind of olive greenish colour', wrote Aubrey. He recalled that Sir Christopher Wren had noticed 'they doe pitch all one way, like arrows shot . . . Sir Christopher thinks they were cast up by a volcano.'[15] Samuel Pepys described them as 'stones of considerable bigness, most of them certainly growing out of the ground'. Local people have been content to call them either grey wethers because they resemble sheep, or 'sazzens' or 'saracens', the heathen stones.

As early as 1644 Symonds found 'the inhabitants calling them Saracens' stones'. This name for the Arabs who fought against the Christian crusaders during the Middle Ages was corrupted into 'sarsens' and became a term of opprobrium for anything ungodlike, and it is significant that as late as the seventeenth century Avebury's stones still had memories of paganism attached to them. Brentnall records that the pillars of the Rollright Stones were also sometimes called the Sarsen Stones even though they were made of oolitic limestone. Interestingly, the prehistoric family vaults of big stone slabs on the Chotanagpur plateau of northern India are known as *sasans*, and are sometimes associated with stone circles. There are many megalithic tombs in the region.[16]

Sarsens were not volcanic nor did they grow out of the ground. More than forty million years ago the gradual deposition of sands and gravel over the uneven sea-bed of the Marlborough Downs resulted in a cemented layer of sandstone on top of the chalk. Slowly the seas evaporated and the sandstone eroded and broke into slabby blocks of sarsen, their undersides resting on the smoothed chalk, their upper surfaces ravaged by rain and freezing ice. Then, during the last Ice Age when Avebury was only just outside the main area of glaciation, constant drizzle and damp caused the chalk beneath the sarsens to soften and a slurry of pebbles, muddy chalk and flints sludged down the slopes of the downs taking thousands of sarsens slithering centimetre by centimetre along the valley-channels with them. Many of these streams have disappeared even in the last hundred years but sufficient remain at Lockeridge, in Clatford Bottom, on Monkton Down and elsewhere to show how many stones there must have been for prehistoric man to use.[17]

They were ideal for building purposes. The blocks were flattish and easier to move than rounded boulders. Although their dull edges made sarsens unsuitable for axes they were durable. 'Those that lie in the weather are so hard that no toole can touch them. They take a good polish.' They had split naturally into either rough pillars or diamond shapes. Above all, they were massive and they were within two miles of Avebury. It was the heaviest stones that were to be selected, the blocks that lay three-quarters buried in the chalk, sarsens so big that they had never been shifted from the summits at the remote heart of the downs. To move these needed organisation.

Long before the first parties set out the communities had been making preparations. These people, many of them descended from the builders of megalithic tombs, knew very well what had to be done if sarsens were to be brought to Avebury. Ropes must be made, rollers and levers fashioned, sledges constructed. Being of fibre or leather or wood, all organic materials, these things have long since decayed although the remains of a timber sled employed to drag a corpse to the cemetery at Dorchester-on-Thames shows that Late Neolithic people near Avebury did know this form of transport.[18]

None of the hardwood levers used to manipulate the stones of the tombs and circles of the British Isles has survived, yet, unexpectedly, some pieces of rope have been preserved, one twisted skein of heather from the famous Neolithic village of Skara Brae being very like the ropes known as 'simmons' used until quite recently in northern Scotland. Closer to Avebury a lightweight grass rope, perhaps intended for tying up a boat, lay in the peat of the Somerset marshes. An even thinner lashing of nettle-fibres still adhered to a flint arrowhead and its shaft.[19]

However effective they were for tying down roof-joists and tethering cattle, it is doubtful whether these fibre ropes would have been strong enough to take the strain of a twenty- or thirty-ton stone and it is likely that cables of plaited leather were made for this purpose. Vikings sometimes wove strips of walrus hide for their ships' rigging, and eighteenth-century Hebridean farmers knew that sealskin thonging was tough enough to drag their horse-drawn plough along. Ropes taut with the weight of laden baskets had scored deep grooves in the sides of mine-shafts at Grimes

65. (*right*) A Kennet Avenue stone.

Graves[20] and, of course, at Avebury itself. Thongs of rawhide a metre or more long, a centimetre square in section, plaited into fifteen-centimetre-thick hawsers possessed considerable tensile strength as long as they were kept supple.

Sledges had to be put together, of elm or oak, two forked tree-trunks, a third of a metre thick, stripped of their bark for the runners, perhaps four thick struts dowelled into place across them, and a long heavy draw-bar for the ropes jointed into position at the front. Men cut down trees with stone axes, lopped them, dragged them to the settlement, shaped them with flint adzes. A tree-trunk of green oak, four metres long and a third thick weighed over six hundredweight and even when seasoned was about a quarter of a ton. A similar length of dry elm was over three hundredweight. Each sledge, as simple and light as possible, must have added a ton or more to the load to be manhandled off the downs. Other men hacked and smoothed more trunks into levers for prising stones free of the ground.

All this was effort and, other than that, did not much diminish the wealth of its society. The passion of the project is revealed shockingly only when one realises the number of cattle that were rounded up and deliberately slaughtered. For one stone alone twenty ropes were needed, each up to twenty metres long and for this perhaps a hundred cows had to be killed. With breakages and the constant wearing-out of ropes many more beasts than this were needed, a culling of stock from each family that must have reduced the herds alarmingly.

The skins of the dead animals had to be flayed, scraped, sliced with finger-thin flints into narrow strips. This was women's work. Half-hearing the distant bellowing of terrified beasts and to a background of chopping and hammering from the men's side of the settlement the women squatted by the huts, pulling thongs tight, interweaving them, the stench of freshly stripped hides always in the air. Other women prepared special food because this was not the prehistoric equivalent of building an office-block or of navvies digging out a canal, this was a religious undertaking vital to the lives of all the people. Before the groups set out there would be celebrations and most probably, like many Indians of North America, the most important chief would invite all the other families in the region to a gift-giving ceremony for which food and drink would have been stored up for weeks, the guests trailing in from miles around to eat and gossip, to accept gifts, to listen to recitations of the chief's ancestors and his own achievements, everyone aware that this was a solemn time in their lives. Like the slaughtering of cattle such a feast or 'potlatch' greatly diminished the accumulated wealth of the chief but it also enhanced his prestige, something far more important to him than economic considerations.[21]

Then, at last, perhaps in the autumn, the first parties set out for the downs, men and women, leaving behind the infants and children, boys to guard the flocks and herds, older women to burn off the stubble in the fields, others to clear the scrub from the place where the circles were to be raised. The sarsens to be taken were not the long pillars but the five-metre wide tabular shapes weighing over twenty tons, stones very like the slabs in megalithic tombs and which would bulk impressively around the ring. Just one pillar was chosen, possibly the first of the stones to be

66. (*left*) A close-up of a Z-Stone inside the South Circle.

selected, nearly seven metres long, forty or fifty tons of rough cylindrical sarsen. Looking at some of these blocks today one senses how such overgrown giants must have seemed immovably welded to the ground, stones that had to be torn with care from Earth's grasp.

On a short track of logs alongside the stone men placed the heavy hardwood sledge. Other people, probably the women who were accustomed to tilling the fields and garden-plots,[22] dug away the surrounding soil until the sarsen was undercut and several levers could be pushed under its edge, dozens of men heaving down to wrench it from its bed, manoeuvring it out and lashing it firmly onto the sledge. A fan of leather cables stretched out from the draw-bar, pairs of men pushing on wooden poles passed at intervals through the ropes, and then with yet more people shoving and levering the sledge from behind the inertia was broken and the load jerked forwards, off the track, onto the grass, dragging cumbersomely over the chalk where scatters of stones were being cleared from its path.

Unless the ground were especially soft rollers would not have been used because although they would have reduced the friction by half they actually saved very little man-power and were sometimes a positive nuisance. Nearly half the men released from hauling the stone would have to be used to shift the rollers back in front of the moving sledge, and whenever it was pulled up one of the many skewed slopes of the downs the sledge could skid sideways off the rollers, tightening the ropes and injuring the work-gang. Sledging heavy stones over the ground without the assistance of rollers was common practice in the ancient world, usually by human beings alone. The Egyptians did occasionally employ oxen. 'This was not usual. Power for most haulings was supplied by a large number of men who dragged the sledges with ropes.'[23] Nor was this just because slaves were available. Oxen were too valuable to be risked. They were also slow, stupid, with sluggish reactions and not easy to control as a team. Men were much more responsive.

In the Sandalwood Islands over five hundred Indonesian natives pulled an eleven-ton stone two miles from its source. In the Egyptian XIIth Dynasty a carving on the wall of the nobleman Jehutihetep's tomb depicted 172 men transporting his sixty-ton statue on a sledge with some unspecified liquid being used to lessen the friction. Thor Heyerdahl watched 180 modern Easter Islanders have a feast of beef, sweet potatoes and pumpkins and then mount an eleven-ton Long-Ear statue onto a forked tree-trunk and drag it away. Experiments near Stonehenge showed that thirty-two teenage boys could pull a ton and a half of stone and sledge for a short distance up a slope. Far away on Malekula Island in the Pacific cannibals heaved a ten-metre-long coral block onto two tree trunks and to the triumphant accompaniment of work-songs tugged it to their village.[24]

The schoolboys in the Stonehenge experiment were able to exert a pull of 110 pounds each for a short while. Easter Islanders managed 136 pounds. Egyptian slaves, either because they were expendable or more feasibly because the mason could not show the entire work-force on his slab, apparently contrived to move an incredible 781 pounds each. Stukeley recalled that his friend, Lord Pembroke to whom his book on Avebury was dedicated, 'computed the general weight of our stones at above fifty-tun, and that it required an hundred yoke of oxen to draw one'.[25]

148

A well-designed sledge, however, would have lessened the friction of the stone to one-tenth of its dead weight so that on flat ground the tractive effort was reduced to about two to three hundred pounds per ton. With every person maintaining an easy daylong pull of fifty pounds a hundred people could have shifted a twenty-ton sarsen on its sledge, each of half a dozen ropes with a safe working strain of a third of a ton being pulled by eight or nine pairs of men. On pronounced slopes such a work-gang might have been doubled involving almost the whole able-bodied population of the Marlborough Downs demonstrating how exacting a commitment in human terms the building of the Avebury circles was.[26]

The downs are by no means level, constantly dipping sharply and twisting into contorted slopes, and it must have been necessary to avoid the steepest hills where the stones would have been impossible to control. The most direct route westwards where the Herepath now descends has occasional gradients of 1:10 or more and had to be shunned. Other westward hillsides were even more precipitous. One route that has been suggested for the transportation of the sarsens is along the Valley of Rocks south-eastwards from Overton Down to Clatford Bottom past the long mound of the Devil's Den, one of the few easy ways to come down from the upper slopes.[27] This gentle valley is strewn with stones. Indeed, Passmore thought that one sarsen on the western bank was so exceptionally large and so isolated that it might have been abandoned by the builders who had started to take it to Avebury. This ingenious and attractive theory may be correct but the stone's situation at the foot of a slight tributary valley makes it likely that it came here naturally, particularly as it is a very unusual shape for a circle stone.[28]

The floor of this valley, moreover, is still so densely littered with sarsens that no stone could have been dragged along it unless the workforce moved along the dangerous side-slopes. A more obvious and closer trail would have been along the Ridgeway which for most of its distance followed a smooth downward slope towards the Kennet Valley. Only near the Sanctuary was there the 1:15 Overton Hill to be descended before the stone-gangs could turn northwards towards Avebury. Crawling at half a mile a day the journey could have been completed in three or four days. Whether from Clatford or along the Ridgeway the massive sarsens would have been dragged along the course of the future Kennet Avenue much as the bluestones of Stonehenge were pulled along the avenue there, a way made sacrosanct by the passage of these pillars.[29]

The work was not always in September sunshine. Sometimes there was grey rain or mist making the grass ankle-wet and treacherous. Sometimes an unpropitious sign stopped the work altogether: the chance flight of an 'unlucky' bird, the howling of a wolf, the breaking of a rope—portents acknowledged as warnings by this superstitious society.

The attitude of mind of the primitive is very different. The nature of the milieu in which he lives presents itself to him in quite a different way. Objects and beings are all involved in a network of mystical perceptions and exclusions . . . If a phenomenon interests him . . . he will think at once, as by a sort of mental reflex, of an occult and invisible power of which the phenomenon is a manifestation.[30]

The builders of Avebury were not slaves driven by the whip. Nor was the project a piecework operation with penalty clauses for the late delivery of a stone or the delayed completion of a circle. The work was freely given by all the people whose dedication came from their own beliefs, to whom time was unimportant and the enterprise everything.

Once the site where the rings would stand had been cleared of undergrowth two stakes were hammered into the ground about 120 metres apart on either side of the knoll's highest point and, using lengths of light rope as radii, people scratched out two huge circles in the chalk. As well as a few huts there may have been a great timber lodge standing here, a Council-House where the affairs of the tribes were discussed by the men. If so, this was removed when the stone circles were built.

Much had been written about the alignment of these rings, some scholars believing that the axis of 340 degrees between the circle-centres was astronomically significant. More probably the planners simply picked out the flattest and most level part of this shallow spur which happened to run south-south-east to north-north-west like most of the hills, ridges and streams in the locality. On either side of this plateau the land fell away so that when Avebury's earthwork was constructed the west and east entrances were several metres lower than the central area making it impossible to see across the enclosure.[31]

Both rings were immense. The destruction of so many stones means that their precise diameters remain uncertain but the South Circle had a radius of about fifty-one metres, perhaps made up of thirty body-fathoms of about 1.7 metres. As long ago as the eighteenth century Stukeley speculated that his 'Druids' had measured in cubits of $20\frac{4}{5}$ inches or fifty-three centimetres, another body-measurement, this time related to the human forearm, six cubits being the length of the staff employed 'when they laid out the ground-plot of these temples'. He observed that the sixth-century BC prophet Ezekiel mentioned a man holding a line of flax and 'in the man's hand a measuring reed of six cubits long' (Ezekiel xl, 5), revealing that the dimensions of the human body had been a widespread means of computing a series of lengths. Until recently market-traders would count yards of cloth by holding the roll loosely against their nose, repeatedly pulling the cloth out tightly with their other hand to the length of their outstretched arm. The natives of Malekula used the span of their fingers, five spans to a measuring rod about a metre long. Stukeley went on to claim that the North and South Circles at Avebury had diameters of 240 cubits, over-estimating their size by some twenty-five metres each although he did remark that they were not very carefully planned: 'Tho' this be the general and stated measure, which was propos'd by the founders, where the stones suited, and of the largest dimensions, yet we must understand this, as in all their works, with some latitude.'[32]

Hypothetical national yardsticks seem to occur in British prehistoric studies about once each century. A hundred years after Stukeley Petrie suggested that the bluestone and sarsen rings at Stonehenge were laid out in Roman or Egyptian feet of about 11·68 inches or thirty centimetres. He was mistaken. Almost a century later Alexander Thom claimed that the diameters of every one of the British megalithic rings from Shetland down to Cornwall, even as far as Brittany, were multiples of

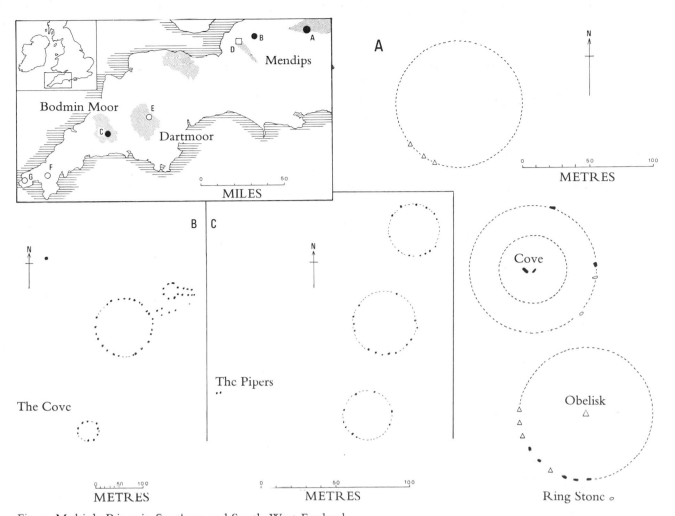

Fig. 7. Multiple Rings in Southern and South-West England.
(A) Avebury; (B) Stanton Drew; (C) The Hurlers; (D) the Priddy henges; (E) the Grey Wethers; (F) Wendron; (G) Tregeseal. The triangles in the Avebury circles represent the concrete markers showing where stones once stood.

his Megalithic Yard, two and a half of which made up a Megalithic Rod of 2.07 metres. The improbable inflexibility of this yardstick has already been discussed. For Avebury Thom stated cautiously that the North Circle is now far too fragmentary for any accurate reconstruction of its size. He observed that the 'south circle is more definite and has a diameter close to 340 feet. This is 50 Megalithic rods', but in his plan both the unknown diameter of the North Circle and the approximate diameter of the South became an exact 340 feet or fifty rods each.[33] Yet all previous surveyors except Stukeley, whose measurements were hopelessly wrong, considered the North Circle to be smaller than the South. Crocker in 1812 assessed their diameters as 83 and 99 metres respectively; Lukis in 1881 as 82 and 98; and Gray in 1912 as 98 and 102 metres. Dr Isobel Smith, having the advantage of the data from Keiller's excavations and a revised plan by the Royal Commission for Ancient and Historical Monuments, accepted Gray's radius of 'close to 170 feet' (51.8 metres) for the South Circle and added for the North Circle that a radius of 160 feet (48.8 metres) 'fits the existing stones as well as the depressions left by the destruction of others'.[34]

Although a radius of 48.8 metres would change the North Circle's diameter from fifty Megalithic Rods to an unconvincing 47.148, spoiling the elegance of Thom's hypothesis, it would be prejudiced to ignore the unanimity of earlier surveyors that this ring really was smaller than its counterpart particularly as in Crocker's time there were more stones present from which to take measurements. Not one of the rings in the other large megalithic complexes in Britain has a diameter identical with its twin. In southern England the three rings at Stanton Drew are all different and this is true of the Priddy henges (4), the Grey Wethers (two stone circles), the Hurlers (3), Wendron (2), and Tregeseal (2). No ring duplicated another.[35] Nor did it matter. Prehistoric people were not over-concerned with accuracy and with their rather casual techniques it was inevitable that their 'stones should be rude and native, untouch'd of tool, and that it was impossible to procure the dimensions exactly'.

Modern over-emphasis on the mathematical and astronomical intentions of stone-circle builders, and the omission of archaeological evidence in several books about megalithic monuments, has transformed the animistic and living world of these prehistoric people into a kind of laboratory whose clinical walls were covered in Euclidean computations. The single support for this comes from statistics. There is no anthropological parallel for such a society. There is not one aspect of Neolithic and Bronze Age life amongst the thousands of artefacts, monuments, settlements, the economies, burial practices, rituals even the personal ornaments of the dispersed communities in Britain to suggest there was an island-wide culture bonding all these societies together, with a national yardstick and an all-powerful priesthood dedicated to a study of the heavens. One suspects with Andrew Lang that some devotees of megalithic science bring their own wish-fulfilments to a study of stone circles, using 'statistics as a drunken man uses lamp-posts—for support rather than illumination'. 'Facts speak louder than statistics' seems a wise observation when one is looking at the zealous and primitive people who built Avebury.

Just avoiding the exact centre where a pit was dug and filled with rich fertile soil[36] they erected the first stone inside the South Circle, the high and thick Obelisk, smashed in the eighteenth century and now represented by a ziggurat-like pyramid of concrete. Far taller than the stones of the circle it became the focus of ceremonies and at least one human cremation was buried by it in the years to come.

Today only five of the lozenge-shaped monsters that made up the South Circle still stand, numbered from 101 in the south to 106 at the west, but even this wrecked arc is long enough to show the efforts of its builders. One by one the sarsens were dragged to Avebury, maybe only ten or twelve a year before the late rains softened the ground and the sledges became unusable. Around the circumference of the circle with spades and antler picks older men and women dug out about thirty irregularly-spaced holes, crude pits with an inclined ramp down which the base of the sarsen was tipped until it rested against stakes rammed in to protect the back of the stonehole from damage. During the hacking out of these positions bits of broken and weathered pottery lying in the grass, the remains of earlier settlement, slipped into the holes, Windmill Hill sherds, thin sandy fragments, coarse Peterborough ware, well over a score of pieces and two or three flints right at the bottom of the pits with not a beaker sherd amongst them, proving the early date of the stone circles.[37]

67. William Stukeley standing by the fallen Obelisk. Immediately above it and in front of the Entrance Stones is the little Ring Stone with a natural perforation in its shoulder.

As each stone arrived it was levered off its sledge and with no shaping or dressing of its base or sides was tilted in its hole until it leaned precariously, propped by heavy timbers, men on a dozen ropes straining to pull it upright. This was a dangerous time. These unwieldy slabs could be the width of a cottage, and thick, their rough uneven bottoms scouring into the chalk so that they resisted movement and it needed the sustained strength of a hundred people dragging in concert, obeying orders, to raise a stone slowly to a vertical position. The operation may have taken some days. In 1934 Keiller experimented by having a skilled foreman, Mr Griffith, and twelve inexperienced men re-erect a fallen Avenue stone, the fourth from the south end, using simulated prehistoric equipment. With stakes, wooden levers but with steel cables instead of rawhide ropes it took them five days even though the stone was relatively small weighing only eight tons. To put up the heavier and more awkward blocks must have taken at least as long and excavations have sometimes showed where thick stakes were driven into the ground in front of a half-lifted stone for the prehistoric labourers to secure their ropes overnight.[38]

Once up the sarsen settled crushingly into its hole. Joists on either side held it straight. Clay was packed in around it and left for some days to show up any movement. If the stone remained stationary the clay was removed and boulder-like sarsen packing-stones were shoved into the hole and battered tightly against the stone's base, sealing the accidental pottery beneath them.

At last, perhaps after two or three years, the ring was finished, a circle of diamond-shaped sarsens, their outer faces shabby with weathered channels, their protected softer sides facing inwards for the best effect. By the centre stood the Obelisk. Outside, to the south-south-east, was a stone about which little is known except that it was large just as many of the outlying stones of stone circles were large. There have

153

68. Stones of the South Circle with the southern Entrance Stones behind them.

been claims that these outliers were always aligned on the sun or moon much as Stonehenge's Heel Stone was related to midsummer sunrise or Long Meg in Cumbria to midwinter sunset but these may be exceptions. Most outliers had no astronomical significance. Neither did the stone at Avebury. It stood too far to the south to coincide with any solar or lunar phenomenon and had only an unspectacular horizon behind it. 'Indeed it is fantastic to imagine that the ill-clad inhabitants of these boreal isles should shiver night long in rain and gale, peering through the driving mists to note eclipses and planetary movements in our oft-veiled skies.'[39] Even if over-stated, the words of that great prehistorian, Gordon Childe, deserve respect.

Outliers quite often had a directional purpose. From Avebury's South Circle its outlying stone, no bank yet interrupting the view, was aligned along the natural north-north-west to south-south-east configuration of the landscape, leading the eye straight down the valley towards the Kennet and the Sanctuary and this may have been intended by the people who put it up.[40] The purpose of the Obelisk is clearer.

Some have thought this central stone to be a phallic symbol, others a representation of the place where the dead were laid in the megalithic tombs, yet others as a stone which embodied the spirits of the dead. As solitary standing stones

154

69. A view of the South Circle looking the other way with the stump of the Ring Stone in the foreground.

were sometimes erected on or near long mounds like Tinglestone cairn in Gloucestershire with its single triangular block of limestone or the Gatcombe chambered tomb with the holed Longstone nearby it is possible that the Obelisk did have funerary associations. Even what was once the tallest prehistoric monolith in Europe, the Grand Menhir Brisé in Brittany, was part of an earthen long barrow as were several other standing stones associated with long burial mounds in the vicinity. In the Pacific islands 'the central object on every altar . . . is a monolith with a smaller cromlech, representing ancestors'.[41]

The enormous size of the South Circle itself, covering as much ground-space as St Paul's Cathedral and ten times the area of the famous dome, an arena big enough to pack in over a thousand cars, and with only one pillar at its centre, was surely meant for a huge number of people. Even today the remaining arc of the south-west quadrant gives some impression of its vastness and although in succeeding centuries other features were added to the interior they hardly affected the spaciousness of this open ring so reminiscent of the circular enclosures at Callis Wold and Whiteleaf Hill with their central mortuary structures. At Avebury the discovery of a male skull and some other skull and rib fragments near Stone 102[42] reinforces the belief that the rites here were closely concerned with death.

155

B   A

C

A. Abury Steeple. B. the cove c Windmill hill.

70. Stukeley's sketch of the North Circle. Since his time the three stones to the right of the Cove have gone.

The same seems true of the adjacent circle which was probably constructed immediately after this on a slight downward slope to the north. The architecture was somewhat different. A great Cove was put up at the centre of the ring with a concentric circle of stones raised around it. Stukeley calculated that there had been thirty sarsens in the outer ring like the South Circle and twelve in the inner 'of the same size and distances. The geometry therefore of them, when laid down on paper, shews, the inner circle must be 100 cubits in diameter, the outer 240.'[43]

Although the size of the ruined North Circle is even more uncertain than that of the South Circle yet, if Gray's estimates were reliable, the outer ring was about ninety-seven metres across, and if a burning-pit discovered in 1964 marks the place of a destroyed stone in the inner ring that circle must have had a diameter of perhaps forty-one metres.[44] What is of some interest when considering the working-methods of the Late Neolithic planners is that they seemed to be counting in threes like the native builders of the long burial mounds, one of the most elementary arithmetical systems. If the diameters are correct, if the stone-numbers are correct and if a body-fathom of 1.7 metres was used, all matters of some speculation, then multiples of three appear too frequently for coincidence. In the South Circle, sixty fathoms across, there were thirty stones. In the North outer ring there may have been twenty-seven stones with twelve others standing in the innermost ring. The circles had diameters respectively of fifty-seven and twenty-four fathoms. There were, of course, three stones in the Cove.[45]

156

71. The Cove. An outer stone of the North Circle is in the background.
72. Another view of the Cove, looking in the opposite direction.

Nowadays, half concealed by houses and with one stone missing, the Cove is almost inconspicuous. Yet, showing how important it once was, after the two rings of the North Circle had been marked out the three mammoth slabs were deliberately erected at their centre, two pillars for the sides with the back slab, nearly fifty cumbrous tons, looming between them. These are perhaps the tallest and most attractive stones at Avebury and must have been tediously picked out from the many sarsen streams of the downs. They were so big that ordinary holes were not adequate for them and long trenches had to be dug with pavings of sarsen blocks spread over the bottoms to prevent the giants from swivelling and toppling as the chalk was crushed beneath their weight. Mrs Cunnington observed the same technique at the Beckhampton Cove where over 150 sarsen cobbles were laid down, some of them heavier than a hundredweight.[46] All of them had to be sledged wearily to Avebury.

The pillars of Avebury's Cove are far apart with intriguingly wide gaps at the corners but the explanation is prosaic. With sarsens nearly seven metres long, over twenty tons of solid rock to be lifted, room had to be allowed at one end for the people levering the stone upwards into its trench, even more space outside where gangs hauled on ropes up to twenty metres long. The two flanking stones had to be at least ten metres apart and even the biggest backstone could not fill the space completely.

With the sleek faces of its unweathered surfaces forming a well-finished interior the Cove faced north-eastwards where the long level of Hackpen Hill stretched two miles away, no notch or summit breaking the line of the horizon. With three stones so far apart and with such short sides the Cove could never have been an observatory for anything precise but it may have been roughly aligned towards the moon's most northerly point, just as at the first Stonehenge contemporary people were setting up yearly markers to plot the eccentricities of the moon's cycle.[47] That the barbarous society that built Avebury and whose ancestors' skeletons lay in the long tombs should have visualised the freely rising moon as a symbol of ancestral spirits being liberated from their dead bones is not improbable when the carvings and the figurines of fertility of these people are remembered. The Cove may have been the focus of an ancestor-cult. When the Revd A. C. Smith and William Cunnington III dug four large holes around it in 1865 they found no human bones but in all the pits and especially near the entrance they came across 'a good deal of British pottery, and many animal bones; sheep, horse, ox and dog', perhaps the remains of prehistoric activity here.[48]

Around the Cove the twelve stones of the inner ring were erected, none of which have survived, and then the pillars of the outer ring, only two still standing, one at the north, another at the east with a fallen distorted lump of sarsen to its south. A sad relic of this wrecked circle lies trapped in a yard by the village lane. Another that stood by the Swindon road well into the nineteenth century suffered the bumps of countless carts and was finally broken up when the road was widened. Fragments can still be seen in the wall north-east of the crossroads.

VII. (*right*) Stones of the South Circle with the Entrance Stones beyond, looking south.
VIII. (*over page*) The Entrance Stones, looking south.

It is uncertain why there should have been two adjacent circles here when one would have been big enough even for a very large population. It is possible that the second ring replaced the first when that became outmoded but this is unlikely as the circles seem of the same period. In both of them their builders used the identical method of supporting the pillars with packing-stones. Alternatively, the rings could have been intended for ceremonies at different seasons, a variation on Stukeley's Solar and Lunar temples for the worship of the sun and moon, a notion popular in the eighteenth century when it was attached variously to stone circles in the Orkneys and to Callanish in the Hebrides.[49] A more recent suggestion is that the North Circle was meant for male adolescents who had proceeded to it from the Beckhampton Avenue, going to a May Wedding. Their sacred marriage was consummated with maidens in the South Circle. 'By dawn, perhaps the virginal blood on the South Circle grass was balanced by blood and flame from the North Circle oxen and rising solar fireball.' As this May Day interpretation depends on the Cove facing twenty degrees farther south than it actually does this nuptial theory is divorced from fact.[50]

It does seem probable that the rings were used for different purposes. Along the south-west peninsula of England from Land's End to Somerset there are several complexes of paired and treble stone circles, and the nearer they are to Avebury the more they resemble it. Whereas double rings like Tregeseal in Cornwall and the Grey Wethers on Dartmoor are unembellished circles Stanton Drew only thirty miles west of Avebury has not only circles but also avenues, an outlying stone and a cove. Nowhere else in the British Isles is there such a concentration of multiple rings. At the Hurlers on Bodmin Moor a paved way led from the central to the south ring making it likely that they were used together. It is reasonable to believe that this was also true at Avebury. If the concentric circle with its Cove represented a circular enclosure with a mortuary house at its centre then the rites with human bones that began here may have been completed elsewhere, perhaps in the adjacent South Circle.

There is some evidence that the people started to build a third circle north-north-west of the others, maybe a hundred years or more after the others. Although Piggott's 1960 excavation proved that such a ring could never have been completed the project might have been abandoned after a few sarsens had been put up. Three empty stoneholes by Avebury's North Entrance were on the circumference of a circle of a similar diameter as the others and the holes were spaced about eleven metres apart like the stones of the North and South Circles. It was clear that at least one stone had actually been erected. 'During the excavations of 1937 a typical stonehole, complete with packing-stones and anti-friction stakeholes, was discovered 12 ft. to the south-west of Stone 46', at right-angles to the circumference of the huge Outer Circle.[51] Almost certainly it was raised before the deep ditch was dug for it was in that area that the rope-gangs must have stood to lift this 'large stone'.

Changes of mind were common amongst British prehistoric societies. In nearly every one of the modern excavations of stone circles there is proof that the site had been modified or abandoned. Stonehenge II was never completed. Nor, probably,

IX. (*left*) The South Circle, looking north-west.

163

THE LIBRARY

🌳 THE SURREY INSTITUTE OF ART & DESIGN
Farnham Campus, Falkner Road, Farnham, Surrey GU9 7DS

73. The Grey Wethers, Dartmoor, from the west. The circles have been restored.

was Callanish. Croft Moraig, Balbirnie, Cairnpapple, Moncrieffe, Berrybrae, all were altered. At Cultoon on the lovely island of Islay pillars that had been laid by their sockets ready for erection had simply been left there amongst the gathering peat. At the foot of two stones that had been put up were deposits of brand-new flint flakes, the 'deliberate offerings to the ancient stones by a superstitious Bronze Age peasantry'.[52]

Prehistoric man was not obsessive about concluding everything neatly. The years it took to build some of his monuments probably contributed to their non-completion or alteration. At Avebury the third ring was never finished. When the bank and ditch were constructed the few standing stones were moved and re-erected in the Outer Circle. At the magnificent ruin of the circle–henge of Stenness in the Orkneys the ditch also was probably quarried after the stone circle was built and this 'may point to the subsequent removal of stones rather than to an uncompleted plan'.[53]

In the bottom of Stenness's ditch by the entrance were sherds of a Grooved Ware bowl with the familiar East Anglian pattern of decoration. People making similar pots would help in building the earthwork at Avebury.

164

CHAPTER SEVEN

The Enclosing of Avebury

*I fully learn'd the scheme and purport of the founders . . . This is done with a sufficient, tho'
not a mathematical exactness. They were not careful in this great measure, where preciseness
would have no effect, seeing the whole circle cannot be taken in by the eye on the same level.*
William Stukeley. *Abury*, 19–20

By THE time the stone circles of Avebury were being erected people making pottery
with grooved decoration were well established in lowland England from the north-
east down to the south coast of Wessex. Distinctive styles in the regions of Yorkshire
and Northumberland, in East Anglia and in Wiltshire show how these herdsmen
were concentrating in the areas of open grassland. Often their thick, flat-based pots
are found with leather-working tools, flint scrapers, knives, awls, but hardly ever
with agricultural equipment like sickles or querns. On the hundreds of sherds from
Durrington Walls there was not one grain impression.[1]

From their regalia Grooved Ware societies seem to have had chiefs and craftsmen.
Antler maceheads are sometimes found. There are others of attractive, naturally
striped stone as well as finely shaped flint axes and delicate articles of jet that reveal a
love of ostentation in these wealthy pastoralists who encouraged the production of
luxuries as trade networks once again expanded.[2] Wandering with their herds across
the plains, past the torpid marshes where water-birds floated amongst the reeds,
living as nomads through the springs, summers, early autumns, maybe in families
that gathered together for the winter at a tribal centre, this new way of life altered
the balance of Neolithic societies. 'The cumulative effects of forest clearance . . .
could have allowed a change from an arduous pattern of cyclic cultivation to a more
stable, mixed pastoral and hunting system in favoured districts during the Late
Neolithic.'[3]

Such a change was bound to influence the people of Avebury. Unlike the
growing of crops, herding demands mobility and encourages initiative to find
water, to guard cattle from wild animals, to prevent the rustling of stock, to fight for
the lushest pastures. Society tended to be governed by men who were responsible for
the herds. 'Male dominance, militarism and independence are found to be
particularly common themes in pastoral socialisation.' Southern England in the Late
Neolithic may have produced more and more bands of aggressive, enterprising
families of herdsmen, at first living peacefully alongside the agricultural natives
while the downs were spacious enough for both, later taking over widening tracts of
the countryside as their herds grew.[4]

Initially the Marlborough Downs seem to have received relatively few of these
wanderers who, with the many other people from eastern England, mingled
hesitantly with the natives but mingled nevertheless so that their new custom of
building circular enclosures for religious activities became integrated with the

DATE BC	AVEBURY	SANCTUARY	STONEHENGE	OTHER EVENTS
3000				
2950				
2900		The first timber building (IA) started.		
2850				
2800				
2750			I. The henge built and the Heel Stone erected.	Silbury Hill started.
2700		IB replaced IA.		
2650				Silbury Hill completed?
2600	Stone circles started.			First great earthworks constructed in southern Britain.
2500	Third circle abandoned. Ditch and bank begun.	Lightweight fence and hut of Phase II.		First Beaker people in southern Britain.
2450		Free-standing timber ring of Phase III.		
2400	Earthwork and Outer Circle completed. Avenues begun.			
2350				
2300	Avenues finished.	Stone circles of Phase IV started.		
2250				West Kennet blocked up.
2200			Blue stones brought from south Wales by Beaker people for Stonehenge II.	
2150				
2100	Beginning of decline in importance.		Sarsens brought from Marlborough Downs for Stonehenge IIIA.	Beaker people expelled from Salisbury Plain.

Fig. 8. The Possible Dates of Building Sequences in the Avebury region and on Salisbury Plain.

continuing traditions of ancestor- and fertility-cults. On Salisbury Plain, however, the changes were more radical. Here the herdsmen with their sun-cults and masculine societies were dominant and different.[5] Although it would take time for such a hierarchical society to develop and although to south and north of Stonehenge the influence of these Grooved Ware people was less their strange ideas and their aggression created fear and doubt.

It could be for this reason that while people were raising Avebury's stone circles other groups to the south were constructing huge earthworks for defence. Unprotected Neolithic settlements previously occupied by Wessex natives were being enclosed within high banks by Grooved Ware groups between about 2600 and 2500 BC. Durrington Walls was enclosed at that time. So was Mount Pleasant. The enclosures were enormous. Knowlton's bank was half a mile long and encircled an area of nearly ten acres or four hectares. Mount Pleasant and Waulud's Bank were bigger. People at Durrington Walls in the heartland of Salisbury Plain trenched out a deep, wide ditch over a mile in length.[6]

Because the banks were built outside the ditches the idea that these earthworks were meant as defences has been rejected yet inner ditches like these had the advantage of preventing village cattle from eroding the banks. A bank the height of two men outside a ditch too wide to jump and limb-breakingly deep provided protection enough. There is little reason to doubt that safety from attack was as much needed now as in earlier centuries. At Meldon Bridge, three hundred miles north of Durrington Walls, the defences were obvious. A massive stockade with one narrow gateway shut off twenty acres of uneven ground, most of it used for grazing, guarded to east and south by water. Directly inside the fortified entrance a totem pole may have stood, replaced several times, finally by a standing stone like Avebury's Obelisk. Human cremated bone had been scattered around it.[7]

From such evidence it appears that these irregular earthworks, usually by rivers in regions long occupied by builders of long burial mounds and causewayed enclosures, combined several functions. Principally they may have been tribal centres where a chieftain lived and where his herds grazed safely during the winter months, most of his followers widely dispersed around the surrounding territory. This might explain the curious preponderance of pig bones at Durrington Walls. All these enclosures were built in open grassland that was ideal for cattle but not for pigs that scavenge best in forests. At Durrington, moreover, 'the skulls of pigs and cattle were poorly represented' suggesting the 'animals were not slaughtered on the site but were brought as carcases or joints of meat'. In primitive societies cattle are valued not for their meat but mainly as 'sources of milk, cheese, hides, dung, fibre, and traction for ploughing'. Pigs are different. Awkward to herd, providing no milk, and eating the same food as man they are luxuries reared chiefly as a delicacy for the feast.[8] Durrington's abundant pig bones may have arrived as gifts of pork to the chief from his followers, a wealth of food very soon returned in the potlatch that the chief would give to prove his own generosity.

74. The bank and ditch at Avebury. Without the stones of the Outer Circle it resembles many other earthwork enclosures in southern Britain.

The prestige of a chief was bound up with his free use of wealth, particularly food. This in turn tended to secure for him a larger revenue from which to display his hospitality, since his followers and relatives brought him choice gifts . . . Apart from lavish entertainment of strangers and visitors, the chief also disbursed wealth freely as presents among his followers. By this means their allegiance was secured and he repaid them for the gifts and personal services rendered to him . . . It was by his accumulation and possession of wealth, and his subsequent lavish distribution of it, that such a man was able to give the spur to . . . important tribal enterprises.[9]

Such exchanges constantly reaffirmed the kinship bonds between the chief and his people. 'To give and to receive gifts is to involve oneself in a network of mutual indebtedness, and so to increase mutual social cohesion and solidarity.'[10]

The construction of riverside defended centres in Wessex was strangely paralleled in North America where the collapsed trading networks of the Hopewell Indians in Ohio were succeeded by Temple Mound societies of the Mississippi culture. Fertile lowlands by the rivers were colonised and people built huge fortifications for their ceremonial temples with small settlements in outlying districts. The largest of the metropolitan sanctuaries at Cahokia near the modern East St Louis was put up alongside a channel of the Mississippi where the traders or *pochteca* could unload their canoes. At its height over a hundred mountainous flat-topped mounds rose here in an area of six square miles enclosed by a heavy palisade from which square towers jutted at regular intervals for archers to fire down on enemies. Trade in elegant pottery and stone carving and in elaborate copperwork extended as far as Wisconsin four hundred miles away. Intensive maize cultivation supported a large population. The art of these Indians shows that wind, sun and fire were important elements of the people's fertility cults with public ceremonies to celebrate the times of sowing and harvesting. In most areas of this culture such rites were probably performed on and around the gigantic temple mounds but in the northern regions natives adhered to the older Hopewell traditions and did not build these new-fangled monuments.

Society was like a pyramid with chieftainship passed on through the female line. As late as the seventeenth century AD Natchez Indians of Mississippi had chiefs, the Great Suns, who inherited their power through the women of their family. Below them were the Nobles who were the warlords and priests. Then came the Honoureds, the important warriors, craftsmen and traders. Only slightly above the status of slaves were the Commoners or Stinkers, the farmers and workers and warriors who were severely repressed but whose children could marry into a higher rank and so escape from their mean birth. It was also possible to climb the social scale by making sacrifices, taking a scalp or performing a brave war-deed.[11] It would be misleading to make over-close comparisons between American Indians and the prehistoric societies of Wessex but there are similarities. Like the early round barrows of Yorkshire some of the Cahokian mounds covered burials, Mound 72, for example, where a totem-pole may have stood, being a domed barrow in which a chieftain, lying on a shell-beaded blanket, was surrounded by several other burials including a group of six young men and women who may have been sacrifices. The central interment and the secondary burials at Duggleby Howe might be comparable.

Gradually, however, barrows for the dead became places for the living. The larger mounds at Cahokia although still associated with death and resembling the funerary barrows had other functions much as Silbury Hill had. The greatest of all, Monks Mound, so-called from a colony of Trappists who grew crops on the lowest of its four terraces, was so big that it took over two hundred years and fourteen stages of enlargement before the last basketload of earth was emptied onto it. Even then it was unfinished 'and military preoccupation might be one reason for the end of the great work'. It was possibly planned as a place for the bones of dead leaders, its flat top supporting a timber charnel-temple with 'idols inside and . . . carved figures on either side of the door'.[12] Silbury Hill, with the Sanctuary so close, may have had an analogous use.

Half a mile west of Monks Mound archaeologists discovered the superimposed locations of four circles of posts put up in succession over a long period. The excavator, Warren Wittry, commented that 'the method of erecting the huge posts at Cahokia was exactly parallel to that used in erecting the posts and stones in Europe'. The second of these rings, built around AD 1000, had forty-seven or forty-eight columns of red cedar, perhaps painted with red ochre and hung with the limbs of enemies or sacrifices.

Near the centre of the circle was a post supposedly for a viewing platform from which an observer could look towards circle-posts marking sunrise at midsummer, midwinter and the equinoxes. In the hole of the midwinter post there was a drinking pot with a sun-symbol on it. As there also seemed to be alignments on the bright star Capella (Alpha Aurigae) Wittry concluded that the circles may have been used 'as sun-calendars where observations of the solstices and equinoxes served to define a tropical year'.

The radius of this second ring was about 62.5 metres measured in sixty units of the 'Cahokian Yard' of 1.04 metres. This was so close to the 'Standard Teotihuacán Unit' of 1.06 metres with which the great Mexican urban and ceremonial centre was laid out that it is likely that Cahokia had links with this ancient Meso-American city explaining how the astronomical knowledge implicit in the timber circles could have been derived from the people of Teotihuacán with their pyramids of the Sun and Moon. Harriet Smith who excavated the Murdock Mound at Cahokia decided, after painstaking analysis, that its ceremonial structures all conformed to a 'module' of five metres (16½ feet), a quarter of the twenty-metre unit that James Marshall, a civil engineer, had deduced at Teotihuacán. Smith added that measurements from forty-two buildings 'prove that pre-Columbian architecture at twelve Mexican sites, from Olmecs to Aztecs, was based on the 16½ foot module'.[13] In passing, one has to point out that such a unit is within a finger-length of six of Alexander Thom's Megalithic Yards and that the radius of Circle 2 is very close indeed to seventy-five Megalithic Yards or thirty Megalithic Rods. Very few people, despite Blacket and his Red Indian Stonehenge-builders, would believe there were any direct connections between an Illinois settlement that was flourishing at the time of the

Norman Conquest and prehistoric British stone circles separated from Cahokia by three thousand years and four thousand miles of Atlantic Ocean. Similarities in the 'yardsticks' of Mesopotamia, Egypt and other civilisations equally do not have to be the result of emigrating surveyors and astronomer–priests.[14] Nor does the illusory 'Megalithic Yard'. Local units of body-measurements seem a simpler answer.

The intricate trade-systems, the timber rings, the funerary ceremonies of the Mississippian Temple Mound cultures did not signify a peaceful existence for the Woodland Indians. After a dark age of over two centuries following the decline of the Hopewell communities there came a period of disturbance. Teotihuacán in Mexico was sacked around AD 700 and a restless movement of population commenced, 'the beginning of a widespread wave of disruption and upheaval that would engulf most of Meso-America', and ultimately it reached northwards into the Ohio and Mississippi valleys where defended centres like Cahokia were formed, suggesting they were set up in hostile territories. 'Many large Mississippian towns seem to have been military as well as commercial centres; the city-states they controlled may have been established by bands of conquering warriors who managed to reduce the local population to serfdom.'[15]

For similar reasons it could have been in alarm at the encroachment of tribes from Salisbury Plain that people at Avebury discontinued work on a third ring and instead began raising an earthwork around the settlement with its two stone circles. Grooved Ware communities certainly were close. At Marden only seven miles away they built an enormous horseshoe-shaped enclosure near the River Avon on an area once occupied by Windmill Hill natives but now taken over by the newcomers whose pottery littered the ditch bottom. Today the tree-covered bank with its facing of sandstone blocks is hardly noticeable but to prehistoric watchers from the downs it must have seemed strong and menacingly near. Its clumsily irregular outline followed the contours much as Avebury's would, surrounding the Hatfield Barrow in an area even bigger than Durrington Walls. In the limited excavations of 1966–7 traces of a large round timber hut were found like others from Durrington where thirty-five have been recorded and it is believed that 'both enclosures were constructed at the same time for similar purposes by people sharing closely comparable cultural traditions'.[16] There was one difference. Whereas earthworks in southern Wessex had ritual henges nearby: Mount Pleasant with Maumbury Rings, Knowlton earthwork and henge, Durrington and Stonehenge; Grooved Ware in every excavated site, no henge is known in the vicinity of Marden. The Hatfield Barrow near its centre may have been the focus of ceremonies in this fortified settlement.

In America the painter George Catlin visited a Mandan village by a river-bank in North Dakota, a timber palisade over five metres high guarding the prairie side. Like Marden it had an inner ditch. 'Running along inside the stockade was a three foot ditch, which further screened their bodies from the view and weapons of attacking enemies.' Here also were round dwellings, timber lodges up to twenty metres across, crowding together around a large circular space at the centre of the village where the people performed their annual religious rites, the Bull Dance and Buffalo Dance, that were expected to make the migrating herds come close enough to the village to be hunted.

170

Catlin strikingly described the place, the medicine- and scalp-poles waving in the wind, buffalo skulls and canoes stacked on the roofs, the green background of the prairie, the chief and his warriors, dogs barking, women cutting out skins, groups chattering by the lodges, people sleeping in the sun. 'The living, in everything, carry an air of intractable wildness about them, and the dead are not buried but dried upon scaffolds.'[17] It is necessary in the mind to reinhabit the deserted, grass-spread emptiness of the Wessex earthworks with bustle and noise and to remind ourselves that here also were huts built by people whose herds grazed the downs up to the dark forests separating their homeland from the hostile lands of their neighbours. Even at Avebury, perhaps the most powerful and densely populated of all the regions, the restlessness of the time was sufficient to cause the people to mark out a roughly circular compound, dig the great ditch, heap up the bank and finally erect the Outer Circle some of whose stones are still standing.

So much has been written about the 'design' of Avebury and the significance of its eccentric shape that it must be stated that there is in fact nothing remarkable about it. All these earthworks were irregular. Knowlton is a deformed ring. Waulud's Bank, described as semi-circular, is well out of true at its south-east. Mount Pleasant resembled a distorted egg. Marden's builders never decided if they were laying out an oval or a rectangle. Durrington Walls looked like a bicycle wheel that had crashed into a railway track.[18] Considering the tools and the working methods of the period as well as the length of time it took to complete these huge structures such misshapen results were inevitable. By tradition their perimeter ditches were dug in segments by individual families or work-gangs whose variable trenches were thinner, longer, deeper, straighter or more crooked as the workers wished, a medley of sections that buckled together like a line of derailed coal-trucks. This was the way that Windmill Hill was dug. It was the way that Stonehenge's ditch was dug and it was one reason for the tortuous plan of Avebury.

Here the people set out an approximate circle from a centre to the east of the dome's highest point. As the two megalithic rings already stood here it is likely that the circumference was staked out from a series of radial offsets additionally hindered by the probable obstruction of huts and lodges scattered haphazardly around the rings. Hardly any of the ground between the stone circles and the ditch has been excavated so that it is still not known whether there was a village here although the broken pottery and animal bones indicate that people did occupy the area. The presence of a settlement would explain both why the earthwork was built here and also why it was so big. Despite their size the two circles take up less than one-sixth of the central plateau's twenty-four acres or ten hectares leaving what are now deserts of grassy field but what may have been land for thatched huts, barns, granaries and cattle-stalls.[19] At every one of the excavated earthworks similar to Avebury wooden buildings have been located: at Durrington Walls, at Marden, at Meldon Bridge, at Mount Pleasant, even at Waulud's Bank where a little hut stood near the bank. The most likely situation for houses at Avebury would have been at the drier north-eastern side, the very area where the earthwork is most irregular.

Avoiding these obstacles gangs gouged out interlocking trenches along the perimeter, dumping the turf and topsoil and chalk untidily along a ring far outside the ditch to make a low bank already wavering and not truly circular. An initial line

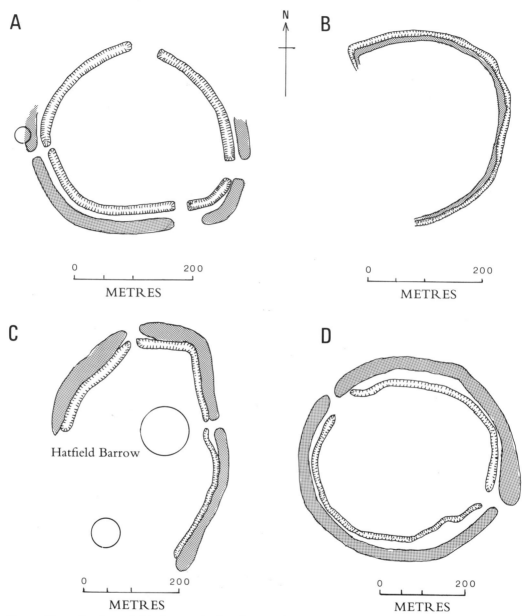

Fig. 9. Great Earthwork Enclosures in Southern Britain.
(A) Mount Pleasant, Dorset; (B) Waulud's Bank, Berkshire; (C) Marden, Wiltshire;
(D) Durrington Walls, Wiltshire.

like this was a guide when the subsequent massive earthwork was constructed, and it must have been this bank, hurriedly thrown up, that was used defensively for years until the larger one was finished. The technique was of great antiquity. It had been used to lay out the spines of long burial mounds, it was used by the builders of Windmill Hill's triple banks, and a small marker-bank lay under the great rampart of Maumbury Rings henge. As with their segmented ditches the natives who put up Avebury's bank followed ancient customs.

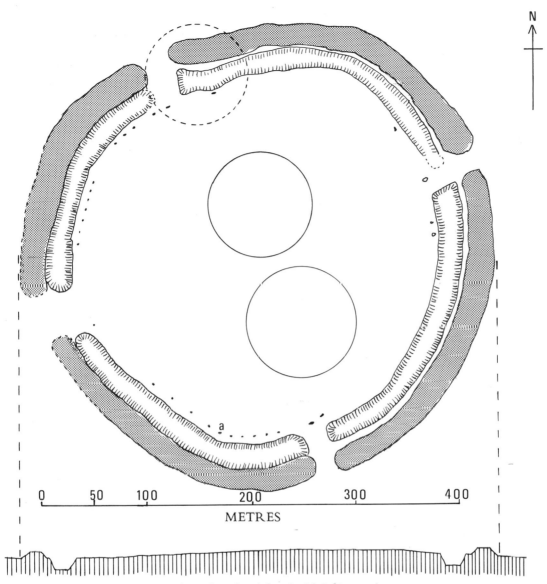

Fig. 10. Plan of Avebury's earthwork today (after Smith I. F., 1965).
The North and South Circles are shown as continuous rings. The position of the intended third circle is shown by a broken ring. Surviving stones of the Outer Circle have been marked in. The Barber's Stone is the sarsen lettered 'a'.

Four gaps were left for entrances, two on the north-north-west–south-south-east axis but well to the west of the highest point so that the surveyors could see between the stones of the circles, two others at right-angles to the axis on a line that passed between the rings. Tall posts could have been used as sighting-devices during these preliminaries, and one hole for a thick and presumably high pole was discovered in the South Entrance. Work on the terminals of the great ditch may have begun at these entrances leaving causeways some fifteen metres wide, almost exactly nine

75. A Neolithic tool-kit. An antler pick, ox shoulderblade and wickerwork basket containing small lumps of chalk.

body-fathoms, once again a multiple of three.[20] Evidently these approaches to Avebury were designed to be impressive. The bank was higher here than anywhere else. The causeways were not merely undug stretches of chalk but were scarped out to be lower than ground level and so make the bank ends appear more overwhelming to the visitor. The ditch was deeper here. The stones of the Kennet Avenue increased in height as they neared the South Entrance. Even today the greatest sarsens of the Outer Circle stand awesomely at the North and South Entrances with another monster lying prostrate by the eastern causeway. Some were placed where they would block a clear view into the enclosure. Although eighteenth- and nineteenth-century alterations to the southern bank, cutting back on the west, adding on the east, have shifted the South Entrance over ten metres to the west it is still possible to observe how Stone 1, the broad Devil's Chair, prevented a direct sight of the interior and this deliberate obstruction was probably true of the other entrances as though the wonders inside Avebury were not to be seen casually.[21]

The emphasis placed upon them suggests that it was these four terminals that were put up first, the marker ditch quarried away and the first bank so quickly covered with rubble that grass had no time to grow on it. The rest of the enclosure must have taken a very long time indeed. Once the turf and earth had been removed from the top of the new ditch the labour became increasingly arduous. The upper layers of rotted chalk had to be prised out, men pushing the prongs of antler picks into the fissures, levering, pulling until the chalk broke and someone could shovel the lumps away, scraping them with a spade or an ox's shoulderblade into a wickerwork pannier that other people, men and women, would haul up, across the wide span of the ditch, across the trampled grass to the sprawling dust-clouded tips of the rising bank. How long it all took can only be conjectured although there are some facts to guide our judgement.

The four ditch-quadrants have a total length of about 1043 metres. The ditch is now twenty to twenty-four metres wide but once it was much narrower, no more than perhaps twelve to fifteen metres with precipitous sides dropping to a bottom less than half the width of the top. Some 94,000 cubic metres of chalk had to be quarried from these ditches and carried over a flat space of variable width before they could be unloaded onto the bank twenty-seven metres wide at its base and, ultimately, six metres or so high. These are average dimensions but they illustrate the compulsive efforts of the people because however the numbers are computed the results show that the building of Avebury took many long and difficult years.

There are several methods for assessing the length of time taken to build the earthwork, not always giving the same answer. Richard Atkinson devised a formula for calculating the man-hours involved in the construction of such an earthwork.

$$\text{Man-hours} = \frac{\text{volume of cubic feet of chalk } (120 + 8L + 2F)}{1000},$$

L being the average height in Imperial Feet that the material had to be lifted, F being the average distance for it to be carried. For Avebury the formula reads:

$$\text{Man-hours} = \frac{3,300,000 \text{ cubic feet } (120 + 8 \times 25 + 2 \times 68)}{1000},$$

about 1,500,000 man-hours. Taking as utterly arbitrary figures a work-force of 250 people labouring ten hours a day for two autumn months Avebury would have taken ten years to complete. Then the task of erecting the Outer Circle could have begun.

Using a different analysis Ashbee and Cornwall concluded that a prehistoric worker might have shifted five hundredweight of chalk in an hour. Avebury's 165,000 tons could have been moved by one hundred full-time labourers in $1\frac{3}{4}$ years or by the same number of people working only sixty days a year in eleven years. With modern tools a gang of four—a pickman, a shoveller and two barrowmen—could dig out a cubic yard or 0.77 cubic metre of virgin chalk in an hour but using primitive tools they would take half as long again. Man-hours = 4 men $\times \frac{3}{2}$ (for the primitive work-rate) $\times$ (circumference of the earthwork in Imperial Feet $\times$ width

$\times$ depth of the ditch), or $4 \times \frac{3}{2} \times 3422 \times 33 \times 30 = 752,840$ hours. Taking the same arbitrary criteria this would mean that 250 people had to work for over twenty years to build Avebury's earthwork alone.[22]

The variables are so indeterminate that it is valueless to speculate further. It is obvious that the span of time involved is enormous and it explains why grass was growing thickly on parts of the marker-bank before it was encapsulated inside the final rampart. In the Meux excavations of 1894 the supervisor recorded a turf-line nine centimetres thick on this internal bank, a depth of topsoil that must have taken at least twenty years, and probably longer, to accumulate, confirming how long the project took. The section drawn by Gray of his bank-cutting in 1914 shows no sign of this inner bank, presumably because being nearer the South Entrance it was buried before turf could form.[23]

Perhaps starting on the opposing north-east and south-west quadrants and working in adjoining segments up to fifty-seven metres long up to a dozen gangs hacked and dug downwards, the sides of the ditch always narrowing but remaining steep, down into the unweathered chalk as hard and resistant as rock, cracking it with fire that scorched the antler picks, smashing it with flint hammers and mauls, smoothing the sides and the bottom of the ditch, tramping out pathways to the places where baskets were heaved up on ropes that scoured channels along the rim, passing the loads beyond an erratic chalk-block wall that prevented the rubble slipping back into the ditch, up the chalk tips, upending the baskets in a cascade of chalk and powder and dust along the undulations of the bank.

At one time it was thought that Beaker people were the architects of Avebury but this has been disproved. Underneath the bank and on the floor of the ditch where any possessions of the builders would have dropped there were no Beaker remains at all, only local material, a few pieces of Windmill Hill and Grooved Ware pottery, many flint tools and flakes including a fine slicing arrowhead, and a lot of Peterborough sherds, mostly plain but a couple with the typical birdbone impressions favoured by these Late Neolithic settlers showing that this great earthwork was constructed by people already living on the Marlborough Downs, a mixture of the original natives and later groups from eastern England that had introduced new forms of monuments and cults into the region.

From the middle of the Neolithic onwards there were bigger structures here than anywhere else. West Kennet and East Kennet were the largest chambered tombs in southern England. Windmill Hill was the largest causewayed camp. Silbury Hill, inspired by different customs, was still the largest man-made mound in Europe. Avebury itself was built by a people driven by megalomania to create a colossal centre where their leaders lived and which would be used by everyone for their communal ceremonies. It was the focus of their private world. The earthwork did not cover an excessive acreage maybe because if it were to be kept reasonably level it could not be extended southwards where the land rose sharply or to east and west where it fell. But the ditch, deep and steep enough to kill any person or animal that tumbled into it, far exceeded the simple demands of a barrier. Its rivals like Marden or Durrington Walls had nothing like its depth. Only the ritual pits at Maumbury

Rings could vie with it showing what overweening zeal had gone into its digging.[24]

The bank, of course, was the ditch in reverse, a core of turves from the first stripping of grass, then layers of fine weathered chalk, then thick cappings of rough chalk blocks from the lowest parts of the ditch poured onto the rippling heaps of rubble whose undulations even infillings of chalk could not obliterate. Some Neolithic earthen long barrows had scalloped profiles for the same reason, Holdenhurst in Hampshire having 'been built round a series of roughly conical dumps of top-soil piled along its axis and covered by gravel',[25] and it was a trait particularly noticeable in some Lincolnshire long barrows like Deadman's Graves where the serpentine humps were never filled in. It shows once again how traditional the building methods used at Avebury were.

One by one the vast sections of the ditch were done, the crude baulks between the sections hacked down and the last loads of rubble dropped onto the bank. The antler picks used in these final stages were laid along the floor of the ditch just as at Durrington Walls where over fifty were piled up near the ditch-end. 'It would have been a very human reaction to throw one's implements into a heap in the relief of having completed such a major undertaking'[26] but this is perhaps too modern an interpretation. In cutting after cutting Gray found antler picks along the bottom of Avebury's ditch, nine in Cutting I 'capable of considerable repair', two in II as well as three ox shoulder-blades, three picks and a rake in VIII, and in Cutting IX by the South Entrance thirty more picks.[27] The prongs or tines of some of these 'bore marks of fire' caused when they were hammered into burned chalk. It is quite likely that these tools that had been employed in desecrating the earth were now being reverently given to her when their work was done. It was a gift rather than a throwing-away. It will be recalled that a cache of picks was placed near the top of the Marlborough Mound and that there was another in the bank of Avebury itself where 'below the crest of the bank a curious box-like structure formed of chalk blocks was discovered which contained twenty deer horn picks of large size, all worn down by use, the tines almost gone'.[28] To the primitive mind it may have seemed that for as long as the tools that had created the Mound and Avebury's bank were combined with the monuments the structures would stand. Offerings of antler picks would keep the ditch sharp and clean.

If that was the expectation it was disappointed. Exposed to wind and rain, the soft upper layers of chalk open to frost, winter by winter the shoulders of the ditch cracked. Lumps of turf, soil and chalk dropped down and according to Gray, who had actually witnessed such weathering at an excavated long barrow, within ten years Avebury's ditch would have had three metres of rubble in it, more still at the sides, and its once-steep profile would have become funnel-shaped with a vertical stem and an ever-widening mouth.[29] It was never cleared out.

If the north-east and south-west quadrants were indeed built first then it is likely that the edges of their ditches were crumbled and creviced long before the other arcs were finished. Here and there the bank had settled, creeping over the flat space that separated it from the ditch, or sinking into even more lumpish bumps. Avebury was not the world's best-constructed monument.

76. The eastern sector of bank at Avebury showing its undulating crest.

Despite its height the unevenness of the chalk-white bank argues against the popular idea that it was once a grandstand where the populace watched the liturgies of their priests inside the stone circles. 'While the vallum all around was cover'd with spectators, it form'd a most noble amphitheater, and had an appearance extremely august.'[30] For once Stukeley was not perceptive. A person squatting on the rubbly bank would have seen very little of the activities inside either ring. The stone circles were well over a hundred metres away and their wide sarsens obscured most of the interiors. Moreover, because Avebury is so much higher at its centre it is not always possible to see into the circles, especially where the bank is lowest. At the north-west only the very tops of the tall Cove stones are visible even from the crest of the bank, and nothing at all can be seen from lower down. Rickman calculated that along the bank's top 'might be seated 2,400 persons' and that with twenty tiers of people neatly disposed around the arena Avebury could accommodate an audience of 48,000, 'about half the number, I believe', who 'might be seated in the . . . Colosseum'.[31]

As such a number of people may have comprised the entire population of western Europe and as three-quarters of them, having travelled hundreds of miles, would have been given seats too low down to see 'the annual festival at Midsummer' Rickman's theory must be rejected. To his credit the combative Fergusson realised Avebury was too big to be meant as an auditorium and commented that if half a million people could be accommodated in the enclosure 'at least five times that of St. Peter's at Rome ... where should such a multitude as this come from?'[32] Unfortunately he was so obsessed with his conviction that Avebury was the burial-place of King Arthur's warriors that he never considered an alternative, that vanished huts and cattle had once filled the space and that the bank was only a barrier and a defence, the stone circles being the places where ceremonies were held.

Without knowing exactly how many workers were involved or how long this project took the sequence of constructional phases at Avebury remains indefinite but there is some evidence that it was after the ditch and bank were completed that the stones of the Outer Circle were dragged through the entrances and erected along the perimeter of the already decaying ditch in a ring that conformed to its irregularities.

If this is correct then Professor Alexander Thom's hypothesis about the design of this Outer Circle is wrong. He has claimed that the ring was mathematically planned by erudite people employing a yardstick of precisely 0.829 metre to set out a right-angle triangle (ABC) around the centre of Avebury with sides measuring 75, 100 and 125 Megalithic Yards. This was used as the design-base for the complicated shape of the outer ring which was not round like the North and South Circles but was an extraordinary mixture of curves, flattened arcs and sharp angles, 'the only ring known to us which consists of circular arcs meeting at an angle instead of running smoothly into one another. It has thus what might be called corners.'[33] To achieve this complexity several long arcs had to be drawn, the two most remarkable each being 622 metres long. One swung from the north-east outside Avebury, climbed

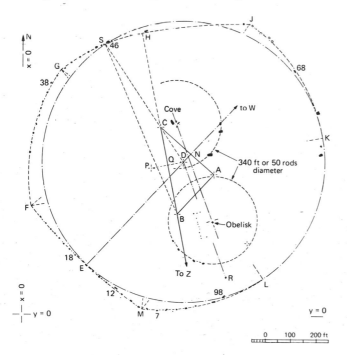

77. The hypothetical geometry of Avebury. (From: A. Thom, 1967). One long arc is supposed to have extended from E out to W 622 metres away. The other arc ran from H, through B, to Z on the lower slopes of Waden Hill a third of a mile away.

over its centre and ended a third of a mile away on the quadrant where the Barber's Stone now stands, that stone incidentally being misplaced by over a metre. The other line started on the high ground to the south-south-east, nearly ten metres above Avebury, and stretched over the same long distance to Stone 50 (H) at the east of the North Entrance.

The asymmetrical outline of the shape is not convincing because it is neither elegant nor explicable in terms of usefulness but Thom, who has plotted it with exceptional care, said that 'the accuracy with which the ring has been set out is clearly remarkable; the stones are all close to the arcs'. It must be added that he was unable to provide any good explanation of why such an involved plan, which 'probably took years of trial and error', should ever have been chosen.[34]

Certainly not all mathematicians and statisticians have accepted it.[35] For the lay reader, uncomfortable in the mystery of higher mathematics, one may simply observe that as the shape of Avebury has no rational explanation in geometrical terms a more likely solution is that the builders just followed the eccentric layout of the ditch.

All this is a long way from Stukeley's comment that Avebury was built 'with a sufficient, tho' not a mathematical exactness' but the sentiments are the same. Other writers, by no means unsympathetic to Thom, have expressed doubts. Wood, who believes in the geometrical and astronomical abilities of 'Megalithic Man', has written, 'It is difficult to accept that there was such a subtle geometrical shape at a time when non-circular rings had hardly begun to evolve. Some archaeologists suspect that Avebury has no systematic layout and the complex interpretation is the result of trying to impose order where none exists.'[36]

Suspicions, of course, are not enough. Neither is prejudice. Although the debate is important because it is fundamental to our beliefs about the abilities and the intentions of the prehistoric people who built and used stone circles its resolution can only come from dispassionately examined evidence. Thom's design seems impracticable not because his arithmetic was wrong—although it may be—but because the Outer Circle could not have been built in the way he imagined. Referring to the two inordinately long radii he wrote, 'the centres for the flat arcs were outside the bank and ditch. It thus seems *likely* that the ring was laid out before the bank and ditch were constructed', the long arcs set out not with an impractical rope but by 'two long rods lifted over one another alternately.[37] It is true that a radial rope nearly half a mile long would have sagged and bent too much for any accuracy but Thom's alternative of leapfrogging rods is not much better. It is incomprehensible how even a genius could measure out hundreds of metres in this way over rough ground from the outer point to Stone 16 with an error of only three centimetres, less than the breadth of two fingers.

Even if such precision were attainable there remains the awkward probability that the bank was standing before the Outer Circle was put up, making it virtually impossible to lay out these long arcs. It is a truism that before there was a ditch it would not have mattered to the builders from which side they erected the sarsens and it is significant that of the eighteen stoneholes where ramps or supporting stakeholes have been recognised 'only Stone 44 appears to have been put up from the ditch side. The remainder had been put up from the front or from a position on the circumference of the circle.'[38] Such consistency demands explanation and the most likely one is that because the ditch did exist it was unnecessarily difficult and dangerous to raise the stones from that side. Even Stone 44 was no exception. This lumpish pillar was the only one that could be hauled upright from the causeway of the North Entrance where the ditch ended. Stone 41, moreover, to the south-west of the Swindon Stone, actually rested on a packing of chalk rubble that had probably been quarried from the ditch indicating that this stone, at least, was later than the earthwork. The positions of the other standing stones, some ten metres in from the rim of the ditch, conformed to its meanderings suggesting that the ditch was there first.

It follows that the bank, composed of ditch material, was also there, and the evidence for the starting of a third stone circle is relevant. One of its stoneholes must have preceded the erection of the Swindon Stone at the North Entrance, demonstrating that the Outer Circle was a secondary feature. So were the bank and ditch because the circumference of the proposed third circle lay under them. The probability, therefore, is that the inner rings of Avebury were the first to be built, occupying land over which it would have been extraordinarily hard to lay out Thom's hypothetical arcs and triangles.

The stones of the Outer Circle were lifted and supported in the same way as those of the smaller rings. The pillars at the middle of the quadrants were relatively little, no more than ten or twelve tons in bulk, but the giants at the entrances were incredible. Two that survive by the south causeway are each big enough to be house walls, metres-thick slabs that are amongst the grossest, most back-breaking megaliths ever heaved upright in prehistoric Britain. One facing the causeway, with a natural ledge like a seat, the background of a million family snapshots, is known as the Devil's Chair. Aubrey mentions another great stone here which 'fell down in Autumn 1684, and broke in two, or three pieces: it stood but two feet deep in the earth'.

At the North Entrance the Swindon Stone weighs over sixty tons and was so heavy that its pointed base pierced half a metre through the bottom of its prepared hole. Known also as the Diamond Stone it is reputed to cross the road when the church clock strikes midnight, perhaps searching for its lost partner 'of a most enormous bulk, fell down and broke in the fall. It measur'd full 22 feet long . . . we saw three wooden wedges driven into it, in order to break it to pieces.'[39] It may have been this sarsen that Stephen Hales described, 'w[ch] is broken in halves is in breadth 11 feet 8 inches, in thickness 6 feet 8 inches, its length 16 feet 8 inches, equal to 1295 cubick feet'.[40] This would make its weight almost ninety tons, nearly twice as heavy as the biggest of the trilithon pillars at Stonehenge, and even allowing for exaggeration or miscalculation the sarsen at Avebury must have been almost impossibly unwieldy. Dragging it from the downs and manipulating it upwards must have demanded not scores but hundreds upon hundreds of people straining upon the timbers and ropes.

Stukeley noticed that the builders 'set the largest and handsomest stones in the more conspicuous part of the temple' but added perspicaciously that the Outer

78. The weathered outer face of the Devil's Chair.

Circle and the bank and ditch were 'not properly the temple' but only its precinct. 'There are strictly, within this great compass, two temples of like form and dimensions.'[41] Around them, enclosing them in the most imposing stone circle in the whole of the British Isles the people raised stone after stone, dragging dozens of sarsens to Avebury, spacing them irregularly alongside the ditch. Altogether there were about ninety-nine or a hundred stones in the ring,[42] years of labour for the fanatical peasants that put them up. They formed a protective barrier around the inner rings but it was still only inside the North and South Circles that ceremonies were performed.

It is difficult for us to comprehend the generations of time taken in the construction of these monuments, over a hundred years between the ditch being started and the last stone of the Outer Circle being put up, four or five lifetimes or more, older people telling vague stories of an ancestor who had a vision of this place. Over the long years new ideas were introduced. New people drifted in. From the east came small parties of Beaker folk, foreigners from the continent, perhaps trading or preaching but too few to have much influence when they first arrived.

In some ways the Beaker people are the most famous of all British prehistoric cultures, yet surprisingly little is known about their way of life. Even the physique of

79. The two great stones at the South Entrance. The Devil's Chair is on the right.

these supposedly thickset, round–headed people, very unlike the slight, lithe natives, has been questioned. Childe visualised them as invaders, warriors who 'eventually established throughout the occupied territories of Great Britain and even Ireland a degree of cultural uniformity never previously achieved'. Jacquetta Hawkes described them as 'energetic conquerors ruthlessly dispossessing the Neolithic communities of their best pastures, and also no doubt of their herds, and sometimes of their women'. Such plundering rapists seem unrelated to Clarke's peasant farmers and fishermen living on 'land snails, pine nuts, whelks, limpets, oysters, crabs, seafish and sea birds'. Beaker people have been called missionaries, traders 'connected with the introduction of metallurgy into western Europe', gypsies, even the architects of the first stone circles although this is now known to be untrue. But they could have introduced cult practices that left no tangible evidence behind, much as the Ghost Dance of the Plains Indians with its ceaseless dancing and visions would be undetectable archaeologically, and this might explain their apparent power in Britain. Living in dispersed settlements of mixed farmers, like cultural chameleons they merged into any locality and only their pots distinguished them from the natives.[43]

One intriguing theory is that they were bee-keepers or, at the least, people who

183

knew that honey could be converted into strong drink. Before the Romans brought hops into Britain various forms of wheaten beer were known but the most common intoxicating drink was mead, made from honey, and some beaker pots from the continent have traces of lime-honey in them. The fragrant, small-leaved lime trees, *Tilia cordata*, once widespread along the streams and valleys of lowland England, attracted bees by their aromatic honey-dew. So did the tall, creamy flowers of meadowsweet. Honey had long been known for its sweetening qualities and many hives must have been robbed to obtain it. Once a man drained the honeycombs he could make alcohol in the form of mead.

Mead is a drink that everybody has heard of but few know much about. Ancient mead was much more intoxicating than wine. Of the doomed sixth-century AD warriors of the *Gododdin* it was said that 'short-lived they were, drunk over the clarified mead'. A hundred years ago Harriet Goodman knew how to make it properly. 'Drain the honey out of a honeycomb. Cover the comb in water in an earthen vessel. Let it stand a week or ten days. Strain. Add 1 oz. of two spices— ginger and cloves, or cinnamon and cloves, to a gallon. Boil it till the flavour is obtained, let it get nearly cold and ferment it.' Mrs Osmonde tried the result and remarked, 'The drinks made by old Mrs. Goodman were all very good . . . but the mead and ale were too strong for me.' Honey with its high content of wild yeast fermented readily and only needed the addition of flavouring to turn it into a pleasant but potent drink. Although spices were unavailable in prehistoric Britain there were several herbs that were just as good.[44] Beaker people knew this. One of their short-necked pots with a burial in Scotland contained the sediment of lime-honey mixed with meadowsweet that would have given the mead 'an agreeable taste and smell'. Bog myrtle had the same effect. One can easily imagine how the knowledge of such a mystery would have made the first Beaker people welcome additions to the eager, if heavy-headed, families of the Marlborough Downs.[45]

When the newcomers arrived they probably gazed in wonderment at stone monuments such as they had never seen before. Fragments of their squat, finely textured vessels have been found in the tops of some stoneholes implying that they helped in the later stages of building. Other sherds fell into the partly filled ditch. Avebury continued to be altered. A stone was added inside the south-west part of the South Circle on a line between the Obelisk and the wide V-topped Stone 103. Two of Stukeley's drawings show it was a wide sarsen half the height of the notched stone behind it. Stukeley thought it was part of a wrecked inner ring. This was not so, nor is any astronomical purpose obvious. But it was put up long after the other pillars of this ring because deep down in one of its stakeholes were several sherds of a short-necked beaker made as late as 2200 BC, at least four hundred years after the first circles were erected.[46]

Another addition to the South Circle was a mysterious row of sarsens to the west of the Obelisk on the same north-north-west to south-south-east axis as the outlying stone and the North and South Entrances. There were twelve of these smallish stones in a line thirty-one metres long, carefully laid out from sighting-posts at either end. Other stones extended eastwards from the north and south corners but as the area on the other side of the Obelisk has not been investigated it is not known if there was a duplicate setting there. Gray discovered what may have been a similar line to the east of the North Circle's Cove. Rectangular settings are known in several other 'ritual' monuments and the Z-Stones as they are known may have been a representation of the former mortuary enclosures in which dead bodies were laid. The stones were erected long after the building of the South Circle and were supported not by the normal sarsen packing-stones but by blocks of chalk from the lower parts of the ditch. The same is true of a perforated sarsen, the Ring Stone, which was substituted

80. A 'European' beaker (19 centimetres high). This elegant pot came from the filled-in north-west chamber of West Kennet chambered tomb.

81. The Z-Stones from the south. The taller concrete pyramid on the right shows where the Obelisk once stood.

for the large outlying stone to the south-south-east of the circle. As the fresh stone was smaller the original pit was partly filled with sarsens and chalk lumps 'in order to display more prominently some feature it possessed, presumably the perforation'.[47] Stukeley who imagined Druids performing sacrifices at Avebury thought the hole in the stone was 'design'd to fasten the victim, in order for slaying it'. Although he saw the Ring Stone as late as 1724 it was gone by the time of Crocker's survey in 1812, smashed by the stone-breakers. Its shapeless stump was found in 1939 alongside its burning-pit, and it now slumps on the grass as meaningless as a melted snowman.

To this time must belong Avebury's avenues. These parallel rows of stones winding up to the enclosure were very like the earthen banked passages, sometimes several miles long, that led to the circular earthworks of the Hopewell Indians, some of them connecting one ceremonial centre with another just as a paved way joined two of the Hurlers stone circles on Bodmin Moor in Britain. Other lines of stones in the British Isles were often built to connect stone circles with water, a river or the sea, and this may have been intended at Avebury where the Kennet Avenue passed very close to the headwaters of the present river. Water being so vital to life it has been an essential part of many religions although, like dancing or prayer, it leaves nothing for the archaeologist to find and its use can only be inferred.

The Beckhampton and Kennet Avenues must have been built at the time when the bank and ditch were almost finished because several of the stones were supported by blocks of Lower Chalk from Avebury's ditch. They have been badly treated. Only one of perhaps two hundred sarsens remains in the Beckhampton Avenue. Even Stukeley saw only its wreckage although 'Mr. Smith, living here, inform'd me, that when he was a schoolboy, the Kennet Avenue was entire from end to end.' John Aubrey certainly saw more, as his plan 'The whole view of Aubury with the Walke, and the lesser Temple appendant to it' shows, and even though several stones were missing around the hamlet of Kennet it is clear from his words that Aubrey believed there had been a continuous avenue from the Sanctuary to Avebury a mile and a half away, 'much about the distance of a noble walke of trees of that length; and very probable this walke was made use of for Processions', a hundred or more pairs of stones 'pitcht on end, about seven feet high'.[48]

Stukeley found only seventy-two stones and had to search out the course of the avenue. 'I was very careful in tracing it out, knew the distinct number of each stone remaining, and where every one stood that was wanting; which often surpriz'd the country people, who remembered them left on the ground or standing, and told me who carried them away. Many of the farmers made deep holes, and buried them in the ground.'[49]

A drawing in his *Abury* shows the ruined Sanctuary, the broken line of the Kennet Avenue leading downhill towards the houses of Kennet and, beyond them, along the lane to Avebury, several pairs of stones where none now stand. Today fewer than half the stones Stukeley saw survive. Yet fieldwork, the reminiscences of elderly farmers, Stukeley's notes, and excavations, mainly those of Keiller and Piggott, have revealed the course of both avenues even if the place where the Beckhampton stones terminated is still uncertain.[50]

82. Stukeley in the ruins of the Sanctuary.

Prospect of the Temple on Overton Hill. 8 July 1725.

TAB. XXI
P.40

The Hakpen, or head of the Snake, in ruins.

Like the ditch and bank the Kennet Avenue was built probably by independent work-gangs whose stretches varied from ninety to 124 metres according to the latest survey,[51] each straightish section kinking onto the next. Trees may still have been growing along the valley between Waden Hill and the Ridgeway, dark oaks at the foot of the downs and, higher to the west, hazels and blackthorns scattered along the edges of the woodland where the avenue passed.

Perhaps because they were so numerous the stones were not very big. Few of them weighed more than seven or eight tons and, when standing, did not dwarf the people as those in the circles did. Spaced fairly regularly and quite constantly some fifteen metres apart the stones were arranged in pairs, pillar opposite diamond, Type A alternating with Type B along each side, the choice of shapes so obvious that the selection and positioning was undoubtedly deliberate. Hundreds of sarsens were needed for the two avenues, still more years of work for a society that had no memory of a time when stones were not being dragged here.

Stukeley suggested that the avenues were composed in imitations of a snake. 'The circle meant the supreme fountain of all being, the father; the serpent, that divine emanation from him which was called the son', the entire Avebury complex being a landscaped representation of the Trinity.[52] A modern and even more eccentric fantasy claimed the pillars and lozenges were alternately positively and negatively charged with electricity by the movement of prehistoric dancers threading in between the stones, the generated current acting as sacred semen to fertilise the crops.[53] If readers find it incredible that anyone could accept such nonsense they have a pleasantly high regard for other people's scepticism. After a recent television serial about Avebury in which children who touched the sarsens disappeared the Department of the Environment custodians were often asked by anxious parents if it was safe for boys and girls to feel the stones.

Sir Norman Lockyer believed the avenues were astronomical instruments, set out long before Avebury's bank because that was too high for the orientations.[54] Recently Michael Dames has proposed that 'the avenue represents a snake on its way from hibernation in the Sanctuary to copulation in the henge' because 'the swelling life-force of human libido and vegetable spring found classic embodiment in the serpent form'.[55] That the figure of this aroused and squirming snake was laid out in straight, lifeless segments is not mentioned. Nor are many other un-writhing avenues in the British Isles like the exactly straight one at Callanish. Stukeley did at least refuse to accept Callanish as straight, denouncing Edward Lhwyd, whose plan he believed it to be, as 'a very bad designer . . . He did not discern the curve of it',[56] which was not surprising.

The Kennet Avenue which, as Aubrey suggested, was surely a processional way, does wander from side to side but this may mean no more than that its builders followed the lie of the land, its course almost duplicating that of the present Winterbourne stream on the other side of Waden Hill meandering down its valley towards Silbury Hill. The avenue may also have been directed towards ancient structures that were to be integrated with it just as the Beckhampton Cove was incorporated into the avenue there. Whether there was a Cove anywhere on the Kennet Avenue is questionable but the presence of an area of ritual activity seems

83. The Kennet Avenue from the north, looking away from Avebury. The 'occupation' area was where the five concrete markers on the right now stand.

quite certain because about half a mile south of Avebury the avenue passed through what the excavators first thought was an occupation site but which, from its scattered sherds, pits and holes, probably had a religious significance.

This ill-defined area lies between the sixth and tenth pairs of stones from where the Kennet Avenue ends today, between stones 33a and b, and 27a and b, the western line of pillars being called 'a', the eastern 'b'. Nothing can be seen but the spot was unusual in that there was a thick layer of Coombe Rock here overlying the chalk and the ground was weirdly pitted with clay-filled hollows and solution holes, natural shafts that tapered down towards the chalk, places where offerings to the earth could be made.

Here they brought the same gatherings of 'dead' material that has been noticed from some round barrows. Hundreds upon hundreds of flint flakes lay near the pits and holes, not from tools made on the spot but waste chippings that the men and women had deliberately collected and carried to this place from their homes. There were flint scrapers, chisel-ended arrowheads, awls, knives. Hundreds of broken, weathered sherds were strewn about, nearly all of them from later Ebbsfleet or Mortlake pots, maybe from a time just before Avebury's stone circles were begun. Two large pits and ten smaller holes were filled with rich soil, sherds, animal bones, flints, charcoal from hazel, blackthorn and, above all, hawthorn trees with their

189

bright spring blossom and autumn fruits. Hazel-nuts were found in one hole. All around the area were lumps of 'foreign' stone: oolitic limestone, greensand, Forest Marble, Portland chert, slate, sandstone. There were even two fragments of Niedermendig lava from Germany.[57]

Such a mixture of material, much of it old or damaged, as well as charcoal from hearths, ox and pig bones from edible parts of the animals, is very reminiscent of the 'spirit-offerings' of broken or 'killed' objects noticed at Whiteleaf Hill, and at this Kennet site some of the motives and beliefs of Avebury's prehistoric peoples can be perceived plainly, depositing into the earth the 'ghosts' of the things they most desired, good flint and stone, broken axes from Cornwall and Wales, fruits, meat-bones, vessels for food and grain, fertile soil. As five holes were lined with clay, liquids may also have been poured out here.

At the centre of the area was the heaviest concentration of flints and pottery and if this was regarded as the focus of such a magical shrine it is understandable that when, several centuries later, the avenue was built a gap was left here. There was never a Stone 30b. Instead, a space was left as though the ground were not to be disturbed.

The avenue was being built at a time when Beaker men were settling around Avebury, and in several cases their burials have been found in front of or even under the sarsens. At Stone 25b the body must have been placed there before the pillar was raised over it, giving a useful check on the date the stone was put up. Although any form of beaker remained fashionable for a long time it is possible to work out a crude average date for burials with these pots. One man lay by Stone 29a with a beaker probably made between about 2500 and 2385 BC. Mrs Cunnington found a skeleton in the Beckhampton Cove, a middle-aged man 'close to and immediately in front of the hole in which the stone had stood', lying with a different type of beaker dated between 2385 and 2230 BC. Since the war a Beckhampton Avenue stone has been discovered in its pit. Under it were the remains of a child with some ox bones, an engraved piece of chalk, flints, and a later beaker of about 2305 to 2160 BC. A similar pot accompanied the mixed-up bones of two adolescents and a man by the Kennet Stone 25b that was erected on top of the burials. Another man, this time with a latish form of Grooved Ware pot, was buried by Stone 22b. The dating is close enough, therefore, to suggest that although Avebury's two avenues took several decades to complete their construction probably centred around 2400–2300 BC.[58]

Other bones were discovered in the avenues but in disturbed conditions and with no pots or artefacts to date them. A man's skeleton with femurs showing signs of cuts made before death was found by Mrs Cunnington by Stone 18b. Fragments of legs or skull occurred by Stones 5b and 25a. All these could be interments by Beaker people who revered the power of the stones but as it is possible, and in one case certain, that the bodies were placed there at the time a stone was being erected it is just as feasible that the burials were dedicatory, even sacrificial. Several of them occur at kinks in the avenue, at the end or beginning of a section—at Stones 5b, 18b and 22b certainly, and possibly at Stones 25a and b also. Rather than the Kennet Avenue being a hallowed Beaker graveyard it may have been the place where Late Neolithic natives, intent on making their fantastic monument even more potent, dedicated the reluctant bodies of visitors to each new stretch of stones. It seems significant that no local ware accompanies these 'burials'. All the pottery was foreign, the possessions of people who may have been strangers to the region.[59]

The Kennet Avenue graves are known because Keiller located and re-erected many of the sarsens but were it not for Stukeley the Beckhampton Avenue would remain unknown, its stones long since torn down for houses and walls. His statements about it have often been doubted but his detailed notes, his drawings of the places where stone-holes could be seen outside the West Entrance and the ground-plan he made, leave no substantial question that this avenue did exist even though Stukeley himself saw only the tumbled ruins of it.

He wrote that it curved westwards from Avebury 'and proceeds by the south side of the churchyard' where two stones still lay in the road. Beyond that it had been denuded for a bridge over the Winterbourne and then could be seen climbing the hill to Avebury Trusloe where 'it enters the open plow'd fields' and made a great sweep southwards towards the Beckhampton Cove. It was a wreck, only 'one stone left standing and one of the cove so that full 201 stones belonging to it are fallen buryed or taken away, a whole mile and a half in length thus adornd with the most stately portico in the world miserably laid waste and widow'd of its old possessors'. The people clearly directed the avenue here towards the ancient Cove to use its rectangular backstone as one of the pillars. This could have been to avoid the labour of erecting a new sarsen but it was more probably an act of piety. The stone was incorporated not into the south but the north line so that the Cove's sideslabs jutted into the avenue itself. Other Beaker people would raise the banks of their own avenue at Stonehenge on either side of the Heel Stone even though it blocked most of the processional way there. The potency of such antique stones must have seemed compelling.

Just beyond the Beckhampton Cove the avenue turned westwards again. The position of one of its buried stones has been found near the modern roundabout and the avenue seems to have ended near some round barrows. 'This point facing that group of barrows and looking up the hill is a most solemn and awful place.' It was from here that Stukeley could see the Sanctuary. 'Here I am sufficiently satisfied this avenue terminated, at the like distance from *Abury*-town, as *Overton-hill* was, in the former avenue, 100 stones on a side, 4000 cubits in length', and his manuscript notes add that 'some of the stones are very large. There seems to be many odd cavitys in the bottom of the downs at the end of bekhampton avenue not commonly seen in other places where perhaps their ceremonys for the dead were performed',[60] maybe referring to solution pockets like those on the Kennet Avenue and thus explaining why the avenue should finish there at a former sacred place.

Near the end of the Beckhampton Avenue was Chapel Field 'full of great stones, many buried under-ground', still waiting for a successor to Keiller to rediscover and set upright again. Guy Underwood believed he knew the exact spot where the avenue had ended, having detected it by water-divining 'at a group of stones beyond the copse known as Fox Covert, as stated by Stukeley'.[61] This is in a field north of the main road, to the east of Harepit Way and half a mile west of the traffic island where the Waggon and Horses now stands on the site of the Hare and Hounds, the ale-house of Richard Fowler, one of the destroyers of this avenue.

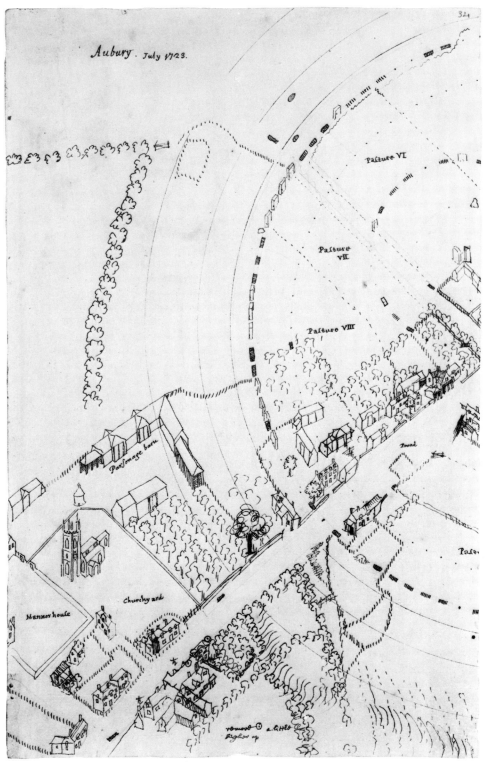

84. Stukeley's plan of Avebury's western entrance. Notice the two stones of the Beckhampton Avenue in the lane.

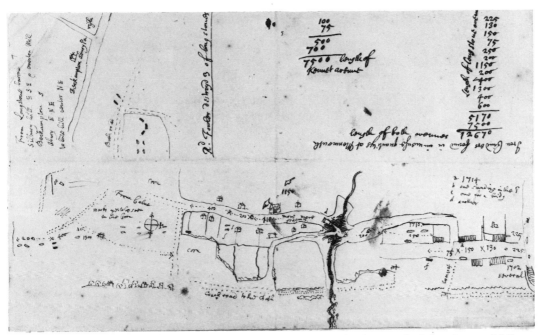

85. Manuscript plan of the Beckhampton Avenue. On it Stukeley has marked the places of fallen stones. He has also calculated the lengths of the Beckhampton and Kennet Avenues as 5170 and 7500 feet respectively, but in his book he made them both 6993 feet long (4000 of his Druid cubits) to fit his theories.

Two and a half miles away the building of the Kennet Avenue terminated at another sacred place. Nearly all the stones that wound up Overton Hill have been taken for the houses around West Kennet but four remain, two standing, behind the hedge at the foot of the hill, and sketches by Aubrey and Stukeley show the general course of this lost segment leading up to the timber circle of the Sanctuary.

The original hut, known to archaeologists as Sanctuary IA and IB, had been replaced by a lightweight fence and central hut in phase II. This short-lived structure was removed when a much heavier building, Sanctuary III, was put up. Sixteen free-standing oak poles, as much as nine or ten metres high, surrounded an inner ring of six posts even taller and set in pits so deep that 'the enlargement near the bottom in many of these holes was made probably to provide space for the digger's knees to enable him to reach the bottom of the hole which otherwise was almost an impossibility'. How Mrs Cunnington managed to re-excavate such awkward cavities 'with a small garden fork' and with decorum she did not state.[62]

On or near the bottom of these deep postholes were a dozen or more sherds of Windmill Hill and Mortlake pots proving the Late Neolithic date of this phase, and it was only higher up that beaker pottery and Grooved Ware appeared. The central building was probably still roofed. It conformed to the circumference of the Sanctuary II that had preceded it, and in several of its holes were shells of damp-loving snails, probably carried here for thatching this strong hut that perhaps was

86. (*over page*) The contrast in the size of the Entrance Stones and the other sarsens of the Outer Circle is very obvious in this photograph taken from the south bank.

still used as a mortuary house.[63] But by the time the Kennet Avenue was being erected even the sturdy posts of Sanctuary III were decaying and they were replaced by the final structure on the site, Sanctuary IV, a concentric circle of stones 'fower or five feet high' according to Aubrey, although even in his time only a few stones were upright and 'most of them (now) are fallen downe'.

The sixteen stones of the inner ring that Stukeley described as 'somewhat bigger than of the outer circle' were set exactly on the circumference of the previous free-standing timber ring and the fact that they were taller than the forty-two sarsens of their surrounding circle suggests that this stone-built structure was a representation in durable sarsen of the timber shrine and circle that had preceded it. These were the stones that Stukeley saw 'carryed downwards towards W. Kennet and two-thirds of the temple plowd up this winter'.[64] Nineteen years later, in 1743, he still remembered the sacrilege.

> This *Overton-hill*, from time immemorial, the country people have a high notion of. It was (alas, it was!) a very few years ago, crown'd with a most beautiful temple of the Druids. They still call it the sanctuary . . . The loss of this work I did not lament alone; but all the neighbours (except the person that gain'd the little dirty profit) were heartily griev'd for it. It had a beauty that touch'd them far beyond those much greater circles in *Abury* town.[65]

As John Aubrey knew the area as Seven-Barrow Hill from the Bronze Age cemetery there one suspects that the name of the 'Sanctuary' was a title foisted on the credulous Stukeley by one of his romantic antiquarian friends.

When Mrs Cunnington excavated the stoneholes she found bits of shattered sarsen in all of them, the work of Farmer Green. She also discovered a mixed

Fig. 11. Plan of Sanctuary II (after Cunnington M. E., 1931). Except for the gateposts at the north-west the posts are much slighter than those of Sanctuary IA and IB. Postholes shaded black are the only ones in which animal bones were found, perhaps the remains of feasts held near the trench with the burned stones in it.

Fig. 12. Plan of Sanctuary III (after Cunnington M. E., 1931).
This was the final structure of timber, and the outer ring may have been a ring of free-standing posts.

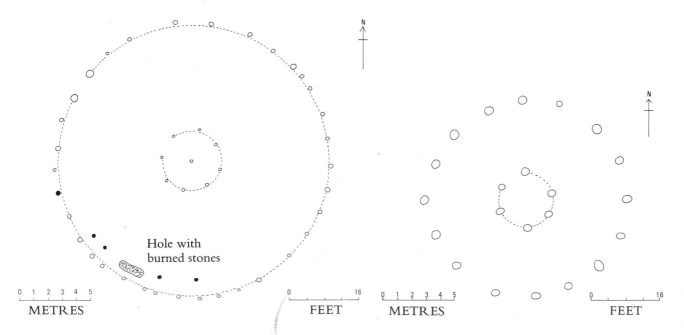

Hole with burned stones

0 1 2 3 4 5
METRES

0 ___ 16
FEET

0 1 2 3 4 5
METRES

0 ___ 16
FEET

87. The Sanctuary. The concrete blocks represent stones. The cylinders shows where posts stood. East Kennet is in the clump of trees in the left background.

collection of Windmill Hill, Mortlake, Grooved Ware and beaker sherds, indicating that this stone circle was built late in Avebury's history. Deep in a hole from which a post of the previous ring had been withdrawn there were bits of Niedermendig lava, the debris of a shattered corn-grinding quern brought by Beaker people from the Rhine.[66] As not one other fragment was noticed anywhere in the Sanctuary it is likely that this was a deposit deliberately placed in the westernmost posthole opposite the burial in the stonehole at the east.

There is no reason to doubt that the Sanctuary's funerary associations continued into this last phase. In a stonehole of the inner ring three pieces of human jaw-bone lay, lost perhaps when a skeleton was removed from the circle. Another discovery reveals the fierce beliefs of the people who were erecting a circle that to them was much more than a simple ring of stones for Sunday prayers. Just as some stones of the Kennet Avenue had Beaker burials by them so here the skeleton of a young person, fourteen to fifteen years old, rested in a shallow grave at the east of the inner ring opposite the posthole with the broken bits of lava. It lay on its right side, head to the south, looking towards the east and the rising sun, its legs crossed, hands placed over the face. People had put the body there before the stone was hauled upright 'for the risk of bringing down the stone would have been considerable had the grave been dug later'. No other burials were discovered 'even though all the ground within . . . was dug over' and 'this solitary somewhat insignificant burial may have been of a dedicatory nature'. Mrs Cunnington's observation seems over-cautious when the evidence of the other Beaker burials is recalled, almost ominously spaced out along the line of the avenue. With these in mind the Sanctuary interment looks less like a burial than the corpse of a human being offered to the rings to give them more power.[67]

197

This probably was the body of a girl. Although the burial is always referred to as a youth the skeletal evidence does not reveal a single strong masculine trait and the method of burial was that used for women. It was a Beaker custom in Wessex to bury women with their heads to the south, men with their heads to the north. A little girl had been sacrificed at Woodhenge and it is likely that another girl had been killed and buried in a sun-directed stonehole at the Sanctuary to give potency to the circles.[68]

When her body was pressed into its grave the people scattered burnt animal bones over it, the teeth and leg-bones of a pig and a young ox, and they set a beaker in front of its knees. This was a bulbous vessel with 'barbed-wire' decoration made by impressing the unfired clay with a flint or bone-splinter wrapped round with thread. Beakers like this have been found along 'the narrow but deep corridor of the Thames/Avon interface ... thus occupying, in very small numbers, a critical neolithic survival area in which Mortlake and Ebbsfleet pottery flourished',[69] another reminder of the eastern links of Avebury's prehistory. The beaker at the Sanctuary belongs to the period when the avenues were being built, for it was almost certainly made within a century of 2300 BC.

Today the Sanctuary is innocuous and unobtrusive and gives no sense of darkness of fear. Nor is its bond with Avebury obvious even though West Kennet, East Kennet and Silbury Hill can all be seen from its enclosure. A few concrete blocks stutter tentatively down the slope where the avenue once passed and then there is nothing. The visitor must negotiate the busy road, passing the hedgerow that hides the four sarsens. Beyond the farm-buildings the lane branches off towards Avebury. Up the slope the stones begin again, the ground falls, one comes to Keiller's marvellous reconstruction and it is possible to walk between the pillars and the diamonds, the land always rising, till the crest is reached. The avenue curves away to the left and the great bank of the earthwork can be seen. No stones survive. There are only pairs of grey markers. Nor can the stone circles be seen. It is not until the very bottom of the slope is reached and the avenue turns sharply to the right that the South Entrance is fully visible. Within it the giant stones of the causeway are framed, yet even here, as one walks up towards the entrance, a sarsen of the South Circle conceals the centre and the Obelisk.

The abrupt twist in the avenue just outside the entrance has puzzled archaeologists ever since Keiller found the holes of the missing stones here. 'Then there is a sharp, awkward turn with 5a and b but no satisfactory junction is effected with the four pairs at the actual entrance.'[70] On plan this is true. Yet on the ground the effect of the dramatically appearing entrance suggests that the people who dragged and raised the pillars quite intentionally veered away from and then back to the earthwork to achieve this view. From this standpoint the swerve of the avenue is not ungainly but, in reality, is an elegant means of ensuring that Avebury was always an awesome and imposing spectacle to anyone approaching it. The kink is not clumsy. It provided an abrupt sight of the South Entrance's gigantic sarsens, previously concealed by high ground, and this would not have been possible had the Kennet Avenue led directly to the earthwork.

From outside the bank the stone circles remained obscure and secret. What happened inside these rings is unknown but some guesses can be made.

88. From inside the south-west quadrant the stones of the Kennet Avenue can be seen approaching the circle.

CHAPTER EIGHT

The Purpose of Avebury

Publick sacrifices, games, hymns, a sabbatical observance being there celebrated; we have just reason to think all the like were observ'd by our Druids at Abury.

William Stukeley. *Abury*, 69.

DEATH and regeneration are the themes of Avebury. The presence of human bones, the pieces of stone, the red ochre, the pockets of fertile earth, the antlers, the shapes of the sarsens, the architecture of the avenues and circles, all are consistent with the belief that Avebury was intended as a temple in which, at various times of the year, the large population could gather to watch and take part in ceremonies of magic and evocation that would safeguard their lives.

Understanding the uncertainty and inadequacy of the evidence archaeologists have always been reluctant to conjecture about the purpose of the British stone circles. Other writers have seen no need for caution. As early as 1723 Twining decided that Avebury was a Roman temple dedicated to Terminus, a god without motion, the Outer Circle being added by Agricola to commemorate his voyage around Britain. John Wood visualised Avebury as one of four minor colleges of the Druids who had a university at Stanton Drew and their capital at Bath. Stukeley followed this with his opinion that Avebury was a representation of the sacred egg and snake. 'The whole temple of Abury may be consider'd as a picture', he wrote, and proceeded to falsify his measurements and plans to mould the facts to his theory.[1]

In the next century Maurice said the circles had an astronomical function and Bowles wrote that 'the inner circles represent, severally, the months, the year, the days and the hours, included in the great circle of eternity, representing the god over the heavens'. In 1840 Rickman imagined the site to be an amphitheatre. Six years later Duke made it part of an incredible planetarium that stretched from Stonehenge (Saturn) through Marden (Mars) to Avebury (Sun and Moon) and beyond. 'The planetary temples, thus located, seven in number, will, if put in motion, be supposed to revolve around Silbury Hill.' Avebury was soon immobilised by Herbert who saw 'nothing in it but great circles and avenues' built in the Dark Ages by people who abandoned their forest shrines 'in which their wooden idols stood, in which their sacrifices were performed, and of which the sacred trees were aspersed with the piacular blood'.[2]

The combative Fergusson rejected temple, observatory, planetarium, Herbert and all, in favour of his own conviction that Avebury was a burial ground. 'Two of Arthur's generals of division lie buried, one in each of the stone circles inside the inclosure', with the commoners underneath the bank 'which however is nothing but a long barrow of circular shape'.[3] Even when this was disproved by Smith's 1865 excavation Fergusson refused to admit that the absence of bodies made Avebury a rather unusual cemetery.

Such idiosyncracies diminished as the date of Avebury and its similarities to other stone circles became apparent but in recent years there has been another gush of eccentricity from writers more interested in mysticism than method, their standards of scholarship being anticipated by Stukeley as 'voluminous enough, but barbarous, poor and impertinent, when compared to the solid performance of learned men'.[4] It is unlikely, for example, that Avebury's church was built on an earlier dragon site, a centre of fertility, or that 'it stands on a ley running between Stonehenge and the stone circle at Winterbourne Abbas'.[5]

For any reader fortunate enough to be ignorant of what ley-lines are claimed to be, a brief explanation must be given. They are non-existent alignments supposedly passing through a variety of sites set out in mysterious straight lines. When first 'detected' they were thought to be old straight tracks for ancient travellers, an improbable proposition in itself considering the irregular pattern of hills, rivers and mires that determined prehistoric man's paths, but when it was realised that many of these 'tracks' disconcertingly plunged into the middle of swamps like the one around Neolithic Salisbury the lines were reinterpreted as spiritual rays with the sacred places, the churches, stone circles and Celtic crosses acting as beacons and dynamos to keep the current flowing. That these beacons belonged to periods as much as four thousand years apart has never deterred the real ley-liner.

The longest of these leys is said to stretch nearly four hundred miles from near Land's End to Lowestoft with Avebury at its midpoint. Devotees insist that such lines are both very accurate because they are exceptionally narrow, less than a metre across, and also so undeviatingly straight that they cannot be the results of uncritical imagination. Devotees are mistaken. So far from the Avebury ley being a thin, concentrated ray it is at least a mile wide, the distance by which it misses an important target, 'one of the oldest, smallest and least accessible of all churches, St. Michael's Brentnor', in fact an ordinary thirteenth-century church built by the monks of Tavistock Abbey. The ley also misses two other significant spiritual centres, Glastonbury Tor and Burrowbridge Mump which it is supposed to cross, passes to the side of all three of the Hurlers stone circles on Bodmin Moor, evades the Cheesewring there, and finally misses Avebury itself by a good quarter of a mile. Fears that it ever existed can surely be allayed.[6]

Ley-lines were first envisaged by Alfred Watkins, a brewery representative whose occupation may have contributed to the development of his ideas. Years ago, in a copy of Watkins' first publication, *Early British Trackways, Moats, Mounds, Camps and Sites*, that fervent Wiltshire archaeologist, A. D. Passmore, scrawled, 'ROT! How any man at any time can have made such a collection of damned nonsense I cannot imagine.' It seems a moderate assessment.

A major reason for the popularity of such 'damned nonsense', apart from people's natural liking for escapist literature, is the lack of better-balanced accounts of what Avebury once was. There are only a few lines about the site in most archaeological books and even those simply describe what can be seen today. Yet if various comments are put together then, like an incomplete jigsaw, an imperfect picture emerges. Gordon Childe thought of Avebury as a cathedral, Stuart Piggott as an open sanctuary associated with a sky-god, Isobel Smith as a monument dedicated to a fertility cult whose practices included the use of stone discs, balls of chalk and human bones. Jacquetta Hawkes wrote of fertility rites involving the earth and the sun although 'what those mysteries were we shall never know'.[7] However generalised these observations there is agreement about a religious centre for fertility cults linked with the earth, the sun, ritual objects and dead bones. Not many years ago Patrick Crampton went further, suggesting that Avebury was not only a temple of the powerful Earth Goddess but also a 'city', the first 'capital—religious, cultural and commercial—of most of southern Britain'.[8]

Long before then Colley March had interpreted Avebury and all other stone circles as places first intended as mortuary enclosures where the dead could be stored. Over the centuries 'the stone circle gradually lost its original defensive function, and became at last associated in only a mystical manner with the ritual of the dead'.[9] The presence of scattered human bones in Avebury's ditch would certainly be explained if they had come from corpses exposed within the earthwork either on the ground or on scaffolds erected outside the huts of the village and March's suggestion, therefore, has some physical evidence to support it.

'We speak from facts, not theory' was the famous introductory claim of Sir Richard Colt Hoare in his *Ancient Wiltshire*[10] but no archaeologist today about to discuss the beliefs of a pre-literate and forgotten people would write with that kind of certainty. It is one thing to examine the actual remains of those people, their pottery, stone axes, skeletons, even the shape of a megalithic ring, because all these can be analysed and some truths about them deduced. People's ideas are different. In one sense they never existed and now only the ruined shrines and temples are left, empty, silent, overgrown, irrevocably changed in appearance just as our own beliefs are irreversibly altered from those of the men and women who built Avebury. Whereas previous chapters have been shaped around a framework of facts with a filling of speculation this chapter is a mist of conjecture in which the few facts, hopefully used as signposts, may in reality be obstacles or diversions that lead us farther and farther from the truth but with no sure path to follow we can only travel optimistically. We cannot bring them to us so we must go back to the people of Avebury, using the architecture, the carvings and the dead bones, the myths as landmarks along the trail. Care has to be taken not to distort the people into copies of ourselves, turning medicine-men, shamans or witch-doctors into astronomer–priests just because the latter fit more comfortably in our modern, technological minds. Witch-doctors may appear somewhat ridiculous and ineffectual, rather disgusting and frightening, primitive, and yet the people of Avebury themselves were primitive and witch-doctors or medicine-men are anthropologically more likely amongst them than astronomer–priests.

A stone circle, starkly simple on its hillside today, may be transformed into a prehistoric Mount Palomar without difficulty, but the wealth of Celtic animal mythology and the images on Scandinavian rock-carvings warn that it may be necessary to have the stones illuminated by night-fires and inhabited by antlered shamans holding axes on high, raising hands with outspread fingers, and performing acts of fertilisation with domestic animals and with humans.[11]

The Neolithic world was a place of spirits and symbols in which a pot deliberately broken took on a new existence just as real as the one it had left. It was a world in which the dead were needed and in which life and death were not separate but were reflections of each other. It was a world in which rites of imitation, like the rain-making ceremonies of the Natchez Indians of America or the natives of Java, gave men some control over the nature-spirits around them. Although it is not possible to reconstruct any one of their ceremonies with precision it is possible in the mind to pass along the avenues, blending the archaeological evidence with our knowledge of other primitive societies to compose a picture of what may have happened at Avebury, moving on towards the circles and the mysteries that surround them. Insights may occur as Shelley hoped:

> I sought for ghosts, and sped
> Through many a listening chamber, cave and ruin,
> And starlight wood, with fearful steps pursuing
> Hopes of high talk with the departed dead.
>
> *Hymn to Intellectual Beauty*

For ease of reading most qualifications and reservations are omitted from this stage onwards but it is hoped the reader will be able to detect what is fact, what speculation. 'Maybe', 'possible', 'could', 'may have been' are words of evasion in a chapter reconstructing the evanescent past and in most instances they have been excised even though professional discretion demanded they should remain.

We can, very hesitantly, picture communal seasonal activities in the circles at autumn, midwinter and spring, led by antlered medicine-men or witch-doctors, the people dancing out the themes of death and rebirth, giving offerings, using human bones, and engaging in rituals of sex to bring back the warmth and richness of the summer soil. Once, thousands of years ago, dressed in their soft skin clothes, the leather decorated with shell and bone and coloured in bright patterns, the people squatted on their heels by the stones, watching ceremonies they knew would make their brief lives safer. Such rites were held at set times of the year, at sowing and at harvest, maybe also at midsummer and midwinter. Centuries later the Celts had four great nature festivals: Oimelg in February when the ewes came into milk; Beltane in May when the cattle could be driven out to the spring grass; Lughnasa for the August harvest; and Samhuin at the end of October when the ghosts of the dead rose in the night to roam the dark, defenceless countryside.

By tradition Lughnasa is linked with Neolithic cairns and stone circles[12] and it is feasible that every one of these festivals was rooted in early agricultural customs when the hazards of crop-growing and cattle-rearing seemed entirely dependent on the whims of capricious forces. Ritual was essential. 'From the preceding examination of the spring and summer festivals of Europe we may infer that our rude forefathers personified the powers of vegetation as male and female'[13] and tried to influence the growth of crops by imitative magic, performing rites before the crops were sown, celebrating in the autumn when the harvest was in.

Such seasonal gatherings were common the world over. In America the Pawnees had a vital forecasting ceremony in February when their medicine-men foretold what the coming year would be like. The Algonquins had a regular festival to celebrate the ripening of fruits and grain. The Temple Mound builders held rituals at the times of sowing and planting. Hariot reported that at a certain time of the year the Virginian Indians came in from their villages, bodies painted, and assembled on a plain 'abowt the which are planted in the grownde certayne posts carved with heads like to the faces of Nonnes couered with theyr vayles', a circle of totem-poles around which the Indians danced for a long while before holding a 'solemne feaste' inside the ring.[14]

That the people of Avebury also had regular agricultural festivals in which rites of fertility were prominent is hinted at from the fragments of their myths that have survived in the much later poetry of the Celts, people descended from the stone circle builders. 'The first Celtic settlements of the British Isles may be dated to the early Bronze Age',[15] and if this is correct then the Iron Age natives were related to those strange Beaker people who helped in the building of Avebury. Professor Christopher Hawkes believed that Iron Age religion was a mixture of Indo-European sky-cults and the old 'megalithic [religion] existing here before them, which could descend through the Bronze Age to their undisputably Celtic successors. Thence came the religion that the Druids administered.'[16] The very fact so many churches and chapels in Britain and Brittany were deliberately built on top of or alongside megalithic monuments suggests that Neolithic beliefs about death

89. Bronze age carvings from the Bohuslän district of Sweden, showing men mating with women and with cattle, presumably in fertility ceremonies.

90. Virginia Indians. The three women in the middle were the loveliest virgins in the tribe.

and fertility lingered well into the mediaeval period. The Irish archaeologist Sean O'Riordain thought that 'apart from a small veneer of Celtic-speaking chieftains and craftsmen, the Irish are basically the people of the Neolithic and Bronze Age who built the great megalithic tombs'.[17]

Despite none of the mythology even of their Iron Age descendants being written down until well into Christian times, there is a core of myths that derives from early prehistoric times. Professor Proinsias MacCana observed that 'it can safely be presumed that all [the various Celtic communities] have assimilated much of the religious thought and usage of the pre-Celtic inhabitants of their several areas'.[18]

It is this core that cautiously used may tell us something of the beliefs of Late Neolithic people. There is a frail tradition of bardic poetry about famous heroes and about gods of nature who lived in the earth or in chambered tombs like New Grange in Ireland, a memory of the times when ancestors whose bones lay in the long mounds were regarded as powerful, god-like spirits.[19] Quite consistently at the heart of these Celtic stories is a regeneration cycle, symbolised by a woman who passed from her husband to a lover and back to her husband within a year, presumably a myth of the fertile Earth, the woman, passing from summer to winter and back again, summer portrayed as a vigorous young man who overcame an older, weaker rival. Winter was equated with barrenness, sterile soil, infertile men, and 'this idea of a sympathetic relationship between the potency of the king and the fertility of the land is supported by Irish texts which hint that a king might be ritually married to the tutelary earth goddess of the tribe'.[20]

Such cycles of cold and warmth, growth and decay, are widespread in early societies, not surprising when one considers how fundamental the richness of the soil is to people, but it is the acting out of the myth as a human drama that distinguishes the poetical mind of the primitive to whom the real world was not merely that in which he lived but 'the Lands of the Living where there is neither death nor sin nor transgression' set 'in a great fairy hill' to which all men aspired.[21]

Prehistoric people lived in a world where reality and the imaginary reflected against each other like the shimmering of crystals, and although we shall never know whether the myths touched on here did derive from much older beliefs of people who used stone circles for their ceremonies it is likely that the two had much in common and that fertility cycles and legends of heroic ancestors were central to the rituals that were performed inside the circles of Avebury.

At these seasonal ceremonies there must surely have been a leader or a priest to guide the people through the stages of the ritual, every phase needing to be enacted exactly as tradition had always had it done. Short of a written or drawn description by an onlooker proof that such men existed is hard to come by just as it is unclear

91. Some of the perforated bone points from Upton Lovell. The longest measures twelve centimetres. The curved object at the bottom is a boar's tusk.

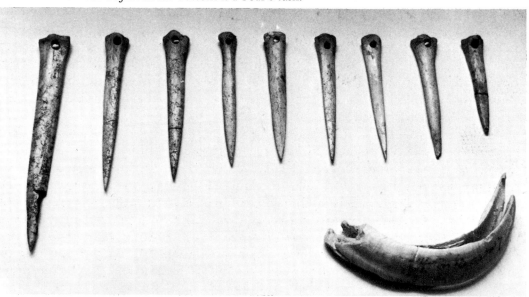

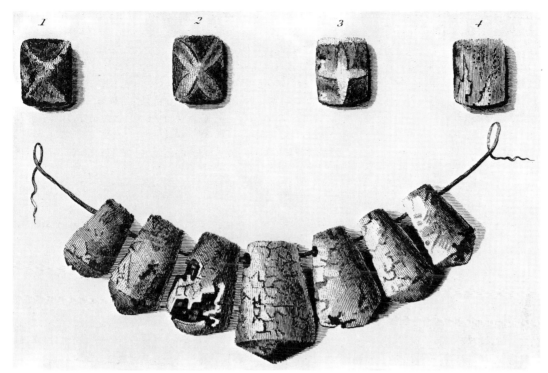

92. The four 'plaques' from the Lake barrow cemetery near Stonehenge. Beneath them is a necklace of amber beads from another round barrow.

whether a tribal chief was also the spiritual minister, although within a large community the two roles may well have been separate.

In 1801 William Cunnington opened a round barrow at Upton Lovell twenty miles south-west of Avebury. In it he discovered a man's skeleton lying full-length on its back, quite different from the customary crouched position of most Early Bronze Age burials, and one which hints at a difference in the man's status. With him were over sixty small animal bones, shaped to a point, perforated at one end and graduated in length for a necklace rather like others from Cambridgeshire, Yorkshire and Wessex. Some perforated boar's tusks lay by his legs. So did some shaped 'cups' of marcasite, granulated nodules of iron pyrites found in the chalk whose striking appearance obviously attracted prehistoric people. There was also a broken macehead or battleaxe, some stones and foreign pebbles.

Necklaces or clothing fringed with perforated animal bones or teeth are known from prehistoric Russia associated with carved T-bone objects like the drumsticks used by present-day shamans for beating on their magical drums and it is possible that at Upton Lovell the unusual burial position and the unique articles of clothing indicate the remains of a shaman or medicine-man. 'One would rightly hesitate before producing an early Bronze Age shaman on Salisbury Plain but the shamanistic element in prehistoric and early historic tradition in both Europe and Asia cannot be ignored.'[22]

Another round barrow at Amesbury covered a burial with deer antlers laid at its head and feet. A cremation at Snail Down near Stonehenge 'was surrounded by a circular wreath of the bones of the red deer within which, amidst the ashes, were five beautiful arrowheads cut out of flint, and a small red pebble'.[23] A burial at Rockbourne in Hampshire had three specially cut lengths of antler, each with a branching tine, placed by the skull. The stag frontlets found at the famous Middle Stone Age settlement of Star Carr in Yorkshire and the antlers carried by the present-day Horn Dancers of Abbots Bromley provide ancient and modern counterparts to the ceremonial antler head-dresses of medicine-men apparelled in bone-fringed garments, their other possessions of maceheads, pebbles, 'cups', laid in their grave with them.

Recognisable scenes of religious activity were carved in the Bronze Age on rocks in Scandinavia, the earliest about 1800 BC a few centuries after Avebury was completed. In several instances priests or witch-doctors seem to be wearing animal skins as though 'becoming' horses, cattle, even goats, or to have birds' masks, and 'sometimes a connection with the sun is manifest'.[24] It is with some despair that one realises that although the participants at Avebury may also have worn antler head-dresses or donned the hides of bulls or other animals, just as primitive societies like the Mandan Indians had done, it is impossible to prove. The profusion of antlers in Avebury's ditch, however, and their secretion in the bank and in the Marlborough Mound do suggest that Neolithic people regarded the annual growth and shedding of stag-horns as symbolic of the cycle of regeneration, and accordingly invested the leaders of their own ceremonies with antler head-pieces.

The burnt bones of a Bronze Age man at Hvidegard in Denmark were accompanied by a leather bag which contained a real witch's brew of bits and pieces: an amber bead, a sea-shell, tweezers, a bronze knife and the lower jaw of a squirrel, a wooden cube, a flint flake, dried roots, bits of bark, a falcon's claw and the tail of a grass-snake.[25] Collections like this, known also from other Scandinavian burials, must surely be the relics of sorcery practices. There is nothing quite like them from Britain but the little perforated ox bones from West Kennet could have been whistles used by witch-doctors to summon up the spirits of the dead.[26]

In 1806 the Revd Edward Duke found 'four ornaments of stained bone' mixed up with cremated bone in a round barrow in the Stonehenge district. These thin, small tablets, each about the size of a thumb-nail, are now in the British Museum. They are rectangular, flat on one side, convex on the other, perhaps cut from one piece of bone. One is entirely plain. The others have lightly scraped-out patterns, star-shaped or crossed or in lozenges, the underside being a mirror image of the face. There are no signs of wear at their edges as there would have been if they had been implements or trimmings for clothing nor is there any evidence that they were ever attached to anything. They are not deeply enough engraved to have been stamps for pottery. When he saw them William Cunnington thought they might have been used for telling the future: 'We might be led to suppose by this circumstance that the custom of casting lots existed amongst the Britons, and that these articles were appropriated to that purpose.'[27] Cunnington may have been right. Carved ox bones for telling the future, tablets, antlers, all of them could have been the equipment of medicine-men for use in the rituals of fertility.

93. Part of Avebury's Outer Circle on a misty autumnal morning.

Fertility rites, antlers and witch-doctors are the background to the faded, blurred reconstruction of what happened at Avebury in prehistoric times. With John Aubrey 'let us imagine then what kind of Countrie this was in the time of the ancient Britons, by the nature of the soile, which is a soure, woodsere land, very natural for the production of oaks especially. One may conclude that this . . . was a shady, dismall wood; and the inhabitants almost as salvage as the Beasts whose skins were their only rayments.' In the forests that still clutched the borders of the cleared land, the wolf lurked, 'as strong as one man but as cunning as seven', ready to attack children and old people, hunting in quiet deadly packs that in the severest winters would turn even upon man himself.[28] To the south of the Marlborough Downs were unfriendly tribes. In every household around Avebury illness was expected and death a commonplace. Outside, the crops and animals were always prone to unexplainable disasters.

It is in this setting that the antlered priests and the people moved along the avenues to their dark winter rituals and daylit summer celebrations where the stones bulked like fossilised men against the sky. In the ceremonies there were three elements: offerings to the earth, human bones, and sexuality; all of them associated with the

209

fertility of the land: the deposits of rich soil, fruits from trees, broken things as part of the harvest festivals, the skulls and dead bones in the chill sterility of midwinter, and the sexuality of sowing and the springtime, the song that Herrick sang

> of May-poles, Hock-carts, wassails, wakes,
> Of bride-grooms, brides and of their bridal cakes.

The elements were all intermixed and no doubt on the occasions when great men died the funeral rites included offerings as well as bones.

The drum-beats and the dances were no more than warm breaths on the window of Time. They have gone but we can be sure they existed. Legends of impious girls who danced on the Sabbath being transformed into a circle of stones are too many to be coincidental.[29] As early as the twelfth century Geoffrey of Monmouth referred to Stonehenge as Chorea Gigantum, the Giants' Dance. As far away as the Shetlands a circle was named Haltadans, 'the limping dance' and three cairns nearby are known as the Fiddlers' Crus (enclosures). At Stanton Drew, close to Avebury, the three circles are nicknamed the Weddings with particular stones identified as the Fiddlers, the Maids and the Bride and Bridegroom.[30] Whether at Land's End or on Bodmin Moor or in Wicklow there are the same stories that people danced in the stone rings whose very shape and size encourages this belief. Avebury need be no different with lines of face-painted men and women circling the sarsens, drums beating, torches burning into the blackness of the night. Near Peshawur in Pakistan, the natives knew nothing of a concentric circle of tall stones except that 'a wedding party, passing over the plain, were turned into stone by some powerful magician'.[31]

The time of year of at least one of the ceremonies is certain for it is only in the autumn that the celebrations for the safe gathering of the harvest could have taken place. The sheer size and uncluttered interiors of the Avebury rings tells us that they were for a great number of people and it is easy to imagine the straggle of families with their offerings and gifts coming in across the September downs to join their relatives and friends at the earthwork for rites of thanksgiving in the years when the crops were good. Equally, in the worst times when the harvests were poor there were acts of propitiation. In Gambia where hundreds of little stone circles lie overgrown in the bush almost nothing is remembered about them even though they are only a few centuries old but the natives believe them to be the home of the Earth Spirit and some villages still hold yearly rituals in them at the times of sowing and harvesting the ground-nuts and millet. Sacrifices of 'black' animals, a cock, a ram, or, best of all, a bull-calf are offered by the men in circles where Iron Age burials lie and where Y-shaped outlying stones stand in line with the spring and autumn sunrises. An early investigator, Captain Maxwell Carroll, noted that 'all the measurements of the circles are multiples of three, while curiously enough one foot may be taken almost exactly as the unit', a reflection of the simple counting-systems and body-measurements of other early societies whose agricultural way of life shaped the nature of their religious activities.

X. (*right*) Stones of the north-west arc of the Outer Circle with the bank beyond, looking north-east.

In Gambia as in Britain communal dancing was the natural way to express the gratitude of the people for a bountiful crop and to play out the dramas of their fertility cults. In Britain whispers of this survive in the legends of petrified merrymakers, especially girls, at a marriage, and in Gambia 'the stone circle is a wedding party turned to stone because the bride was found not to be a virgin'. Like the 'Megalithic Yard' at Cahokia this is not evidence of megalithic missionaries spreading across the world. To the contrary, it shows the fundamental likenesses that exist between primitive communities engaged in the growing of crops.[32]

At Avebury and elsewhere in the British Isles the 'offerings' of objects, many of them deliberately broken, show how people expected to communicate with the world of spirits about them, sometimes combining the autumn offerings with rites of death, fertility and sacrifice. At Pond Cairn, Coity, four or five days' journey westward from Avebury, the people of the small community whose leader had died undertook a series of complicated ceremonies that were brilliantly reconstructed by the archaeologist Sir Cyril Fox. At the place chosen for burial a circular rubble bank was built. A child was killed, her body burnt, the bones washed and scattered in a pit at the centre of the ring. The cremated ashes of the chieftain were put into an urn and placed over the child's remains alongside a shallow trench shaped in the likeness of a phallus. A central stack of turves was raised over these burials. Around this the people walked or danced, their faces streaked with charcoal that was thrown over them, their feet trampling the ground hard while, at the east, facing west towards the setting autumn sun, someone brought burning charcoal, lit a fire in a deep hollow in the bank and threw sheaves of wheat and barley into it. Death, sacrifice, fertility, dancing and autumn offerings merged in these rites. 'Was he a "corn king"—an embodiment of the corn spirit?'[33]

At Avebury there is no such unequivocal evidence but the burial of smashed pots, waste flints, earth, hazel-nuts and the twigs of fruit-bearing trees in the fissures of the Kennet Avenue show that the people had a similar belief about the need to give the 'spirits' of valued objects and food to the ghosts of the dead dwelling in the ground who had the power to provide or withhold their goodness as they wished. These were offerings of thanks and appeasement to the forces controlling the destinies of the men and women and with whom the dead could speak.

This would also explain the exceptional depth of the ditch, far deeper than any ordinary defence required but explicable if the people, like those of Maumbury Rings, wished to penetrate to the core of the earth in order to bury their antler picks as dedications that would give magical protection to the stone circles. It is noteworthy that virtually all the objects in the first collapse of chalk-rubble were picks and rakes. If these were only discarded tools it is difficult to explain how several lay well over a metre above the bottom of the ditch.

Whatever their depth they could have been buried as dedicatory objects had the bottom of the ditch been deliberately back-filled to seal these symbols of regeneration within it. In contrast, in the layer of fine silt above the rubble, a layer that only slowly accumulated over the centuries of Avebury's use as a temple, there

XI. (*left*) The North Entrance, with the 'Swindon Stone' and the Marlborough Downs beyond, looking east. The three concrete obelisks show where stones of the intended third circle stood.

were no picks or rakes but lots of pieces of unworked antler, broken pottery, flint scrapers, knives, cores and flakes, and human bones, especially jaw-bones. This collection is so different that it seems this silty layer received not merely domestic rubbish but also offerings of prized, often broken objects, donated to the spirits safeguarding the enclosed stone circles.

At the centre of the South Circle where the Obelisk stood several pits were dug to receive not broken objects but deposits of fine, dark-brown soil, entirely free of chalk, pockets of rich earth symbolising the fertility that the people so much desired.[34] If, as some scholars have thought, the Obelisk was a pillar embodying the spirits of ancestors then autumn offerings there would be doubly potent.

There have been many instances of harvest food being given to the dead for this reason. The African Bantus believed that the souls of their dead chiefs controlled the rain and so gave them harvest corn in the expectation of good weather the following year. Prayers were made asking their ancestors to protect the crops, drive away illness and evil spirits, and no food was eaten by the living until their chief had sacrificed a bull and placed pots of fresh beer and porridge in the house where the skulls of his ancestors rested.[35] In such customs thanksgiving offerings and ancestor cults merged at harvest time. At Avebury similar ceremonies are possible.

It is also likely, from the stories of malevolent ghosts and birds of ill omen, that other ceremonies took place at a colder time of the year in November or at the lifeless midwinter when the nights were long and frightening. This was the time when protection was needed and when the people came to the hard stones of the circles with care, watching every gesture of their leader until they entered the safety of the rings. A circle was a barrier. It 'also serves the purpose of preserving profane man from the danger to which he would expose himself by entering it without due care. The sacred is always dangerous to anyone who comes into contact with it unprepared, without having gone through the "gestures of approach" that every religious act demands.'[36] At a time when human skulls were being carried along the avenues for rituals inside the stone circles the people must have felt perilously vulnerable to the ghosts around them in those winter nights, and they kept cautiously to every ordained word and movement of the ceremony.

Once inside the Outer Circle they saw the Ring Stone, the isolated pillar outside the South Circle where the original sarsen had been substituted during the Beaker period by a flattish block with a small natural hole near its top eastern corner.[37]

Imposing outlying stones are known in other stone circles, notably at the Rollright Stones, at Long Meg & Her Daughters, and, of course, at Stonehenge where the Heel Stone's relationship to the midsummer sunrise has led to the supposition that all outliers were intended as astronomical markers.[38] Fieldworkers well know that the majority of these stones that look so astronomically persuasive on plans are actually far too small ever to have been used as sighting-devices though they could have acted as directional guides before avenues were built. Indeed, the enclosing of the Heel Stone within a round bank when Stonehenge's avenue was constructed could be a good example of an earlier feature being replaced by a more ambitious means of directing the eye towards water as so many avenues seem to do. From Stukeley's sketch the Ring Stone was too little for astronomical use and quite probably it was substituted for a taller pillar when the bank was heaped up and people could no longer see directly down the Kennet valley but, instead, had to walk along the line of the new avenue of stones.

While debating the purpose of the Ring Stone it is appropriate to ask whether Avebury offers any support for the idea that it and the other 'great henges of Wessex were inhabited centres . . . in and near which lived a permanent population of non-agricultural specialists such as priests, astronomers, wise men, poets and all their attendant craftsmen and servants'.[39]

Of stone circles it has been written, 'neither can there be much doubt that many, if not most, of the scores of other stone rings of Britain would, if carefully examined, also be found to be exactly positioned in relation to astronomically useful, distant features on the horizon'.[40] This is plausible only in the study. Many circles are far out on gently undulating moors or deeply set in valleys or hard by featureless seas, none of whose landscapes provide 'useful, distant features', or else are surrounded by such saw-toothed skylines that every notch offers a potential target.[41] At Avebury the Ring Stone was not aligned on anything of astronomical interest as several frustrated astronomers can testify.

It is fair to remark that the removal of so many stones may have destroyed what sight-lines there were. They certainly have been looked for. Duke can be ignored with his preposterous planetarium 'to form on the face of the land the diagram of the entire system of the Universe'[42] but the opinion of Sir Norman Lockyer, former Director of the Solar Physics Observatory, does deserve consideration. He decided that the Kennet Avenue was aligned on the rising of the star Alpha Centauri, to warn that the November sunrise was approaching 'while the sunrise in May was provided for in the Beckhampton Avenue'.[43] The association of the sun with the important festivals of Beltane and Samhuin was sensible. Unfortunately, as Lockyer perceived, 'the existence of the bank would have prevented any star rise being seen from the circle'. For his theory to work the avenue had to be put up long before the bank, a belief which has been disproved.

The astronomer Fred Hoyle looked at Avebury hopefully. 'Following what I felt to be exciting results coming from the eclipse interpretation of Stonehenge, I tried (quite hard) to apply similar ideas to Avebury. The result was a failure . . . given the plan of Avebury, it would be possible to invent many hypotheses about the purpose of this monument'.[44] This is true of some other astronomical theses about stone circles.

> He his fabric of the Heavens
> Hath left to their disputes—perhaps to move
> His laughter at their quaint opinions wide
> Hereafter, when they come to model Heaven,
> And calculate the stars; how they will wield
> The mighty frame, how build, unbuild, contrive
> To save appearances . . .
>
> John Milton. *Paradise Lost*. VIII. i. 76.

Thom has suggested that the northward line through the centres of the South and

North Circles was orientated towards the setting of the star Deneb (Alpha Cygni).[45] Later he noted that this alignment was parallel to the line from the Ring Stone to his centre of the site. 'Standing at the obelisk on the line of the centres and looking through the stones of the Cove, one would be looking along the line to the place where Deneb "set" about 1600 BC.'[46] The faintness of Deneb, so dim that it cannot be observed down to the horizon, and the improbability of a date some eight hundred years after the Ring Stone was put up greatly dilutes the probability of this alignment and, in its present state at least, Avebury cannot be regarded as a scientific observatory.

What, then, was the Ring Stone? In the British Isles holed stones can be found by themselves or incorporated in chambered tombs or, sometimes, in stone circles, and folklore associates two traditions with them, one that the stone has curative powers, particularly of bone disorders like rickets in children, the other that it was at such stones that young couples should be betrothed. Perhaps combining these beliefs some Irish pillars were reputed to ensure an easy childbirth if the woman's clothing were passed through them. At the Hole of Odin outside the stones of Stenness on Orkney, as late as the eighteenth century men and girls plighted their troth by clasping hands through the hole, and a contemporary report stated 'that after this they proceeded to Consummation without further Ceremony'.[47]

Such practices reach back to the depths of prehistory when bones of skeletons were passed through the 'porthole' entrances of some chambered tombs and when the artificial hole itself had the significance of the entry to the Other World. Even when megalithic tombs were no longer used the tradition of passing dead bones through a hole in a stone prior to employing them in the people's ceremonies persisted.

The themes of Avebury are death and regeneration. As the people moved from the avenues through the entrances with their colossal stones they passed by the ditch where human jaw-bones lay. Five mandibles and a fragment of a skull were discovered by the South Entrance in the topmost layer of rubble. 'They suggest a close relationship between the individuals, for they bear a close resemblance to each other. The chins, moreover, are strong and firm.'[48] If families were living inside the earthwork then physical similarities might be expected between the skeletons. All the mandibles were weathered 'as if they had been exposed on the surface at some time'.[49] Amidst the clavicles, femurs and other long bones there were only three little bits of cranial bone, entirely compatible with the belief that while the other bones were casually disposed of, some tumbling into the ditch or being buried in it much as the human bones at Maumbury Rings were placed in the pits there[50] the skulls were treated differently, being removed for fertility cults in which the spirits of ancestors were vital.

While a grassed-over long mound or a chambered tomb might still have been the shrine in each family's territory the taking of skulls from places like West Kennet, the discovery of bones and skulls at Windmill Hill, the human jaw-bones at the Sanctuary and the great number of bones in the ditch at Avebury suggest that human remains, especially skulls, were carried along the avenues to the stone circles. Three fragments of a skull were actually discovered inside the South Circle itself.[51]

In the early years some bones were taken from the timber Sanctuary on Overton Hill but by the time the Kennet Avenue was constructed the Sanctuary was being transformed into an open stone circle. The transportation of bones could still have started there by tradition but the site had become only the symbol of a charnel-house. Over its long centuries Avebury had many changes of ritual and one can speak only generally of the ceremonies held within its enclosure.

Not only were skulls brought to Avebury for rites of fertility but corpses were probably laid for a while in the rings before being taken away for burial. Stukeley commented that 'all the long barrows point to Abury'[52] and it is noticeable that Avebury is at the centre of several burial areas. The long mounds, particularly the megalithic tombs, lie on the perimeter of a crude ring three to four miles in radius. The round barrow cemeteries crowd closer, some within a mile, others like the line on Overton Hill at the end of the Kennet Avenue, or the Beckhampton group and the cluster at the foot of Cherhill two miles from the circles where the Beckhampton Avenue is supposed to have ended. Bodies were carried along the avenues to the burial grounds just as, on other occasions, skulls were taken up to Avebury.

To those prehistoric people the head seemed the home of the spirit which would inhabit it as long as the skull was undamaged and for this reason some skulls in tombs like Belas Knap were broken by heavy blows and in a long mound at Warminster Cunnington reported that a skull had been 'beaten into pieces before burial' to release its ghost. The removal of skulls from West Kennet and the presence of crania and long-bones at Windmill Hill were the results of people taking the caged spirits of ancestors to a place where they could be used. Jaw-bones were presumably of less significance, explaining why some were left at the Sanctuary. At the causewayed enclosure of Hambledon Hill many isolated skulls were found buried in the ditches whereas pits with 'ritual fillings' of broken axes, sherds, antlers and mandibles were confined to the interior.[53] There were no jaw-bones at Windmill Hill amongst the skull debris except for one infant's mandible and it was obviously only after the flesh had gone and the jaws dropped off that the skulls were brought here. At the henge of Gorsey Bigbury in Somerset, some forty miles west of Avebury, a man, woman and child had been buried in the ditch and it was not until it was skeletal that the woman's skull was disinterred and reburied right against the entrance, perhaps to watch over it. 'Although an upper molar was found, there was no trace of the mandible or lower dentition.'[54]

When a circle with a long row of stones leading up to it was excavated near the Gambia River earlier this century a whole cemetery of skulls was discovered, each stone having a skull near its base with three more carefully buried at the centre of the ring of tall stones.[55] At Avebury the skulls may have been decorated. Two lumps of haematite or red ochre were found at the Sanctuary, and in stone circles like Gretigate and Druids Temple in north-west England similar bits of 'raddle' lay near the cremations. Several Yorkshire round barrows had ochre in them. In the grave of a youth at Garton Slack were two walnut-sized lumps of yellow ochre, 'the sides and corners of which being clearly rounded by use',[56] and the corpses may have been painted in totemistic patterns before burial. Body-painting at times of ceremony as well as warfare is almost normal practice amongst early societies. There must be a possibility that both the skulls and the faces of the people carrying them along the avenues at Avebury were meticulously coloured as the occasion decreed.

The funerary associations of Avebury's stone circles are revealed not only by the human bones but by some of the most easily ignored and also mysterious objects found there, the stone discs. About the size of a hand's palm and roughly flaked around its edges one of sandstone rested near the stonehole at Avebury's third circle and another of sarsen lay in the north-west area of the earthwork. Several more were excavated at Windmill Hill and one came from the forecourt of West Kennet. It is their relationship with the dead that is intriguing because many have been found in the British Isles in stone circles with cremations, from chambered tombs and round barrows, sometimes deep in the ashes of a pyre.[57] Their presence at Avebury supports the belief that rites connected with the dead were enacted there, these crude stone plaques perhaps being akin to the *churingas* of Australian aborigines, painted tablets that represented the souls of the dead and their journey to the afterworld.

In May 1911 Gray found a similar disc deep in the collapsed rubble of the ditch opposite the Barber's Stone. It had been burned at one edge, maybe because it had been placed with a body during the scorching of the bones. The rarity of stone objects at Avebury makes the discovery of discs like this with its strong links with death all the more impressive.[58]

On the island of Ambryn near Malekula on the opposite side of the world to Avebury where the natives also built stone circles the bodies of great men were not buried but were laid out in a house, the women and children sleeping there, tending the body, removing the worms, until it was possible to take away the skull and long-bones and hang them up. Eventually the skull was carried to the sacred place of the clan at which time the soul of the dead man could go to the Land of the Dead if it were able to follow the intricate, dangerous maze that led to it. Sometimes the skulls were used in rites from which women were excluded.[59]

That the rituals involving human bone at Avebury were held in the darkness of midwinter is unproveable but the fact that its two Coves, themselves in the likeness of tomb entrances, were connected with the night, the North Circle Cove facing towards the moon's most northerly rising, the Cove at Beckhampton towards the sunrise at midwinter, suggests that nocturnal winter activities were once performed here. To go much further is to speculate too far. Whereas the South Circle with its central Obelisk could have been the place for rites of springtime regeneration, the tall sarsen being an image of the ancestors and fecundity of the earth, the North Circle with its Cove was possibly the place for winter rituals when the dead had offerings brought to them in the 'forecourt' of the Cove itself. A little more may be said.

At the village of Sarembal on Malekula a stone circle, two avenues and dancing were integrated in ceremonies of initiation, one avenue half a mile long leading westwards to a ring of tallish stones, the islanders' dancing-ground like another at Epmunbangg where Deacon witnessed the celebrations that accompanied the raising of a phallic tree-trunk gong. Men danced around the centre of the ring, the women at its edge. 'They were decorated with shell-disc woven armlets, their faces were painted, and scented leaves were stuck in their armbands.' Away from the men

218

94. The ruined chamber of Lugbury chambered tomb seventeen miles west of Avebury. Like the Shelving Stones, without its long mound it is very like a Cove.

the women danced in groups, the men stamping in a circle anti-clockwise, the women dancing to and fro 'with a lilting pit-a-pat step' into the evening and beyond the sunset. 'So from the dusk to dawn, without respite, the dance went on. As darkness gathered, torches of reeds were thrust into the glowing embers, and handed to the dancers who, holding them aloft, continued their circling.'[60]

These former cannibals had structures rather like Avebury's Obelisk and its enclosing Z-Stones if that feature did once form a square around the central pillar. Layard described the rectangular enclosure of four posts called 'the grave' the men put up around a wooden statue or standing stone that was inhabited by the ancestral spirit.[61] In some parts of the island these tall monoliths stood by dolmens, settings of stones that symbolised both tomb, the mother's womb and the Cave of the Dead into which a dead man's ghost had to pass on its way to the after-world.[62] Avebury's Coves could have been the counterparts of these dolmens.

These Coves are so like the entrances of long chambered tombs around Avebury that it is feasible they were raised as imitations of those forecourts. Two other Coves, one at Stanton Drew in Somerset roughly aligned towards extreme moonrise, another at Arbor Low in the Peak District facing the maximum moonset, were put up in areas of megalithic tombs. Indeed, the bones of a man were found alongside Arbor Low's Cove by St. George Gray in 1901.[63] Perhaps significantly in terms of what has previously been said about medicine-men and priests the body lay extended on its back like the skeleton at Upton Lovell with its perforated bone points. 'No relics were found with the skeleton.' The stoneholes of a third Cove were detected at the circle–henge of Cairnpapple in Scotland, a site with many similarities to Arbor Low, both the Coves having scraps of human bone in pits near them. Nothing was found in some desultory digging at Stanton Drew's Cove. 'No charcoal or other mark of fire was discovered.'[64]

The restricted size of these Coves means that they could never have been used for scientific observation of the heavens. Yet there is no reason to doubt the interest of prehistoric people in the movements of the sun and moon, the most obvious symbols of warmth and cold, light and darkness, life and death in their world, and the union of the moon with the ceremonies of death in these Coves provides us not only with information about the nocturnal nature of some rites but also with an added glimpse of the poetic vision of these people.

Whether, then, from the west along the Beckhampton Avenue or southwards from the Sanctuary, one can imagine torchlit processions as the moon rose, fleshless skulls carried into the inner ring of the North Circle like the Whiteleaf Hill and Callis Wold mortuary ditches, acts of propitiation around the Cove to prevent the spirits of the dead from revisiting the living in the barren winter nights, the token burials of a newly dead chieftain before his corpse was borne down the avenue to the place where it would be buried and a round barrow heaped over his grave.

> And many a time, within the woods alone,
> Have I sat watching on the heaps of stone
> Where dwell the giants dead; and many a time
> Have my pale lips uttered the impious rhyme,
> That calls the dead from their unchanged abode.
>
> William Morris. *Life & Death of Jason.* xv. 449.

Primitive life is encircled by the year and its seasons. With the coming of spring and the preparations for sowing the new crops the third and perhaps most vital ritual took place, and the assembled evidence, however fragmentary it is, from the stones themselves, from the figurines and the carvings, from the Obelisk, from related prehistoric societies, and from legends, all suggests that sexuality was an important aspect of this agricultural ceremony.

The destruction of the Beckhampton Avenue means that the shapes of its sarsens are unknown but the alternating pillars and lozenges of the Kennet Avenue—not a feature, incidentally, of the earlier circles—are so obvious that it must be presumed that there was an intended symbolism in the juxtaposition of tall cylindrical stones and low, broad slabs. The suggestion that these represented male and female sexual organs has much to commend it with the whole avenue fashioned in the image of fertility, the excited participants at the spring festival moving between these evocative stones towards the great rings of Avebury, passing the sarsens where bodies lay buried, three of them at the foot of 'female' stones.[65]

Assertions of sexuality may titillate the mind and yet not convince it. Despite Eliade's claim that 'it must be remembered what a close connection there is between woman and sexuality on one hand and tilling and the fertility of the soil on the other' this does not prove that people at Avebury tried to influence the yield of the earth by copulating together. The sexual appearance of the avenue pillars and diamonds may be illusory although the male lines and female triangles incised on some Gambian stone circles shows that such symbolism can exist in the minds of primitive agriculturalists.[66] In any case, the proper evidence of the carved chalk phallus and pregnant woman in the flint mines of Grimes Graves must not be forgotten, placed where the flint had petered out. Nor must one ignore the squat, breasted figurine with extended penis from the Somerset marshes, buried where the ground was treacherous and unsafe. Surely these are examples in which symbols of sexuality were expected to make places better for human beings. At the Dorset henge of Maumbury Rings over forty tapering pits plunged deep into the earth around the inside of the bank, nearly all of them containing offerings of human bones, or sherds, or pieces of carved chalk and unused antler. In one there was a huge chalk phallus that had been scraped and smoothed with a serrated flint. It lay within a few centimetres of the antlered skull of a red deer propped against the wall rather like the woman's statuette at Grimes Graves.[67] This combination of male organ and what is generally believed to be the 'female' symbol of the antlers implies a belief that homeopathic magic, the ritual imitation of an action, would create whatever was desired.

> For four days before they committed the seed to the earth the Pipiles of Central America kept apart from their wives in order that on the night before planting they might indulge their passion to the fullest extent; certain persons are even said to have been appointed to perform the sexual act at the very moment when the first seeds were deposited in the ground.

Frazer gave other examples of this bond between human mating and the fecundity of the soil, concluding that 'it would be unjust to treat these orgies as a mere outburst of unbridled passion; no doubt they are deliberately and solemnly organised as essential to the fertility of the earth and the welfare of man'.[68]

The time of spring-sowing is the very time that the stags browsing at the margins of the dense forests around Avebury, heads raised at the scent of wolves, were losing their grey winter coats and shedding their antlers, events that were probably imitated by the antlered medicine-men costumed in deer hides. So numerous are the antler picks found in the earthworks like Avebury and Durrington Walls that it is a minor mystery where prehistoric man got them from. Foresters can go for weeks without seeing a single shed antler, and to have accumulated hundreds suggests an intensive search of the trackless, threatening woodlands at the time of shedding before the red deer eat them. The rutting of deer in autumn, their division into separate herds of stags and of pregnant does through the winter, the birth of the calves in May could have been the acts of a cyclical drama that was played out by men and women in the belief that the mating of human beings would influence the yield of the harvest.

95. The 'Sacred Marriage' on the Maltegard pot-lid.

It has even been suggested that the Obelisk was a phallic pillar like some later stones in prehistoric Ireland. It is possible. Single standing stones were often associated with the dead as can be seen from the vast pillars standing at the heads of long mounds in Brittany. In Britain some stand outside the entrances to chambered tombs, others actually inside like the smoothed, round-headed stone in the chamber of Bryn Celli Ddu on Anglesey. In stone circles central stones are quite firmly linked with death by their burials at their bases[69] and it will be recalled that an urn was found close to the Obelisk.

An identification with death and ancestral spirits does not preclude a further identity as a fertility symbol. The two can be complementary. On Malekula the sacred stones which are set at the centre of many village dancing-grounds are regarded as clan totems and as ancestral stones yet at least one of these important monoliths was known as the 'Penis of the Ambat'.[70] Whether such associations existed at Avebury is doubtful. The links between the Obelisk and death are fairly clear making its interpretation as an ancestor-stone more probable. The presence of the holed Ring Stone is a more likely indication of the fertility rites that took place in the circles.

One tantalising whisper of the ancient merging of fertility cults, death, sexual activities and holed stones comes from a prosaic object, a pot-lid from Denmark. Made of sandstone and with a roughly shaped edge like the stone discs from Wessex this had a well-finished perforation at its centre and was the lid of a Bronze Age cremation urn from Maltegard. Engraved on it the matchstick figure of a man, his extended penis touching the edge of the hole, holds out his hands to a woman on the other side of the perforation. Behind her is a May Tree, the forerunner of the Maypole, that symbol of fecundity described by Philip Stubbes, the puritan, as a 'stinking Idol' because of the depravity he knew accompanied its raising in the villages of Elizabethan England, when 'all the young men and maides, old men and wives, run gadding over-night to the woods, groves, hills and mountains, where they spend the night in plesant past-times'.[71]

The whole scene from Maltegard, sometimes called the Sacred Wedding, is encircled by what may be a wreath of spring flowers. If the central hole represented the underground presence of the rich Earth for whom such mating was essential, the holed Ring Stone could have stood for the same principle of ritual mating at the time of sowing. The Maltegard lid demonstrates that death in the form of the cremated bones, life and generation were not separate concepts in the prehistoric mind.[72]

Amongst the Bronze Age rock-carvings in Scandinavia there are many compositions of men brandishing axes underneath the wheel-discs of the sun. That these were men is unmistakeable from their erect organs, a condition which implies that sexual activity was fundamental to the rites. Scenes on many rocks make this quite certain because acts of copulation are explicitly shown. 'The part would be played, perhaps by a priest, who would be considered for the occasion to embody the deity. Sometimes the engraving reveals clearly that the fertilising of animals was thought to be of paramount importance'.[73] Unmistakable carvings on many rocks around Bohuslän have men and animals or men and long-haired women coupling. On the surface of a stone at Hoghem there is a 'spring wedding between a man and a woman, and a man mating with a cow', and another at Litsleby portrays a highly phallic man and an ox-team ploughing the third furrow of a field.

It is obvious that he is engaged in the first ploughing of the year to awaken the earth's fruitfulness after the sleep of winter with the phallus of the plough, the ploughshare ... The man's enormous phallus and the highly exaggerated reproductive organs of the oxen speak for themselves. The branch [in his hand] is a 'may tree', a feature of the spring fertility cult.[74]

The likelihood of similar rites of imitative magic to enhance the fertility of the earth and the herds having taken place inside stone circles like Avebury is increased by the many legends of marriages that are attached to them, not only in Britain but in

several parts of the world. Not only are the Gambian rings and the stones at Peshawur petrified wedding parties but a circle at Asota in the foothills of the Himalayas is said to be a group of women raped by bandits who, themselves, were transformed into boulders as they fled up the hillside.[75] Stones in Brittany and elsewhere in the megalithic regions of France were reputed to have the power to make sterile women fruitful.[76] Legends of the wedding at Stanton Drew, about 'going to the stanes' at Callanish in the Hebrides where the cuckoo sang its May song of spring from the circle,[77] the stone dancers of the Nine Maidens, the Eight Rocks, Belstone, the Nine Stones all point to spring rituals inside Avebury's circles in which the themes of death, sexuality and regeneration were strong. It is too fanciful to speak of a Ring of Death and a Ring of Life and the titles would, anyway, misrepresent the thinking of the alien and distant people who raised the stones. It is just possible to see their wraiths, grey as the stones themselves and lost against their outlines but hard as we may try there is nothing else. Stukeley knew this. 'Indeed in these works of antiquity, I would be as temperate as possible in multiplying conjectures; and to nothing more can I pretend in this case . . . for we want sufficient *data*. A future age may pronounce with more certainty.'[78]

Throughout southern and western Britain people were engaging in rites like those

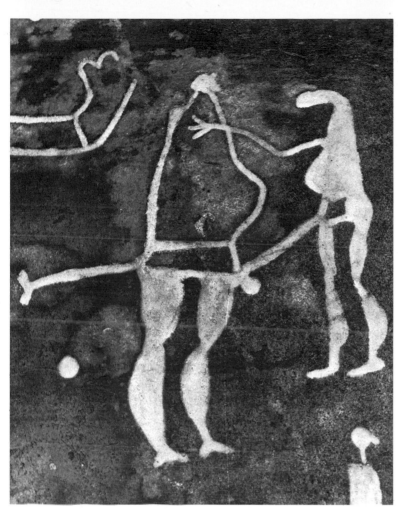

97. Rock-carving of a man and woman. From Hvarlös, Bohuslän, Sweden.

at Avebury if the presence of centre stones, avenues and Coves can be interpreted as revealing similar beliefs. Axe-traders from Cornwall or Cumbria would understand the import of the tall Obelisk even though the Cove would be strange to them. In the variety of its architecture and the complexity of its ceremonies Avebury was a cosmopolitan centre only partly matched at that time by its cousin at Stanton Drew where in an area of long chambered mounds a great stone circle was flanked by two smaller rings with an outlying stone on the high ridge to the north-east and a Cove, its flanking stones split from the same block of conglomerate, at the edge of a terrace to the west. Two short avenues joined outside the rings where the ground sloped down to a shallow river. For once Stukeley was generous. 'Mr. Aubrey, that indefatigable searcher-out of antiquities, is the first that has observed it',[79] he wrote of Stanton Drew. Almost every feature of Avebury is reproduced here but in a fragmented way as the elements were rearranged by an individual community. The same is largely true at Arbor Low where the bank and ditch enclosed a toppled ring of stones with a collapsed Cove inside it. An unobtrusive earthen bank wanders away from the henge's entrance towards the empty mound of Gib Hill. Although there is no central stone at Arbor Low there are reports of a holed stone being connected with the circle.[80]

The further from Avebury the fewer the features in common, something which could be expected in those days of difficult travel, but the themes of death and fertility, expressed differently in every region, seem common to many stone circles in the British Isles in rituals undertaken by people concerned by the fragility of their existence. We have no need to be told that Arbor Low 'could be the "central support" of the British ley system' or that 'a very sincere man, now dead, spent a night at Arbor Low stone circle, where he awakened to be told by "ghosts" of Atlanteans that it had been erected by them', an experience which suggests that he had gone to sleep in high spirits.[81] The men and women of prehistoric Britain deserve better than this silliness.

One matter barely touched upon is the question of sacrifices because the evidence is untrustworthy, but it is unlikely to be coincidence that at some henges burials have been discovered at the entrances as though guarding them. At Llandegai in North Wales cremations were found in pits outside both the henges there. At Durrington Walls, close to Stonehenge, the leg-bone of a man lay in the ditch by the south causeway. This may have been no more than the casual discarding of an unwanted bone like some of those at Avebury but this could not be true of the burials at Gorsey Bigbury in Somerset where a man, woman and child, physically like many of the Beaker people in Britain, had been carefully buried in a stone cist at the west end of the ditch only for the young woman and child to be disinterred, probably by a Grooved Ware community who knew exactly where they lay, when their flesh had rotted. The skull of the man, a person of great muscular strength, was left in the cist. The rest of his bones and the woman's were scattered in the earth around it. Just the skulls of the woman and child were reburied at the east of the entrance. These were certainly not normal burials and the fact that these Beaker people were buried here well before 'the main beaker occupation' some years later suggests that the bodies were dedicatory offerings in the henge rather than the reverent disposal of a well-loved family group.[82]

At the earthwork of Marden, the Grooved Ware settlement only a few miles south of Avebury, the body of a young woman who may have suffered from recurrent malnutrition in her childhood was put in the ditch right alongside the north entrance. Again, this could have been an ordinary burial but, if so, it is remarkable that the body of yet another young woman should have been found by Gray by Avebury's south entrance, buried there like the skeleton at Marden some time after the ditch was dug. The dwarf at Avebury had been placed inside an oval setting of sarsens, one of them being the broken half of a ring-stone that might have been the remains of the first outlier of the South Circle, replaced when the bank was erected.

The woman lay in the fine silt, her teeth worn down, one missing, and with her were some flints, some broken pottery, a sheep's foot-bone and a small crudely shaped ball of chalk just like those fertility objects with the antlers at Grimes Graves.[83] She lay with her head to the south, a common Beaker practice in Wessex when burying women, as has been noticed with the burial in the Sanctuary stone circle.[84]

Every one of these 'burials' appears to be of a Beaker person. Beaker pottery was

226

98. Aerial view of Stanton Drew, Somerset, from the north, showing the small north-east ring and the great Centre Circle which is about the same size as the inner rings at Avebury. Slight remains of avenues can be seen to the left of each ring.

recovered at Llandegai and at Gorsey Bigbury in monuments built by native people. 'The ghosts of strangers, being unfamiliar with the country, are much less likely to stray away from their skulls' and so make better guardians observed Frazer when writing of the ancient practice of sacrificing strangers at the time of harvest.[85] Strangers were, moreover, regarded as representatives of the corn-spirit.

The skeletons of these young women lying in their graves by the entrances of prehistoric earthworks tell us that life then was savage, harsh and short, ridden with fears, and that death was not distant but always within a shadow's length of the men and women of Avebury.

99. (*over page*) Three stones of the South Circle. It was near the middle one that human skull fragments were discovered.

CHAPTER NINE

After Avebury

They speak of different times, or perhaps of different people, new successions from the continent, that drove out the former possessors who performed these works, more northward and westward.

William Stukeley. *Abury*, 49.

AFTER nearly five unbroken centuries of labour the giant monuments were finished, first Silbury Hill, then the sarsen circles, the ditch, the bank, the Outer Circle, the long stretches of the avenues, finally the stone rings of the Sanctuary. Grass was growing over the scars where the stones had been dragged. Twenty generations of men and women had died since the building started and now it was done, a complex of enormous works to be used by the whole population of the Marlborough Downs. Year after year the ceremonies were performed through the autumns and winters of decade after decade as though time would always be the same. Yet it would not last.

Society was changing. The custom of taking corpses to the communal tomb with its jumble of bones was slowly replaced by individual burials under circular mounds of chalk, the dead beneath their round barrows taking personal possessions with them into the other world. Wealth was now apparent. For the first time metal ores were being worked, and little copper knives became articles of prestige. Gold ear-rings and buttons with gold cappings, copper pins, archers' wristguards of beautifully polished stone, these were luxury goods that, however rare they were, showed how riches and power centred on the chiefs and their leading warriors. Already the very vastness of Avebury, lacking any conspicuous place to act as the focus for a garishly ornamented leader, may have seemed inappropriate for the new ways.

Because it is their burials that often have the richest grave-goods it seems likely that some of this social change was caused by Beaker people even though there were never many of them. For the whole of the seven hundred years when beakers were being made in the British Isles fewer than thirty pots have been discovered in the Avebury district, some as early as 2500 BC, four perhaps as late as 1800 BC, and their makers, physically so different from the slender, short, long-headed natives, may have obtained power through their murderous short bows and knives even though their numbers were small.[1] At Avebury, as well as the complete vessels buried by the stones of the Kennet Avenue other early sherds were found in the upper levels of the ditch, dropped there years after the earthwork was built and when the human bones and flints were already covered by wind-blown earth and chalk and rotted grass.[2] These smashed bits of beaker were not offerings but casual breakages and at Avebury the only evidence that Beaker people used the rings for their own ceremonies may be the burial of the young woman by the South Entrance.

230

100. Alan Sorrell's reconstruction of Avebury. There should be a concentric ring inside the North Circle. The 'kink' in the Kennet Avenue near the southern entrance is well shown.

The condition of her teeth and the childhood malnutrition of the other woman at Marden expose the myth of any golden age in prehistoric Britain. The inflamed facial bones of a child under a round barrow on Overton Hill near the Sanctuary, the arthritic state of three skeletons in the same mound, and the suggestion of anaemia and rickets in a fourth child demonstrate the instability of life in those days. At Charlton Marshall in Dorset three round barrows were dug into in the early nineteenth century. From one came the remains of 'a hardy fellow whose skull was cracked, probably by a stone axe, but the fracture ossified and he got well without a surgeon'.[3] These people, taller and more robust than the aboriginal inhabitants of the Marlborough Downs, were just as prone to sickness, accident and childhood death and they had the same desperate need for intercession with the malignant powers around them.

At first, Beaker burials were in pits with no barrows over them, flat and featureless graves in which the body was laid, crouched up as though asleep, head to the north, quite different from the burials in northern England and Scotland where the Beaker custom was to put men on their left side, head at the east and facing south, women on their right, head westwards, also looking to the south. In this, as with the long mounds and the Coves, the links between death and sun can readily be detected. Both William Cunnington I and John Thurnam noticed the habit Beaker people in Wessex had of placing heads of male corpses to the north, presumably to look towards either the rising or the setting sun. 'We have frequently found the body deposited in a cist, with the legs and knees drawn up, and the head placed towards the north', wrote Sir Richard Colt Hoare, Cunnington's patron, and Thurnam noted that in four out of five round barrows the skull lay to the north.[4] He also observed that in those barrows where the head was not at the north it was often to the west of south, 'pointing probably to the greater number of deaths in winter when the sunrise is to the south of east',[5] a sensible interpretation based on his own experience as a country doctor.

Such obsession with the orientation of a corpse in its grave shows unarguably both how these prehistoric people associated the sun with death and also how their alignments were symbolic, the dead man sealed in his pit where no sunrise could penetrate, his lifeless eyes looking towards another sunrise in another world. Like the broken flints and the shattered pots of the previous Neolithic Age his release from life enabled him to enter another existence but now taking his undamaged beaker and knife and perfect arrowheads with him.

New cult-practices werre being introduced, intermixing with the former beliefs or, sometimes, superseding them. As the idea of the 'single grave' became established the long mounds were gradually abandoned, the fragmentary skeletons in them covered over with thick layers of rubble and earth. There was no desecration.

The modern visitor to the West Kennet long barrow, when he gazes admiringly at the enormous sarsens that obstruct the entrance and when he wonders why access to the passage is so awkward and devious, is looking at a tomb that was deliberately blocked up maybe a thousand years after it was built. Some time after the last burial native people carried basketloads of clean chalk, panniers of soil dirty with charcoal and ash, scatters of animal bones, flints, broken bits of the local Peterborough pots,

101. The façade of West Kennet. The largest stone and its flankers were put up to block off the original curved forecourt.

some Grooved Ware, some beakers, the remnants of occupation that by tradition was a fitting accompaniment to the spirits of the dead. All this was piled into every chamber and in the passage, up to the roof, filling the tomb with this rich, dead collection of broken artefacts, food and soil. 'The total bulk of the filling must have amounted to at least 2,500 cubic feet', so many hundreds of loads that they must have been carried by people who thought it appropriate to seal off this ancient shrine in such a way, filling it with the sort of offerings the dead had always been given.[6]

Yet it was being closed simply because these beliefs were no longer strong. Exactly when it was done is uncertain but the variety of beaker sherds suggest that a date around 2250 BC would not be unlikely, soon after the Kennet and Beckhampton Avenues were completed, when Beaker people had been in the Avebury region for two hundred years and when they may have become the dominant group. But it was native expertise that raised two huge stones outside West Kennet's entrance in line with the passage and then set up three even bigger sarsens straight across the curved forecourt, closing it, filling the space with hundreds of small boulders until it was no longer possible to see the chamber, passage or entrance. It was the end of the megalithic tomb and although the old beliefs must have lingered on for generations it was also the end of one form of ancestor cult. No longer were skulls and femurs to be used in the ceremonies. Now the important dead were given their own private graves where they would lie undisturbed.

Over the years that bridged the end of the Late Neolithic and the beginning of the Early Bronze Age it became more and more common to heap a round barrow over the grave, a circular mound twenty metres or more across, the height of two men but with no passage or entrance to the burial. Often these barrows stand on the skyline because their builders set them not on the summit of the hills and ridges but

102. A cemetery of round barrows at Lambourn, Berkshire.

slightly down the slope where they would be visible from below. William Stukeley, that remarkable field archaeologist, was the first to realize this. 'I observe the barrows upon Hakpen Hill and others are set with great art not upon the very highest part of the hills but upon so much of the declivity or edge, as that they make app.[earance] as above to those in the valley.'[7]

Today from Avebury one can see such barrows studding the line of the Ridgeway along which the traders and travellers passed. Others were put up within the overgrown enclosure on Windmill Hill. Stukeley dug into one in 1724 and his sketch of it and the decorated urn he extracted still survives although the rotted human bone has disappeared.[8]

Often on Salisbury Plain but only infrequently on the Marlborough Downs several barrows were set out in a row, linear cemeteries extending further and further as new barrows were added over the years like the splendid lines of plain and ditched mounds at Winterbourne Stoke near Stonehenge. A rare group like this exists on Overton Hill by the Sanctuary, John Aubrey's 'Seaven-Barrowes' which were known as the *Seofon-beorgas* as early as the tenth century AD. Built in the Early Bronze Age the mounds still stand by the Ridgeway, outlines blurred by grass, sides rounded by weather, their bases sliced by the plough. An ordinary one hides by the hedge south of the busy road, its contents of skeletons, wooden coffin, bronze knife, axe and pin long since removed. Others to the north, in the fenced field, run northwards, ditched and banked, robbed of their urns, cremated bone and

234

exotic ornaments. The rich contents suggest that these were the graves of chieftains but when both men and women and children are found in them one may also think of inherited status in which women fully shared and from which children were not excluded, the bodies under barrows that were sometimes made even more conspicuous by the wide space in which they stood, encircled by a bank and ditch that kept the respectful onlooker at a distance.[9] Stukeley had no doubt. 'They are assuredly the single sepulchres of kings, and great personages, buried during a considerable space of time, and that in peace. There are many groups of them together, and as family burial places.'[10]

It is noteworthy that whereas over all Wessex fewer than one barrow in twelve had a bank and ditch around it the Avebury region had the much higher proportion of one to seven including three on Overton Hill.[11] If such 'fancy' barrows are early one might conclude that at the beginning of the Early Bronze Age Avebury still enjoyed more wealth and power than the regions to its south. Stukeley, perhaps referring to one of these rich barrows, recorded that the 'Landlord of the *White Hart*', the ale-house at the foot of Overton Hill, 'says the head lay north in the barrow they opened'.[12]

As the skill of metalsmiths increased, mixing tin with copper to produce bronze, so the splendour of the burials increased. At Hemp Knoll, not three miles south west of Avebury, people who must have gone to the stone circles for the ceremonies there dug out a massive grave, over two metres square and nearly as deep, removing fifteen tons of solid chalk to make a vault in which they built a wooden room for the dead man. On his wrist was an archer's wristguard of smoothed green slate. His belt was fastened with a toggle of carved, polished bone. A short-necked beaker, possibly brimming with mead, was placed by his feet. More grimly, the body of a little child was set down near him. All this was part of the new belief in the dead taking their most valued belongings with them but, showing how old traditions persisted, when the grave was partly back-filled the mourners spread an ox-hide, hoofs and skull still attached, over the burial just as people had done nearly two thousand years before at the long barrow of Fussells Lodge. At the end of the elaborate interment a large round barrow was built over it. Under a similar barrow at Winterbourne Monkton two ox skulls were put on the body of another Beaker man.[13]

Other ox-remains on the Marlborough Downs, at Beckhampton, Manton and Monkton Down point to a growing cult of the bull, perhaps as a totem animal, quite distinct from the stag-cult hinted at by the antlers or skulls so often found under round barrows around Stonehenge or in Dorset where two bodies at Chaldon Herring were seated upright with antlers on their shoulders.[14] Such differences between the people of Avebury and Salisbury Plain may be yet another reflection of the tribal divisions and antagonisms which were strengthening as the population grew and as land became even scarcer.

Herds of cattle grazed on the plains, intermingling with small flocks of brown, long-coated sheep. Wheat was still grown but now barley also was cultivated, and for the first time crops were planted on the higher downs in fields walled with stones cleared from the land. Competition for marginal soils and for trade magnified tensions between regions and intensified the feeling of belonging and identification

103. Soay sheep at the Butser Experimental Farm, Hampshire. These are the closest relatives to British prehistoric sheep alive today.

that is so strong a feature of tribalism. In the great circles of Avebury rites that emphasised the unity of the tribe, the strength of the chief, the power of the tribal gods must by now have been important parts of the ceremonies, possibly the witch-doctors or priests dressed in bull-hides, wearing bull-masks, dancing in mimes of the tribe's ancestors and their heroic deeds.

Within the great regions the clan-territories were maintained, their petty chieftains striving to emulate the glory and authority of the tribal leader. Several outlying stone circles were built, like village churches within the diocese of a cathedral.

Near Avebury was the Broadstones ring at Clatford, finally destroyed in the 1880s but noticed and described by Aubrey. 'In a Lane from Kynet towards Marleborough, doe lie fall'n down, eight huge stones in a Circle', to which Stukeley added that the sarsens lay 'at a flexure in the river' near the point where the dry valley of Clatford Bottom reached the Kennet only half a mile south of the Devil's Den chambered tomb.[15] The proximity of Bronze Age temple to the earlier Neolithic shrine suggests that both may have been built at the edge of a territory whose boundaries remained unaltered for centuries.

Peasants, warriors, women with their children, the brightly-clothed and glittering chieftain once came to this ring of stones by the river where the land sloped, spread with sarsens, from the downs, the people coming at a time of death,

236

bringing the body here, or at harvest, or to avert a feared danger. Their voices and movements gave the ring a meaning. Now the stones themselves have gone and the only sound and motion is the slow flowing of the Kennet.

This circle was about an hour's walk east of Avebury, far enough away to justify a separate monument for clan use. Almost the same distance to the south was an uncertain little ring in Langdean Bottom, very small but with the wreckage of a possible avenue of stones leading to it. Much farther away, nine miles north of Avebury, are the fallen pillars of the Coate Circle, prostrate and three-quarters covered by turf but when A. D. Passmore probed the ground he found several were up to three metres long. Like Langdean there was the suggestion of an avenue leading to the ring from the north.[16] It has been thought that Richard Jefferies first recognised the remains of this ring and, undoubtedly, he had an affinity with the people who had moulded the ancient landscape before him.

> There were grass grown tumuli on the hills to which of old I used to walk, sit down at the foot of one of them, and think. Some warrior had been interred there in the ante-historic times. The sun of the summer morning shone on the dome of sward, and . . . I felt at that moment that I was like the spirit of the man whose body was interred in the tumulus.[17]

In the case of Coate, however, it was John Aubrey, two hundred years before Jefferies, who wrote that 'at Brome near Swindon in Wiltshire', hardly a mile from Coate, 'in the middle of a pasture ground called Long-stone is a great Stone ten foot high (or better) standing upright', the ruin of a circle with a row of stones 'in a right line' leading to it.[18]

Very close indeed to Avebury near the ritual site on the Kennet Avenue and alongside a possible long barrow is the surviving stone of a large ring of twelve sarsens whose filled-up holes were noticed by the 'zealous antiquarian', Mr Falkner of Devizes in 1840.[19]

The most impressive of the lesser centres stood at Winterbourne Bassett, an hour's walk north from Avebury, where a huge concentric circle was erected, two-thirds the size of the Avebury circles. Stukeley saw its remains with a 'single, broad flat, and high stone' outside to the west. By 1881 every stone had fallen and the Revd A. C. Smith probed the ground, returning the following year with his friend, the Revd W. C. Lukis, to determine where the pillars had stood. They located a tumbled stone near the middle but could not find the outlier although there were other collapsed sarsens to the east of this once-splendid ring. Today a few stones lie without order or meaning in a long, hedged field. As in all these minor rings Time and the indifference of local farmers has destroyed them and only Avebury survives as a memento of the lives of prehistoric people who raised the stones four thousand years ago. Like Clatford and Falkner's Circle there was an earthen long barrow close to the Winterbourne Bassett circle, and less than a mile west nine sarsens covering prehistoric burials were hauled away in 1854.[20]

Every one of these outlying rings was built near a source of stone. Where, to the west of Avebury, there was none there were no stone circles although the existence of long and round barrows testifies to the presence of prehistoric people there. It

104. The north-west arc of the Outer Circle.

may be that timber rings, the posts long perished, were put up. The same is probably true of Salisbury Plain where only two unimposing stone circles were built, one at Tisbury in a rare and tiny area of Portland and Purbeck stone.[21] The other was the first ring at Stonehenge.

By 2200 BC the makers of some distinctive elegant burnished beakers were masters of Salisbury Plain, their copper knives, well-made wristguards, their pairs of gold-capped conical buttons and polished belt-toggles all indicating the aristocratic appearance of these people who dominated the local population. Even their clothing was different for their decorated buckles 'seem to be . . . for narrow strap-like belts, used to keep fastened wrap-around garments of the sarong or loin cloth type, which we know from the Danish bogs to have been the normal male garb in slightly later times'.[22]

Already these Beaker warriors had established trading links with Ireland, bringing copper and gold from the Wicklows, recrossing the seas back to south-west Wales, sailing towards the landmark of the misty Preseli mountains. Perhaps because they had seen the impressive stone circles surrounding New Grange or had travelled far to the west to the monstrous bank and stones of the Lios where, as at New Grange, sherds of their beakers have been found, one of their leaders must have decided that a stone circle should be added to the old earthwork at Stonehenge.

238

105. The South Circle, with the village beyond.

What resentment this may have caused among the native descendants of its Neolithic and Grooved Ware builders cannot be known although it was these skilful woodworkers who had built the solidly constructed Woodhenge, still standing two miles away, and they may well have wondered why stones had to be brought into a region with so much timber.[23]

What is significant is that when the eighty or so stones were brought to the henge they were not dragged from the nearest plentiful source, the Marlborough Downs, but from the Preselis, nearly two hundred miles away, along the route these Beaker traders travelled every year. It was a commitment which must have taken a hundred or more years to fulfil even if one stone every year was ferried along the swirling coastline of South Wales. One must presume that the sarsens around Avebury were not available to the Stonehenge people. Yet the new circle was planned as a concentric ring like those to the north, at Winterbourne Bassett, the Sanctuary and the North Circle at Avebury itself, and with an avenue leading up to it like several others on the Marlborough Downs. One wonders if it was a conscious attempt to imitate those rings. If so, it failed. The avenue led from water but was made of chalk. No stones lined its white bank and ditches. But just as people had built the Beckhampton Avenue around the Cove so the outlying Heel Stone was encircled with a ditch and incorporated into the avenue. 'The Heel Stone was doubtless

239

hedged round, for the new builders, with all kinds of taboos and restrictions', and had to be respected.[24]

It is true that the task of transporting so many Welsh bluestones was the most awesome stone-movement ever undertaken in prehistoric Britain but the result was not especially impressive. The concentric stone circle at Stonehenge, when finished, would have covered less than half the area of the Sanctuary and would have been only one-seventh the size of Winterbourne Bassett. Fifteen Stonehenges could have been fitted comfortably into Avebury's North Circle.[25] John Aubrey's comparison between Avebury and the final, well-known structure at Stonehenge would have been even more relevant to this little bluestone ring. 'This old Monument [at Avebury] does as much exceed in bignes (greatness) the so renowned Stoneheng, as a Cathedral doeth a parish church: so that by its grandure one might presume it to have been an Arch-Temple of the Druids.'[26]

The inhabitants of Salisbury Plain had to watch the interior of their own henge transformed. If they disliked the work they could not prevent it. Their Beaker masters carried not only quiversful of hunting arrows with barbed and tanged flint heads but also had a deadlier javelin-head type. 'These heavy arrowheads possibly represent a man-killing missile.'[27]

Avebury maintained its accustomed prestige. Rich Beaker graves like that of the old man on Roundway Down showed that luxuries continued to reach there from west, east and farther north from the Peak District, Yorkshire, even from southern Scotland. Ceremonial centres like Arbor Low and Cairnpapple near Edinburgh have so many likenesses to Avebury that they demonstrate the extent of the contacts and the respect that any chieftain of the great circles and earthwork enjoyed. Indeed, the links may have become even closer over the years for there are many similarities between the users of short-necked beakers in north-east England and the Marlborough Downs.

The chance preservation of organic material in one burial near Driffield in Yorkshire permits us a glimpse of the wealth and importance of those people. Under a round barrow a tall man was buried in a sandstone cist whose capstone was so heavy that in 1851 it needed eight men and a windlass to shift it. Head to the east, facing south, the man was huddled up, a superb grey slate guard on his right wrist held in place by four bronze, gold-covered pins. At his side was his bronze dagger in a wooden sheath. Two amber beads had fallen by his neck. His corpse had been carefully wrapped in a woollen cloak or shroud, some of the earliest woven textile to be discovered in Britain. Behind his legs was his beaker. All this was splendid regalia but, as if to remind us of the alien thinking of these remote people, a hawk's skull without its body had been set down in front of his body.[28]

It was such people from the east that travelled along the Thames Valley, the long-established route to Avebury, perhaps actively engaged in the trading of black Yorkshire jet, North European amber, maybe gold and copper too. In this there would have been active rivalry with the people of Salisbury Plain.[29]

106. (*right*) Avebury. The isolated Stone 50. The mounds and hollows are the results of later fieldwalls and quarries.

The long-standing differences between the people living on the Marlborough Downs, trading and mingling with others from the east, and the natives of Salisbury Plain, reaching out westwards towards Cornwall, Wales and Ireland, would in any society have resulted either in integration or warfare.

Only forty miles south-west of Stonehenge was the earthwork enclosure of Mount Pleasant in Dorset. Here, at the very time that work on the first stone circle at Stonehenge ceased around 2100 BC, an enormous stockade of heavy posts was put up along the inner rim of the ditch. It was almost immediately burned down.[30] At Stonehenge the bluestone ring, only two-thirds finished, was abandoned, an antler pick dropped in a half-dug stonehole, the standing stones pulled down and dragged from the henge.

Archaeology can recover only part of the story. Precisely what had happened is not certain but maybe it was at this time that Beaker people were driven out of Salisbury Plain. Hardly any beakers from the period after 2100 BC have been found in central Wessex, contrasting strongly with the large numbers discovered there from earlier periods. They do, however, occur in the surrounding areas as though their makers had been driven from the prosperous grasslands around Stonehenge and it has been speculated that their displacement coincided with the rise of the famous Wessex chieftains with their riveted bronze daggers, elaborate maceheads and their ornaments of gold and amber.[31]

These new leaders may have been warriors from the continent, adventurers seizing control of the lucrative trade-routes in southern England, but it is more likely that these were native people who had risen against their masters. Pottery from their graves, collared urns and diminutive pygmy cups, always derives from older local forms, quite different from the beakers that had previously accompanied rich burials in Wessex. 'The problem here is, how can one ever demonstrate conquest, using archaeological data?'[32]

One pointer is in the rebuilding of Stonehenge. As soon as the bluestones had been taken away a new circle was begun of enormous stones with carefully shaped slabs along their tops. Within this ring five towering paired pillars surmounted by lintels stood in a horseshoe aligned towards the south-west and the setting sun. No other stone circle was like it because this was not properly a stone circle, it was a monument of wood-workers who treated the stones as they would have treated blocks of timber, shaping mortise-and-tenon joints, hacking out pegs, smoothing surfaces, rebating the undersides, chamfering the edges so that the stones would fit precisely together. It was megalithic carpentry. It was novel. One fact makes it a shout of supremacy by the inhabitants of Salisbury Plain. Its stones were sarsens, dragged from the Marlborough Downs, maybe by the people of Avebury themselves.

Whether it was conquest or a joining together of two great tribal areas must for now be an unanswered question but the very design of Stonehenge, in no way attempting to imitate the rough austerity of Avebury, suggests that its architects were determined to build the circle in their own fashion, very probably like others of timber whose lintelled posts have not survived. The project must have taken years to complete. 'This most time-consuming repetitive task may . . . indicate a slave-

242

107. Avebury from the Ridgeway. It is among the trees in the centre of the picture.

class, in the sense of a group without land or cultivation- or grazing-rights.'[33] Whereas the people of northern Wiltshire had long been accustomed to moving and erecting the sarsens there was no tradition of stone-working on Salisbury Plain where there was not even one megalithic tomb or standing stone, and it is quite possible that the thirty-, forty- and fifty-ton sarsens were drudgingly hauled over the miles to Stonehenge by the unwilling forced labour of Avebury's people, watched over by aggressive conquerors.

Certainly, in bleak contrast to the rich Wessex cemeteries around Stonehenge, the Avebury area has very few lavish burials from this period, one or two glass beads from the barrows on Overton Hill and at Bishops Cannings and one bronze dagger and an axe from a tree-trunk coffin at West Overton. There is just one magnificent collection of wealth from the round barrow at Manton where the body, maybe of an old woman dressed in a woollen garment and wrapped in a shroud, had articles of bronze, amber, shale, steatite and gold buried with her. The barrow was excavated by Maud Cunnington and her husband in 1906 and a Mr Bucknall kept the skeleton in the shed of his nearby cottage for a while, giving a visitor a fingerbone from it. Almost immediately poor circulation forced him to have one of his own fingers amputated. It is said that he used it to replace the one he had given away and then hurriedly put the skeleton back into its barrow to the confusion of future archaeologists and pathologists.[34]

The isolation of this one rich burial points to a decline in the wealth of the region in agreement with the idea that it was Stonehenge people who now dominated the trade and riches of Wessex. Very little Bronze Age pottery has been found at Avebury and only a few round barrows nearby show that the great stone circles still had some attraction.[35] Peasants worked the fields in Fyfield Down and elsewhere but the countryside was quiet and unbustling, its glories slowly forgotten. By the Middle Bronze Age the Kennet Avenue was no longer used and a field wall was built across it, a quite different story from Stonehenge where prehistoric field-systems stopped short of the avenue, respecting its sanctity.[36] And whereas lots of broken Iron Age pottery has been recovered from Stonehenge none at all has been found at Avebury and it seems that the stones and the earthwork were deserted, the bank overgrown, the ditch thick with trees.[37] A Roman visitor to Avebury would have found it abandoned.

It was a sombre ending for a monument of such splendour, its stone weather-stained, leaning, grass clawing at the sarsens, the enclosure half-hidden by bushes and trees, dark sanctuaries where the wildcat could stalk, shelter for the nervous deer, leaves settling and decaying in the ditch, cold winter winds blowing off the downs across the desolation, the people gone away for ever. The Japanese Haiku poet, Imozeni, expressed the melancholy of it.

> Not a voice or stir . . .
> Darkness lies on fields and streets
> Sad : the moon has set.

But at the end of this book about the mysteries and meanings of Avebury let the last words be with William Stukeley, its first and greatest chronicler.

> Therefore I thought it fully worth while, to bestow some pains on these temples of theirs, as the only monuments we have left, of the patriarchal religion; and especially in regard to their extraordinary grandeur and magnificence, equal to any of the noted wonders of the world.
>
> *Abury*, iii.

XII. (*right*) Stones of the south-west arc, looking south.

Abbreviations

AER	Annual Excavation Report H.M.S.O.
Ant	Antiquity
Ant J	Antiquaries' Journal
Arch	Archaeologia
Arch J	Archaeological Journal
Arch R	Archaeological Review, Council for British Archaeology, Groups XII and XIII
BAJ	Bedfordshire Archaeological Journal
C Arch	Current Archaeology
CBACE	Council for British Archaeology Calendar of Excavations
GM	Gentleman's Magazine
IAF	Irish Archaeological Forum
JAS	Journal of Archaeological Science
JDANHS	Journal of the Derbyshire Archaeological and Natural History Society
JHA	Journal for the History of Astronomy
JRAI	Journal of the Royal Anthropological Institute
PAI	Proceedings of the Archaeological Institute
PPS	Proceedings of the Prehistoric Society
PSAL	Proceedings of the Society of Antiquaries of London
PSANHS	Proceedings of the Somerset Archaeological and Natural History Society
PSAS	Proceedings of the Society of Antiquaries of Scotland
PUBSS	Proceedings of the University of Bristol Spelaeological Society
SAF	Scottish Archaeological Forum
TLCAS	Transactions of the Lancashire & Cheshire Antiquarian Society
VCH	Victoria History of the Counties of England
WAM	Wiltshire Archaeological and Natural History Magazine

XIII. (*left*) The great sarsen in the Valley of Rocks on the Marlborough Downs, looking north.

Notes

References are of two forms. In the case of a minor reference, full details are given. The more important works which are often referred to are quoted under the author's surname followed by the date of publication in brackets and then the page reference, e.g. Stukeley W. (1743), 35.

Full details of these major references are given in the Bibliography which follows these Notes.

NOTES TO THE INTRODUCTION

1. G. Cocchiara. *Il Mito del Buon Selvaggio*. Messina, 1948. 7. For a discussion of 'hard' and 'soft' primitivism and the ways in which 17th- and 18th-century antiquarians compared the prehistoric inhabitants of the British Isles with the recently discovered Indians of North America, see: S. Piggott. *The Druids*. London, 1968. 96–9, 136–42; *Ruins in a Landscape*. Edinburgh, 1976. 150–5.
2. Stukeley W. (1743).
3. Julius Caesar. *War Commentaries* (ed. R. Warner). New York, 1960. Book VI, 2, 123.
4. J. Ivimy. *The Sphinx and the Megaliths*. London, 1974.
5. J. Fergusson. *Rude Stone Monuments in All Countries*. London, 1872. 86.
6. Smith A. C. (1867), 214.
7. Thom A. (1967), (1971).
8. Thom A., Thom A. S. & Foord T. R. (1976), 191.
9. MacKie, E. W. (1977), 151.
10. M. Dames. *The Avebury Cycle*. London, 1977. 9.
11. Long W. (1858a); (1858b); (1862).
12. Aubrey J. (1665–97). See also: his *Natural History of Wiltshire* (ed. K. G. Ponting). Newton Abbot, 1969.
13. Smith I. F. (1965).
14. A. F. Aveni (ed.). *Native American Astronomy*. Austin, Texas, and London, 1977. xvi.

NOTES TO CHAPTER ONE

1. A. H. Burne. *The Battlefields of England*. London, 1950. 1–10.
2. J. R. L. Anderson. *The Oldest Road: An Exploration of the Ridgeway*. London, 1975. 91.
3. Hoare R. C. (1821), 57.
4. J. Hawkes. *A Guide to the Prehistoric and Roman Monuments in England and Wales* (rev. edn). London, 1973. 109.
5. S. Piggott. *British Prehistory*. London, 1949. 119.
6. E. C. Baity. 'Archaeoastronomy and Ethnoastronomy so far'. *Current Anthropology* 14, 1973, 389–449. 396.
7. W. Cunnington III. 'Account of a Barrow on Roundway Down near Devizes'. *WAM* 3, 1857, 185–8. 187. Annable F. J. & Simpson D. D. A. (1964), 38, nos. 59–63. Clarke D. L. (1970), 503, no. 1135.
8. Piggott S. (1962), 25, 81, 82.
9. Gray H. St. G. (1935), 145–7.

NOTES TO CHAPTER TWO

1. J. L. Todd. 'Note on Stone Circles in Gambia'. *Man* 3, 1903, 164–5. J. L. Todd & G. B. Wolbach. 'Stone Circles in the Gambia'. *Man* 11, 1911, 161–4. H. Parker. 'Stone Circles in Gambia'. *JRAI* 53, 1923, 173–228. 222.
2. Gray H. St. G. (1935), 155–7.
3. A. Robertson. 'Roman Coin Hoards from non-Roman Sites'. *WAM* 65, 1970, 199–200.
4. L. Alcock. *Arthur's Britain*. London, 1971. 109–11, 70–1, 371 n. 4. J. Morris, in *The Age of Arthur*. London, 1973. 113, suggests Solsbury Hill, 2 miles NE of Bath, a hill-fort which stands on a steep-sided hill. A. H. Burne. *The Battlefields of England*. London, 1950. 1–10.
5. E. G. H. Kempson. 'The Anglo-Saxon Name for the Avebury Circle'. *WAM* 56, 1955, 60–1; 'Waledich'. *ibid*, 190. *The Cartulary of Cirencester Abbey, Gloucestershire*. III. (ed. M. Devine). Oxford, 1977, nos. 737, 738.
6. L. Alcock. *Arthur's Britain*. London, 1971. 335.
7. D. J. Bonney. 'The Pagan Saxon Period', in *VCH* I, 2. 468–84. 479.
8. M. Deanesly. *The Pre-Conquest Church in England*. London, 1961. 81.
9. E. Ekwall. *English River-Names*. Oxford, 1928. 227–8.
10. W. Johnson. *Byways in British Archaeology*. Cambridge, 1912. 1–100. Chapters 1 and 2, 'Churches on Pagan Sites'.
11. J. M. Kemble. 'Notices of Heathen Interment in

the *Codex Diplomaticus*'. *Arch J* 14, 1857, 119–39. no. 54. *Cod. Dipl.* 1120.

12. A. H. Burne. 'Ancient Wiltshire Battlefields'. *WAM* 53, 1950, 397–412. 411.

13. K. Cameron. *English Place-Names*. London, 1969. 112. Ekwall E. (1959), 19, has a similar translation. J. E. B. Gower, A. Mawer and F. M. Stenton, in *Place-Names of Wiltshire*. Cambridge, 1939. 293–4, suggest, 'the prehistoric stronghold by the River Avon'.

14. For the Avebury font, see: A. G. R. Buck, 'Some Wiltshire Fonts, I'. *WAM* 53, 1949–50, 458–70. H. C. March. 'Note on Portions of a Cross-shaft'. *PSAL* 25, 1912–13, 177–9. Long W. (1858), 51.

15. N. Cohn. *Europe's Inner Demons*. London, 1975. 165–79.

16. P. Saintyves. *Corpus du folklore préhistorique en France et dans les colonies françaises*, III. Paris, 1936. 336, 375.

17. ed. M. Devine (note 5), 1051, no. 738; 1050, no, 737.

18. Gray H. St. G. (1935), 132.

19. Keiller A. (1939b), 9.

20. A. Meyrick. 'An Early 18th-Century Visitor to Avebury'. *WAM* 57, 1958–60, 225–6.

21. L. V. Grinsell. *Folklore of Prehistoric Sites in Britain*. Newton Abbot, 1976. 105, 106, 165. Pp. 113–22 are about sites in Wiltshire.

22. W. Camden. *Britannia* (ed. E. Gibson). London, 1695. 111.

23. A. Powell. *John Aubrey and His Friends*. London, 1963. O. L. Dick has edited, *Aubrey's Brief Lives*. London, 1949. For Aubrey as a scholar, see: M. Hunter. *John Aubrey and the Realms of Learning*. London, 1975. See also: Aubrey J. (1665–97), c. 25, 38, for another version of the Colet story.

24. His 'Monumenta Britannica', which has yet to be published, was written between about 1665 and 1697. The manuscript is in the Bodleian Library, Oxford, MS. Top. Gen. c.24, c.25. Extracts from the first part, the 'Templa Druidum', appear in Long W. (1858a), 311–18; (1858b), 3–10; (1861), 244–7.

25. The July plan may still exist. In the Royal Society library a plan of Avebury (Roy. Soc. MS. 131. 67) is inscribed, 'By Mr. Awbrey, july 8, 1663', the date of Aubrey's meeting with Charles II. In the Bodleian Library, Oxford, MS. Top. Gen. c.24, 40, there is another plan of Avebury with an early draft of the introduction to the 'Monumenta Britannica' on its back.

26. Aubrey J. (1665–97), c.24, 35. Col. R. Symonds. *Diary of the Marches of the Royal Army*, 1644 (ed. C. E. Long). London, 1859. 151.

27. S. Piggott. *The Druids*. London, 1968. 136–42.

28. Aubrey J. (1665–97), c.25, 21.

29. G. de Beer. *Hannibal*. London, 1969. 182.

30. Piggott S. (1950), 45. Stukeley W. (1717–48), 9–65. This 'Commonplace Book' of Stukeley's includes his transcription, 'From Mr. Gale's notes out of Mr. Aubury's Collections', dated Dec. 10. 1718. It is in the library of the Wiltshire Archaeological and Natural History Society, Devizes Museum.

31. Stukeley W. (1743), Tabs XV, XXIV, XXXIV.

32. Stukeley W. (1722–4), 9a.

33. Long W. (1858), 65.

34. Piggott S. (1950), 105, 114, 129. Stukeley W. (1922–4), 8b, where distances between Beckhampton, Silbury and Kennet are revised from 8000 paces to 7500, and from 7000 to 6000.

35. J. Fergusson. *Rude Stone Monuments in All Countries*. London, 1872. 150n. See also: A. Herbert. *Cyclops Christianus*. London, 1849. 106. J. Rickman. 'On the Antiquity of Avebury and Stonehenge'. *Arch* 28, 1840, 399–419. 401.

36. Piggott S. (1950), 124–31, 183.

37. Stukeley W. (1722–4), 7, 33, 244b; (1724), 39, 59, 63, 109.

38. Stukeley W. (1722–4), 244b.

39. Stukeley W. (1740), 6, 12, 15; (1743), 19–20, 31. Thom A., Thom A. S. and Foord T. R. (1976), 190, in which Rods of $2\frac{1}{2}$ Megalithic Yards (6 ft $9\frac{1}{2}$ ins or 2.07 m) are proposed.

40. Stukeley W. (1743), 53.

41. Aubrey J. (1665–97), c.24, 40. On his plan he noted the measurement from the inner edge of the western ditch across to the east as 60 perches of $16\frac{1}{2}$ ft or 990 ft (302 m). Stukeley (1743), 19, estimated the distance as 800 Druid Cubits of 20.8 ins or 1387 ft (423 m). The average diameter (Smith I. F. (1965), 193) is actually about 1140 ft (348 m).

42. A. Law. 'Caleb Baily, The Demolisher'. *WAM* 64, 1969, 100–6.

43. Long W. (1858b), 22–3.

44. Long W. (1878), 331.

45. Hoare R. C. (1821), 69–86, pl. XIII.

46. R. H. Cunnington. *From Antiquary to Archaeologist*. Aylesbury, 1975. A biography of William Cunnington I, the first of a remarkable family of Wiltshire archaeologists. See also: B. M. Marsden. *The Early Barrow Diggers*. Aylesbury, 1974. 12–24, 51–64, for an account of early excavations in Wiltshire.

47. Long W. (1858a–1878). King B. (1878); (1879).

48. Smith A. C. (1861–1885).

49. J. G. D. Clark. 'The Preservation of Avebury'. *PPS* 3, 1937, 467.

50. Thom A., Thom A. S. and Foord T. R. (1976), 191.

51. Grinsell L. V. (1957). For a synthesis of current archaeological thinking about Wiltshire prehistoric sites, see: Piggott S. (1973).

NOTES TO CHAPTER THREE

1. A. Herbert. *Cyclops Christianus: Or An Argument to Disprove the Supposed Antiquity of the Stonehenge and Other Megalithic Erections in England and Brittany.* London, 1849.
2. Aubrey J. (1665–97), c.24, 44–5.
3. Stukeley W. (1743), 27–8.
4. Burl A. (1976), 229. S. P. O'Riordain. 'Lough Gur Excavations: The Great Stone Circle (B) in Grange Townland'. *Proceedings of the Royal Irish Academy* 54C, 1951, 37–74. 47.
5. J. Hunter. 'Present State of Abury, Wilts'. *GM* 99.2, July 1829, 3–7.
6. Smith A. C. (1867).
7. J. Fergusson. *Rude Stone Monuments in all Countries.* London, 1872. 74–5.
8. Smith A. C. (1885), 160, figs 90–3. On p. 143 he calls the pottery from his own excavation at Avebury 'British'.
9. Smith I. F. (1865), 226.
10. W. Greenwell. *British Barrows.* Oxford, 1877. 508. J. R. Mortimer. *Forty Years Researches in British and Saxon Burial Mounds of East Yorkshire.* London, 1905. 102, fig. 248.
11. Lukis W. C. (1882); (1883). Avebury is described on pp. 344–6. Smith A. C. (1885), 139–42.
12. Lukis W. C. (1882), 153. Gray H. St. G. (1935), 103.
13. H. C. March. 'A New Theory of "Stone Circles"'. *TLCAS* 6, 1889, 98–111. 107.
14. Pass A. C. (1887).
15. Gray H. St. G. (1935), 103–4. Passmore A. D. (1935). The excavation was 113 m SSW of the East Entrance, and measured 43 × 2.4 m.
16. R. Bradley. 'Maumbury Rings, Dorchester: The Excavations of 1908–13'. *Arch* 105, 1975, 1–98. 4.
17. Gray H. St. G. (1935). Interim and more detailed reports of each season's work were published in the *Annual Reports* of the British Association for the Advancement of Science: 1908, 401–11; 1909, 271–84; 1911, 141–52; 1915, 174–89; 1922, 326–33.
18. Gray H. St. G. (1935), 145.
19. *Ibid*, 114.
20. S. Piggott. 'The Pottery from the Avebury Excavations', in: Gray H. St. G. (1935). 136–41.
21. H. A. W. Burl. 'Dating the British Stone Circles'. *American Scientist* 61.2, 1973, 167–74.
22. Gray H. St. G. (1909), 408.
23. Gray H. St. G. (1916), 179.
24. Gray H. St. G. (1935), 109–10.
25. A. Fahkry. *The Pyramids.* Chicago, 1969. 252. I. E. S. Edwards. *The Pyramids of Egypt.* Harmondsworth, 1947. 243. The pyramids of the pharaohs Userkaf, Neferefre and Unas were smaller and that of Sahura not much bigger than the 'Avebury' pyramid.
26. Passmore A. D. (1922).
27. M. Dames. *The Avebury Cycle.* London, 1977. 133–4.
28. J. Dyer. 'A Secondary Neolithic Camp at Waulud's Bank, Leagrave'. *BAJ* 2, 1964, 1–15. 4–5.
29. G. J. Wainwright, J. G. Evans and I. H. Longworth. 'The Excavation of a Late Neolithic Enclosure at Marden, Wiltshire'. *Ant J* 51, 1971, 177–239. 187.
30. Gray H. St. G. (1935), 133–4.
31. Cunnington M. E. (1913a).
32. Clarke D. L. (1970), 501, no. 1051, fig. 233, p. 310. The pot is Clarke's type, 'North/Middle Rhine'. According to Lanting J. N. and van der Waals J. D. (1972), fig. 1, it belongs to their Step 3 of *c.* 1900–1800 bc (*c.* 2385–2230 BC). Its presence by the Cove Stone provides a valuable date for the time before which the stone must have been erected. The beaker is in Devizes Museum, no. 451.
33. Cunnington M. E. (1913a), 7–9; and *ibid*, E. H. Goddard, 9–11.
34. Cunnington M. E. (1913b).
35. Cunnington M. E. (1931).
36. Keiller A. and Piggott S. (1936), 420.
37. Smith I. F. (1965), 251.
38. Keiller A. and Piggott S. (1936), 424. This was a burial with a beaker of Clarke's 'Developed Northern' (N2) type. See: Clarke D. L. (1970), 501, no. 1071; p. 343, no. 515. It falls within Lanting and van der Waals' Step 4, *c.* 1850–1750 bc, about 2300–2150 BC.
39. S. Piggott. 'The Pottery from the Avebury Excavations', in: Gray H. St. G. (1935), 136–41. 137.
40. The Avebury stones are numbered according to Isobel Smith's (1965) classification, p. 175. For the Outer Circle, Stone 1 is the huge stone at the South Entrance from which stones are numbered clockwise, including concrete markers, round to the gigantic Stone 98 immediately to the east of Stone 1. The South and North Inner circles begin with Stones 101 and 201 respectively. The Kennet Avenue is numbered from pair 1, now destroyed, at the South Entrance, the one on the left as the viewer faces south, being 1a, the one on the right, to the west, being 1b. The first complete pair is 13a, 13b.
41. Keiller A. (1937); (1939b), 5.
42. D. E. Chapman. *Is This Your First Visit To Avebury?* (3rd edn). London, 1947. 9.
43. H. A. W. Burl. 'Henges: Internal Features and Regional Groups'. *Arch J* 126, 1969 (1970), 1–28. 6–7.
44. Chapman (note 42), 11.

45. Smith I. F. (1965).
46. Young W. E. V. (1948); (1950).
47. Vatcher F. de M. and L. (1968), 6; (1969a), 25; (1969b), 127.
48. Piggott S. (1964).
49. Vatcher F. de M. and L. (1969b), 25; *AER*, 1969, 11–12.
50. F. de M. Vatcher. 'Recent Archaeological Investigations in the Avebury Area'. (forthcoming).
51. Burl A. (1976).
52. J. and C. Hawkes. *Prehistoric Britain*. Harmondsworth, 1943. 55.

NOTES TO CHAPTER FOUR

1. J. G. Evans and I. F. Smith. 'Cherhill'. *Arch R* 2, 1967, 8–9. The site gave a date of 5280±140 bc (BM-447) for the Mesolithic occupation. It is now built over.
2. Piggott S. (1973), 286.
3. Smith I. F. (1965), 24–8. Three post-sockets and possibly two more were noticed in a line 3 m long with a hearth to the west. A date of 2950±150 bc (BM-73) came from some charcoal nearby.
4. Overton Hill: *PPS* 32, 1966, 151; Hemp Knoll: *Arch R* 2, 1965, 7; Bishops Cannings: *ibid*, 1964, 7; Hackpen Ridge: *WAM* 48, 1939, 90–1; Roughridge Hill: *WAM* 60, 1965, 133; Avebury Down: *PSAL* 31, 1918–19, 78–108; Waden Hill: *WAM* 56, 1955–6, 167–71.
5. Evans J. G. (1975), 118. Whittle A. W. R. (1977), 238.
6. This cyclical pattern was well known amongst Neolithic farmers. The large village of Köln-Lindenthal is thought to have been reoccupied seven times. See: S. Piggott. *Ancient Europe*. Edinburgh, 1965. 52.
7. H. Hodges. *Artifacts*. London, 1964. 150–2.
8. For a discussion of the nature of early prehistoric societies in western Europe, see: A. P. Phillips. 'The evolutionary model of human society and its application to certain early farming populations of western Europe', in: Renfrew C. (ed.) (1973), 529–38. See also: M. J. Schwartz and D. K. Jordan. *Anthropology: Perspective on Humanity*. New York, 1976. 382–90, 580–93.
9. R. Wernick. *The Monument Builders*. London, 1975. 73.
10. Instances of Neolithic disease and accident are too numerous to list as they appear in almost every excavation report of Neolithic burials. Readers interested should refer to: J. Cameron. *The Skeleton of British Neolithic Man*. London, 1934. W. F. Bernfield. 'The Physique of Neolithic Man'.
Transactions of the Cardiff Naturalists' Society 91, 1961–3, 17–22. D. R. and P. Brothwell. *Food in Antiquity*. London, 1969. C. Wells. *Bones, Bodies and Disease*. London, 1964. P. A. Janssens. *Palaeopathology*. London, 1970.
11. Wor Barrow, Crichel Down: Piggott S. (1954), 49; Fengate: F. Pryor. 'A Neolithic Multiple Burial from Fengate, Peterborough'. *Ant* 50, 1976, 232–3; Ascott-under-Wychwood: *C Arch* 24, 1971, 8; Tulloch of Assery: J. W. P. Corcoran. 'Excavation of the Chambered Cairns at Loch Calder, Caithness'. *PSAS* 98, 1967, 1–75. 44; West Kennet: Piggott S. (1962), 25.
12. A. B. Deacon. *Malekula: A Vanishing People in the New Hebrides*. London, 1934. J. Layard. *Stone Men of Malekula*. London, 1942.
13. Eliade M. (1958), 260.
14. *Ibid*, 260, 332, 354–61.
15. J. G. Frazer. *The Magic Art and the Evolution of Kings*. London, 1911. 98–113, *Aftermath*. London, 1936. 153–6.
16. Eliade M. (1958), 331.
17. J. G. Frazer. *Spirits of the Corn and of the Wild*, I. London, 1912. 238–69; *The Golden Bough*. London, 1922. 399, 401–38. For sowing, see: pp. 28, 35, 136–40, 577. Eliade M. (1958), 341–7.
18. Eliade M. (1958), 352–3. References to ancestor cults are numerous. See: J. G. Frazer. *The Golden Bough, VIII. Bibliography and General Index*. London, 1936. 158.
19. P. Ashbee. *The Earthen Long Barrow in Britain*. London, 1970. 161–8.
20. J. Mellaart. *Earliest Civilisations of the Near East*. London, 1965. 86–90. For other examples of excarnation, see: J. G. Frazer. *Taboo and the Perils of the Soul*. London, 1911. 372–4. For a recent examination of the excarnated bones in a megalithic tomb, see: J. T. Chesterman. 'Burial Rites in a Cotswold Long Barrow'. *Man* 12, 1977, 22–32.
21. T. Hariot. *A Briefe and True Report of the New Found Land of Virginia*. Frankfort, 1590. Illus. XXII.
22. H. McCracken. *George Catlin and the Old Frontier*. New York, 1969. 99. For the Sioux and Choctaws, see: O. La Farge. *A Pictorial History of the American Indian*. London, 1956. 157, 27.
23. Willey G. R. (1966), 269–70. Snow D. (1976), 42.
24. B. Fagan. *Elusive Treasure: The Story of Early Archaeologists in the Americas*. London, 1978. 305.
25. Ashbee (note 19), 161–8. G. Daniel. *The Prehistoric Chamber Tombs of England and Wales*. Cambridge, 1950. 65–80. J. X. W. P. Corcoran. 'The Cotswold–Severn Group', in: Powell, Corcoran, Lynch and Scott (eds). *Megalithic Enquiries in the West of Britain*. Liverpool, 1969. 13–104, 292–5.

THE LIBRARY

 THE SURREY INSTITUTE OF ART & DESIGN

Farnham Campus, Falkner Road, Farnham, Surrey GU9 7DS

26. Piggott S. (1973), 286.
27. R. J. C. Atkinson. 'Old Mortality: Some Aspects of Burial and Population in Neolithic England', in: J. M. Coles and D. D. A. Simpson (eds). *Studies in Ancient Europe*. Leicester, 1968. 83–93.
28. Thom A. (1967), 34–55.
29. Piggott S. (1962), 15.
30. R. J. C. Atkinson, 'Waylands Smithy'. *Ant* 39, 1965, 126–33. P. Ashbee. 'The Fussells Lodge Long Barrow Excavations, 1957'. *Arch* 100, 1966, 1–80; Ashbee (note 19), 52.
31. R. Hicks. 'Thom's Megalithic Yard and Traditional Measurements'. *IAF* 4 (1), 1977, 1–7. M. Reiche. 'Ancient Peru Link with Stonehenge'. *Daily Telegraph*, 31 May 1976. A. Burl and P. Freeman. 'Local Units of Measurement in Prehistoric Britain'. *Ant* 51, 1977, 152–4.
32. A. Burl. 'Intimations of Numeracy in the Neolithic and Bronze Age Societies of the British Isles'. *Arch J* 133, 1976 (1977), 9–32. 29.
33. Hicks (note 31), 2.
34. J. R. Mortimer. *Forty Years' Researches in British and Saxon Burial Mounds in East Yorkshire*. London, 1905. 103.
35. S. Piggott. 'Heads and Hoofs'. *Ant* 36, 1962, 110–18.
36. For an analysis of the motivations of a society in such a state of stress, see: V. Reynolds. 'Ethology of Social Change', in: Renfrew C. (ed.) (1973), 467–80. 472.
37. G. Connah. 'Excavations at Knap Hill, Alton Priors, 1961'. *WAM* 60, 1965, 1–23; 'Radiocarbon Dating and Laboratory Examinations from Knap Hill'. *WAM* 64, 1969, 113–4. The antlers gave a date of 2760±115 bc (BM-205).
38. I. F. Smith. 'Neolithic Pottery from Rybury Camp'. *WAM* 60, 1965, 127. D. J. Bonney. 'All Cannings: Rybury Camp'. *WAM* 59, 1964, 185.
39. J. G. D. Clark. 'Neolithic Bows from Somerset, England, and the Prehistory of Archery in North-West Europe'. *PPS* 29, 1963, 50–98. Bows preserved in the peat of the Somerset Levels have come from Meare Heath, dated to 2700±120 bc (*c.* 3485 BC) and Ashcott Heath, 2675±120 bc (*c.* 3460 BC). Such bows had an accuracy of about sixty metres. *Ibid*, p. 59.
40. P. W. Dixon. 'Badgeworth, Gloucs. Crickley Hill'. *CBACE*, January 1978. 109.
41. A. J. E. Cave, in: A. Keiller and S. Piggott. 'Excavation of an Untouched Chamber in the Lanhill Long Barrow'. *PPS* 4, 1948, 122–50. 131–50. Aubrey J. (1665–97), c.25–58. He calls Lanhill, Hubba's Low. The same page mentions Lugbury.
42. Piggott S. (1962), 82–4.
43. Corcoran (note 25), 100. Whittle A. W. R. (1977), 55–8. But see: Piggott S. (1962), 59–61, for reasons supporting the idea that the multiplication of chambers may indicate 'some change in social structure'.
44. Piggott S. (1962), 24. P. Drewett. 'The Excavation of an Oval Burial Mound of the Third Millennium bc at Alfriston, East Sussex'. *PPS* 41, 1975, 119–52. 139–40.
45. L. H. Wells, in: Piggott S. (1962). 79–89. 81. See also: J. G. Frazer. *The Magic Art and the Evolution of Kings*. London, 1911. 148, 150.
46. Piggott S. (1962), 49. W. Greenwell. *British Barrows*. Oxford, 1877. 136–40. Mortimer (note 34), 23–42. 28.
47. J. G. Evans. 'Land Mollusca from the Neolithic Enclosure on Windmill Hill'. *WAM* 61, 1965, 91–2; *Land-Snails in Archaeology*. London, 1972. 246. G. W. Dimbleby, in: Smith I. F. (1965), 34–8.
48. I. F. Smith. 'Causewayed Enclosures', in: D. D. A. Simpson (ed.). *Economy and Settlement in Neolithic and Early Bronze Age Britain and Europe*. Leicester, 1971. 89–112. R. Palmer. 'Interrupted Ditch Enclosures in Britain'. *PPS* 42, 1976, 161–86. A. W. R. Whittle. 'Earlier Neolithic Enclosures in North-West Europe'. *PPS* 43, 1977, 329–48. For Cherhill, see: Evans and Smith (note 1). For Overton Hill, see: E. C. Curwen. 'Neolithic Camps'. *Ant* 4, 1930, 22–54. 41.
49. Smith I. F. (1965), 6.
50. Hambledon Hill, 2790±90 bc (NPL-76); High Peak, 2860±150 bc (BM-214); Knap Hill, 2760±115 bc (BM-205); Windmill Hill, 2580±150 bc (BM-74); Orsett, 2791±113 bc and 2635±82 bc (BM); Cherhill, 2765±90 bc (BM-493); Abingdon, 2780±135 bc (BM-348); plus six other dates from the inner ditch that run from 3110 bc to 2500 bc with an average of 2810±132 bc. The rather later date for Windmill Hill came from a sample mixed from the Outer and Middle ditches. Otherwise the determinations from the sites range consistently from 2860 to 2760 bc, the approximate equivalents of 3650 to 3540 BC in real years.
51. D. R. Brothwell, in: Smith I. F. (1965), 138–40.
52. Smith I. F. (1965), 116.
53. For the Hopewell Culture, see: Snow D. (1976), 48–56. Willey G. R. (1966), 273–80. A. M. Josephy. *The Indian Heritage of America*. London, 1972. 88–90. R. Claiborne. *The First Americans*. N.P., 1976. 131–5.
54. P. Drewett. 'The Excavation of a Neolithic Causewayed Enclosure on Offham Hill, East Sussex, 1976'. *PPS* 43, 1977, 201–41. 225.
55. Smith I. F. (1965), 137. J. G. Frazer. *Balder the Beautiful*, I. London, 1913. 91 n.4.
56. N. Thomas. 'A Neolithic Chalk Cup from

Wilsford in the Devizes Museum: and Notes on Others'. *WAM* 54, 1951–2, 452–63.

57. For stone discs, see: Smith I. F. (1965), 115–16, 123–4. Piggott S. (1954), 145. A. S. Henshall. *The Chambered Tombs of Scotland*, I. Edinburgh, 1963. 130, 149; II. Edinburgh, 1972, 110, 348, 441, 503. Burl A. (1976), 59. L. V. Grinsell. 'Somerset Barrows, II: North and East'. *PSANHS* 115, 1971, 44–137. 96.

58. Smith I. F. (1965), 132.

59. Piggott S. (1954), 42. The discovery of this figurine was made in 1939 in Pit 15 where the usual seam of good flint nodules was absent because of a geological fault. See also: V. G. Childe. *Prehistoric Communities of the British Isles*. London, 1940. 39–40. R. R. Clarke. *Grime's Graves*. London, 1963. 22–3. It must be added that some archaeologists suspect that the tableau was a hoax played on the excavator, A. L. Armstrong, by his workmen. As the excavation was never properly published the controversy remains unresolved. There is only the briefest mention of it in: *British Association for the Advancement of Science*. Dundee, 1939. 75.

60. McCracken (note 22), 106.

61. Daniel (note 25), 120–1. H. J. Fleure and G. J. H. Neely. 'Cashtal yn Ard, Isle of Man'. *Ant J* 16, 1936, 373–95. 394–5.

62. A. W. R. Whittle. 'Resources and Population in the British Neolithic'. *Ant* 52, 1978, 34–42. Whittle A. W. R. (1977), 30. For details of individual sites, see: J. G. Evans. *Land-Snails in Archaeology*. London, 1972. (Horslip: 261; South Street: 257; Waylands Smithy: 265; Beckhampton: 248).

63. K. D. Thomas, in: Drewett (note 44), 150.

64. Piggott S. (1962), 29.

65. J. W. Porter. 'The Mitchell Site and Prehistoric Exchange Systems at Cahokia: AD 1000±300'. *Explorations into Cahokia Archaeology*. Urbana, Illinois, 1969. 137–64. 160.

66. Willey, G. R. (1966), 280.

NOTES TO CHAPTER FIVE

1. F. A. Hibbert and R. A. Jones. 'Vegetational History of the Somerset Levels', in: *Somerset Levels Project*, I. 1975. 8–10. For the god-dolly, see: J. M. Coles and F. A. Hibbert. 'Prehistoric Roads and Tracks in Somerset, England. I. Neolithic'. *PPS* 44, 1968 (1969), 238–58. 254–7.

2. J. G. Evans. *Land-Snails in Archaeology*. London, 1972. 242–74.

3. The relevant dates are: for Wiltshire—Durrington Walls, 2320±125 bc (NPL-192); Silbury Hill, 2365±110 bc (SI-910B); Beckhampton, 2307±90 bc (BM-506a); and elsewhere—Alfriston, Sussex, 2360±110 bc (HAR-940); Halling, Kent, 2230±190 bc (BM-249); Giants Hill, Lincolnshire, 2370±150 bc (BM-192); Fengate, Cambridge-shire, 2240±90 bc (HAR-779); Broome Heath, Norfolk, (2217±78 bc (BM-755). There are also four relevant determinations from Grimes Graves, Norfolk, 2340±150 bc (BM-97), 2320±150 bc (BM-87), 2300±130 bc (BM-377), 2203±64 bc (BM-944).

4. G. W. Dimbleby and J. G. Evans, in: G. J. Wainwright. 'The Excavation of a Neolithic Settlement on Broome Heath, Ditchingham, Norfolk, England'. *PPS* 38, 1972, 1–98. 86.

5. Coles and Hibbert (note 1), 251.

6. A. S. Kennard, in: Cunnington M. E. (1931), 332–4. J. G. Evans, in: Musson C. R. (1971), 371 n. 2. Nearly 500 shells were taken from about 35 postholes. Most of them indicated damp grassland conditions.

7. R. J. C. Atkinson. 'The Dorset Cursus'. *Ant* 29, 1955, 4–9. 9. P. Ashbee. 'The Fussell's Lodge Long Barrow Excavations, 1957'. *Arch* 100, 1966, 1–80. 36.

8. Barford: A. Oswald. 'Excavations for the Avon/Severn Research Committee at Barford, Warwickshire'. *Transactions of the Birmingham Archaeology Society* 83, 1969, 1–64. 19–27; Dorchester: R. J. C. Atkinson, C. M. Piggott and N. K. Sandars. *Excavations at Dorchester, Oxford*, I. Oxford, 1951. 8; Fengate: F. Pryor. *Excavations at Fengate, Peterborough, England*. Toronto, 1974. 6; Windmill Hill: Smith I. F. (1965), 30–3.

9. A. Burl. 'Intimations of Numeracy in the Neolithic and Bronze Age Societies of the British Isles'. *Arch J* 133, 1976, 9–32. A. E. Berriman. *Historical Metrology*. London, 1953. For the measurements of West Kennet, see: Piggott S. (1962), 15.

10. C. Hawkes. 'An Early Bronze Age Urn from Milton, Northants'. *Ant J* 47, 1967, 198–208. 204.

11. Willey G. R. (1966), 269.

12. D. Coombs. 'Callis Wold Round Barrow, Humberside'. *Ant* 50, 1976, 130–1. J. R. Mortimer. *Forty Years Digging*. London, 1905. 161–3. T. G. Manby. 'Long Barrows of Northern England: Structural and Dating Evidence'. *SAF* I, 1970, 1–27. 14–16.

13. V. G. Childe and I. F. Smith. 'Excavation of a Neolithic Barrow on Whiteleaf Hill, Bucks'. *PPS* 20, 1954, 212–30. 220.

14. W. Greenwell. *British Barrows*. London, 1877. 11. Mortimer (note 12), lxx. P. Ashbee. *The Bronze Age Round Barrow in Britain*. London, 1960. 55.

15. W. Johnson. *Byways in British Archaeology*. Cambridge, 1912. 292.

16. Mortimer (note 12), 23–42.

17. For the skeletal evidence from this barrow, see: J. G. Garson, in: *ibid*, 30–40. For platycnemia and the evidence for squatting facets, see: C. Wells. *Bones, Bodies and Disease*. London, 1964. 131–4, 190. J. Cameron. *The Skeleton of British Neolithic Man*. London, 1934. 179–86. For sandals, see: Piggott S. (1954), 141–2.

18. Mortimer (note 12), 352.

19. T. Bateman. *Ten Tears Digging*. London, 1861. 18. B. M. Marden. *The Early Barrow Diggers*. Aylesbury, 1974. 35.

20. I. F. Smith. 'Excavation of a Bell Barrow, Avebury G55'. *WAM* 60, 1965, 24–46. 32, 42. For the environment of West Kennet, see: Evans (note 2), 263. I. F. Smith and D. D. A. Simpson. 'Excavation of a Round Barrow on Overton Hill, North Wiltshire'. *PPS* 32, 1966, 122–55. 151.

21. Piggott S. (1962), 49–51. J. V. S. Megaw. 'Penny Whistles and Prehistory'. *Ant* 34, 1960, 6–13.

22. E. M. Clifford. 'The Excavation of Nympsfield Long Barrow, Gloucs.' *PPS* 4, 1938, 188–213. 204. As well as at Nympsfield ochre has been found with cremations at the stone circles of Gretigate C, Cumbria, and the Druids Temple, Lancashire; at Rodmarton chambered tomb; and in several Yorkshire round barrows: Goodmanham, nos 118, 121; and Garton Slack, nos 40, 43.

23. Smith A. C. (1885), 78, 84–5.

24. *Ibid*, 85. Smith I. F. (1965), 74, 78.

25. J. B. Davis and J. Thurnam. *Crania Britannica*, II. London, 1865. 58.

26. These beakers belong to Clarke's S2/W category. See: Clarke D. L. (1970), 504, nos 1185–6. They are now in Devizes Museum (D.M. 470–6).

27. For the Sanctuary, see: Cunnington M. E. (1931). For discussions of the building sequence, see: Musson C. R. (1971). Piggott S. (1940). For the durability of timber houses, see: J. M. Coles. *Archaeology by Experiment*. London, 1973, 59–63. Wainwright G. J. and Longworth I. H. (1971), 220–5.

28. For the Megalithic Yard, see: Thom A. (1967), 34–55. For the radii of the Sanctuary, see: pp. 38–9, Table 5.1, listed as S5/2 where a non-existent ring has been included. For the Sanctuary as a priest's house, see: J. E. Wood. *Sun, Moon and Standing Stones*. Oxford, 1978. 195. For criticism of the Megalithic Yard, see: D. G. Kendall. 'Hunting Quanta', in: F. R. Hodson (ed.). *The Place of Astronomy in the Ancient World*. London, 1974. 231–66. P. R. Freeman. 'A Bayesian Analysis of the Megalithic Yard'. *Journal of the Royal Statistical Society* 139, 1976, 20–55. A. Burl and P. Freeman. 'Local Units of Measurement in Prehistoric Britain'. *Ant* 51, 1977, 152–4. R. Hicks. 'Thom's Megalithic Yard and Traditional Measurements'. *IAF* 4, 1, 1977, 1–7.

29. Stukeley W. (1743), 46. Smith A. C. (1885), 177–8.

30. Aubrey J. (1665–97), c.24, 13–14, 44. Hoare R. C. (1821), 63. D. R. Brothwell, in: Piggott S. (1962), 95.

31. Stukeley W. (1743), 33.

32. M. Dames. *The Avebury Cycle*. London, 1977. 74–81.

33. A. B. Deacon. *Malekula: A Vanishing People in the New Hebrides*. London, 1934. 564–85. Aubrey J. (1665–97), c.24, 38.

34. Piggott S. (1962), 27.

35. G. E. Daniel. *The Chamber Tombs of England and Wales*. London, 1950.

36. R. B. Onians. *The Origins of European Thought*. Cambridge, 1951. 256, 260–3, 269.

37. Stukeley W. (1743), 43. J. Ivimy. *The Sphinx and the Megaliths*. London, 1974. 84–5, 158. G. E. Daniel. *The Idea of Prehistory*. Harmondsworth, 1964.

38. Stukeley W. (1743), 49.

39. Hazel fragments from the core of the primary mound: 2145 ± 95 bc (I-4136). Pieces of turf from the covering mound, excluding one anomalously high assay: 2725 ± 110, 2620 ± 120, 2580 ± 110, 2515 ± 130, 2365 ± 110 bc (SI-910A, C, D, CH, B). Deer antlers in the ditch bottom: 1899 ± 43 bc (BM-842); 1802 ± 50 bc (BM-841). There is also one very late date from a mixture of antlers from earlier excavations: 800 ± 100 bc (I-2795).

40. Dean J. Merewether. 'Examination of Silbury Hill'. *PAI* Salisbury volume, 1849, 73–81.

41. *Ibid*. See also: C. Tucker. 'Report of Examination of Silbury Hill'. *PAI*, 1849, 297–303, for a denial of the theory that Silbury was a burial place. Smith A. C. (1861). For the recent excavations, see: Atkinson R. J. C. (1967); (1969); (1970). For an imaginative but erratic interpretation of the significance of this mound, see: M. Dames. *The Silbury Treasure*. London, 1976.

42. Merewether (note 40). R. J. C. Atkinson (pers. comm., 1978).

43. D. Williams. 'A Neolithic Moss Flora from Silbury Hill, Wilts.' *JAS* 3, 1976, 267–70.

44. The 'date' from the primary core of 2145 ± 95 bc means there is a 2:1 chance that the material died between 2240 and 2050 bc. Two standard deviations improves the probability level to 95.4 per cent that the material died between 2335 and 1955 bc (3035 and 2460 BC). The latest 'date' from the ditch, 1802 ± 50 bc can, in the same way, be expanded to 1902–1702 bc (2390–2100 BC). There is almost an overlap around 2400 BC suggesting that all the phases at Silbury Hill could have been built within a few years of each other, perhaps a century from start to finish.

45. Pass A. C. (1887). Information about the prehistoric water level was kindly provided by Professor R. J. C. Atkinson (pers. comm., 23 May 1978).

46. A., A. S., and A.S. Thom. 'Stonehenge'. *JHA* 5, 1974, 71–90. 89.

47. For Tan Hill, see: H. W. Timperley. *The Vale of Pewsey*. London, 1954. 67. T. Storey-Maskelyne. 'Tan Hill Fair'. *WAM* 34, 1905–6, 426–32.

48. M. B. Cotsworth. *The Rational Almanack*. New York, 1902. A. Davidson. 'Silbury Hill', in: M. Williams (ed.). *Britain: A Study in Patterns*. London, 1971. 20–8.

49. For prehistoric work-rates on earthworks, see: R. J. C. Atkinson. 'Neolithic Engineering., *Ant* 35, 1961, 292–9. Coles (note 27), 73. P. Ashbee and I. W. Cornwall. 'An Experiment in Field Archaeology'. *Ant* 35, 1961, 129–34. E. M. Clifford. 'The Cotswold Megalithic Culture', in: C. F. Fox and B. Dickins (eds) *The Early Cultures of North-West Europe*. Cambridge, 1950. 21–40. 35.

50. Hoare R. C. (1821), 6–7.

51. Approximate volumes of these great mounds in cubic metres: Wold Newton, 750; Duggleby Howe, 3,200; Hatfield, 10,000; Marlborough, 53,000; Silbury, 250,000. A small bowl barrow of the Early Bronze Age had about 60 cubic m of material in its tumulus. The passage-grave of New Grange in Ireland, with a flat top and near-vertical sides, contained about 60,000 cubic m.

52. Hoare R. C. (1812), 194. L. V. Grinsell. *The Archaeology of Wessex*. London, 1958. 110.

53. For the Marlborough Mound, see: H. C. Brentnall. 'Marlborough Castle'. *WAM* 48, 1937–9, 133–43. 140–2, 143. A. G. Bradley, A. C. Chambers and J. W. Baines. *A History of Marlborough College*. London, 1923. 3–5. J. Aubrey, in: W. Camden. *Britannia* (ed. E. Gibson). London, 1695. 112. Stukeley W. (1776a), 63–4. Hoare R. C. (1821), 15.

54. Stukeley W. (1743), 42–3.

55. Smith A. C. (1861), 179 n. 2.

56. K. Mendelssohn. *The Riddle of the Pyramids*. London, 1976. 140.

57. Evans (note 2), 268.

NOTES TO CHAPTER SIX

1. Stukeley W. (1743), 35.

2. From calculations at the remaining stone it seems the cove faced approximately 128° where a nearby hillock rises. At latitude 51.4°, the combination of an azimuth of 128.39° and a horizon altitude of 1.4° produces a declination of 23.98°, that of the midwinter sunrise. Short of excavating what remains of the hole of the backstone nothing more definite can be claimed.

3. Aubrey J. (1665–97), c.25, 63. W. Camden. *Britannia* (ed. E. Gibson). London, 1695. 112.

4. Stukeley W. (1722–4), 3.

5. Burl A. (1976). For Stenness, see: J. N. G. Ritchie. 'The Stones of Stenness, Orkney'. *PSAS* 107, 1975–6 (1978), 1–60. For New Grange, see: C. O'Kelly. *Illustrated Guide to New Grange*. Wexford, 1971. J. Patrick. 'Midwinter Sunrise at New Grange'. *Nature* 249, 1974, 517–19.

6. For recent ideas about the distribution of stone axes, see: W. A. Cummins. 'The Neolithic Stone Axe Trade in Britain'. *Ant* 48, 1974, 201–5; 'Stone Axe Trade—or Glacial Erratics'. *C Arch* 61, 1978, 42–3. See also: L. Keen and J. Radley. 'Report on the Petrological Identification of Stone Axes from Yorkshire'. *PPS* 37, 1971, 16–37. 29–30.

7. M. J. Swartz and D. K. Jordan. *Anthropology: Perspectives on Humanity*. New York, 1976. 383–90. V. Reynolds. 'Ethology of Social Change', in: Renfrew C. (ed.) (1973), 467–80. A. P. Phillips. 'The Evolutionary Model of Human Society and Its Application to Certain Early Farming Populations of Western Europe', in: *ibid*, 529–38. 529–30.

8. Swartz and Jordan (note 7), 580–93.

9. For maceheads at Windmill Hill and Avebury, see: Smith I. F. (1965), 110–11, 227; West Kennet: Piggott S. (1962), 48; Crosby Garrett and Cowlam: W. Greenwell. *British Barrows*. London, 1877. 390, 217; Duggleby Howe: J. R. Mortimer. *Forty Years Digging*. London, 1905. 28; Liff's Low: T. Bateman. *Vestiges of the Antiquities of Derbyshire*. London, 1848. 42. For the association with Grooved Ware, see: F. Roe. 'Stone Maceheads and the latest neolithic cultures of the British Isles', in: J. M. Coles and D. D. A. Simpson (eds). *Studies in Ancient Europe*. Leicester, 1968. 145–69. 156–9. T. G. Manby. *Grooved Ware Sites in the North of England*. Oxford, 1974. 92–101.

10. H. Bayley. *The Lost Language of Symbolism*. London, 1951.

11. M. Dames. *The Avebury Cycle*. London, 1977. 185–209.

12. B. le Poer Trench. *Temple of the Stars*. London, 1973. 63, 67, 79, 81.

13. Stukeley W. (1743), 18.

14. Evans J. G. (1975), 75, 142–7.

15. Aubrey J. (1685), 44.

16. H. C. Brentnall. 'Sarsens'. *WAM* 51, 1946, 419–39. 426. P. Singh. *Burial Practices in Ancient India*. Varanasi, India, 1970. 104, 137, 154.

17. Evans J. G. (1975), 60–1. Brentnall (note 16), 424. Smith A. C. (1885), 127–9. M. J. Clark. *Fyfield Down: Geomorphological Trail*. Newbury, 1976.

M. J. Clark, J. Lewin and R. J. Small. 'The Sarsen Stones of the Marlborough Downs and their Geomorphological Implications'. *Southampton Research Series. Geography* 4, 1967, 3–40.

18. R. J. C. Atkinson. *Stonehenge*. London, 1956. 108.

19. For ropes in Britain, see: D. V. Clarke. *The Neolithic Village at Skara Brae, Orkney: 1972–3 Excavations*. Edinburgh, 1976. 25. J. M. Coles, F. A. Hibbert and B. J. Orme. 'Prehistoric Roads and Tracks in Somerset. 3. The Sweet Track'. *PPS* 39, 1973, 256–93. 288–9, 291.

20. J. G. D. Clark. *Prehistoric Europe: The Economic Basis*. London, 1952. 83–4. Atkinson (note 18), 114.

21. R. Claiborne. *The First Americans*. Netherlands, 1976. 70–6. J. Beattie. *Other Cultures*. London, 1966. 198–9. M. Sahlins. *Stone Age Economics*. London, 1974. 260–3.

22. M. Harris. *Cows, Pigs, Wars and Witches*. London, 1977. 41, 55. Sahlins (note 21), 54–5. J. G. Frazer. *The Golden Bough*. London, 1915. I, 141, 282; VI, 206; VII, 118; VIII, 279; X, 24.

23. A. Fahkry. *The Pyramids*. Chicago and London, 1969. 12.

24. Sandalwood Islands: J. M. Coles. *Archaeology by Experiment*. London, 1973. 88; Egypt: I. E. S. Edwards. *The Pyramids of Egypt*. Harmondsworth, 1947. 216–7; Easter Island: T. Heyerdahl. *Aku-Aku*. Harmondsworth, 1960. 139–40. R. Story. *The Space-Gods Revealed*. London, 1976. The latter comments on von Däniken's claim that only extra-terrestrial visitors could have moved the statues; Stonehenge: Atkinson (note 18), 108–10; Malekula: J. Layard. *Stone Men of Malekula*. London, 1942. 582–3. See also: R. J. C. Atkinson. 'Neolithic Engineering'. *Ant* 35, 1961, 292–9.

25. Stukeley W. (1743), 17.

26. Atkinson (note 18), 109; *Ant* 35, 1961, 293.

27. O. G. S. Crawford. 'Notes on Fieldwork round Avebury, December 1921'. *WAM* 87, 1922. 52–63.

28. Brentnall (note 16), 421. The stone is at SU 134706. See also: Clark (note 17, 1976), 8A, no. 17.

29. Keiller A. and Piggott S. (1936), 418. Atkinson (note 18), 57.

30. L. Lévy-Bruhl. *La Mentalité Primitive*. London, 1947. 17–18.

31. The highest point at Avebury near the NE corner of the crossroads is 160 m above sea-level. Corresponding heights of the four entrances are: south, 161; west, 155; north 158; east, 157 m.

32. Stukeley W. (1743), 20. For calculations of the Druids' Cubit, see: Stukeley W. (1740), 6, 7, 12, 15; (1743), 19–20, 31. For Malekula, see: A. B. Deacon. *Malekula: A Vanishing People in the New Hebrides*. London, 1934. 31.

33. W. M. F. Petrie. *Stonehenge: Plans, Description and Theories*. London, 1880. 22–3. Thom A., Thom A. S., and Foord T. R. (1976), 191, fig. 1, 185.

34. Smith I. F. (1965), 198, 201.

35. Burl A. (1976), 341, 342, 345, 347. For Knowlton, see: S. and C. M. Piggott. 'Stone and Earth Circles in Dorset'. *Ant* 13, 1939, 138–58. For Priddy, see: E. K. Tratman. 'The Priddy Circles, Mendips, Somerset: Henge Monuments'. *PUBSS.* 11, 1967, 97–125. 101–2.

36. Smith I. F. (1965), 201. Gray H. St. G. (1935), 131–2.

37. Smith I. F. (1965), 226–7.

38. Keiller A. and Piggott S. (1936), 419.

39. V. G. Childe. *The Bronze Age*. Cambridge, 1930. 164.

40. For the history of the outlying stone at Avebury, see: Smith I. F. (1965), 202–3. For outlying stones of stone circles, see: Burl A. (1976).

41. For Breton standing stones associated with earthen long barrows, see: S. Piggott. 'The Long Barrow in Brittany'. *Ant* 11, 1937, 441–55. For Le Grand Menhir Brisé (Er Grah) and its long barrow, see: E. Hadingham. *Circles and Standing Stones*. London, 1975. 158, 162. For the Pacific Islands, see: J. Layard. 'The Journey of the Dead', in: *Essays Presented to S. Seligman*. London, 1934. 116.

42. Smith I. F. (1965), 204, 229.

43. Stukeley W. (1743), 23.

44. Smith I. F. (1965), 223n. The hole was '60 ft. south of Stone 1 of the Cove', making it about 20.7 m south of the circle's centre.

45. *Ibid*, 198. Following Gray, Smith suggests 29 stones for the South Circle but with the average spacing she indicates of 10.8 m, not 11 m, there would have been 30 stones. The North Circle would have had a maximum of 27 or 28 stones with another 12 in its inner ring. With a body-fathom of about 1.7 m the diameter of the South Circle (102.4 m) would have measured 60.2 fathoms; the North Circle (97.5 m), 57.4 fathoms, and its inner ring (41.5 m), 24.4 fathoms.

46. For the Beckhampton Cove, see: Cunnington M. E. (1913a), 2. For the Avebury Cove, see: Smith A. C. (1867), 210.

47. C. A. Newham. *The Astronomical Significance of Stonehenge*. Leeds, 1972. Burl A. (1976), 305.

48. Smith A. C. (1867), 210–11.

49. Piggott S. (1950), 100–1, 112–14.

50. M. Dames. *The Avebury Cycle*. London, 1977. 173. For the hypothetical 70° azimuth of the Cove, see: p. 163.

51. Keiller A. (1939), 5. Piggott S. (1964). Smith I. F. (1965), 203, 221, fig. 74.

52. For a description of Cultoon by its excavator, see: E. MacKie. *The Megalith Builders*. London, 1977.

102–4. For other abandoned sites, see: Burl A. (1976). The northern henge at Priddy was never finished. See: Tratman (note 35), 102. Other instances are numerous. Even Arbor Low might be included. See: B. Barham. 'Arbor Low and the Holed Stone'. *JDANHS* 50, 1928–9, 79, 84.

53. Ritchie (note 5), 16. For the Grooved Ware sherds, see: pp. 11, 20.

NOTES TO CHAPTER SEVEN

1. For Grooved Ware economy, see: Wainwright G. and Longworth I. H. (1971), 235–306. T. G. Manby. *Grooved Ware Sites in the North of England.* Oxford, 1974. 77–101. For some other sites, see: C. L. Matthews. *Occupation Sites on a Chiltern Ridge,* I. Oxford, 1976. 11–18. A. M. ApSimon *et al.* 'Gorsey Bigbury, Cheddar, Somerset'. *PUBSS* 14, 1976, 155–83. 174, 180, 164–7.

2. Manby (note 1), 98.

3. *Ibid*, 101.

4. M. J. Swartz and D. K. Jordan, *Anthropology Perspective on Humanity.* New York, 1976. 387–90. See also: A. Fleming. 'Models for the Development of the Wessex Culture', in: Renfrew C. (ed.) (1973). 571–85. 581.

5. M. Eliade. *Patterns in Comparative Religion.* London, 1958. 124–53. 149, 150.

6. Wainwright G. and Longworth I. (1971), 13–22.

7. C. Burgess. 'Meldon Bridge: A Neolithic Defended Promontory Complex near Peebles', in: Burgess C. and Miket R. (1976). 151–80. See also: *Discovery and Excavation in Scotland, 1977.* Edinburgh, 1977. 27.

8. For pig bones at Durrington Walls, see: Wainright G. and Longworth I. (1971), 189. For the usefulness of pigs, see: M. Harris. *Cows, Pigs, Wars and Witches.* London, 1977. 36–7.

9. R. Firth. *Economics of the New Zealand Maori.* Wellington, 1959. 133. In his interesting *Science and Society in Prehistoric Britain.* London, 1977. 160–9, Euan MacKie interpreted the pig bones as offerings from peasants to astronomer–priests living in the precinct of Durrington Walls.

10. J. Beattie. *Other Cultures.* London, 1966. 201.

11. For the Temple Mound (Mississippi) Culture, see: Willey G. R. (1966), 292–310. Snow D. (1976), 60–75. For a more popular account, see: R. Claiborne. *The First Americans.* Netherlands, 1976. 135–53.

12. For Mound 72, Cahokia, see: M. L. Fowler, 'The Cahokia Site', in: *Explorations into Cahokia Archaeology.* Bulletin 7, Illinois Archaeological Survey. Urbana, Illinois, 1969. 1–30. 19–26. For Monks Mound, see: N. A. Reed. 'Monks and Other Mississippian Mounds', in: *ibid,* 31–42. M. L. Fowler. *Cahokia: Ancient Capital of the Midwest.* Addison-Wesley Module 48. Reading, Mass., 1974. J. A. Brown (ed.). *Perspectives in Cahokia Archaeology.* Bulletin 10. Urbana, Illinois, 1975.

13. For the Cahokian timber circles, see: D. Norrish. 'Woodhenge—work of a genius'. *Cahokian.* Feb. 1978. Collinsville, Illinois. W. L. Wittry. 'An American Woodhenge'. *The Explorer* 12 (4), 1970, 14–17; 'The American Woodhenge', in: (note 12, 1969), 43–8. For a discussion of Cahokia and its astronomy, see: E. C. Krupp. 'Cahokia: Corn, Commerce and the Cosmos'. *Griffith Observer* 41 (5), 1977, 10–20. For Cahokian units of measurement, see: H. M. Smith. 'The Murdock Mound, Cahokia Site', in: (note 12, 1969), 49–88. 79. For measurements at Teotihuacán, see: R. Millon. 'Teotihuacán'. *Scientific American* 216 (6), 1967. 38–48.

14. E. MacKie. *Science and Society in Prehistoric Britain.* London, 1977. 53–70.

15. Snow D. (1976), 60. Claiborne (note 11), 138.

16. G. J. Wainwright. 'The Excavation of a Late Neolithic Enclosure at Marden, Wilts.' *Ant J* 51, 1971, 177–239. 225. For structures at Durrington Walls, see: P. D. Catherall. 'Henge Monuments: Monument or Myth?' in: Burgess C. and Miket R. (1976), 1–10. 1. Charcoal from Marden's ditch gave a date of 1988+48 bc, (*c.* 2500BC).

17. H. McCracken. *George Catlin and the Old Frontier.* New York, 1969. 85.

18. All these earthworks have been planned. For Mount Pleasant, see: G. J. Wainwright. 'Mount Pleasant'. *C Arch* 23, 1970, 230–3. A largescale plan kindly sent me by Dr Wainwright reveals its eccentricities even more clearly. For Knowlton, see: S. and C. M. Piggott. 'Earth and Stone Circles in Dorset'. *Ant* 13, 1939, 138–58. 153; Durrington Walls: Wainwright G. and Longworth I. (1971), 13; Waulud's Bank: J. Dyer. 'A Secondary Neolithic Camp at Waulud's Bank, Leagrave'. *BAJ* 2, 1964, 1–15. 2.

19. Today the area within the ditch at Avebury covers about 23.8 acres (9.6 hectares). To this should be added about $1\frac{1}{4}$ acres to allow for the weathering of the ditch rim because as much as 5 m of the inner lip may have eroded. The four quadrants of the ditch measure approximately: SE, 278 m; NE, 284 m; NW, 203 m; SW, 278 m; a total of 1043 m. The North and South Circles occupy respectively about 1.8 and 2.1 acres, less than 4 acres out of an area of some 25 acres.

20. The entrances were about 50 ft (15.2 m) wide. See: Smith I. F. (1965), 195. This would be 8.97 fathoms of 1.7 m each.

21. *Ibid*, 181–2.

22. R. J. C. Atkinson. 'Neolithic Engineering'. *Ant* 35, 1961, 292–9. P. Ashbee and I. W. Cornwall. 'An Experiment in Field Archaeology'. *Ant* 35, 1961, 129–34. C. Griffiths. 'Work Study', in: R. Bradley and A. Ellison. *Rams Hill: A Bronze Age Defended Enclosure and Its Landscape*. Oxford, 1975. 225–8. See also: J. M. Coles. *Archaeology by Experiment*. London, 1973. 69–74.

23. Gray H. St. G. (1935), 104, pl. XL, fig. 3, 122.

24. Average ditch depths for earthworks comparable with Avebury are: Rams Hill, 1.0 m; Waulud's Bank, 2.0 m; Windmill Hill, 2.5 m; Marden, 3.0 m; Durrington Walls, 5.5 m. Avebury's ditch was a fairly consistent 9 m deep. At Maumbury Rings, however, the pits with their ritual deposits averaged 10 m in depth. See: R. Bradley. 'Maumbury Rings, Dorchester: The Excavations of 1908–13'. *Arch* 105, 1975, 1–98. 8–11.

25. P. Ashbee. *The Earthen Long Barrow in Britain*. London, 1970. 41.

26. Wainwright G. and Longworth I. (1971), 22.

27. Gray H. St. G. (1935), 113, 115, 121, 126, 148–55.

28. Passmore A. D. (1935), 288.

29. Gray H. St. G. (1935), 120. 124. A similar process occurred in the chalk pits of Grimes Graves and has also been recorded at the experimental earthwork on Overton Down a mile to the east of Avebury. Today's ditch at Avebury is perhaps twice as wide and half as deep as it was originally.

30. Stukeley W. (1743), 25.

31. J. Rickman. 'On the Antiquity of Abury and Stonehenge'. *Arch* 28, 1840, 399–419. 405–6.

32. J. Fergusson. *Rude Stone Monuments*. London, 1872. 68.

33. Thom A., Thom A. S. and Foord T. R. (1976). 184–5.

34. *Ibid*, 188. For Thom's doubts, see: p. 190, 'How was Avebury set out?'

35. P. R. Freeman. 'Thom's Survey of the Avebury Ring'. *JHA* 8, 1977, 134–6. I Angell. 'An Algorithm for Fitting Circles and Ellipses to Megalithic Stone Rings'. *Science & Archaeology* 20, 1977, 11–16. 14. I. O. Angell and J. S. Barber. 'The Application of Curve Fitting Techniques to the Study of Megalithic Stone Rings'. *Computer Applications in Archaeology*, 1977, 10–20.

36. J. E. Wood. *Sun, Moon and Standing Stones*. Oxford, 1978. 48.

37. Thom, Thom and Foord (Note 34), 190.

38. Smith I. F. (1965), 248 n. 1.

39. Stukeley W. (1743), 22.

40. Stukeley W. (1722–4), 109b. His 'Prospect of Abury', p. 218, shows the Swindon Stone and its fallen companion which lies parallel with and overlapping the road. The sketch is dated August 1722.

41. Stukeley W. (1743), 21, 23.

42. The stones have an average spacing of 10.5 m. see: Smith I. F. (1965), 196. The irregular circumference of the Outer Circle measures about 1062 m of which some 61 m were taken up by the 4 entrances. One great stone stood in each. This would leave space for 95 or 96 stones along the ditch quadrants plus 4 on the causeways, 99 or 100 altogether. See also: A. Burl. 'Intimations of Numeracy in the Neolithic and Bronze Age Societies of the British Isles'. *Arch J* 133, 1976 (1977), 9–32, 28, 29.

43. For views about British Beaker societies, see: V. G. Childe. *Prehistoric Communities of the British Isles*. London, 1940. 91–118. 91, 101. J. and C. Hawkes. *Prehistoric Britain*. London, 1947. 54. Clarke D. L. (1970), 68. H. J. Case. 'The Beaker Culture in Britain and Ireland', in: R. Mercer (ed.). *Beakers in Britain and Europe*. Oxford, 1977. 71–101. 80. Another idea, that the brachycephalic Beaker people might have been planetary space-travellers appeared in: T. C. Lethbridge. *The Legend of the Sons of God*. London, 1973. 110.

44. For mead, see: C. Wilson. *A Book of Booze*. London, 1974. 146–7. F. White (ed.). *Good Things in England*. London, 1968. 351. For a recipe for sweet mead, see: R. Heesom (ed.). *Farmhouse Kitchen*. Leeds, 1975. 161–2. For the use of honey, see: E. Crane (ed.). *Honey: A Comprehensive Survey*. London, 1976. For references to mead-drinking in the Dark Ages, see: K. H. Jackson. *The Gododdin*. Edinburgh, 1969. 35–7 etc.

45. J. H. Dickson. 'Bronze Age Mead'. *Ant* 52, 1978, 108–13. For the Beaker burial, see: A. S. Henshall. 'A Dagger-Grave and other Cist Burials at Ashgrove, Methilhill, Fife'. *PSAS* 97, 1964, 166–79. The beaker belonged to the Final Southern group (Clarke D. L. (1970), 406, 517), *c.* 2100–1850 BC. For another Bronze Age alcoholic drink, see: P. V. Glob. *The Mound People*. London, 1974. 60.

46. For Stone D, see: Smith I. F. (1965), 198–9. Stukeley W. (1743), Tabs XVI, XVII. The beaker sherds, one of them part of a base with 'horizontal lines, apparently drawn with a point' (Smith I. F. (1965), 227), are most similar to Clarke's (1970), 'Developed Northern' Group, dated in Wessex by Lanting and van der Waals to their Step 4, 1850–1750 bc (*c.* 2300–2150 BC).

47. For the Z Stones, see: Smith I. F. (1965), 199–201. D. E. Chapman. *Is This Your First Visit to Avebury?* London, 1947. 11. For the setting in the North Circle, see: Gray H. St. G. (1935), 108, n. 3. Smith I. F. (1965), 202. Smith A. C. (1867), 212. For the Ring Stone, see: Smith I. F. (1965), 202–3. Stukeley W. (1743), 25, Tabs XVI, XVII.

48. John Aubrey's 'Monumenta Britannica' quoted in Long W. (1858), 316, where there is a somewhat

inaccurate transcript of Aubrey's notes on Avebury. See: Aubrey J. (1665–97), c.24, 34–5.

49. Stukeley W. (1743), 29–30.

50. For research into the avenues, see: Stukeley W. (1743), 18–37. Long W. (1858), 63–5; (1878), 327–35. King B. (1879). For the excavations, see: Keiller A. and Piggott S. (1936). Smith I. F. (1965), 206–17, 223, 229–43. Stukeley made several drawings of both avenues and there is an invaluable plan of the Beckhampton Avenue in Stukeley W. (1722–4), 231, f. 7. The first sketch of the Kennet Avenue was a schematic one by Aubrey.

51. Thom A. and Thom A. S. (1976).

52. Stukeley W. (1743), 54.

53. J. and C. Bord. *The Secret Country*. London, 1976. 17, 51.

54. N. Lockyer. *Stonehenge and Other British Stone Monuments Astronomically Considered*. London, 1909. 354–61, 368–9. See also: E. H. Goddard. 'Avebury: Orientation of the Avenues'. *WAM* 35, 1907–8, 515–17, for a refutation of Lockyer's theories.

55. M. Dames. *The Avebury Cycle*. London, 1977. 85

56. Stukeley W. (1743), 62. The plan of Callanish was probably not by Lhwyd who did not visit the circle but Stukeley's source is uncertain. The sketch in his 'Commonplace Book' (Stukeley W. (1717–48), 46) is quite unlike the earliest known plan by Martin Martin in his *A Description of the Western Isles of Scotland*, 1703. See also: Piggott S. (1950), 114–15. G. and M. Ponting. *The Standing Stones of Callanish*. Stornoway, 1977. 11.

57. This 'occupation area' was discovered in 1934. See: Keiller A. and Piggott S. (1936). Smith I. F. (1965), 210–16, 233–43, 251–2.

58. The beakers have been dated following the chronology of Lanting J. N. and van der Waals J. D. (1972) which itself has been recalibrated from the bristlecone-pine tables of R. M. Clark. 'A Calibration Curve for Radiocarbon Dates'. *Ant* 49, 1975, 251–66. The types of beakers follow the nomenclature of Clarke D. L. (1970)—(i) Kennet Avenue stone 29a: 'European' beaker, no. 1070. Clarke confused this with the burial by Stone 18b (Cunnington M. E. (1931b)) where there was no pot. (ii) Beckhampton Cove: 'North Middle Rhine' beaker, no. 1051; (iii) Beckhampton Avenue stone: 'Developed Northern' beaker, no. 1073; (iv) Kennet Avenue stone 25b: 'Developed Northern' beaker, no. 1071. The Beckhampton Cove beaker is in Devizes Museum, (D.M. 451). The others are in the Avebury Museum. For a discussion of the Beaker burials, see: Smith I. F. (1965), 209–10, 229–31.

For plans showing the kinks in the avenue, see: *ibid*, fig. 71. Thom A. and Thom A. S. (1976), 194.

59. The exclusion of strangers from religious ceremonies and even the killing of them at times of sowing or harvesting is recorded amongst some early societies. See: J. G. Frazer. *The Golden Bough*. London, 1935, III, 101–13; VII, (many references).

60. Stukeley's is almost the only evidence for the Beckhampton Avenue. See: Stukeley W. (1743), 34–7. His sketches and notes in the Bodleian Library, Oxford, must be consulted by any serious student. These give much more information about the stones. See: Stukeley W. (1722–4), 9a, 25b, 32b, 36b, 223. Invaluable plans are given in: Stukeley W. (1724), 39, 59, 63, 109. For the recent location of stones in this avenue, see: Young W. E. V. (1948); (1950). Vatcher F. de M. and L. (1968); (1969b).

61. G. Underwood. *The Pattern of the Past*. London, 1969. 84.

62. Cunnington M. E. (1931), 319, 320–1. At the Sanctuary there are 6 rings of postholes and 2 rings of stoneholes, the inner of which conforms to the outer ring of posts. Mrs Cunnington lettered the rings A to G, A being the outermost. They seem to be the relics of several phases of rebuilding but the relative brevity of Mrs Cunnington's excavation report and the inadequacy of her drawn sections make it impossible to reconstruct the sequence. In this book it is suggested that Sanctuary IA consisted of timber rings D and E, of 12 and 8 posts respectively, with diameters of 10.5 and 5.9 m. This roofed building was almost identically reproduced in phase IB. Sanctuary II was the lightweight ring B, the small inner ring F with a central post, all slender and rather flimsy. There were 34 posts in ring B and 8 in ring F, the diameters of the rings being 19.8 and 4.2 m. Sanctuary III, the final timber structure, was much more substantial, ring C, 14.3 m across, having 16 strong posts set around the 6 heavy posts of ring G, 3.7 m across. Sanctuary IV was the concentric stone circle, ring A, 39.5 m, having 42 stones, and ring C, the same diameter as ring C in Sanctuary III, 14.3 m, consisting of 16 stones.

63. J. G. Evans, in: Wainwright G. J. and Longworth I. H. (1971), 371 n. 2.

64. Stukeley W. (1722–24), 8b, written on 13 May 1724. See also: Aubrey J. (1665–97), c.24, 43–4.

65. Stukeley W. (1743), 31–2.

66. Cunnington M. E. (1931), 332. Smith I. F. (1965), 212, 234, 246. Clarke D. L. (1970), 100.

67. Cunnington M. E. (1931), 313.

68. For details of the Sanctuary skeleton, see: Sir Arthur Keith. 'Report on Human Remains from the Sanctuary', in: Cunnington M. E. (1931), 330. Although Keith refers to 'the bones those of a lad' none of his measurements unequivocally supports

this. The stature of 1.5 m or 5 ft also suggests that this might have been a girl. As no details of the pelvis, the best indicator of sex, are given the question must be left open.

Research into the alignment of prehistoric burials has been hampered by the imprecise accounts of early antiquarians who rarely bothered to indicate whether the head was to north or south or which way it faced. Recent studies, however, have shown that such orientations were important to certain prehistoric groups. See: A. Tuckwell. 'Patterns of Burial Orientation in the Round Barrows of East Yorkshire'. *Bulletin of the Institute of Archaeology* 12, 1975, 95–123. For Beaker burials in Wessex, see: Lanting J. N. and van der Waals J. D. (1972), 37. For problems of interpretation, see: P. J. Ucko. 'Ethnography and Archaeological Interpretation of Funerary Remains'. *World Archaeology* 1, 1969, 262–80. 271–4.

69. Clarke D. L. (1970), 137. This 'Barbed Wire' beaker is Clarke's no. 1063. Lanting J. N. and van der Waals J. D. (1972) would place such pots in Wessex within their Steps 3 and 4, *c.* 1900–1750 bc (*c.* 2385–2160 BC). The beaker is in Devizes Museum (D.M. 488) as are the sherds of 'All-Over-Corded' beaker also found at the Sanctuary (Clarke, no. 1064F; D.M. 487).

70. Smith I. F. (1965), 208.

NOTES TO CHAPTER EIGHT

1. T. Twining. *Avebury in Wiltshire. The Remains of a Roman Work*. London, 1723. For John Wood, see: S. Piggott. *The Druids*. London, 1968. 149–50.
2. Revd T. Maurice. 'On the Indian Origin of the Druids'. *Indian Antiquities* VI, 1801, 118. Revd W. L. Bowles. *Hermes Britannicus*. London, 1828. J. Rickman. 'On the Antiquity of Abury and Stonehenge'. *Arch* 28, 1840, 399–419. Revd E. Duke. *The Druidical Temples of the County of Wilts*. London, 1846. 6. A. Herbert. *Cyclops Christianus*. London, 1849. 108–9.
3. R. J. Fergusson. *Athenaeum*, 23 Dec. 1865. For the development of this controversy, see the same author in: *Quarterly Review* 215, July 1860, 209; *Athenaeum*, 27 Jan. 1866; and the replies of Sir John Lubbock, *ibid*, 6 Jan. 1866, and Professor Tyndall. *ibid*, 17 Feb. 1866. In 1867 Smith published the results of his excavation (Smith A. C. (1867)) but Fergusson ignored the evidence and restated his opinions in his *Rude Stone Monuments*. London, 1872. 65, 86–9.
4. Stukeley W. (1776a), 2.
5. J. Michell. *The View Over Atlantis*. London, 1973. 60–1.

6. Michell (*ibid*, 64) admits that this line does miss some of its 'targets' but this fact is not mentioned in: J. and C. Bord. *Mysterious Britain*. St Albans, 1972. 176; nor in: J. Wilcock. *A Guide to Occult Britain*. London, 1977. 160.
7. V. G. Childe. *Prehistoric Communities of the British Isles*. London, 1940. 101. S. Piggott. *British Prehistory*. London, 1949. 119. Smith I. F. (1965), 251. J. and C. Hawkes. *Prehistoric Britain*. Harmondsworth, 1943. 55.
8. P. Crampton. *Stonehenge of the Kings*. London, 1967. 43.
9. H. C. March. 'A New Theory of "Stone Circles"'. *TLCAS* 6, 1888 (1889), 98–111. 108.
10. Hoare R. C. (1812), 7.
11. Burl A. (1976), 87.
12. M. MacNeill. *The Festival of Lughnasa*. Oxford, 1962. 296–306, 346.
13. J. G. Frazer. *The Magic Art and the Evolution of Kings*, II. London, 1911. 97. Frazer, in Chapter XI, gives many examples of people engaging in sexual intercourse to influence the fertility of the earth. For other references to rites at times of sowing and harvest, see his: *Spirits of the Corn and of the Wild*, I, II. London, 1912.
14. T. Hariot. *A Briefe and True Report of the New Found Land of Virginia*. Frankfort, 1590. fig. XVIII.
15. M. Dillon and N. K. Chadwick. *The Celtic Realms*. London, 1967. 214. In Chapter IX there is a discussion of the relationships between the branches of the Indo–European language in such diverse areas as Ireland, Spain, Portugal, central Asia and India. For an early prehistoric origin for the Celts, see also J. X. W. P. Corcoran. 'The Origins of the Celts', in: N. K. Chadwick. *The Celts*. Harmondsworth, 1970. 24–6. C. W. Lewis. 'The Historical Background of Early Welsh Verse', in: A. O. H. Jarman and G. R. Hughes (eds). *A Guide to Welsh Literature*, I. Swansea, 1976. 11–50. 12.
16. C. F. C. Hawkes, in: J. M. Wallace-Hadrill and J. McManners (eds). *France: Government and People*. London, 1957. 16.
17. G. Daniel. *Megaliths in History*. London, 1972. 16.
18. P. MacCana. *Celtic Mythology*. London, 1970. 19.
19. Dillon and Chadwick (note 15), 142–5. Daniel (note 17), 13ff.
20. J. Gantz (trans.). *The Mabinogion*. Harmondsworth, 1976. 18.
21. K. H. Jackson. *A Celtic Miscellany*. Harmondsworth, 1971. 145. See also: MacCana (note 18), 91.
22. S. Piggott. 'From Salisbury Plain to South Siberia'. *WAM* 58, 1962, 93–7. 96. Hoare R. C. (1812), 75. Piggott S. (1954), 360–4.
23. Hoare R. C. (1812), 183.

24. P. Gelling and H. E. Davidson. *The Chariot of the Sun*. London, 1969. 115.

25. P. V. Glob. *The Mound People*. London, 1974, 114–16.

26. J. V. S. Megaw. 'Penny Whistles and Prehistory'. *Ant* 34, 1960, 6–13. Piggott S. (1962), 48.

27. Hoare R. C. (1812), 212. The tablets are illustrated there. The round barrow was never clearly identified by Duke but was probably Wilsford South G50a, at SU 11064011. See: Grinsell L. V. (1957), 198. Extracts about the tablets in a letter from Cunnington to Hoare are quoted in: R. H. Cunnington. *From Antiquary to Archaeologist*. Aylesbury, 1975. 98–100. Duke's excavation 'report' is given in: H. Goddard. 'Notes on Barrows at Lake, from MS. Note Book by the Rev. E. Duke'. *WAM* 38, 1908. 582–6. 584. The tablets are in the Department of Prehistoric and Romano–British Antiquities of the British Museum, nos 95. 7. 23. 48–51.

28. J. Clarke. *Man is the Prey*. London, 1971. 170-9.

29. Burl A. (1976), 84–6.

30. Geoffrey of Monmouth. *The History of the Kings of Britain* (trans. L. Thorpe). Harmondsworth, 1966. 196 (Book VIII, 10–11). L. V. Grinsell. *Folklore of Prehistoric Sites in Britain*. Newton Abbot, 1976. For Stanton Drew, see: L. V. Grinsell. *The Folklore of Stanton Drew*. St Peter Port, Guernsey, 1975.

31. Fergusson (note 3, 1872), 452–3.

32. For agricultural rites in the Gambian stone circles, see: H. Parker. 'Stone Circles in Gambia'. *JRAI* 53, 1923, 173–228. 222–5. For links with a sun-cult, see: Sir R. H. Palmer. 'Stone Circles in the Gambia Valley'. *JRAI* 69, 1939, 273–83. For a summary of recent findings and the Wedding folk-story, see: D. Evans. 'Stonehenges of West Africa'. *Country Life*, 16 Jan. 1975, 134–5. For other references to these little-known sites, see: Chapter II, Note 1, here.

33. C. Fox. *Life and Death in the Bronze Age*. London, 1959. 105–27. 123.

34. Smith I. F. (1965), 201.

35. J. G. Frazer. *Adonis, Attis, Osiris*. London, 1914. 60–1, 161–3, 175–91.

36. M. Eliade. *Patterns in Comparative Religion*. London, 1958. 370.

37. In Stukeley (1743), 32, Tab. XVII, this stone can be seen between two sarsens of the South Circle, much smaller than any other stone in the picture. The crest of the bank rises high above it, hiding the natural skyline.

38. For a corpus of stone circles with outlying stones and a discussion of their possible function, see: Burl A. (1976).

39. MacKie E. W. (1977), 162–3.

40. E. W. MacKie. *The Megalith Builders*. London, 1977. 104.

41. Burl A. (1976), 50–4, 76.

42. Duke (note 2), 68.

43. N. Lockyer. *Stonehenge and Other British Stone Monuments Astronomically Considered*. London, 1909. 360.

44. F. Hoyle. *On Stonehenge*. London, 1977. 92, 41.

45. Thom A. (1967), 104–5, 100 (S5/3).

46. Thom A., Thom A. S. and Foord T. R. (1976), 191.

47. E. W. Marwick. 'The Stone of Odin', in: J. N. G. Ritchie. 'The Stones of Stenness, Orkney'. *PSAS* 107, 1975–6 (1978), 1–60. 24–34. 33. For holed stones and stone circles, see: Burl A. (1976), 332. For legends about them, see: Grinsell (note 30, 1976), 15, 142–3, 221. For chambered tombs, see: J. Thurnam. 'On Ancient British Barrows'. *Arch* 42, 1869, 161–244. 242–3. For a general account of holed stones, see: R. R. Brash. 'On Holed Stones'. *GM*, Dec. 1864, 686–700.

48. W. Wright, in: Gray H. St. G. (1935), 146.

49. *Ibid*, 148 n. e.

50. R. Bradley. 'Maumbury Rings, Dorchester: The Excavations of 1908–13'. *Arch* 105, 1976, 1–98. 18, 25.

51. Smith I. F. (1965), 229.

52. Stukeley W. (1724), 59.

53. R. Mercer (Pers. comm., August 1977).

54. A. M. ApSimon *et al.* 'Gorsey Bigbury, Cheddar, Somerset'. *PUBSS* 14 (2), 1976, 155–83. 173.

55. J. L. Todd and G. B. Wolbach. 'Stone Circles in the Gambia'. *Man* 11, 1911, 161–4.

56. J. Mortimer. *Forty Years' Digging*. London, 1905. 229.

57. These little-known objects have been found in many funerary contexts—in a pyre at Charlton Horethorne, Somerset: L. V. Grinsell. 'Somerset Barrows, II'. *PSANHS* 115, 1971, 44–137. 96; in stone circles: Burl A. (1976), 59; in chambered tombs: Piggott S. (1954), 145, 176. A. S. Henshall. *The Chambered Tombs of Scotland*, I. Edinburgh, 1963. 130, 149; II, Edinburgh, 1972. 110, 348, 441, 503; in round barrows: P. Ashbee. 'Tregulland Barrow'. *Ant J* 38, 1958, 174–96. For West Kennet, see: Piggott S. (1962), 48. For Windmill Hill: Smith I. F. (1965), 123–4. For Avebury: *ibid*, 228.

58. Gray H. St. G. (1935), 121. Smith I. F. (1965), 124, 251.

59. A. B. Deacon. *Malekula: A Vanishing People in the New Hebrides*. London, 1934. 580–5, 707–9.

60. Deacon (note 59), 516. For a description of the Sarembal dancing-ground, see: pp. 28–30. For further details of this New Hebridean megalithic society, see: J. Layard. *Stone Men of Malekula*. London, 1942. Unconvincing arguments about the

diffusion of 'megalithic cultures' from a single European or Mediterranean source appear in: W. J. Perry. *The Megalithic Culture of Indonesia.* Manchester, 1918. G. R. Levy. *The Gate of Horn.* London, 1963.

61. Layard (note 60), 699–707.

62. *Ibid*, 218, 272. Levy (note 60), 154–7.

63. Gray H. St. G. (1903b), 481. See also: J. G. Garson. 'Short Report on the Human Skeleton Found in the Stone Circle of Arbor Low in 1901', in: *ibid*, 490–1.

64. Burl A. (1976), 279, 281. For Cairnpapple, see: S. Piggott. 'The Excavations at Cairnpapple Hill, West Lothian'. *PSAS* 82, 1948, 68–123. For Stanton Drew and its Cove, see: C. W. Dymond. *The Ancient Remains at Stanton Drew in the County of Somerset.* Bristol, 1896. 13n.

65. Males were found at Stones 18b, 22b and 29a, all 'female' stones. The adult and two adolescents underneath Stone 25b ('male') could not be definitely sexed. See: D. R. Brothwell, in: Smith I. F. (1965), 230–1.

66. Palmer (note 32), 274.

67. Bradley (note 50), 20, 25, 33–45.

68. J. G. Frazer. *The Magic Art and the Evolution of Kings.* II. London, 1911. 98–100.

69. Burl A. (1976), 124–5, 205–8.

70 Deacon (note 59), 596, 635. For the sex and fertility magic of these people, see: pp. 233, 518, 635.

71. Philip Stubbes. *The Anatomie of Abuses.* London, 1583. For notes on may-poles and May festivals, see: C. Hole. *British Folk Customs.* London, 1976. 128–38.

72. For the Maltegard disc, see: O. Klindt-Jensen. *Denmark Before the Vikings.* London, 1957. 80. Glob (note 25), 167. H. R. E. Davidson. *Scandinavian Mythology.* London, 1969. 32–3.

73. Gelling and Davidson (note 24), 68.

74. Glob (note 25), 149–50. Gelling and Davidson (note 24), 74, 79. For further discussion of this Scandinavian art, see: H. Kühn. *The Rock Pictures of Europe.* London, 1966. 168–206.

75. D. H. Gordon. 'Megalithic Stones, Asota'. *Ant* 13, 1939, 464–5.

76. Eliade (note 36), 220–7.

77. G. and M. Ponting. *The Standing Stones of Callanish.* Stornoway, 1977.

78. Stukeley W. (1743), 52.

79. Stukeley W. (1776b), 169. For a detailed description of Stanton Drew, see: Dymond (note 64).

80. B. Barham. 'Arbor Low and the Holed Stone'. *JDANHS* 50, 1928–9, 79–84. 83.

81. P. Screeton. *Quicksilver Heritage.* London, 1974. 48, 158.

82. For the Llandegai burials, see: C. Houlder. 'The Henge Monuments at Llandegai'. *Ant* 42, 1968, 216–21. 218. For Durrington Walls, see: Wainwright G. and Longworth I. (1971), 191. For Gorsey Bigbury, see: ApSimon (note 54), 159, 162, 170–3.

83. For the burials at Marden, see: G. Wainwright. 'The Excavation of a Late Neolithic Enclosure at Marden, Wiltshire'. *Ant J* 51, 1971, 177–239. 189. R. Powers reported on 'The Human Remains' in: *ibid*, Appendix IV, 235–6. The burial at Avebury is reported in: Gray H. St. G. (1935), 145–7.

84. Gray H. St. G. (1916), 179. Lanting J. N. and van der Waals J. D. (1972), 32, fig. 1; 37.

85. J. G. Frazer. *Spirits of the Corn and of the Wild*, I, London, 1912. 242, 217, 225 etc.

NOTES TO CHAPTER NINE

1. The total of 29 beakers comes from Clarke D. L. (1970), 500–5, using the parishes of Alton Priors, Avebury, Bishops Cannings, Beckhampton, Calne Without, Cherhill, Overton, Savernake Column and Winterbourne Monkton. Of the seven chronological Steps of Lanting J. N. and van der Waals J. D. (1972), Step 1 (2520–2383 BC) has three beakers, from West Kennet, Windmill Hill and from the ditch at Avebury. Step 2 (2455–2305 BC) has four, from Avebury, Windmill Hill, the Sanctuary, West Kennet. Step 3 has four, Step 4, three. Step 5 (2230–2035 BC) has eight 'Developed Southern' beakers; Step 6, three; and Step 7 (1975–1835 BC) has four, ugly misshapen vessels.

2. Gray H. St. G. (1935), 138, fig. 7, no. 279. These are not from a late long-necked beaker (Smith I. F. (1965), 229) but from a 'Finger-Nail' decorated beaker (Clarke D. L. (1970), 501, no. 1054F) usually associated with the early 'All-Over-Corded' beakers (*ibid*, 58). Near them may have been sherds of another early 'European' beaker. The position of such pottery in the late weathering layers proves that the ditch had been dug long before there was any major Beaker presence in the Avebury region.

3. I. F. Smith and D. D. A. Simpson. 'Excavation of a Round Barrow on Overton Hill, North Wiltshire'. *PPS* 32, 1966, 122–55, 146. For Charlton Marshall, see: A. Mee. *The King's England. Dorset.* London, 1967. 39.

4. For the alignments of skeletons, see: A. Tuckwell. 'Patterns of Burial Orientation in the Round Barrows of East Yorkshire'. *Bulletin of the Institute of Archaeology* 12, 1975, 95–123, particularly pp. 109–13. For Cunnington, see: Hoare R. C. (1812), 24, 78, 102. For Thurnam, see: J. Thurnam. 'On Ancient British Barrows, especially those of Wiltshire and the Adjacent Counties. Part II. Round Barrows'. *Arch* 43, 1871, 285–552. 315–22,

where he notes that 64 per cent of Wessex round barrows contained bodies with their heads to the north.

5. Thurnam (note 4), 323. See also Lanting J. N. and van der Waals J. D. (1972), 37.

6. Piggott S. (1962), 29.

7. W. Stukeley. *Avebury Drawings* (Keiller MSS.), quoted in: Piggott S. (1950), 71. Piggott noted that this observation of false cresting was not repeated until 1943 when Sir Cyril Fox commented on it in *Arch J* 99, 22.

8. Stukeley W. (1722–4), 226; (1743), 45.

9. A Fleming. 'Models for the development of the Wessex Culture', in: Renfrew C. (ed.) (1973), 571–85. 579. See also: the same author's, 'Territorial Patterns in Bronze Age Wessex'. *PPS* 37, 1971, 138–66.

10. Stukeley W. (1740), 43.

11. Fleming (note 9, 1971). The totals for Wessex are 2335 round barrows which include 100 'Bell' and 80 'Disc' barrows. Of the 400 round barrows near Avebury there are 40 Bells and 18 Discs.

12. Stukeley W. (1722–4), 94.

13. For Hemp Knoll, see: M. E. Robertson-Mackay. 'Bishops Cannings 81. Hemp Knoll'. *AER*, 1965, 7. For Fussells Lodge, see: P. Ashbee. 'The Fussells Lodge Long Barrow Excavations, 1957'. *Arch* 100, 1967, 1–80. S. Piggott. 'Head and Hoofs'. *Ant* 36, 1962, 110–18. For Winterbourne Monkton 9, see: Grinsell L. V. (1957), 200, who stresses that this barrow is not to be confused with the nearby Disc, Winterbourne Monkton 10.

14. L. V. Grinsell. *Dorset Barrows*. Dorchester, 1959. 51.

15. S. Piggott. 'Destroyed megaliths in North Wiltshire'. *WAM* 52, 1947–8, 390–2. The Broadstones circle at Clatford probably stood around SU 165688 near Barrow Cottages. Stukeley's unpublished field-notes mention that two barrows were visible from the ring. Aubrey J. (1665–97), c.24, 43.

16. A. D. Passmore. 'Notes on an Undescribed Stone Circle at Coate, near Swindon'. *WAM* 27, 1894, 171–4. Langdean Bottom, if it was a circle, lay at SU 118657, and Coate, by Day House Farm, at SU 181824. It may have been a very large ring, as much as 68 m across.

17. R. Jefferies. *The Story of My Heart*. London, 1946. 20, Chapter III.

18. Aubrey J. (1665–97), c.24, 67.

19. Smith A. C. (1885), 147–8. The Circle stood at SU 109693. The surviving stone by the hedge is just over a metre high. The long barrow of Avebury 21, 45 m long and 18 wide, was at SU 110692, not 100 m away, even closer than the Devil's Den to the Broadstones.

20. Winterbourne Bassett stood at SU 094755. For references, see: Stukeley W. (1722–4), 216; (1743), 45. Smith A. C. (1885), 76–8. Lukis W. C. (1883), 347.

21. For Tisbury, see: Hoare R. C. (1812), 251. It stood at ST 951299 but its tall central stone was removed and is now in the grounds of Wardour Castle 2 miles away. See also: R. S. Barron. *The Geology of Wiltshire*. Bradford-on-Avon, 1976. 125, 139.

22. Clarke D. L. (1970), 113. The beakers belong to his 'Wessex/Middle Rhine' group.

23. The average of two Carbon-14 assays provides a good date for the time when the building of the Stonehenge bluestone ring ended: 1620 ± 110 bc from an unfinished stonehole, and 1720 ± 150 bc for the beginning of the next phase, the sarsen circle. These average 1670 bc (*c.* 2060 BC). Two earlier Carbon-14 assays from antlers in the Avenue, 1728 ± 68 bc and 1770 ± 70 bc (*c.* 2160 BC), show that work on the bluestone ring may have begun as early as 2200 bc (see: R. J. C. Atkinson. 'Some new measurements on Stonehenge'. *Nature* 275, 1978, 50–2). Two dates from Woodhenge, 1867 ± 74 bc and 1805 ± 54 bc, both from material in the ditch, average 1836 bc (*c.* 2276 BC) hardly 75 years earlier. The heavy timbers of Woodhenge should still have been standing when the bluestones were first brought to Stonehenge.

24. R. J. C. Atkinson. *Stonehenge*. London, 1956. 67.

25. With diameters of 26.2 m; 39.5 m; 71.3 m; and 103.6 m respectively the concentric rings of Stonehenge II, Sanctuary IV, Winterbourne Bassett and the North Circle at Avebury had internal areas of: 539 square m; 1225; 3993; and 8430, in ratios of 1; 2.27; 7.4; and 15.6.

26. Aubrey J. (1665–97), c.24, 33. There are two versions of this celebrated quotation. This is the one Aubrey used in his description of Avebury. The other, cited in Chapter II, comes from c.24, 24, and is Aubrey's account of Charles II's conversation with Dr Charleton about how the latter had heard Aubrey speak of Avebury.

27. Clarke D. L. (1970), 98.

28. J. R. Mortimer. *Forty Years Digging*. London, 1905. 271–5. The barrow is his Driffield C. 38 on the north side of the Gypsey Race at TA 02.56. In Clarke D. L. (1970), 506, the beaker is no. 1265, a 'Developed Northern' beaker.

29. Clarke D. L. (1970), 174.

30. For Mount Pleasant, see: G. Wainwright. 'Mount Pleasant'. *C Arch* 23, 1970, 320–4. First started as an earthwork enclosure around 2100 bc (2670 BC) the defensive palisade was added about 2100 BC from a computation of two assays of 1687 ± 63 bc and 1695 ± 43 bc. For evidence of its destruction, see:

R. Burleigh, I. H. Longworth & G. J. Wainwright. 'Relative and Absolute Dating of Four Late Neolithic Enclosures'. *PPS* 38, 1972, 389–407. 399–400.

31. Clarke D. L. (1970), 227–8, 233.

32. Fleming (note 9, 1973), 578.

33. H. Case. 'The Beaker Culture in Britain and Ireland', in: R. Mercer (ed.). *Beakers in Britain and Europe*. Oxford, 1977. 71–101. 80.

34. For the excavation of the Manton Barrow, Preshute G. 1a, see: M. E. Cunnington. *An Introduction to the Archaeology of Wiltshire*. Devizes, 1949. 105–111; *WAM* 35, 1908, 1–20. The articles are in Devizes Museum, nos D.M. 907–28.

For Mr Bucknall, see: R. H. Cunnington. 'The Manton Barrow Legend'. *WAM* 50, 1944, 483–4.

35. Smith I. F. (1965), 229, 242–3.

36. For the Avebury avenue, see: Grinsell L. V. (1957), 31–2. For Stonehenge, see: C. Bowen, in: P. Fowler (ed.). *Recent Work in Rural Archaeology*. Bradford-on-Avon, 1975. 44–56, and 33.

37. Many Iron Age sherds were found in stoneholes at Stonehenge. See: Atkinson (note 24), 91. None was found at Avebury by either Gray or Keiller. See: Gray H. St. G. (1935), 135. Smith I. F. (1965), 243.

Bibliography

Very few books have been devoted solely to the topic of Avebury's prehistoric stone circles. To my knowledge there are only these works.

T. Twining. *Avebury in Wiltshire, the Remains of a Roman Work*. London, 1723.

W. Stukeley. *Abury, a Temple of the British Druids*. London, 1743.

W. Long. *Abury Illustrated*. Devizes, 1858.

M. Dames. *The Avebury Cycle*. London, 1977.

There are, of course, many other books which include descriptions of Avebury, the most detailed of which is: I. F. Smith. *Windmill Hill and Avebury*. Oxford, 1965.

For books concerning both Stonehenge and Avebury the reader should refer to the compendium by W. J. Harrison. 'A Bibliography of the Great Stone Monuments of Wiltshire—Stonehenge and Avebury'. *WAM* 32, 1901, 1–69.

Besides these there are other important sources that are referred to frequently in this book. To save space they are cited by author and date only in the Notes but are listed in full below.

Annable F. K. and Simpson D. D. A. (1964). *Guide Catalogue of the Neolithic and Bronze Age Collections in Devizes Museum*. Devizes.

Atkinson R. J. C. (1967). 'Silbury Hill'. *Ant* 41, 259–62.

———(1969). 'The Date of Silbury Hill'. *Ant* 43, 216.

———(1970). 'Silbury Hill, 1969–70'. *Ant* 44, 313–14.

Aubrey J. (1665–97). 'Monumenta Britannica'. Bodleian MS. Top. Gen. c.24–5.

———(1685). *The Naturall Historie of Wiltshire* (publ. John Britton). London, 1847.

———(1862). *Wiltshire: The Topographical Collections of John Aubrey* (ed. Canon J. E. Jackson).

Burgess C. and Miket R. (1976). *Settlement and Economy in the Third and Second Millennia B.C.* Oxford.

Burl A. (1976). *The Stone Circles of the British Isles*. London.

Clarke D. L. (1970). *Beaker Pottery of Great Britain and Ireland*. I, II. Cambridge.

Cunnington M. E. (1913a). 'The Re-erection of Two Fallen Stones and Discovery of an Interment with Drinking Cup, at Avebury'. *WAM* 38, 1–8.

———(1913b). 'A Buried Stone in the Kennet Avenue'. *WAM* 38, 12–14.

———(1913). 'The "Sanctuary" on Overton Hill, near Avebury'. *WAM* 45, 300–35.

Ekwall E. (1959). *The Concise Oxford Dictionary of English Place-Names*. Oxford.

Eliade M. (1958). *Patterns in Comparative Religion*. London.

Evans J. G. (1975). *The Environment of Early Man in the British Isles*. London.

Freeman P. R. (1977). 'Note: Thom's Survey of the Avebury Ring'. *JHA* 8, 134–5.

Gray H. St. G. (1901). 'On the Excavations at Arbor Low, August, 1901'. *British Association. 71st Report*. Glasgow. 427–40.

————(1903a). 'On the Excavations at Arbor Low. May–June, 1902'. *ibid, 72nd Report.* Belfast, 1902. 455–66.

————(1903b). 'On the Excavations at Arbor Low, 1901–2'. *Arch* 58, 461–98.

————(1907). 'Excavations at the Stripple Stones, East Cornwall, 1905'. *British Association. 76th Report.* York, 1906. 371–82.

————(1908). 'On the Stone Circles of East Cornwall'. *Arch* 61, 1–60.

————(1909). 'The Avebury Excavations, 1908'. *British Association. 78th Report.* Dublin, 1908. 401–13.

————(1910). 'The Avebury Excavations, 1909'. *ibid, 79th Report.* Winnipeg, 1909. 273–84.

————(1912). 'The Avebury Excavations, 1911'. *ibid. 81st Report.* Portsmouth, 1911. 142–52.

————(1916). 'The Avebury Excavations, 1914'. *ibid, 85th Report.* Manchester, 176–89.

————(1923). 'The Avebury Excavations, 1922'. *ibid, 90th Report.* Hull. 327–33.

————(1935). 'The Avebury Excavations, 1908–1922'. *Arch* 84, 99–162.

Grinsell L. V. (1957). 'Archaeological Gazetteer'. In: *VCH Wilts.* I, 1. 21–279.

Harrison W. J. (1901). 'A Bibliography of Stonehenge and of Avebury'. *WAM* 32, 1–169.

Hoare Sir R. C. (1812). *The Ancient History of South Wiltshire.* London.

————(1821). *The Ancient History of North Wiltshire.* (1819). London.

Keiller A. (1939a). 'Avebury: Summary of Excavations, 1937 and 1938'. *Ant* 13, 223–33.

————(1939b). *Avebury: Summary of Excavations, 1937 and 1938.* Morven Institute of Archaeological Research.

————and Piggott S. (1936). 'The West Kennet Avenue: Excavations, 1934–5'. *Ant* 10, 417–27.

King B. (1878). 'Abury Notes'. *WAM* 17, 132.

————(1879). 'Avebury. The Beckhampton Avenue'. *WAM* 18, 377–83.

Lanting J. N. and van der Waals J. D. (1972). 'British Beakers as seen from the Continent'. *Helinium* 12, 20–46.

Long W. (1858a). 'Abury'. *WAM* 4, 307–63.

————(1858b). *Abury Illustrated.* Devizes.

————(1861). 'Fac-Similes of Aubrey's Plans of Abury'. *WAM* 7, 224–7.

————(1862). *Abury Illustrated. With Additions.* Devizes.

————(1878). 'Abury Notes'. *WAM* 17, 327–35.

Lukis W. C. (1882). 'Report on the Prehistoric Monuments of Stonehenge and Avebury'. *PSAL* 9, (1882–3), 141–57.

————(1883). 'Report on the Prehistoric Monuments of Wiltshire and Somerset'. *ibid,* 344–55.

MacKie E. W. (1977). *Science and Society in Prehistoric Britain.* London.

Merewether J. (1849). 'Examination of Silbury Hill'. *PAI,* Salisbury volume. 73–81.

Musson C. R.(1971). 'A Study of Possible Building Forms at Durrington Walls, Woodhenge and the Sanctuary', in: Wainwright G. J. and Longworth I. H. (1971), 363–77.

Pass A. C. (1887). 'Recent Explorations at Silbury Hill'. *WAM* 23, 245–54.

Passmore A. D. (1922). 'The Avebury Ditch'. *Ant J* 2, 109–11.

———(1935). 'The Meux Excavation at Avebury'. *WAM* 47, 288–9.

Piggott S. (1940). 'Timber Circles: A Re-examination'. *Arch J* 96, 193–222.

———(1950). *William Stukeley. An 18th-Century Antiquary*. Oxford.

———(1954). *Neolithic Cultures of the British Isles*. Cambridge.

———(1962). *The West Kennet Long Barrow Excavations, 1955–6*. London.

———(1964). 'Excavations at Avebury, 1960'. *WAM* 59, 28–9.

———(1973). in: *VCH* I, 2. 'The First Agricultural Communities, *c.* 3000–1500 BC', 284–332; 'The Later Neolithic, *c.* 2000–1500 BC', 333–51; 'The Wessex Culture of the Early Bronze Age', 352–75.

Renfrew C. (ed.) (1973). *The Explanation of Culture Change: Models in Prehistory*. London.

Smith A. C. (1861). 'Silbury'. *WAM* 7, 145–91.

———(1867). 'Excavations at Avebury'. *WAM* 10, 209–16.

———(1869). 'A Report of Digging made in Silbury'. *WAM* 11, 113–18.

———(1885). *A Guide to the British and Roman Antiquities of the North Wiltshire Downs*. Devizes.

Smith I. F. (1960). 'Excavations at Windmill Hill, Avebury, Wilts. 1957–8'. *WAM* 57, (1958–60), 149–62.

———(1964). 'Avebury: The Northern Inner Circle'. *WAM* 59, 181.

———(1965). *Windmill Hill and Avebury: Excavations by Alexander Keiller, 1925–39*. Oxford.

Snow D. (1976). *The American Indians: their Archaeology and Prehistory*. London.

Stukeley W. (1717–48). 'Commonplace Book'. Autograph MS. Devizes Museum.

———(1722–4). 'Druidical Remains etc.' Prints and Drawings by W. S., Gough Maps 231. Bodleian Library, Oxford.

———(1724). MS. Eng. Misc. b65. Bodleian Library, Oxford.

———(1740). *Stonehenge. A Temple Restor'd to the British Druids*. London.

———(1743). *Abury, a Temple of the British Druids, with Some Others Described*. London.

———(1776a). *Itinerarium Curiosum. Centuria I*. London.

———(1776b). *Ibid, Centuria II*. London.

Thom A. (1967). *Megalithic Sites in Britain*. Oxford.

———(1971). *Megalithic Lunar Observatories*. Oxford.

———and Thom A. S. (1976). 'Avebury (2): the West Kennet Avenue'. *JHA* 7, 193–97.

———and ——— and Foord T. R. (1976). 'Avebury (1): A New Assessment of the Geometry and Metrology of the Ring'. *JHA* 7, 183–92.

Thurnam J. (1861). 'Examination of a Chambered Long Barrow at West Kennet, Wiltshire'. *Arch* 38, 405–21.

Vatcher F. de M. (1976). *The Avebury Monuments*. London.

———and Vatcher L. (1968). 'Avebury: Avenue Stones'. *Arch R* 3, 6.

———(1969a). 'Avebury: School Site'. *ibid*, 4, 25.

———(1969b). 'Avebury: Beckhampton Avenue'. *WAM* 64, 127.

Wainwright G. J. and Longworth I. H. (1971). *Durrington Walls: Excavations, 1966–8.* London.

Whittle A. W. R. (1977). *The Earlier Neolithic of Southern England and its Continental Background.* Oxford.

———(1978). 'Resources and Population in the British Neolithic'. *Ant* 52, 34–42.

Willey G. R. (1966). *An Introduction to American Archaeology. I. North and Middle America.* New Jersey.

Williams D. (1976). 'A Neolithic Moss Flora from Silbury Hill, Wiltshire'. *JAS* 3, 267–70.

Young W. E. V. (1948). 'Beckhampton, Wilts.' *Archaeological News Letter* I, 5, 6.

———(1950). 'A Beaker Interment at Beckhampton'. *WAM* 53, 1950, 311–27.

Index

Where a subject has many page references the main reference is given in **bold type**. Page numbers for illustrations are given in *italics*.

271

274